Fruits Basket™

Volume 17

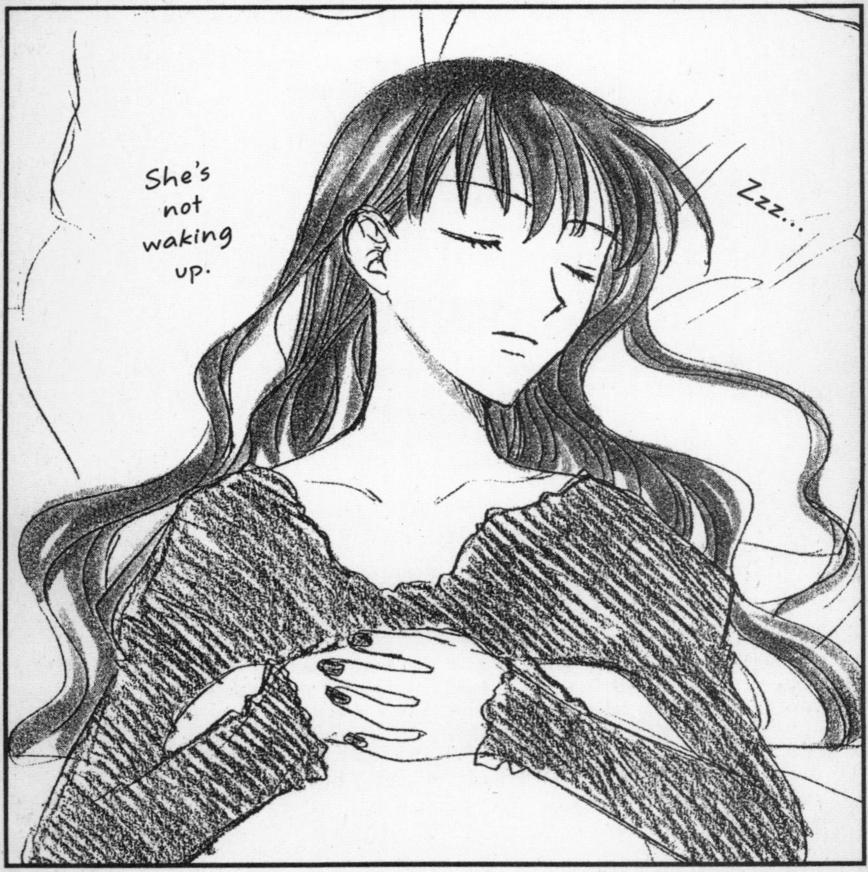
She's not waking up.
Zzz...

Natsuki Takaya

Fruits Basket Volume 17
Created by Natsuki Takaya

Translation - Alethea & Athena Nibley
English Adaptation - Lianne Sentar
Copy Editor - Stephanie Duchin
Retouch and Lettering - Star Print Brokers
Production Artist - Vicente Rivera, Jr.
Cover Design - Christian Lownds

Editor - Paul Morrissey
Digital Imaging Manager - Chris Buford
Pre-Production Supervisor - Erika Terriquez
Art Director - Anne Marie Horne
Production Manager - Elisabeth Brizzi
Managing Editor - Vy Nguyen
VP of Production - Ron Klamert
Editor-in-Chief - Rob Tokar
Publisher - Mike Kiley
President and C.O.O. - John Parker
C.E.O. and Chief Creative Officer - Stuart Levy

A  Manga

TOKYOPOP and ⟨⟩ are trademarks or registered trademarks of TOKYOPOP Inc.

TOKYOPOP Inc.
5900 Wilshire Blvd. Suite 2000
Los Angeles, CA 90036

E-mail: info@TOKYOPOP.com
Come visit us online at www.TOKYOPOP.com

ISBN: 978-1-59816-799-3
First TOKYOPOP printing: August 2007
10 9 8 7 6 5 4 3 2 1
Printed in the USA

Fruits Basket

Volume 17

By
Natsuki Takaya

HAMBURG // LONDON // LOS ANGELES // TOKYO

Fruits Basket™

Table of Contents

Filler Sketch

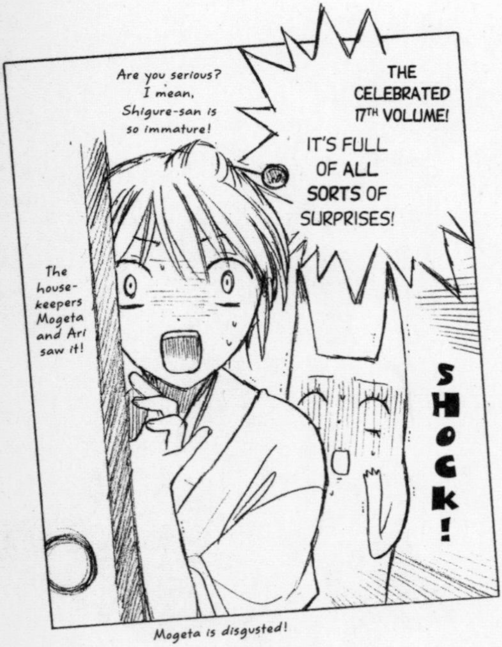
THE CELEBRATED 17TH VOLUME!
IT'S FULL OF ALL SORTS OF SURPRISES!
Are you serious? I mean, Shigure-san is so immature!
SHOCK!
The house-keepers Mogeta and Ari saw it!

Mogeta is disgusted!

STORY SO FAR...

Hello, I'm Tohru Honda and I have come to know a terrible secret. After the death of my mother, I was living by myself in a tent, when the Sohma family took me in. I soon learned that the Sohma family lives with a curse! Each family member is possessed by the vengeful spirit of an animal from the Chinese Zodiac. Whenever one of them becomes weak or is hugged by a member of the opposite sex, they change into their Zodiac animal!

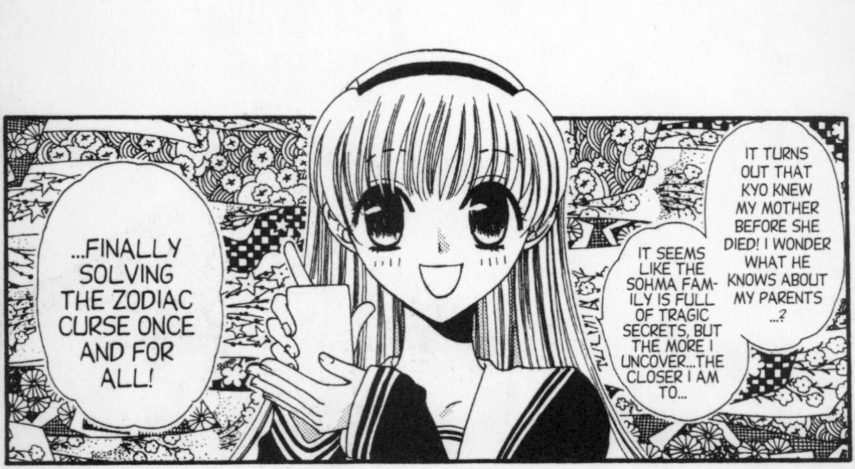
IT TURNS OUT THAT KYO KNEW MY MOTHER BEFORE SHE DIED! I WONDER WHAT HE KNOWS ABOUT MY PARENTS ...?
IT SEEMS LIKE THE SOHMA FAMILY IS FULL OF TRAGIC SECRETS, BUT THE MORE I UNCOVER...THE CLOSER I AM TO...
...FINALLY SOLVING THE ZODIAC CURSE ONCE AND FOR ALL!

Tohru Honda

The ever-optimistic hero of our story.
An orphan, she now lives in Shigure's
house, along with Yuki and Kyo, and is
the only person outside of the family
who knows the Sohma family's curse.

Yuki Sohma, the Rat

Soft-spoken. Self-esteem issues.
At school he's called "Prince Yuki."

Kyo Sohma, the Cat

The Cat who was left out of the Zodiac.
Hates Yuki, leeks and miso. But mostly
Yuki.

Kagura Sohma, the Boar

Bashful, yet headstrong. Determined to
marry Kyo, even if it kills him.

Fruits Basket Characters

Mabudachi Trio

Shigure Sohma, the Dog

Enigmatic, mischievous and a little perverted. A popular novelist.

Hatori Sohma, the Dragon

Family doctor to the Sohmas. Only thing he can't cure is his broken heart.

Ayame Sohma, the Snake

Yuki's older brother. A proud and playful drama queen...er, king. Runs a costume shop.

Saki Hanajima

"Hana-chan." Can sense people's "waves." Goth demeanor scares her classmates.

Arisa Uotani

"Uo-chan." A tough-talking "Yankee" who looks out for her friends.

Tohru's Best Friends

Hiro Sohma, the Ram (or sheep)

This caustic tyke is skilled at throwing verbal barbs, but he has a soft spot for Kisa.

Momiji Sohma, the Rabbit

Half-German. He's older than he looks. His mother rejected him because of the Sohma curse. His little sister, Momo, has been kept from him most of her life.

Hatsuharu Sohma, the Ox

The nicest of guys, except when he goes "Black." Then you'd better watch out. He was once in a relationship with Rin.

Kisa Sohma, the Tiger

Kisa became shy and self-conscious due to constant teasing by her classmates. Yuki, who has similar insecurities, feels particularly close to Kisa.

Fruits Basket Characters

Isuzu "Rin" Sohma, the Horse

She was once in a relationship with Hatsuharu (Haru)...and Tohru leaves her rather cold. Rin is full of pride, and she can't stand the amount of deference the other Sohma family members give Akito.

Ritsu Sohma, the Monkey

This shy kimono-wearing member of the Sohma family is gorgeous. But this "she" is really a he!! Crossdressing calms his nerves.

Akito Sohma

The head of the Sohma clan. A dark figure of many secrets. Treated with fear and reverence.

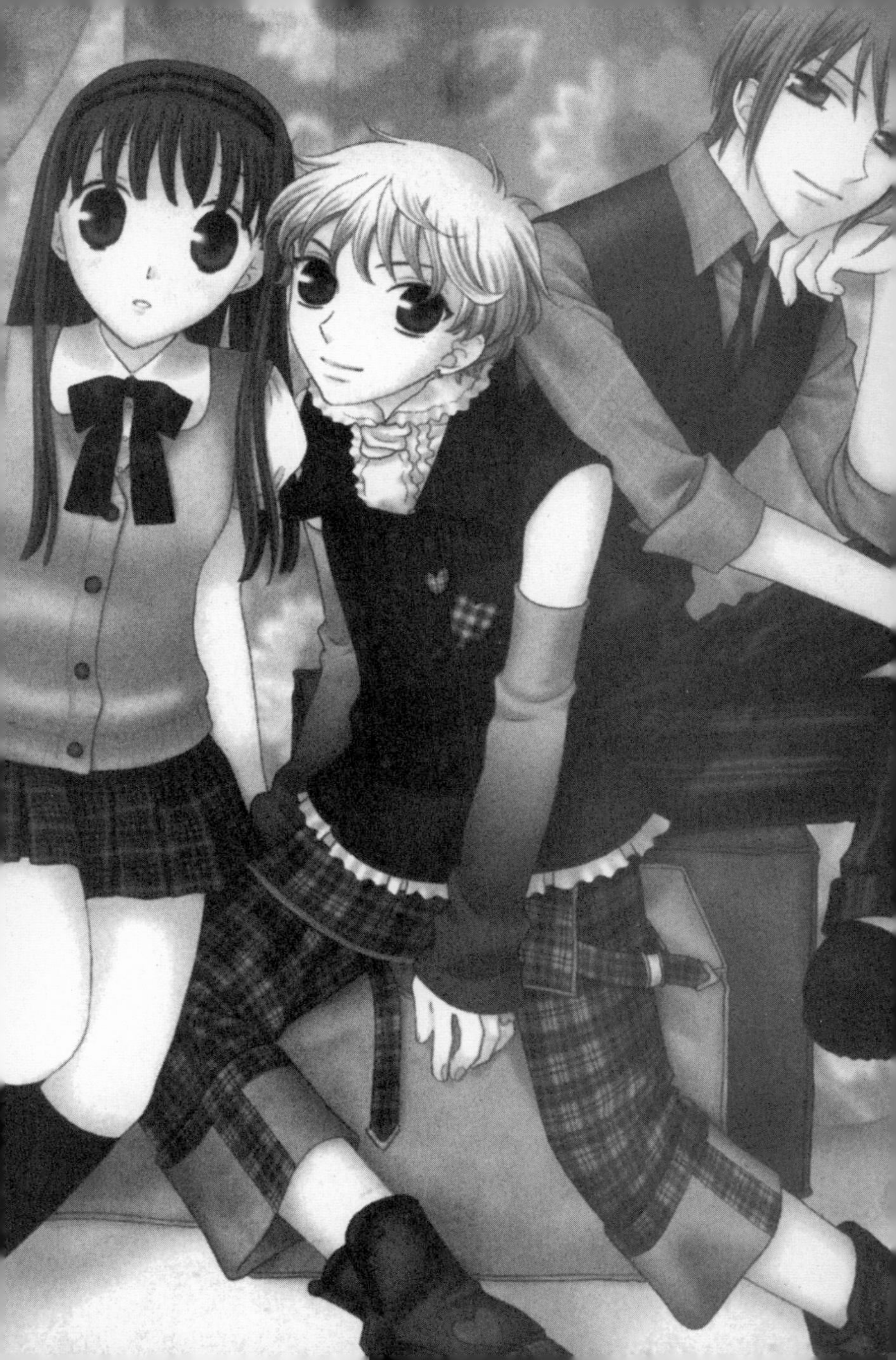

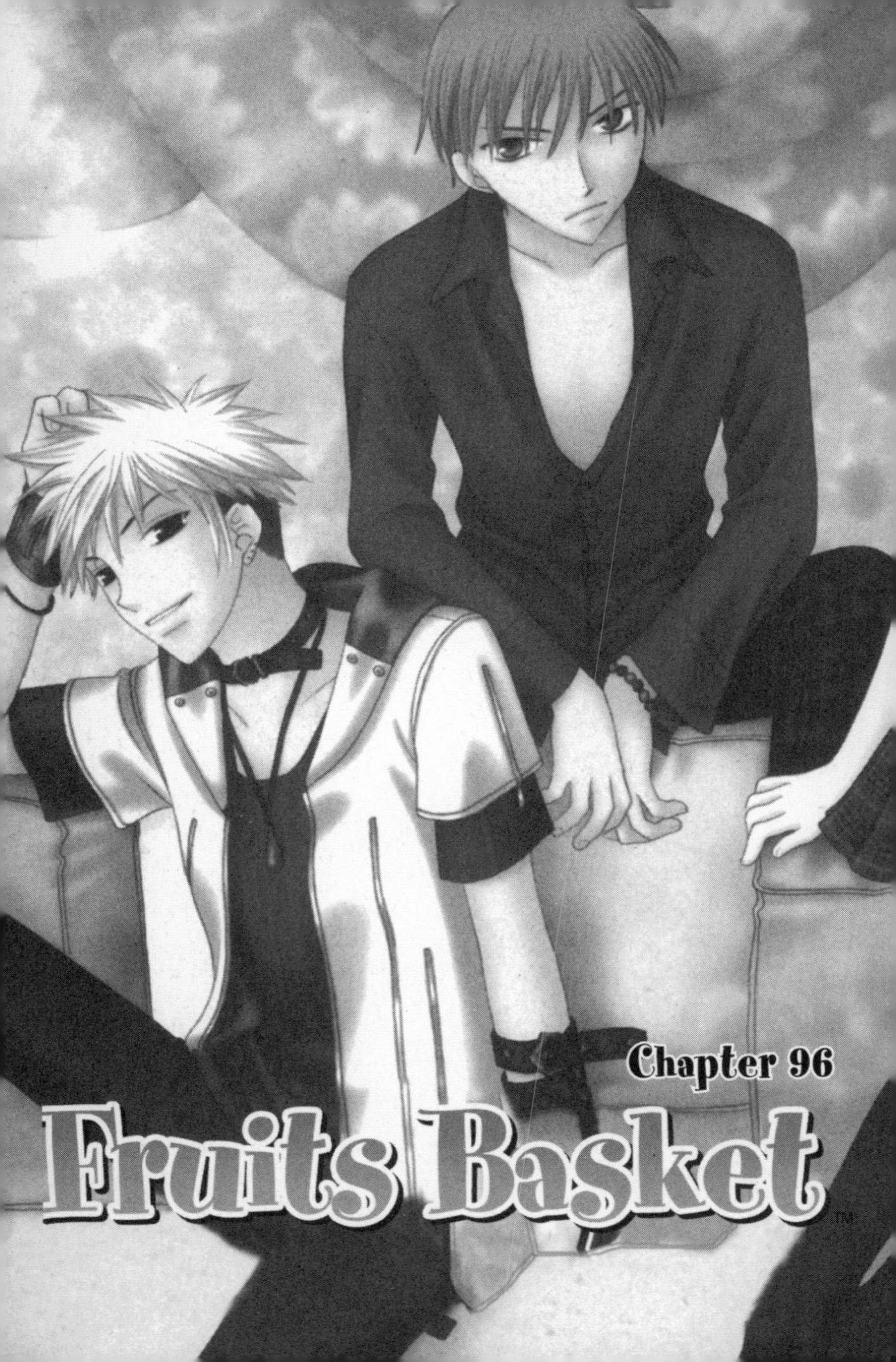
Chapter 96
Fruits Basket™

Filler Sketch

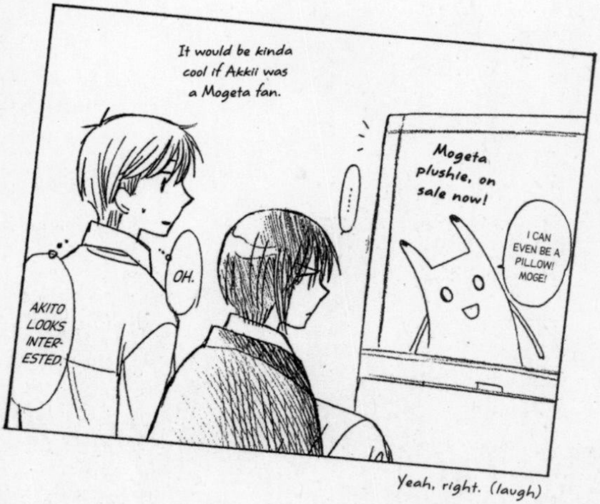
It would be kinda cool if Akkii was a Mogeta fan.
Mogeta plushie, on sale now!
I CAN EVEN BE A PILLOW! MOGE!
.....
OH.
AKITO LOOKS INTER-ESTED.

Yeah, right. (laugh)

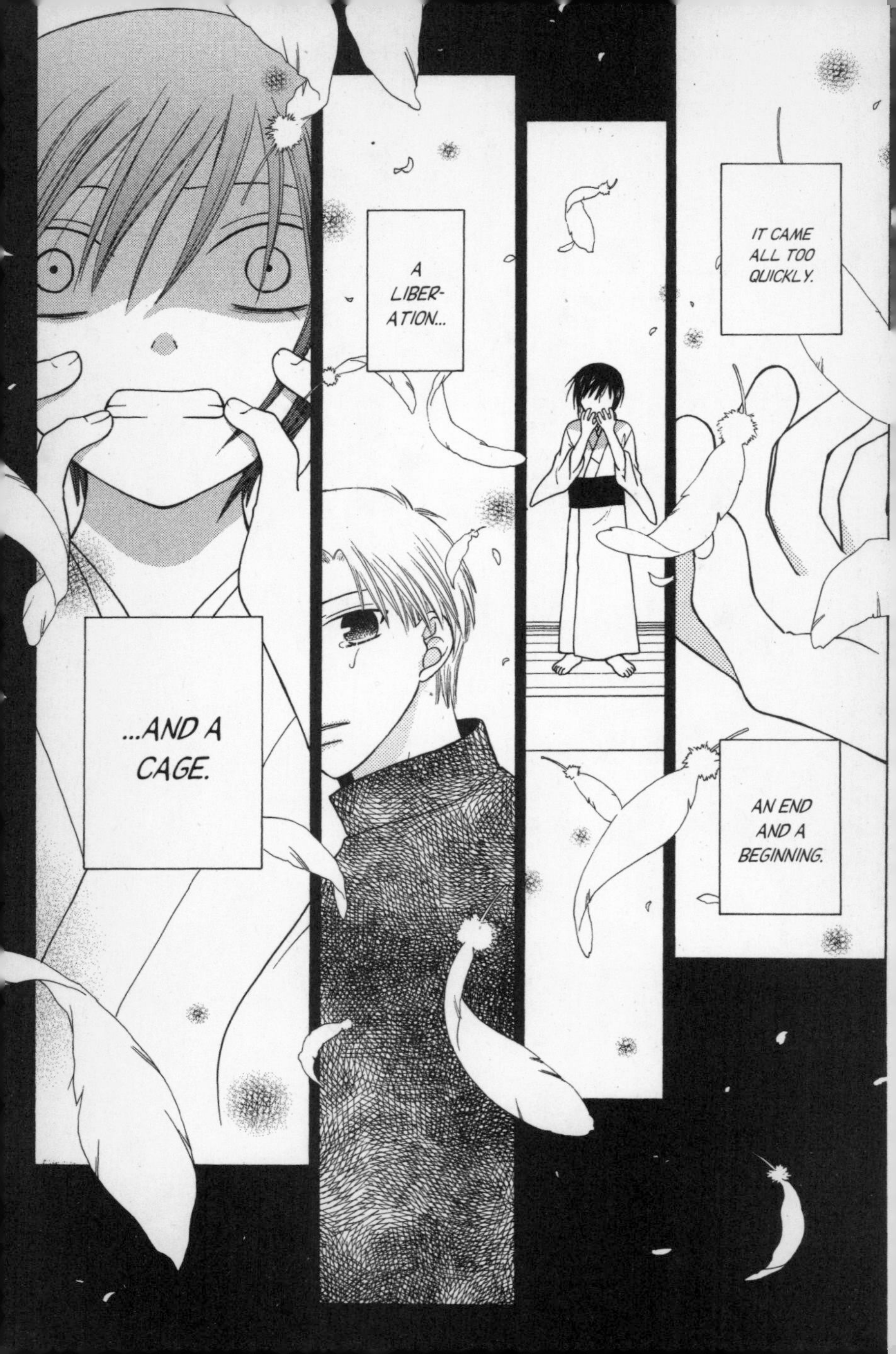
IT CAME ALL TOO QUICKLY.
AN END AND A BEGINNING.
A LIBER-ATION...
...AND A CAGE.

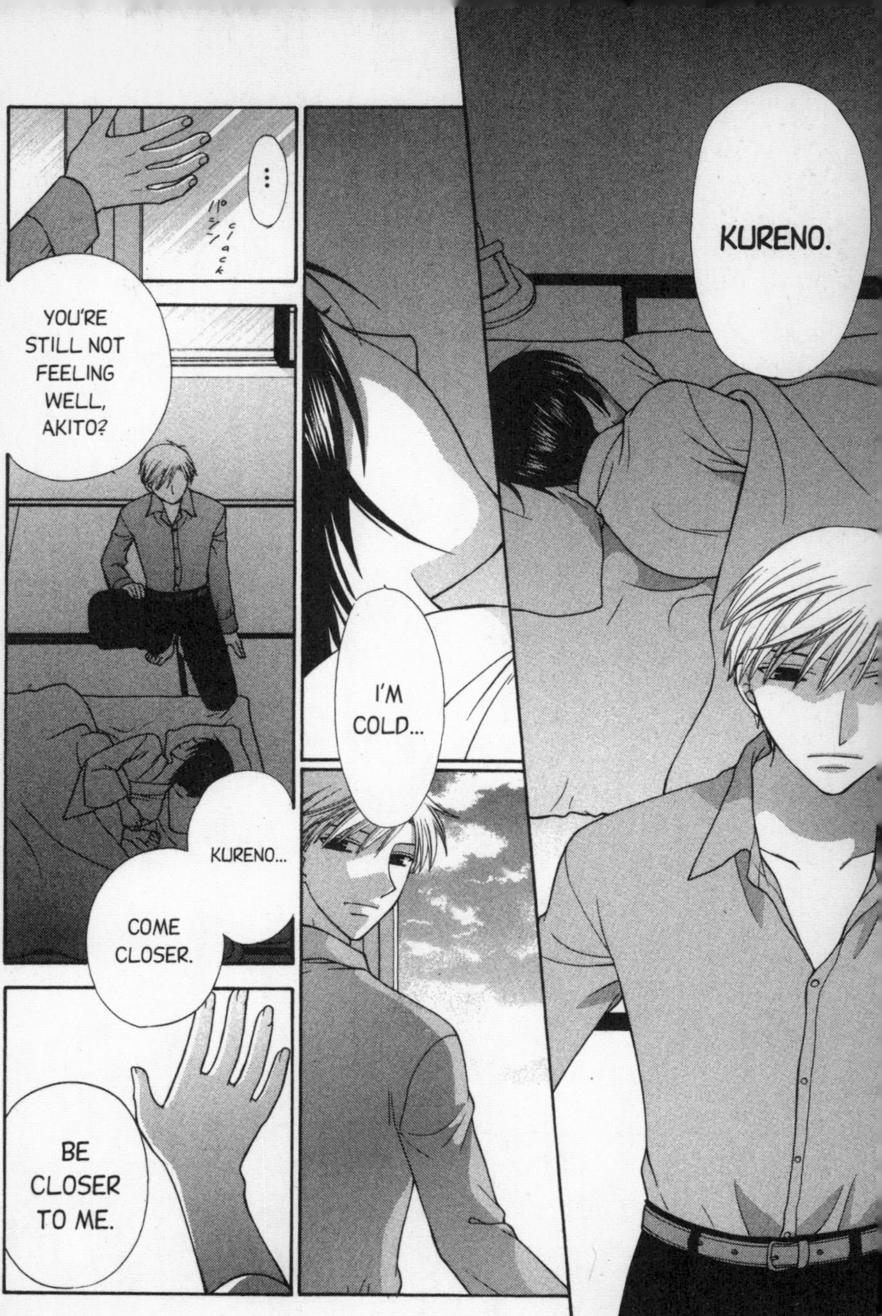
KURENO.
I'M COLD...
...
clack
YOU'RE STILL NOT FEELING WELL, AKITO?
KURENO...
COME CLOSER.
BE CLOSER TO ME.

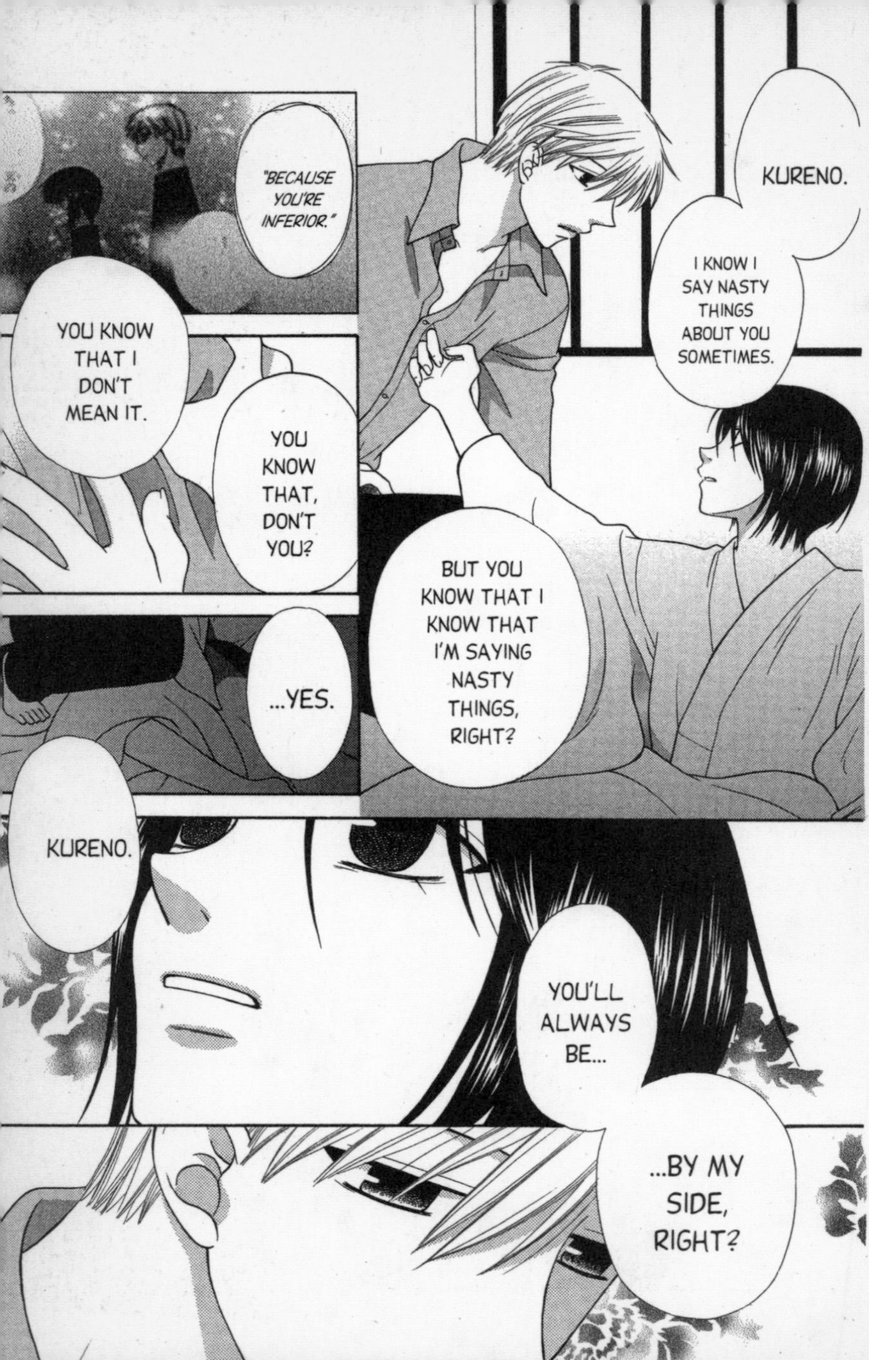
KURENO.
I KNOW I SAY NASTY THINGS ABOUT YOU SOMETIMES.
BUT YOU KNOW THAT I KNOW THAT I'M SAYING NASTY THINGS, RIGHT?
"BECAUSE YOU'RE INFERIOR."
YOU KNOW THAT I DON'T MEAN IT.
YOU KNOW THAT, DON'T YOU?
...YES.
KURENO.
YOU'LL ALWAYS BE...
...BY MY SIDE, RIGHT?

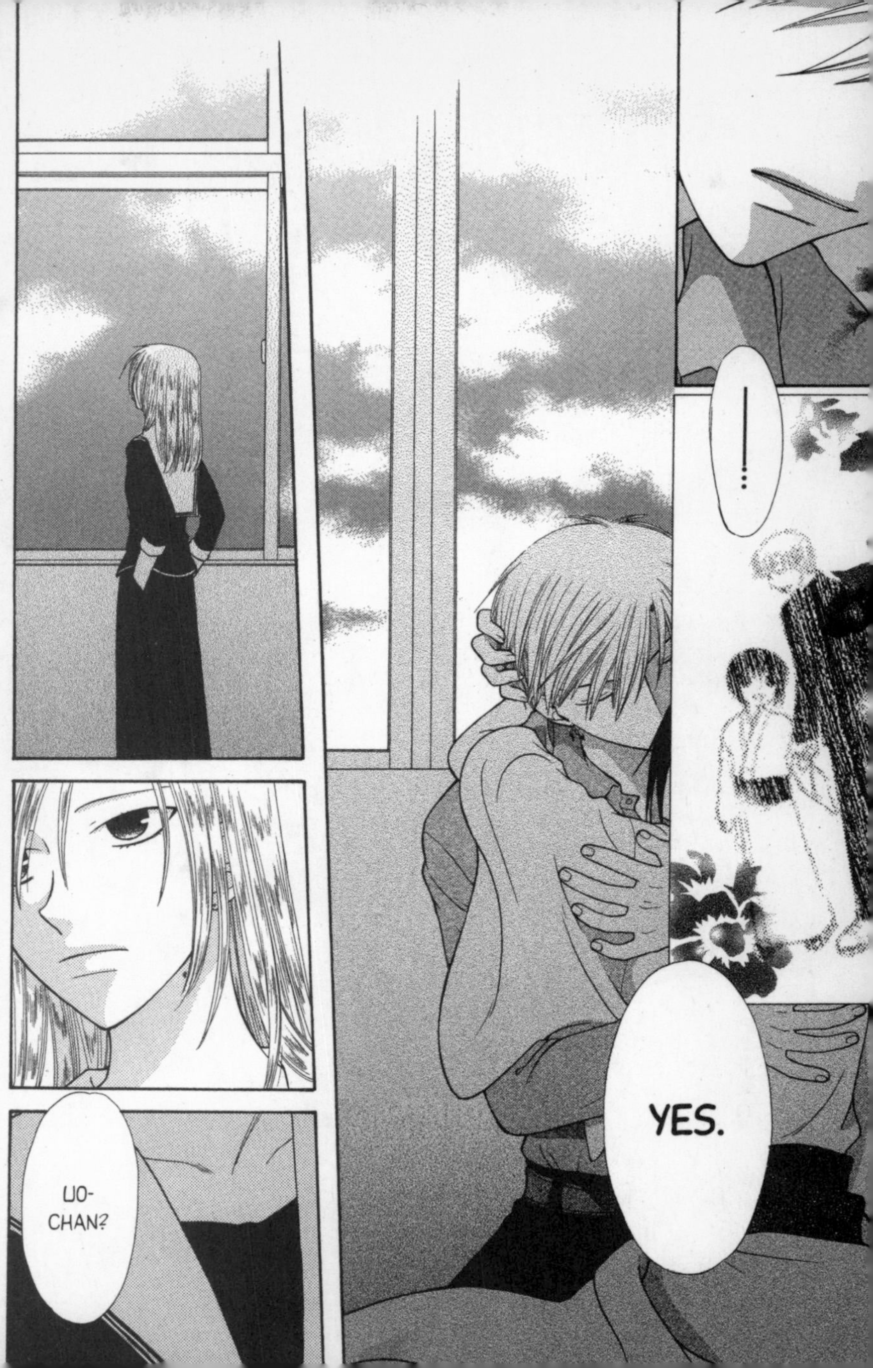
!...
YES.
UO-CHAN?

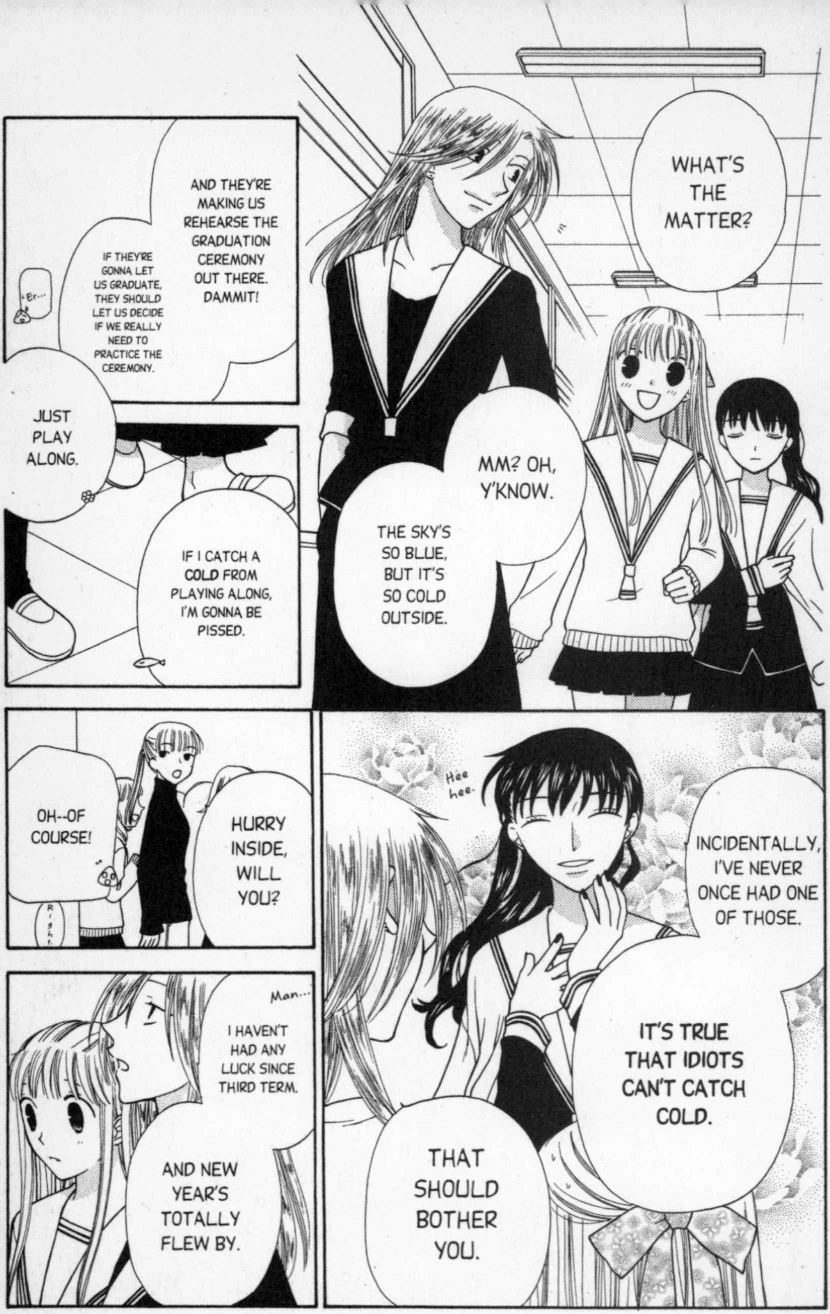
WHAT'S THE MATTER?
MM? OH, Y'KNOW.
THE SKY'S SO BLUE, BUT IT'S SO COLD OUTSIDE.
AND THEY'RE MAKING US REHEARSE THE GRADUATION CEREMONY OUT THERE. DAMMIT!
IF THEY'RE GONNA LET US GRADUATE, THEY SHOULD LET US DECIDE IF WE REALLY NEED TO PRACTICE THE CEREMONY.
Er...
JUST PLAY ALONG.
IF I CATCH A COLD FROM PLAYING ALONG, I'M GONNA BE PISSED.
INCIDENTALLY, I'VE NEVER ONCE HAD ONE OF THOSE.
Hee hee.
IT'S TRUE THAT IDIOTS CAN'T CATCH COLD.
THAT SHOULD BOTHER YOU.
HURRY INSIDE, WILL YOU?
OH--OF COURSE!
Right.
Man...
I HAVEN'T HAD ANY LUCK SINCE THIRD TERM.
AND NEW YEAR'S TOTALLY FLEW BY.

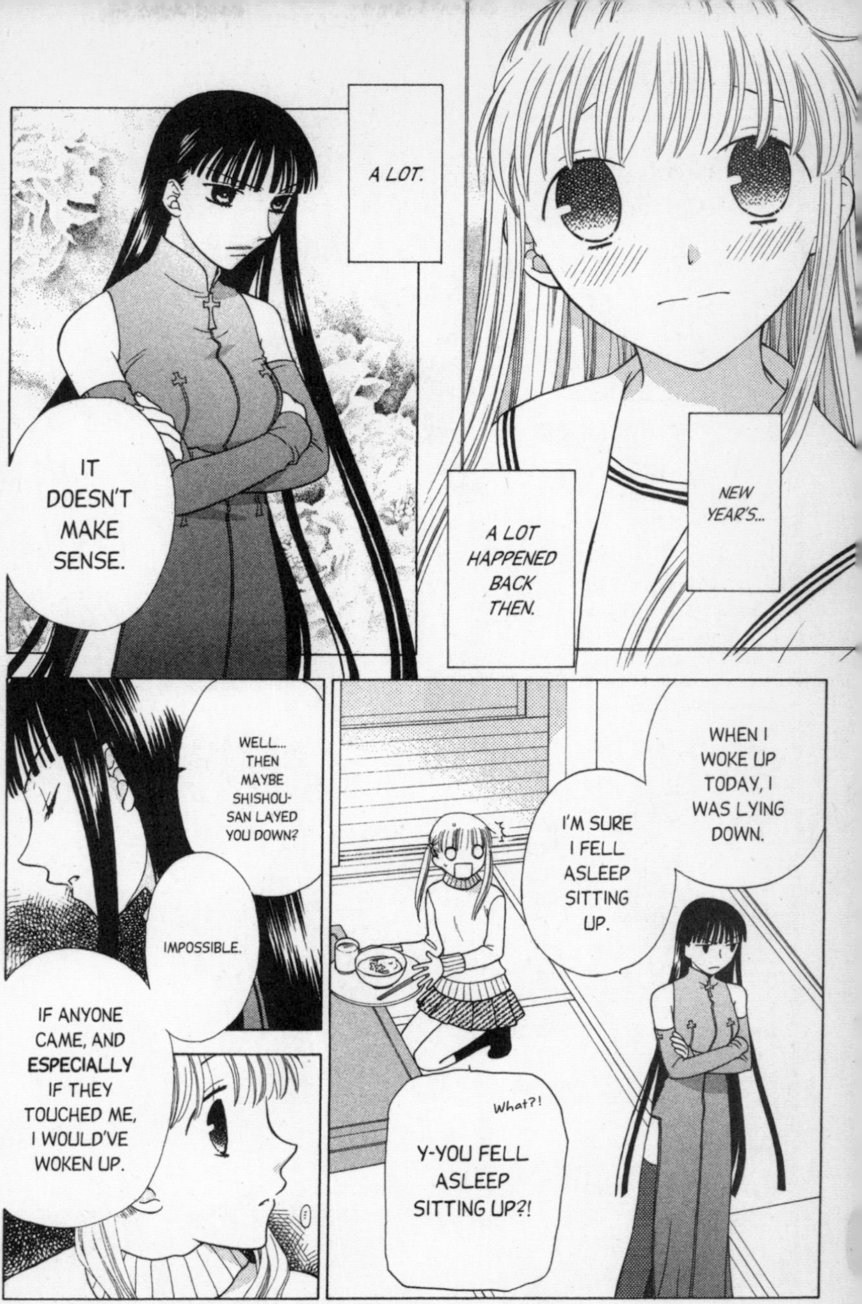
NEW YEAR'S...
A LOT HAPPENED BACK THEN.
A LOT.
IT DOESN'T MAKE SENSE.
WHEN I WOKE UP TODAY, I WAS LYING DOWN.
I'M SURE I FELL ASLEEP SITTING UP.
What?!
Y-YOU FELL ASLEEP SITTING UP?!
WELL... THEN MAYBE SHISHOU-SAN LAYED YOU DOWN?
IMPOSSIBLE.
IF ANYONE CAME, AND ESPECIALLY IF THEY TOUCHED ME, I WOULD'VE WOKEN UP.
...

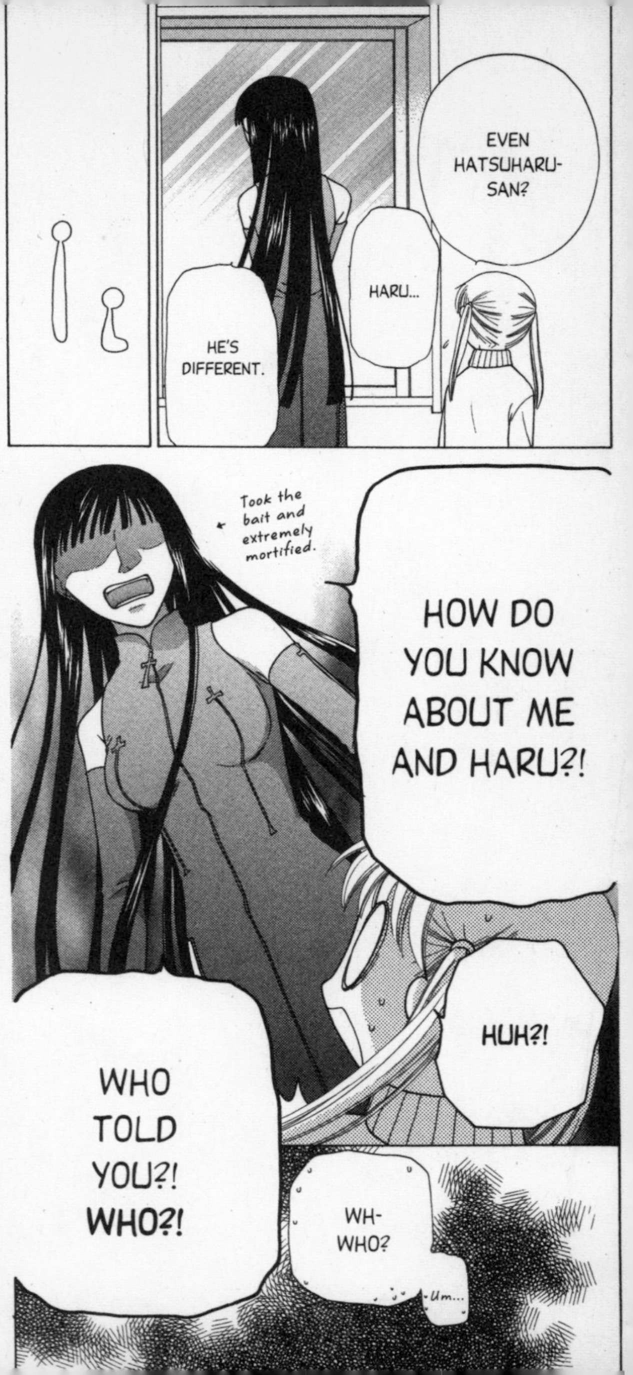
EVEN HATSUHARU-SAN?
HARU...
HE'S DIFFERENT.
HOW DO YOU KNOW ABOUT ME AND HARU?!
Took the bait and extremely mortified.
HUH?!
WHO TOLD YOU?! WHO?!
WH- WHO?
Um...

Fruits Basket 17

Pleased to meet you and hello. This is Takaya, presenting Volume 17. The cover is Hana-chan!

...Somehow it's been no time at all. I feel like time's passing by very quickly these days; I don't know if it's because I'm pushing forward or if it's because of my age. There are a lot of games on sale that I want to play, too, but I don't have the time, so I feel like they're piling up...

There may be people who think, "If you're not going to play it now, buy it later!" but I want to have it on hand. (How can I say what I mean here?) So that someday, when I have time, I can start playing. I wonder if anyone can understand that feeling (laugh).

Well then, please enjoy Furuba 17!

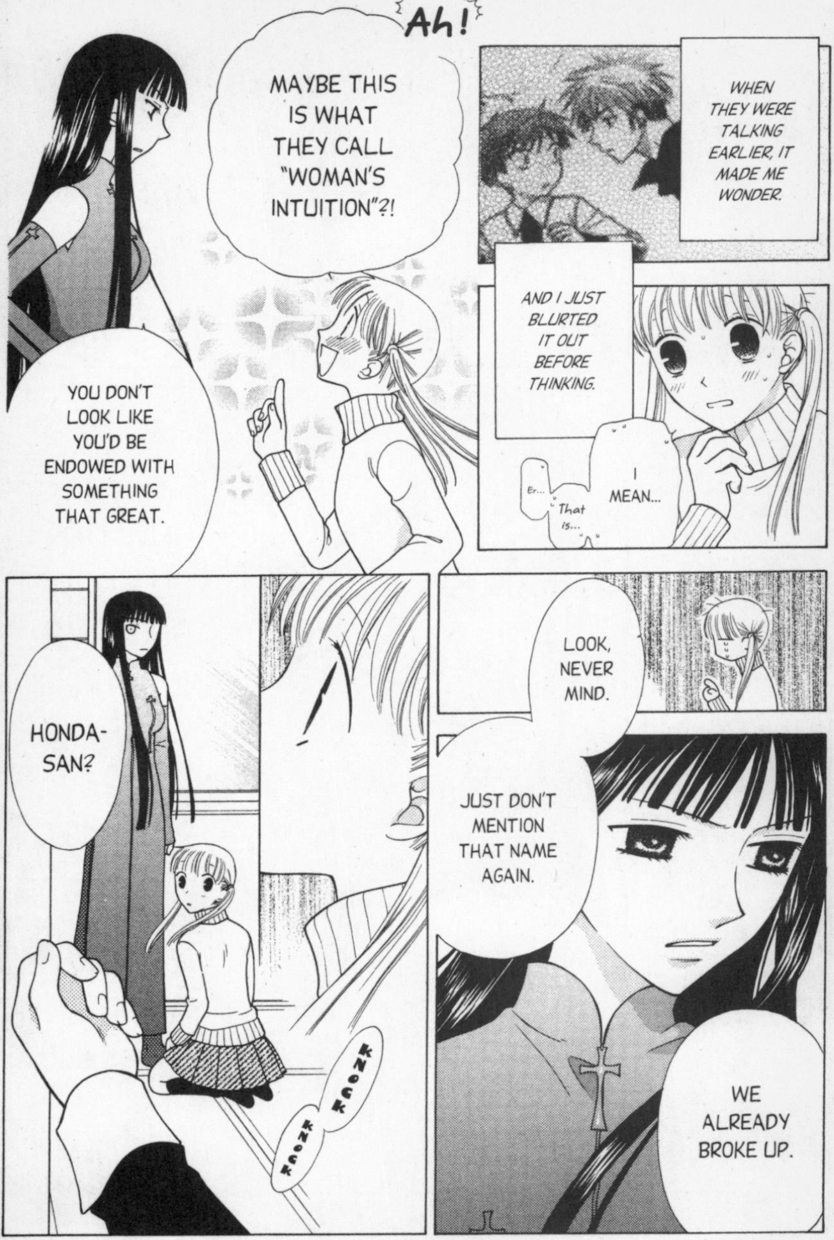

WHEN THEY WERE TALKING EARLIER, IT MADE ME WONDER.
AND I JUST BLURTED IT OUT BEFORE THINKING.
I MEAN...
Er...
That is...
Ah!
MAYBE THIS IS WHAT THEY CALL "WOMAN'S INTUITION"?!
YOU DON'T LOOK LIKE YOU'D BE ENDOWED WITH SOMETHING THAT GREAT.
LOOK, NEVER MIND.
JUST DON'T MENTION THAT NAME AGAIN.
WE ALREADY BROKE UP.
HONDA-SAN?
KNOCK
KNOCK

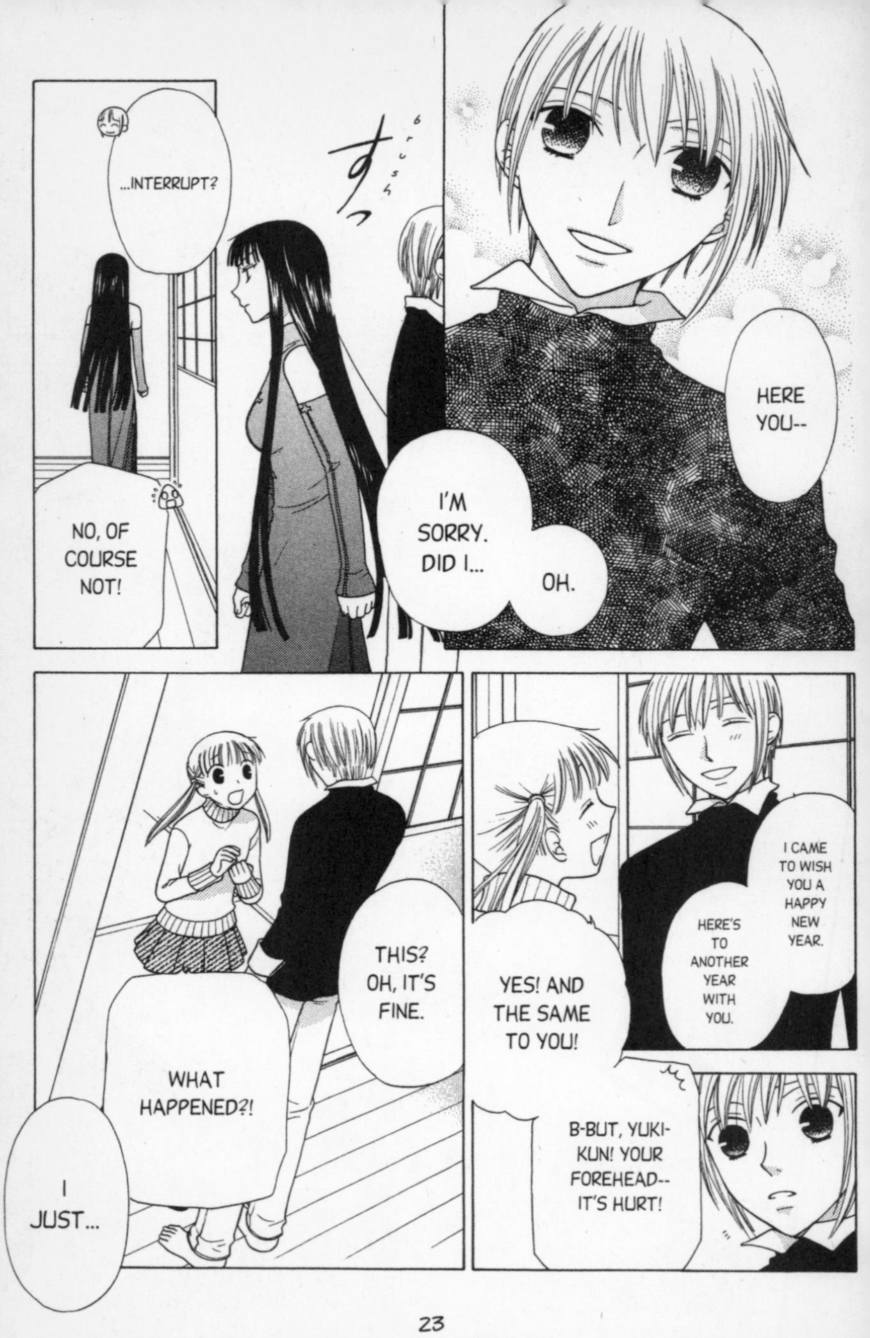
HERE YOU--
OH.
I'M SORRY. DID I...
brush
...INTERRUPT?
NO, OF COURSE NOT!
I CAME TO WISH YOU A HAPPY NEW YEAR.
HERE'S TO ANOTHER YEAR WITH YOU.
YES! AND THE SAME TO YOU!
B-BUT, YUKI-KUN! YOUR FOREHEAD-- IT'S HURT!
THIS? OH, IT'S FINE.
WHAT HAPPENED?!
I JUST...

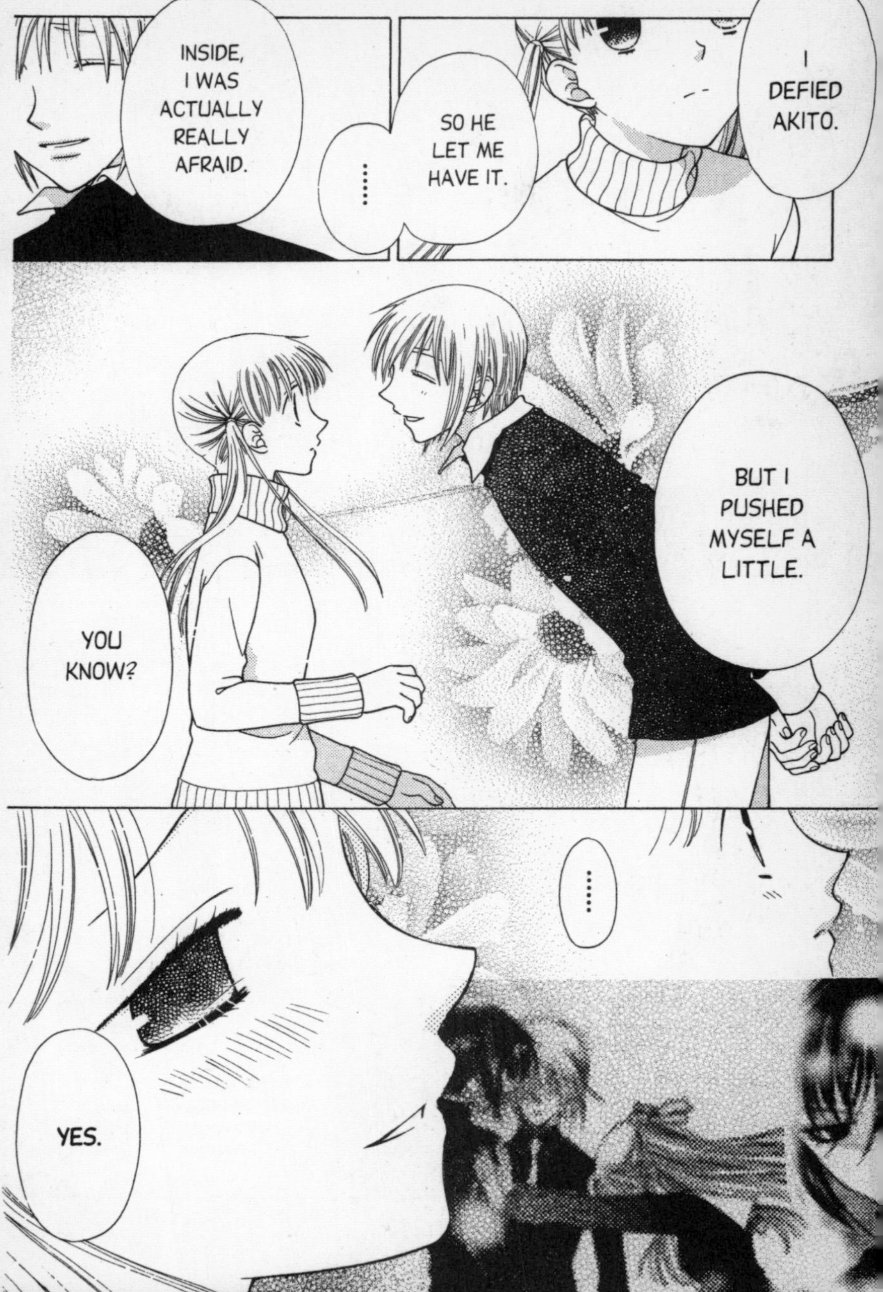
I DEFIED AKITO.
SO HE LET ME HAVE IT.
......
INSIDE, I WAS ACTUALLY REALLY AFRAID.
BUT I PUSHED MYSELF A LITTLE.
YOU KNOW?
......
YES.

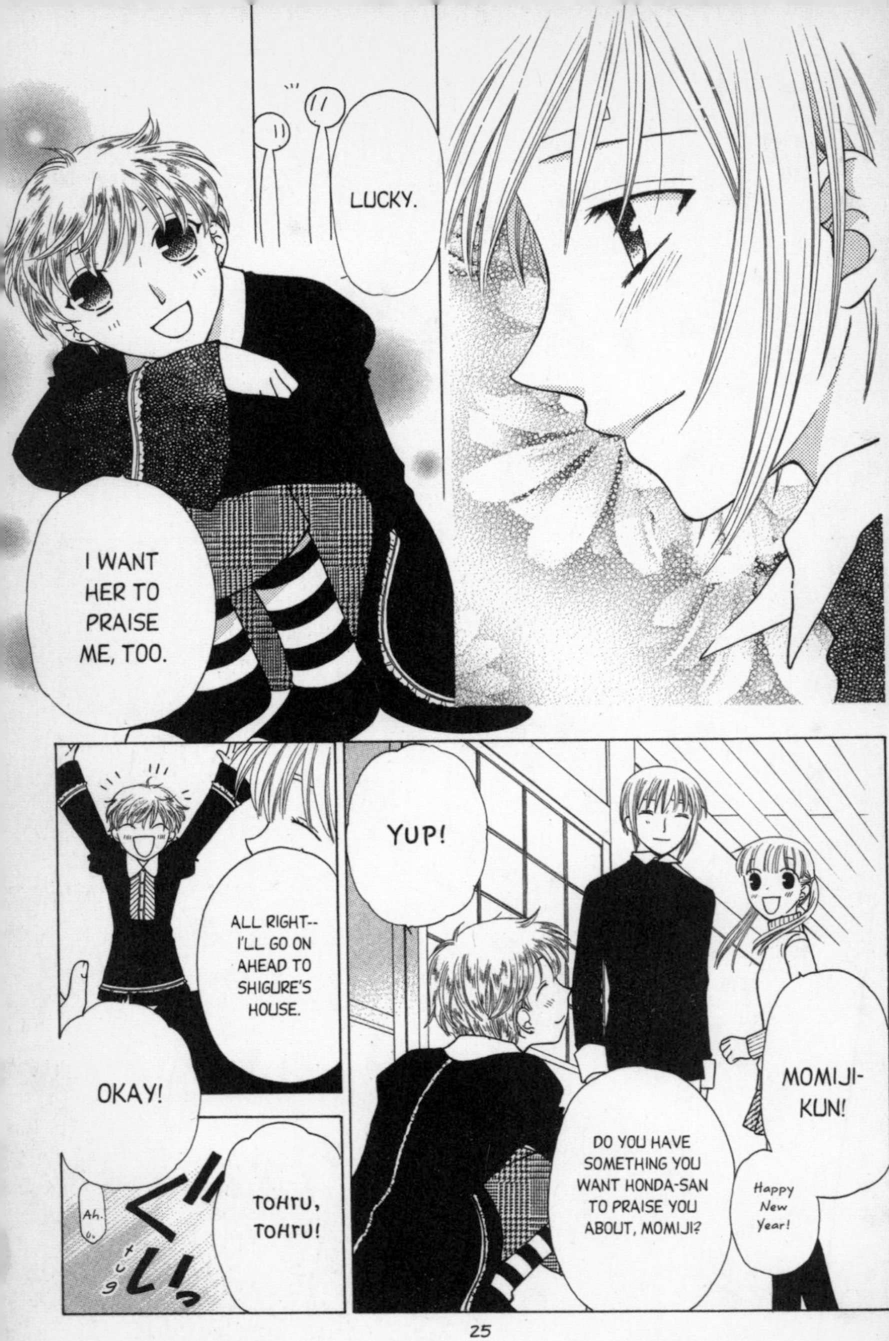
LUCKY.
I WANT HER TO PRAISE ME, TOO.
MOMIJI-KUN!
Happy New Year!
DO YOU HAVE SOMETHING YOU WANT HONDA-SAN TO PRAISE YOU ABOUT, MOMIJI?
YUP!
ALL RIGHT-- I'LL GO ON AHEAD TO SHIGURE'S HOUSE.
OKAY!
TOHRU, TOHRU!
Ah. U.
くいっ
tug

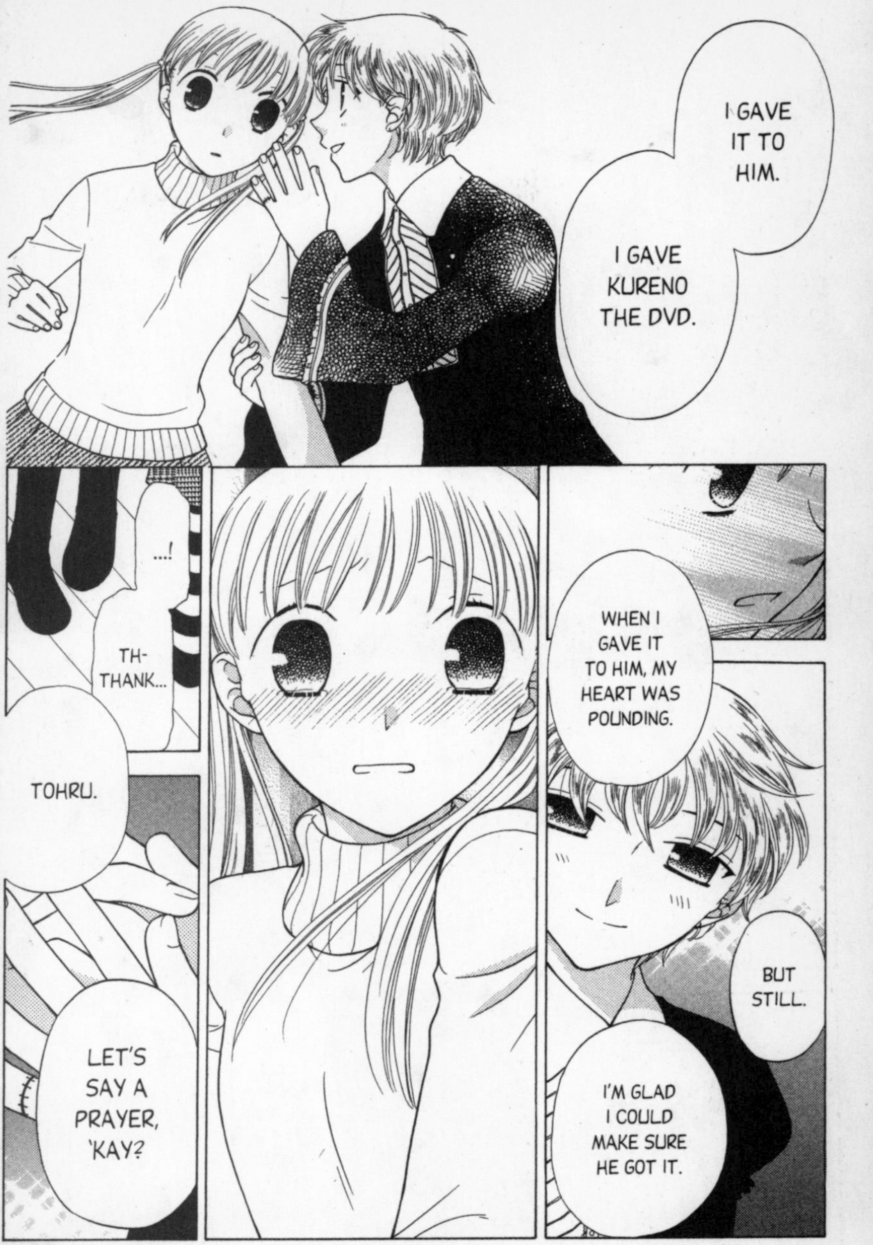

I GAVE IT TO HIM.
I GAVE KURENO THE DVD.
WHEN I GAVE IT TO HIM, MY HEART WAS POUNDING.
BUT STILL.
I'M GLAD I COULD MAKE SURE HE GOT IT.
...!
TH- THANK...
TOHRU.
LET'S SAY A PRAYER, 'KAY?

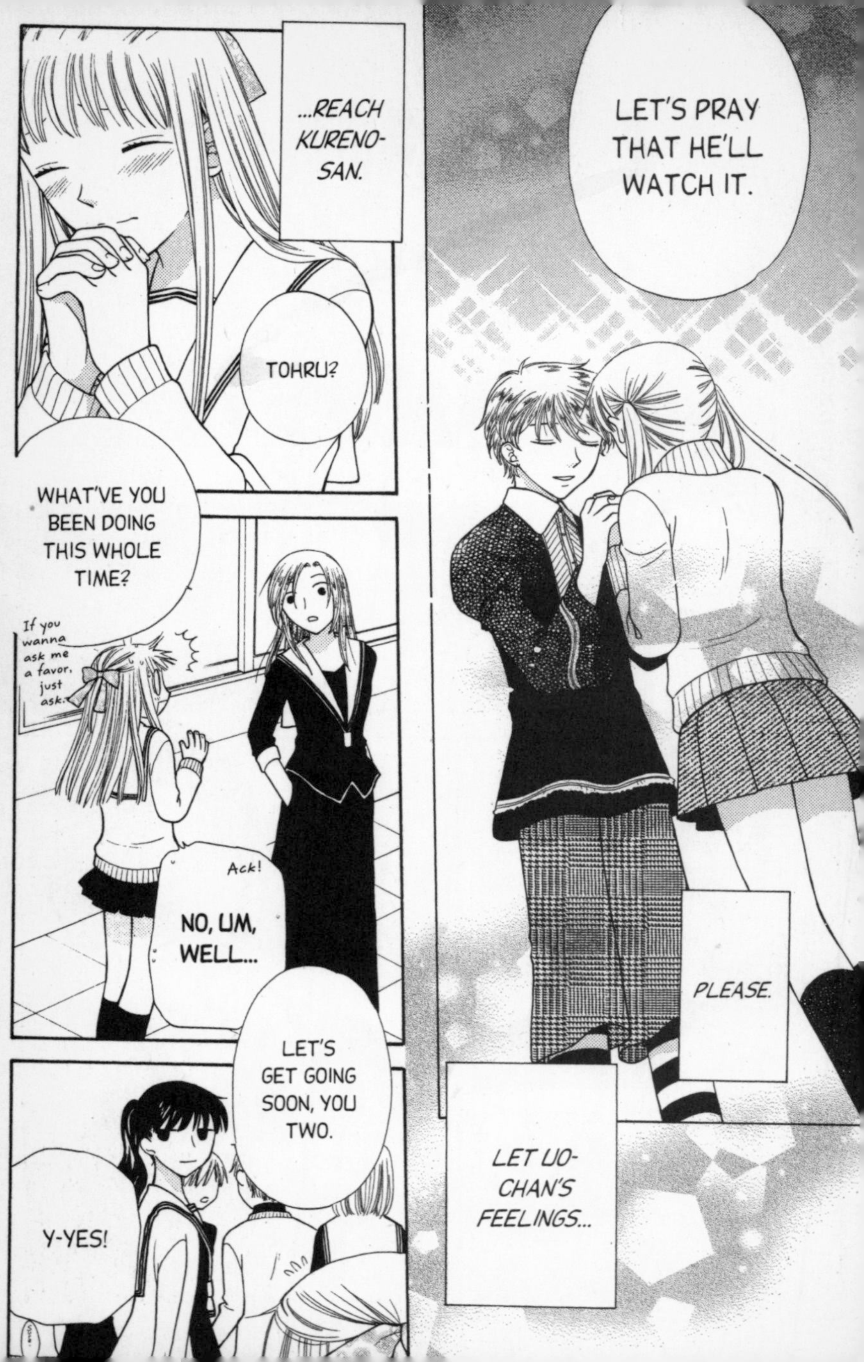
LET'S PRAY THAT HE'LL WATCH IT.
PLEASE.
LET UO-CHAN'S FEELINGS...
...REACH KURENO-SAN.
TOHRU?
WHAT'VE YOU BEEN DOING THIS WHOLE TIME?
If you wanna ask me a favor, just ask.
Ack!
NO, UM, WELL...
LET'S GET GOING SOON, YOU TWO.
Y-YES!

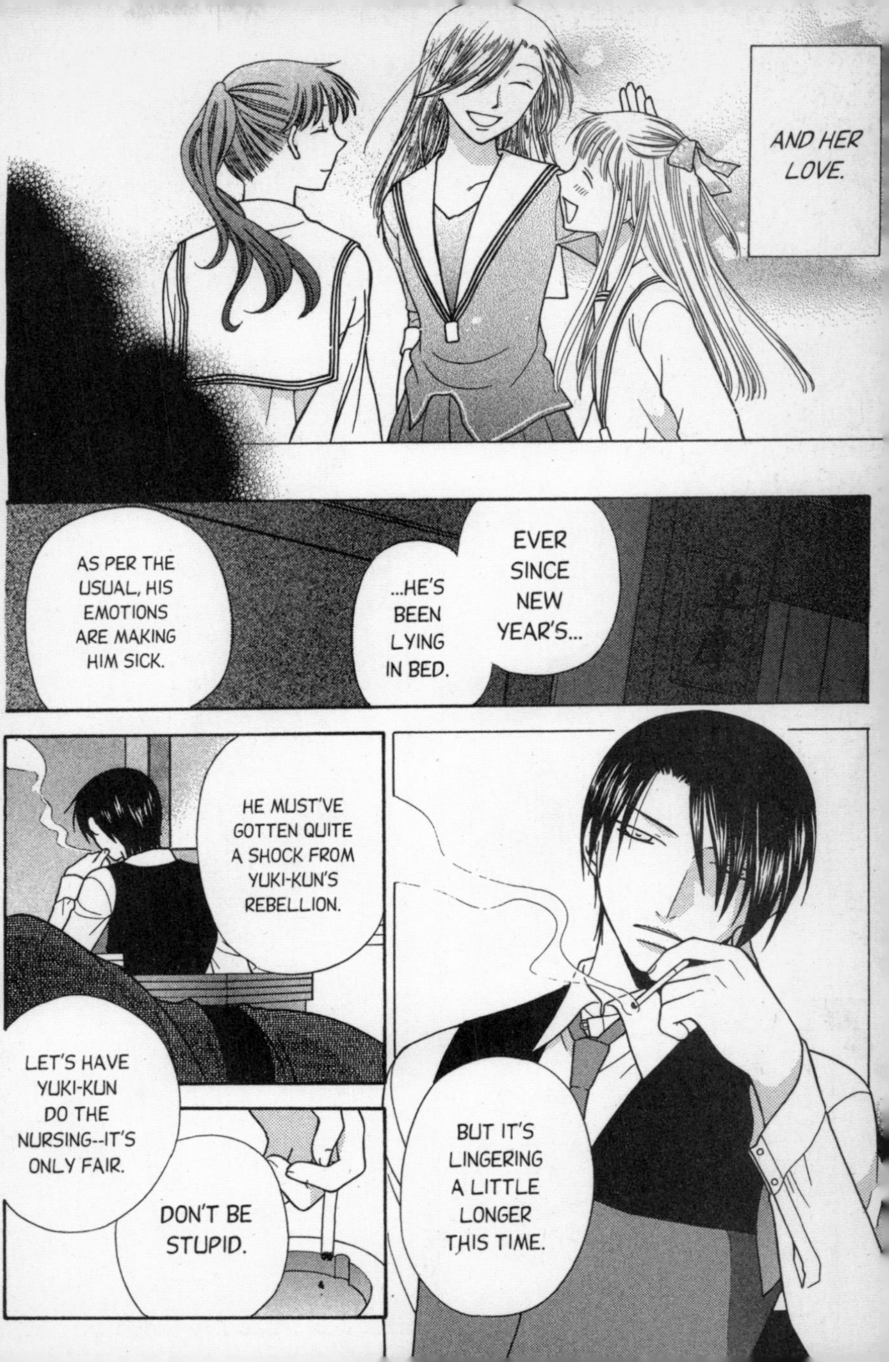
AND HER LOVE.
EVER SINCE NEW YEAR'S...
...HE'S BEEN LYING IN BED.
AS PER THE USUAL, HIS EMOTIONS ARE MAKING HIM SICK.
BUT IT'S LINGERING A LITTLE LONGER THIS TIME.
HE MUST'VE GOTTEN QUITE A SHOCK FROM YUKI-KUN'S REBELLION.
LET'S HAVE YUKI-KUN DO THE NURSING--IT'S ONLY FAIR.
DON'T BE STUPID.

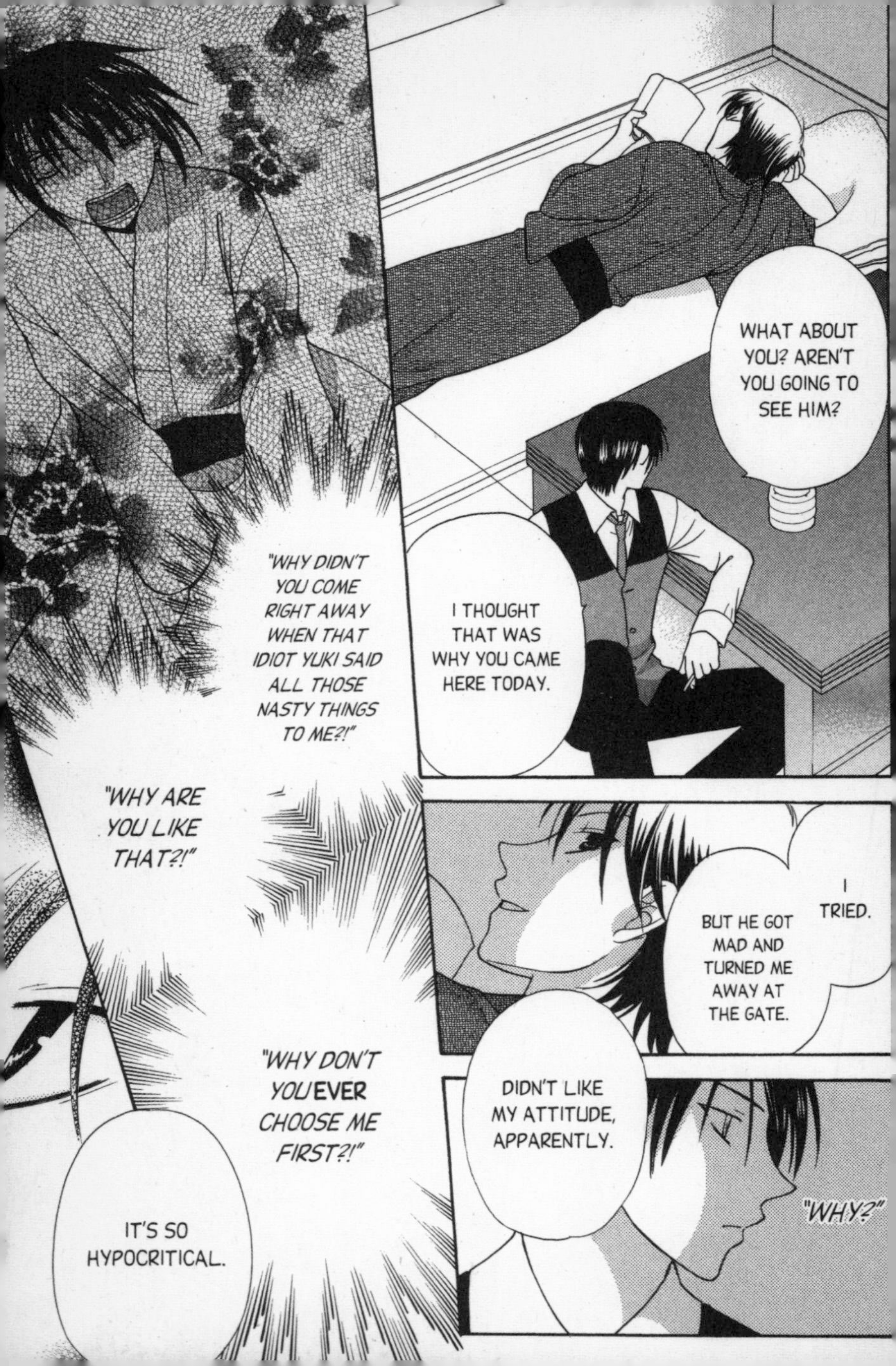
WHAT ABOUT YOU? AREN'T YOU GOING TO SEE HIM?
I THOUGHT THAT WAS WHY YOU CAME HERE TODAY.
I TRIED.
BUT HE GOT MAD AND TURNED ME AWAY AT THE GATE.
DIDN'T LIKE MY ATTITUDE, APPARENTLY.
"WHY?"
"WHY DIDN'T YOU COME RIGHT AWAY WHEN THAT IDIOT YUKI SAID ALL THOSE NASTY THINGS TO ME?!"
"WHY ARE YOU LIKE THAT?!"
"WHY DON'T YOU EVER CHOOSE ME FIRST?!"
IT'S SO HYPOCRITICAL.

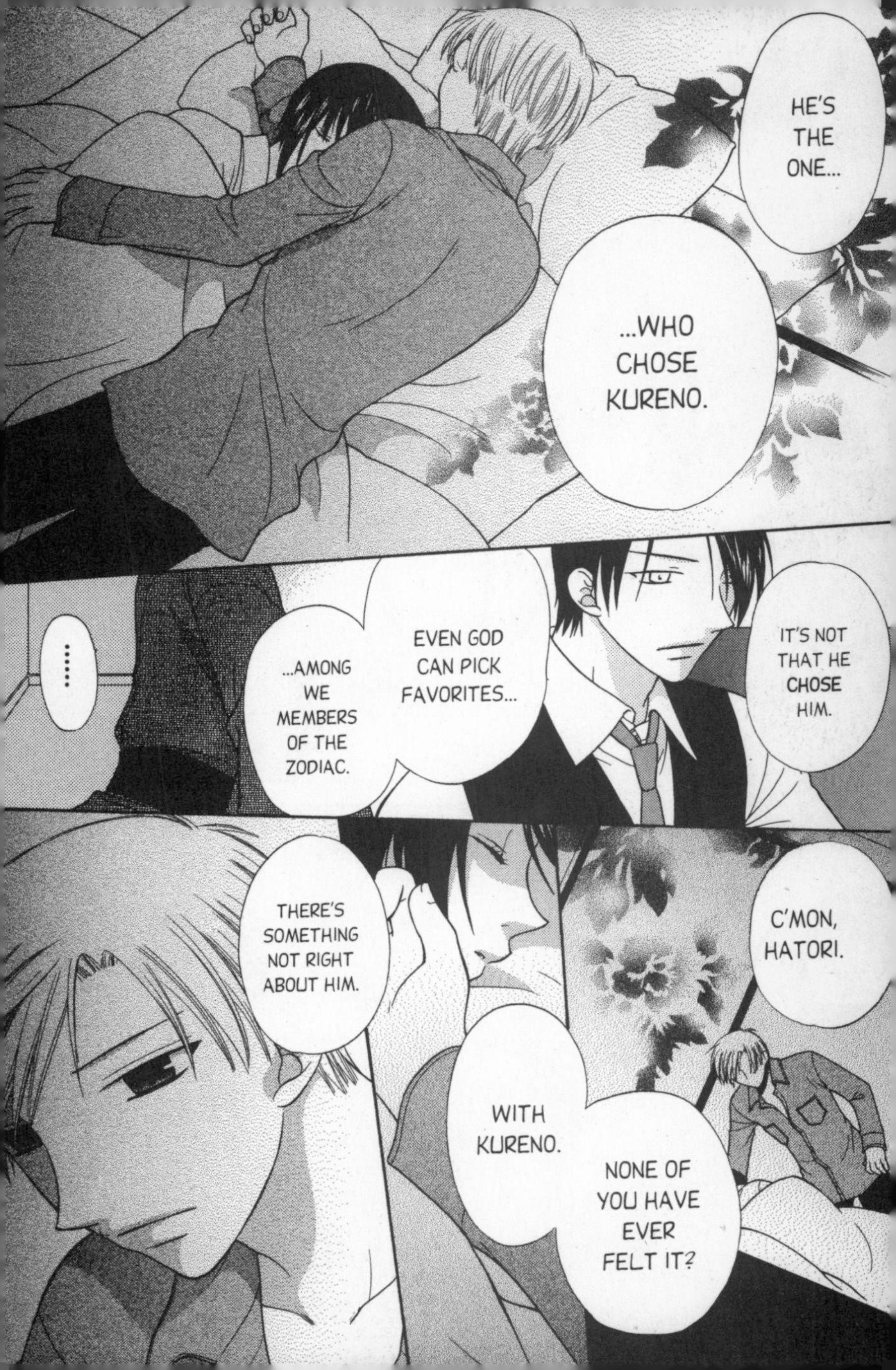
HE'S THE ONE...
...WHO CHOSE KURENO.
IT'S NOT THAT HE CHOSE HIM.
EVEN GOD CAN PICK FAVORITES...
...AMONG WE MEMBERS OF THE ZODIAC.
......
C'MON, HATORI.
NONE OF YOU HAVE EVER FELT IT?
WITH KURENO.
THERE'S SOMETHING NOT RIGHT ABOUT HIM.

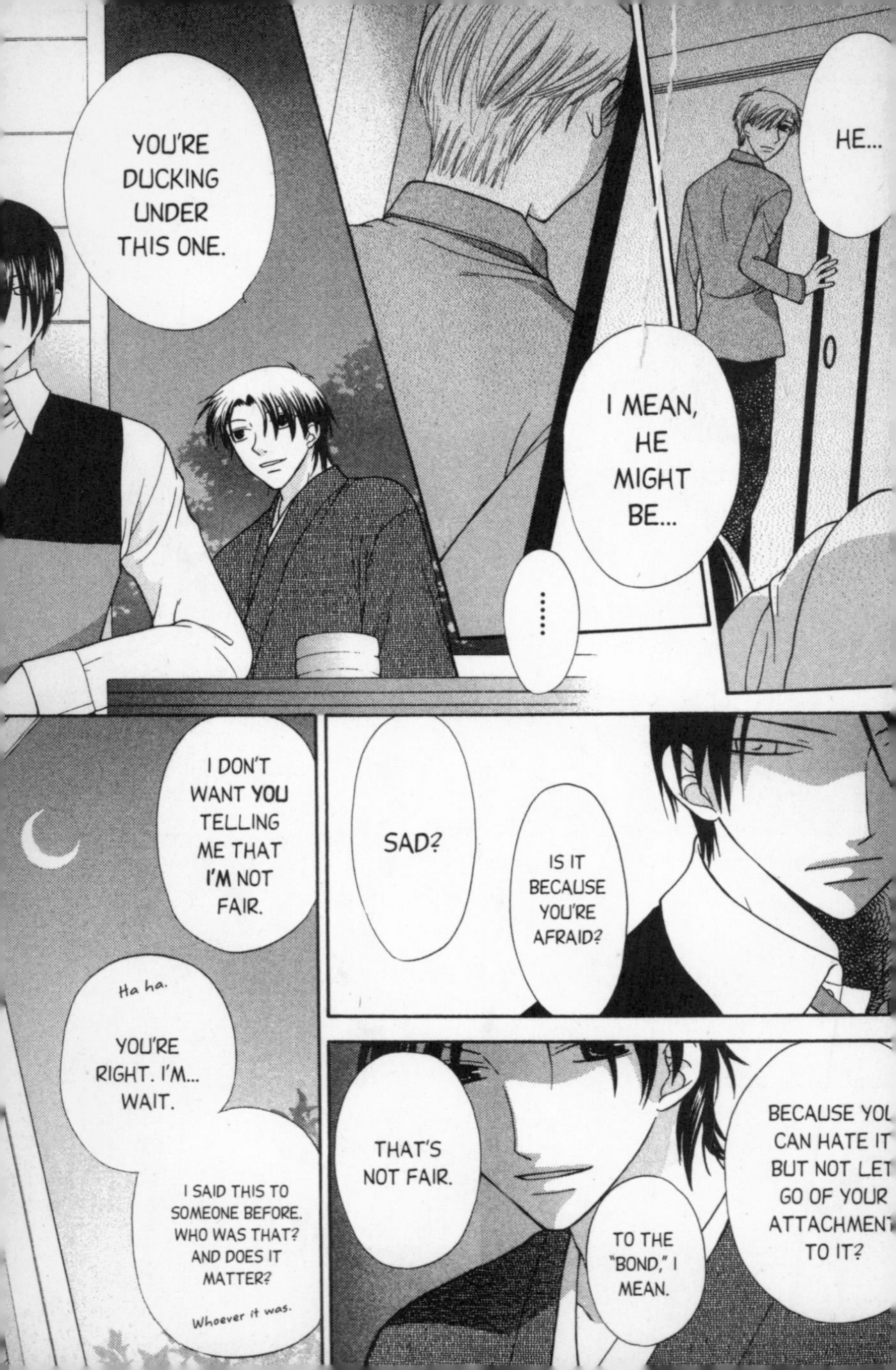
HE...
I MEAN, HE MIGHT BE...
......
YOU'RE DUCKING UNDER THIS ONE.
SAD?
IS IT BECAUSE YOU'RE AFRAID?
BECAUSE YOU CAN HATE IT BUT NOT LET GO OF YOUR ATTACHMENT TO IT?
TO THE "BOND," I MEAN.
THAT'S NOT FAIR.
I DON'T WANT YOU TELLING ME THAT I'M NOT FAIR.
Ha ha.
YOU'RE RIGHT. I'M... WAIT.
I SAID THIS TO SOMEONE BEFORE. WHO WAS THAT? AND DOES IT MATTER?
Whoever it was.

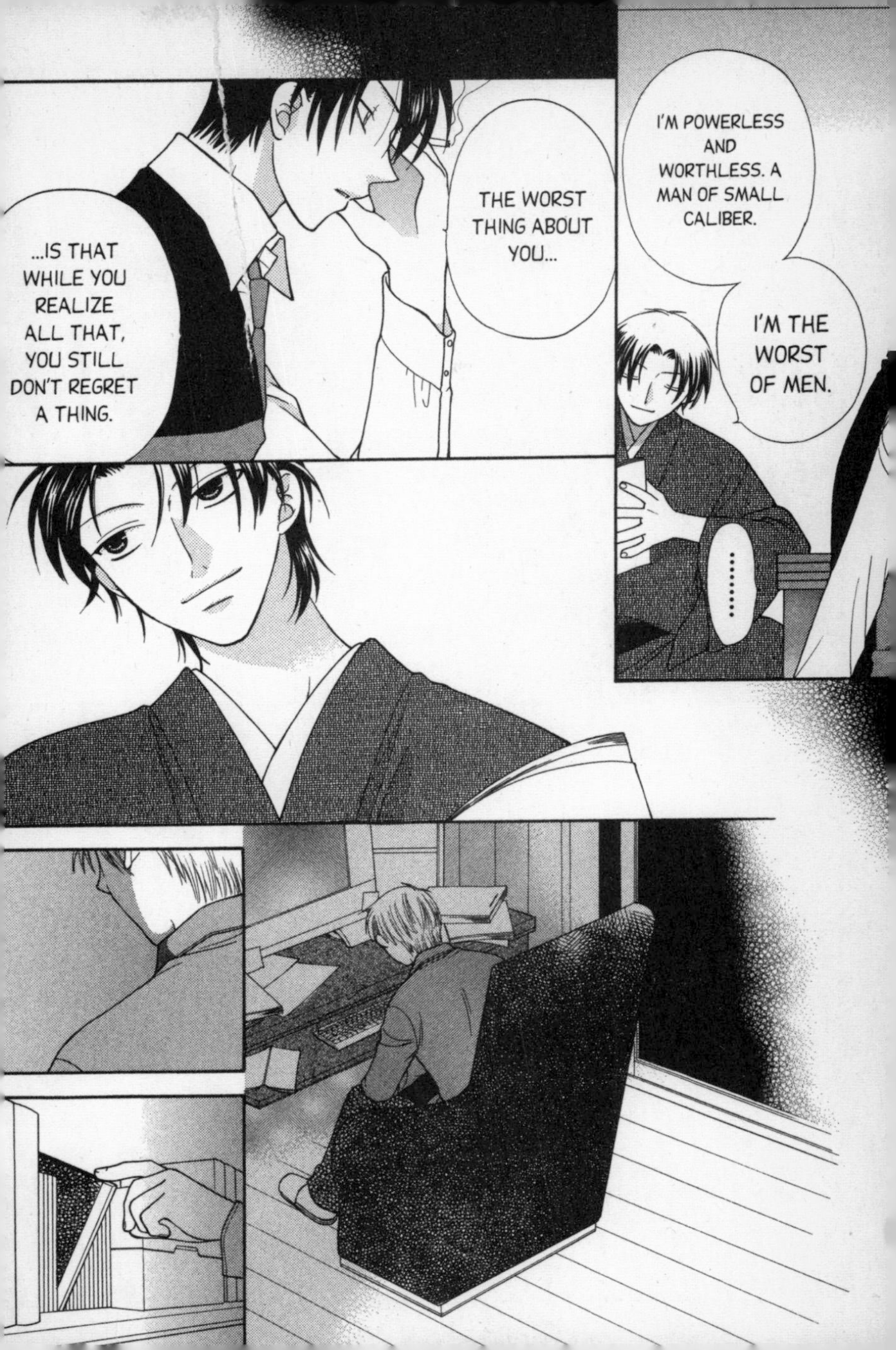
I'M POWERLESS AND WORTHLESS. A MAN OF SMALL CALIBER.
I'M THE WORST OF MEN.
......
THE WORST THING ABOUT YOU...
...IS THAT WHILE YOU REALIZE ALL THAT, YOU STILL DON'T REGRET A THING.

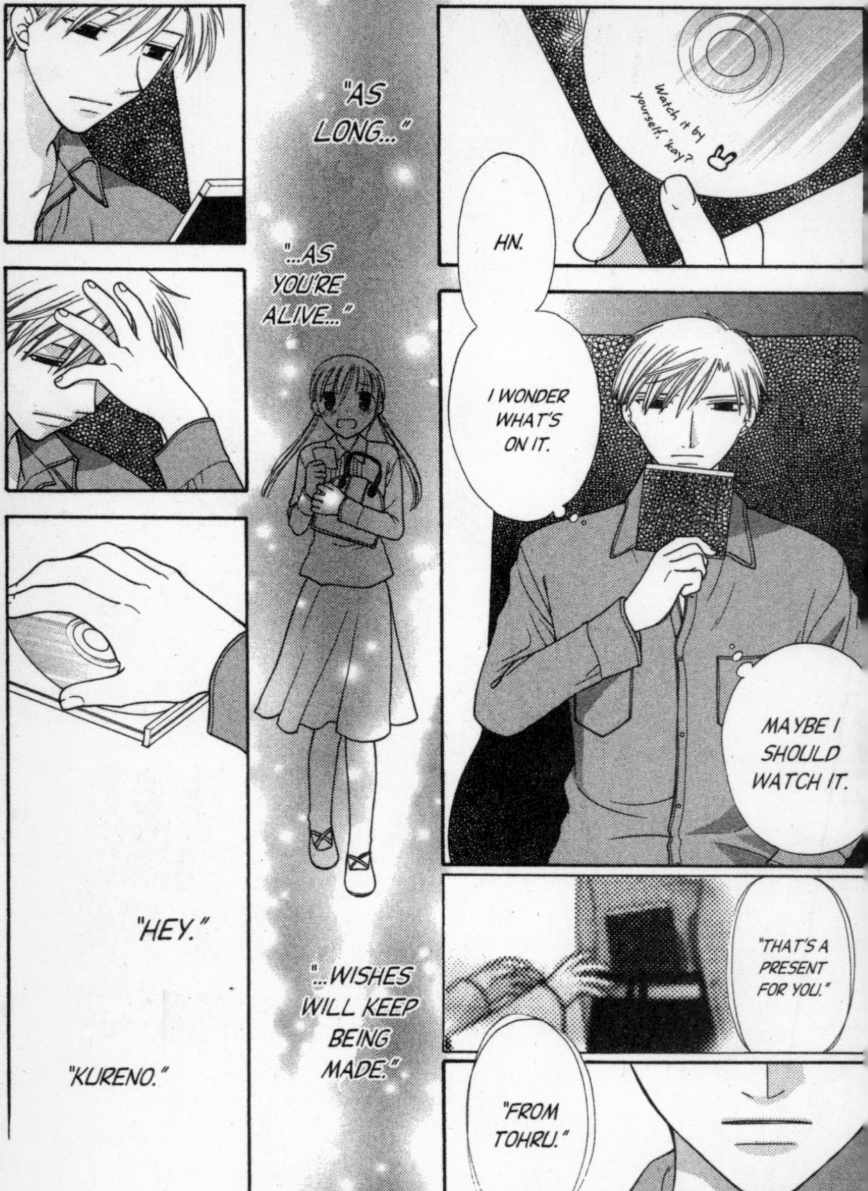
Watch it by yourself, 'kay?
HN.
I WONDER WHAT'S ON IT.
MAYBE I SHOULD WATCH IT.
"THAT'S A PRESENT FOR YOU."
"FROM TOHRU."
"AS LONG..."
"...AS YOU'RE ALIVE..."
"...WISHES WILL KEEP BEING MADE."
"HEY."
"KURENO."

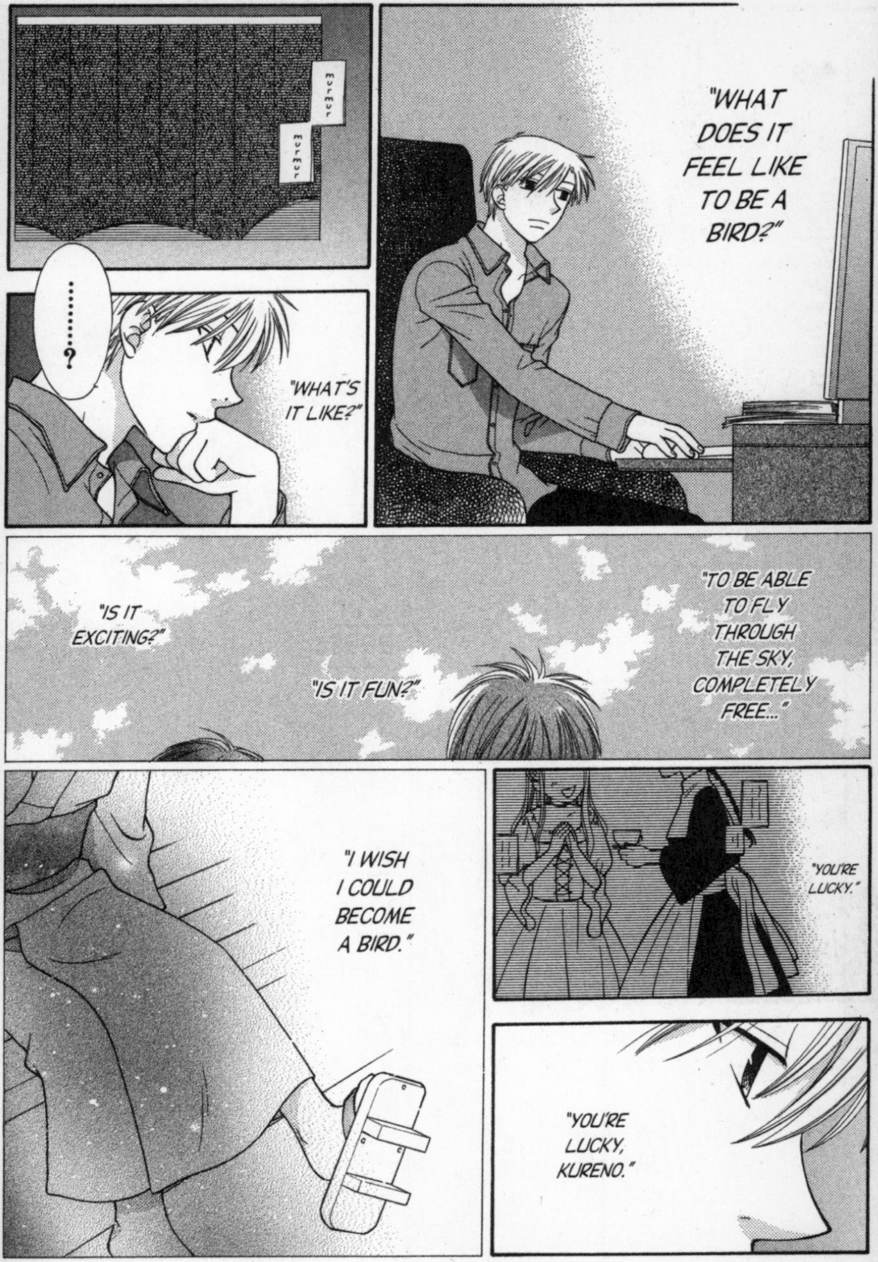
"WHAT DOES IT FEEL LIKE TO BE A BIRD?"
murmur
murmur
......?
"WHAT'S IT LIKE?"
"TO BE ABLE TO FLY THROUGH THE SKY, COMPLETELY FREE..."
"IS IT FUN?"
"IS IT EXCITING?"
"YOU'RE LUCKY."
"YOU'RE LUCKY, KURENO."
"I WISH I COULD BECOME A BIRD."

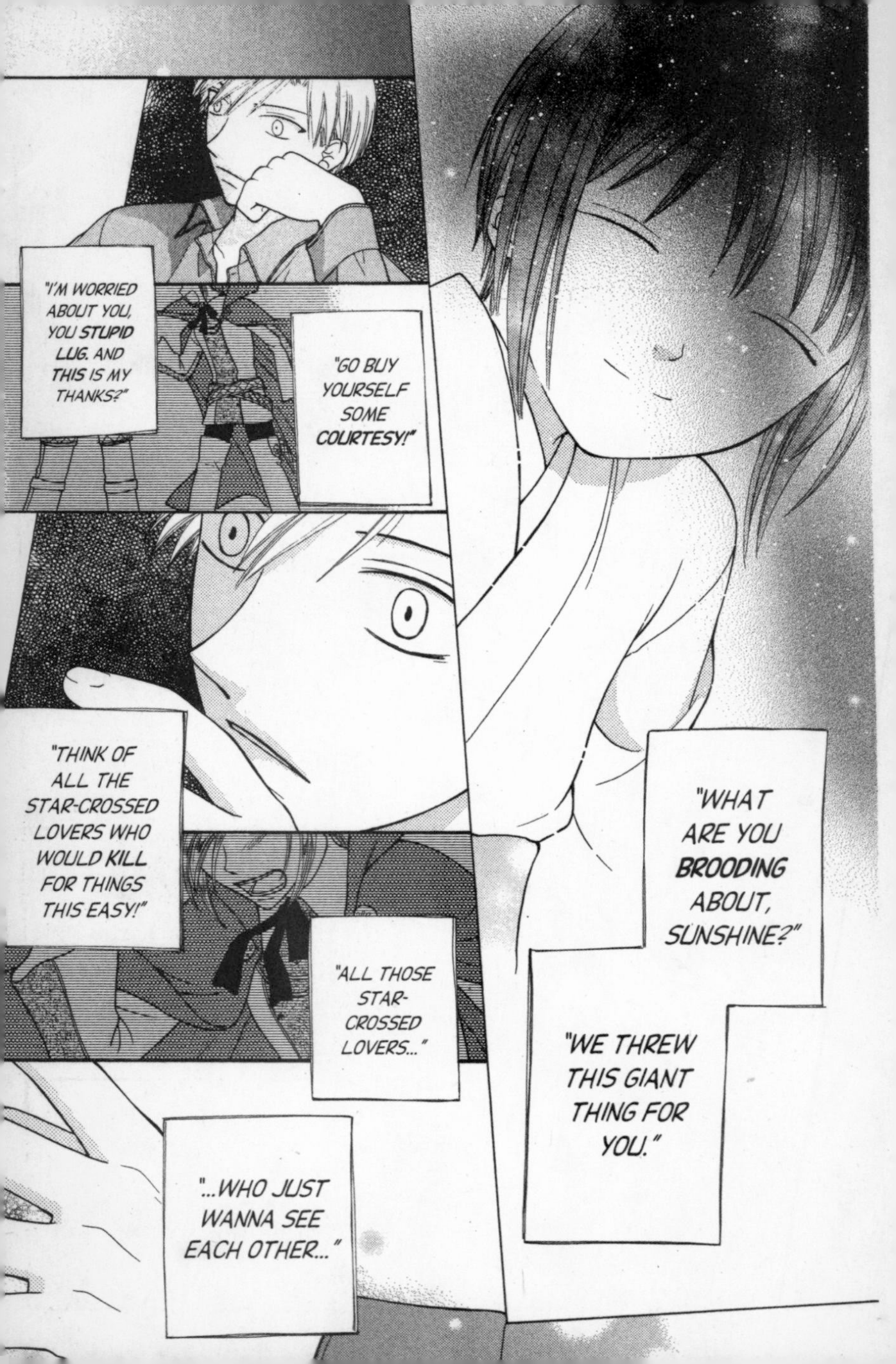
"WHAT ARE YOU BROODING ABOUT, SUNSHINE?"
"WE THREW THIS GIANT THING FOR YOU."
"I'M WORRIED ABOUT YOU, YOU STUPID LUG. AND THIS IS MY THANKS?"
"GO BUY YOURSELF SOME COURTESY!"
"THINK OF ALL THE STAR-CROSSED LOVERS WHO WOULD KILL FOR THINGS THIS EASY!"
"ALL THOSE STAR-CROSSED LOVERS..."
"...WHO JUST WANNA SEE EACH OTHER..."

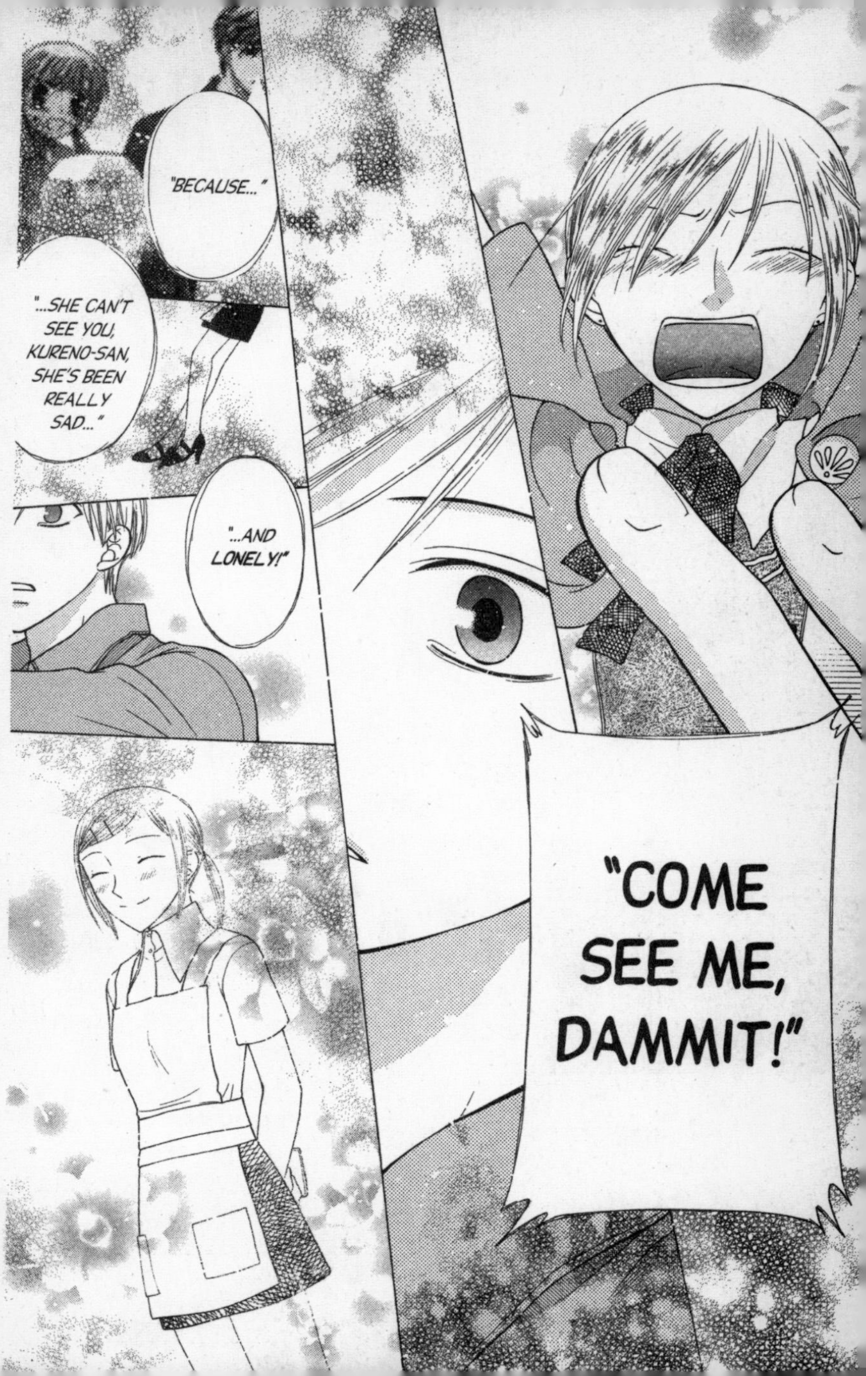
"COME SEE ME, DAMMIT!"
"BECAUSE..."
"...SHE CAN'T SEE YOU, KURENO-SAN, SHE'S BEEN REALLY SAD..."
"...AND LONELY!"

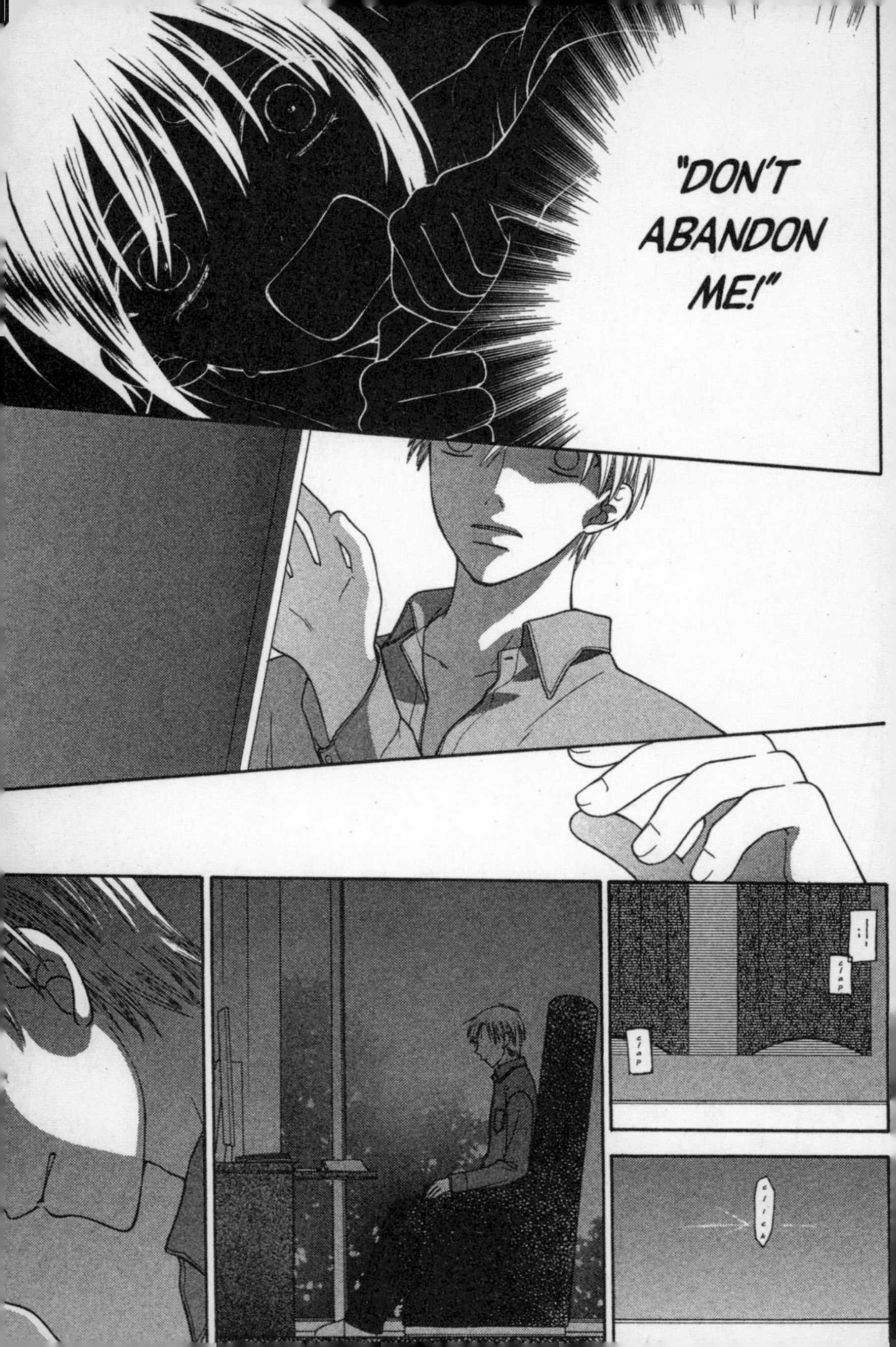
"DON'T ABANDON ME!"
clap
clap
click

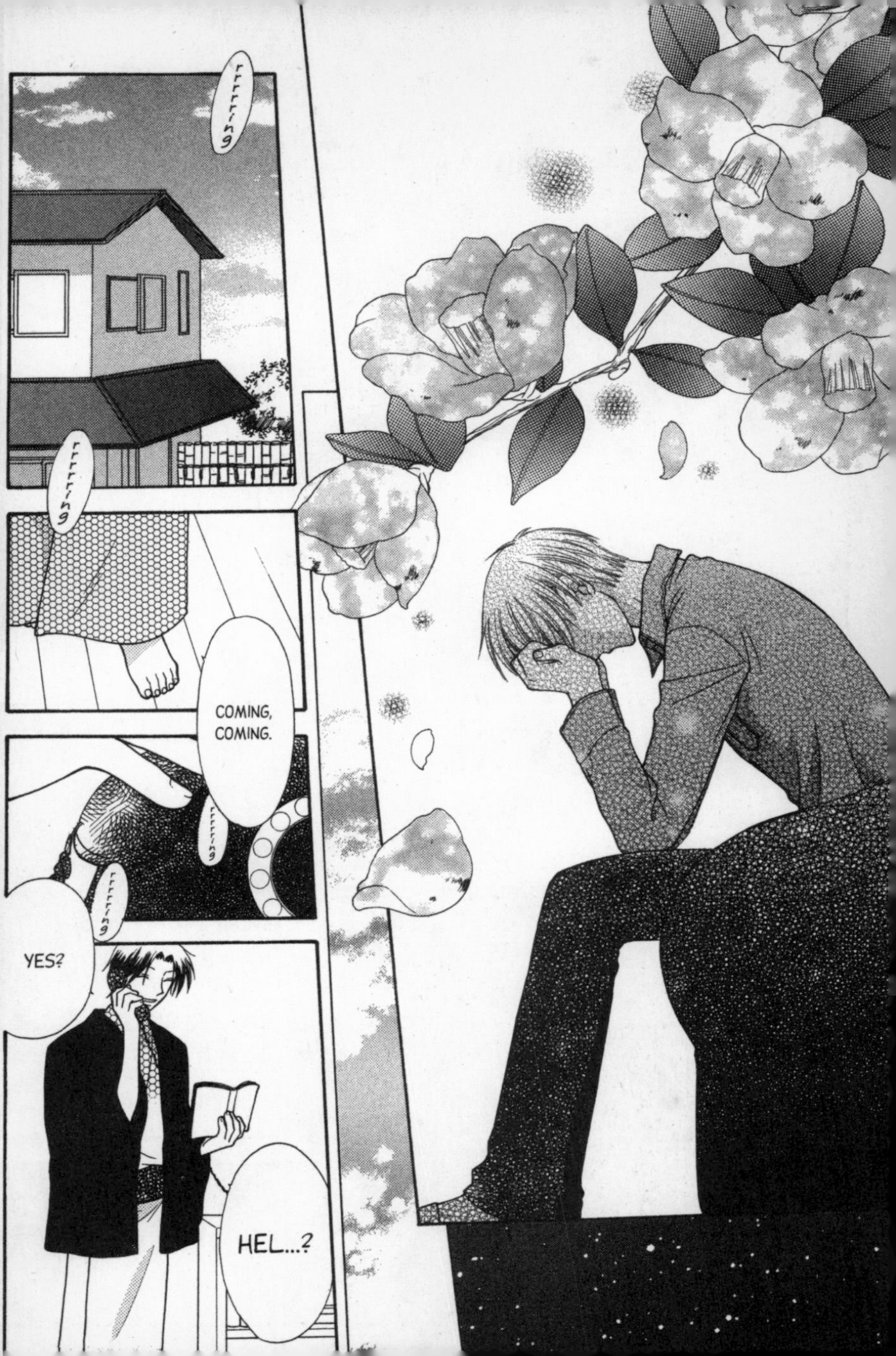
rrrring
rrrring
COMING, COMING.
rrrring
rrrring
YES?
HEL...?

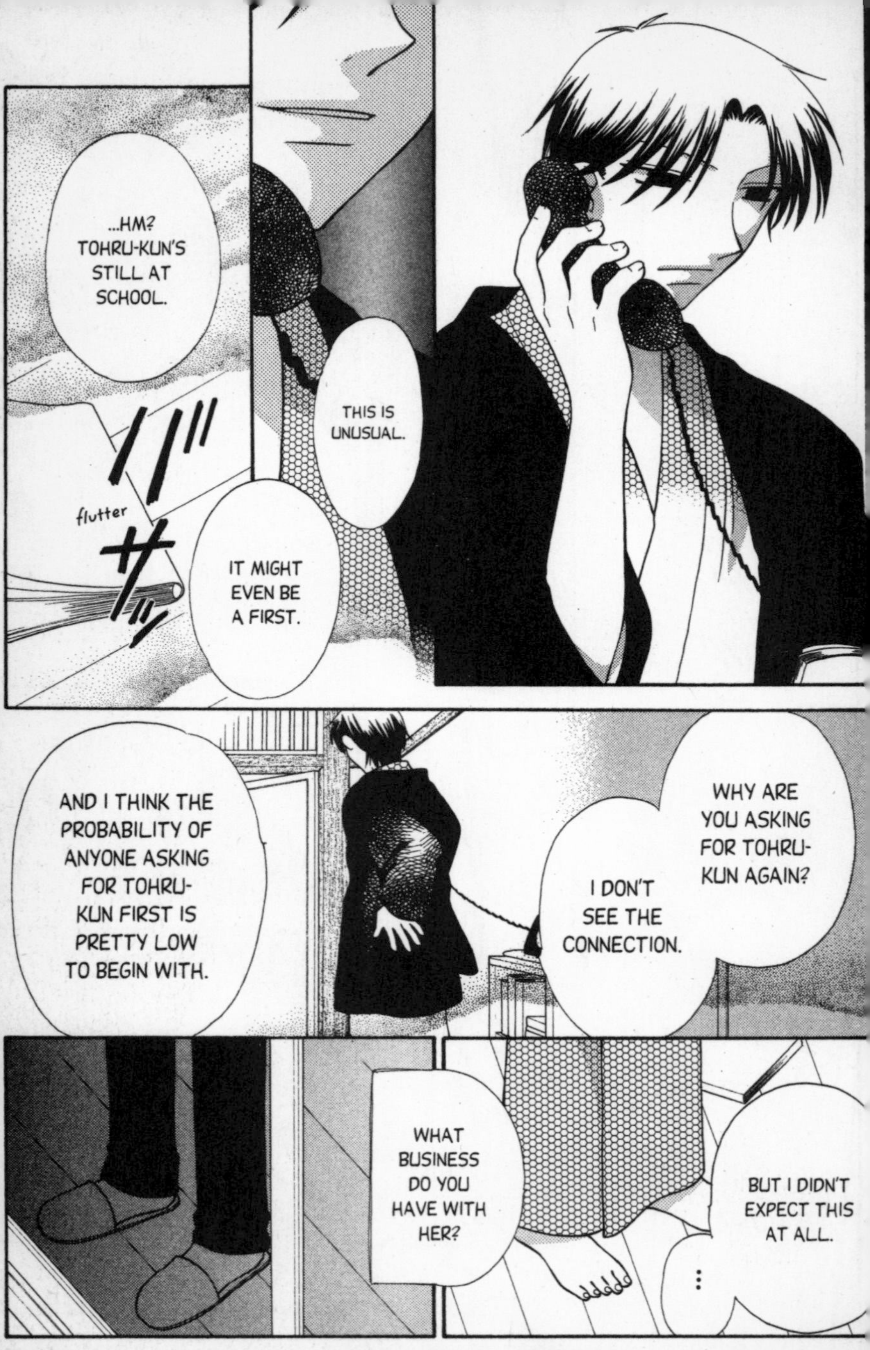
...HM? TOHRU-KUN'S STILL AT SCHOOL.
flutter
THIS IS UNUSUAL.
IT MIGHT EVEN BE A FIRST.
AND I THINK THE PROBABILITY OF ANYONE ASKING FOR TOHRU-KUN FIRST IS PRETTY LOW TO BEGIN WITH.
I DON'T SEE THE CONNECTION.
WHY ARE YOU ASKING FOR TOHRU-KUN AGAIN?
WHAT BUSINESS DO YOU HAVE WITH HER?
BUT I DIDN'T EXPECT THIS AT ALL.
...

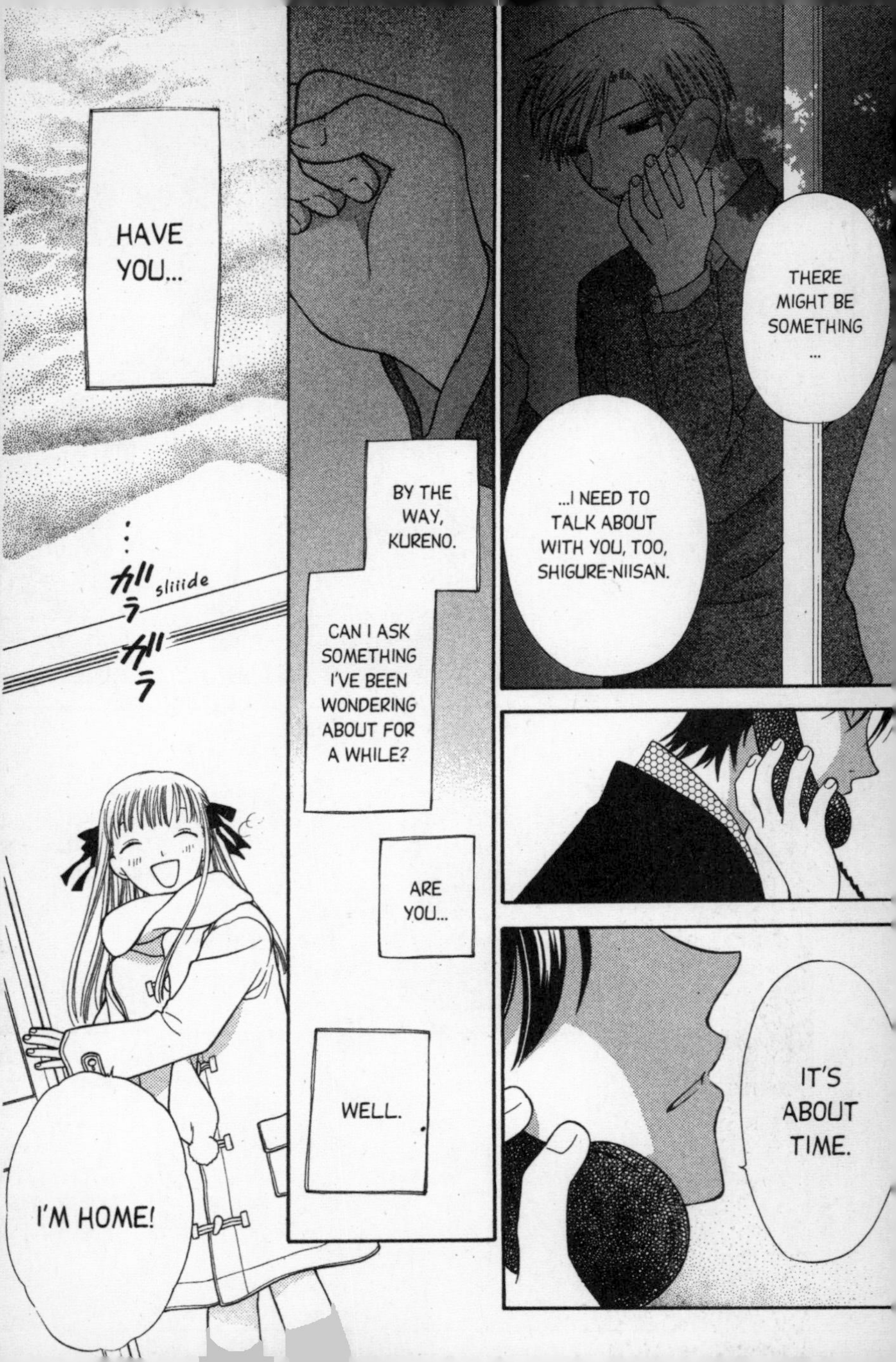
THERE MIGHT BE SOMETHING ...
...I NEED TO TALK ABOUT WITH YOU, TOO, SHIGURE-NIISAN.
IT'S ABOUT TIME.
BY THE WAY, KURENO.
CAN I ASK SOMETHING I'VE BEEN WONDERING ABOUT FOR A WHILE?
ARE YOU...
WELL.
HAVE YOU...
...
ガラ sliiide
ガラ
I'M HOME!

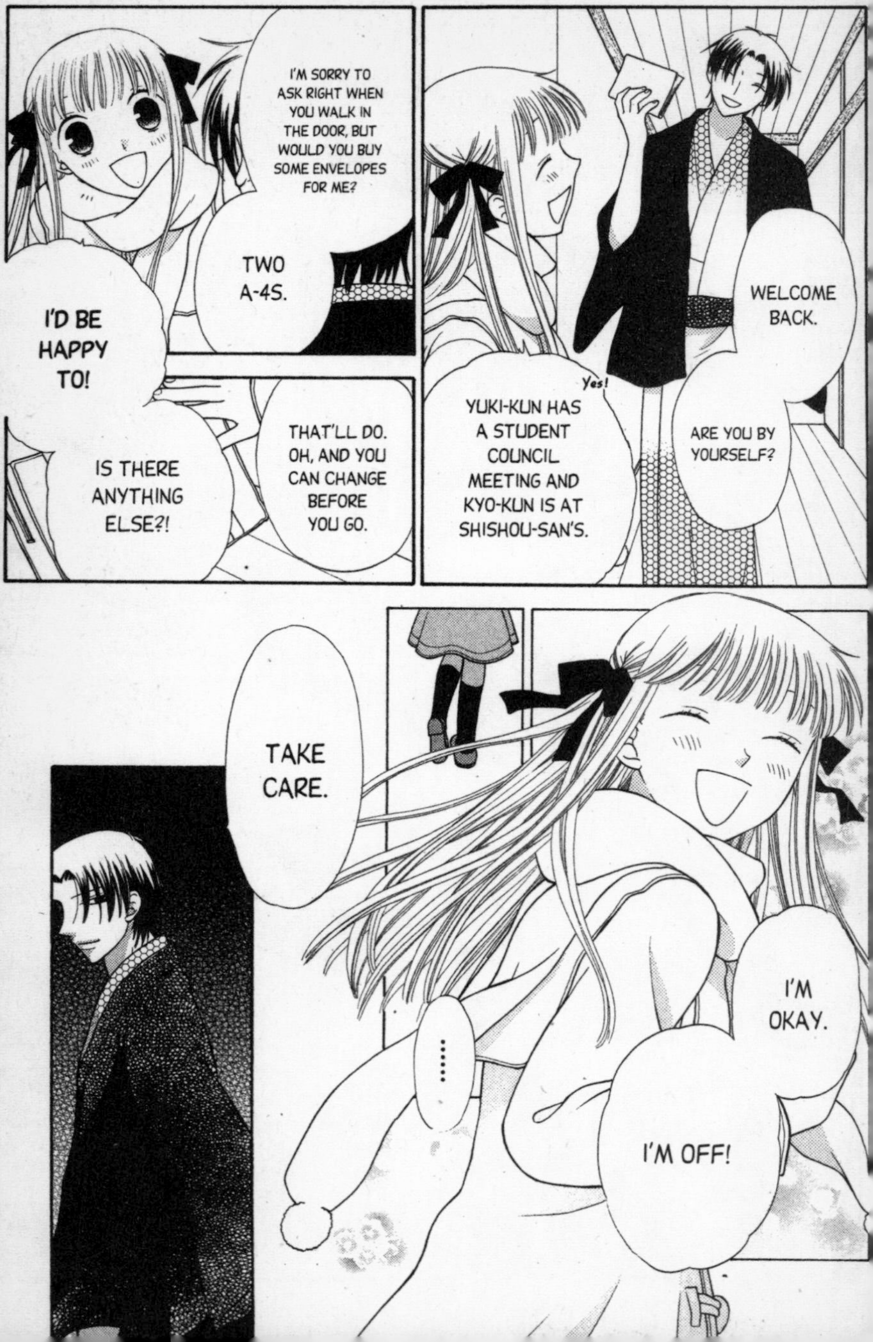
WELCOME BACK.
ARE YOU BY YOURSELF?
Yes!
YUKI-KUN HAS A STUDENT COUNCIL MEETING AND KYO-KUN IS AT SHISHOU-SAN'S.
I'M SORRY TO ASK RIGHT WHEN YOU WALK IN THE DOOR, BUT WOULD YOU BUY SOME ENVELOPES FOR ME?
TWO A-4S.
I'D BE HAPPY TO!
IS THERE ANYTHING ELSE?!
THAT'LL DO. OH, AND YOU CAN CHANGE BEFORE YOU GO.
I'M OKAY.
I'M OFF!
TAKE CARE.
......

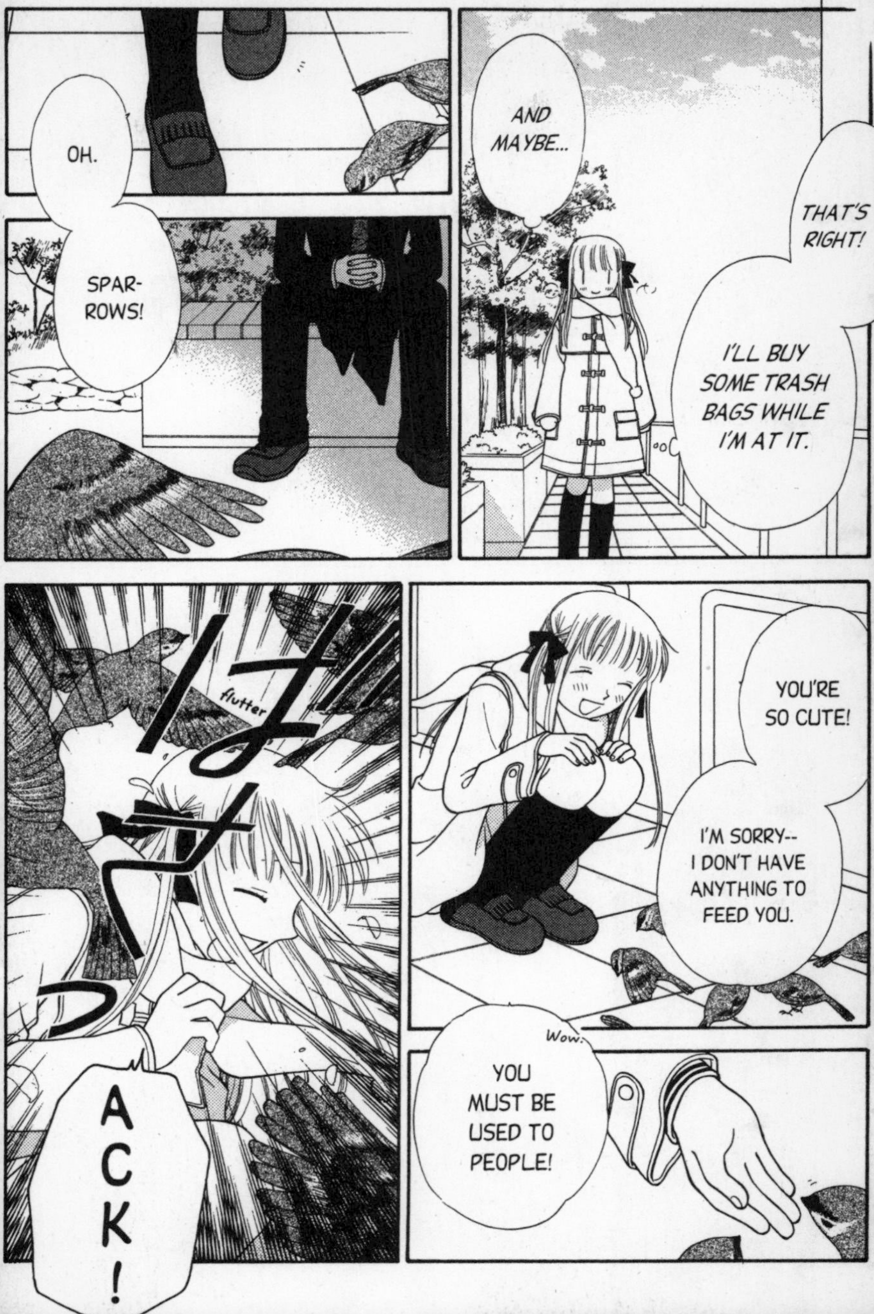
THAT'S RIGHT!
I'LL BUY SOME TRASH BAGS WHILE I'M AT IT.
AND MAYBE...
OH.
SPARROWS!
YOU'RE SO CUTE!
I'M SORRY-- I DON'T HAVE ANYTHING TO FEED YOU.
Wow.
YOU MUST BE USED TO PEOPLE!
flutter
ACK!

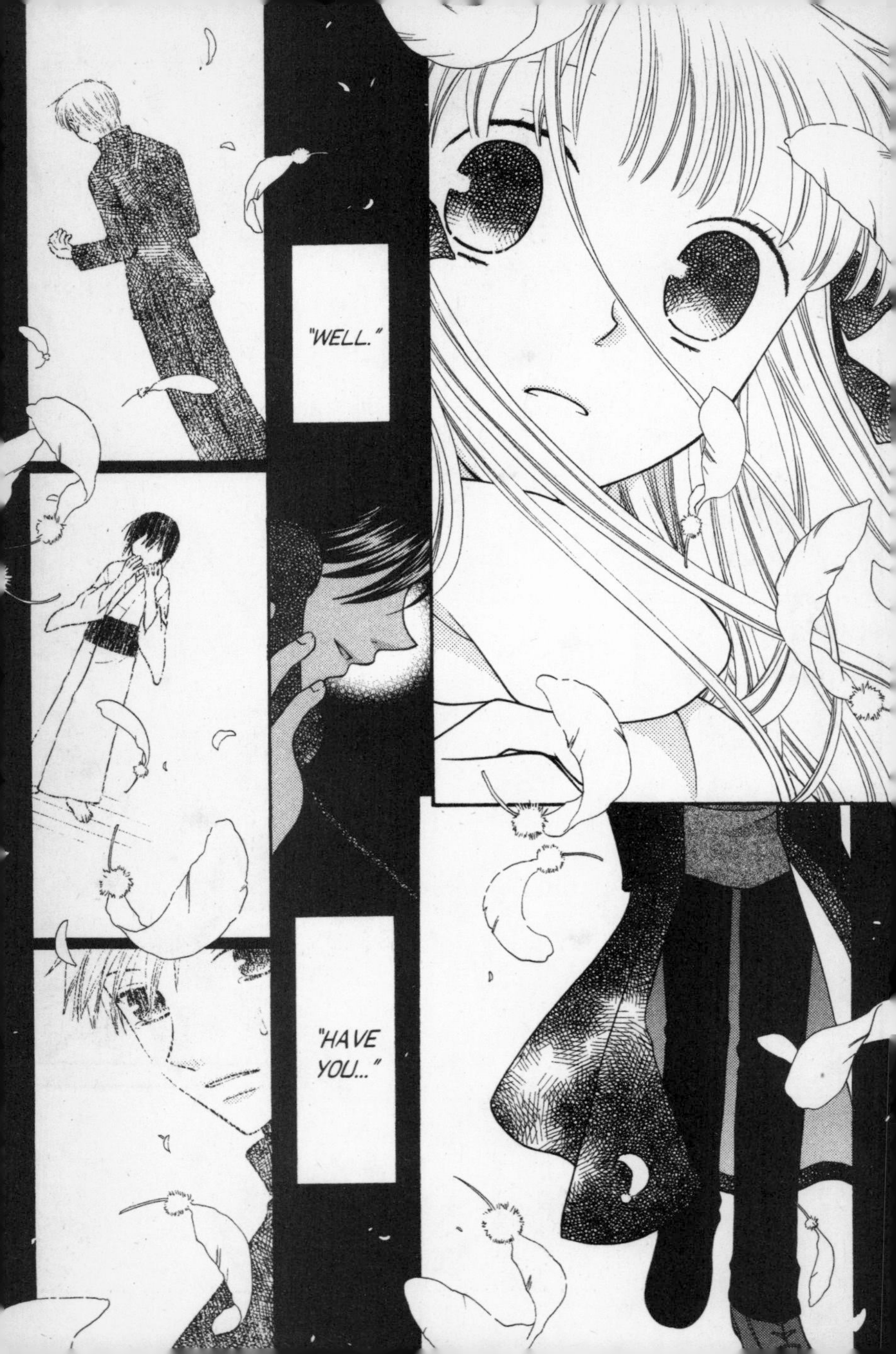
"WELL."
"HAVE YOU..."

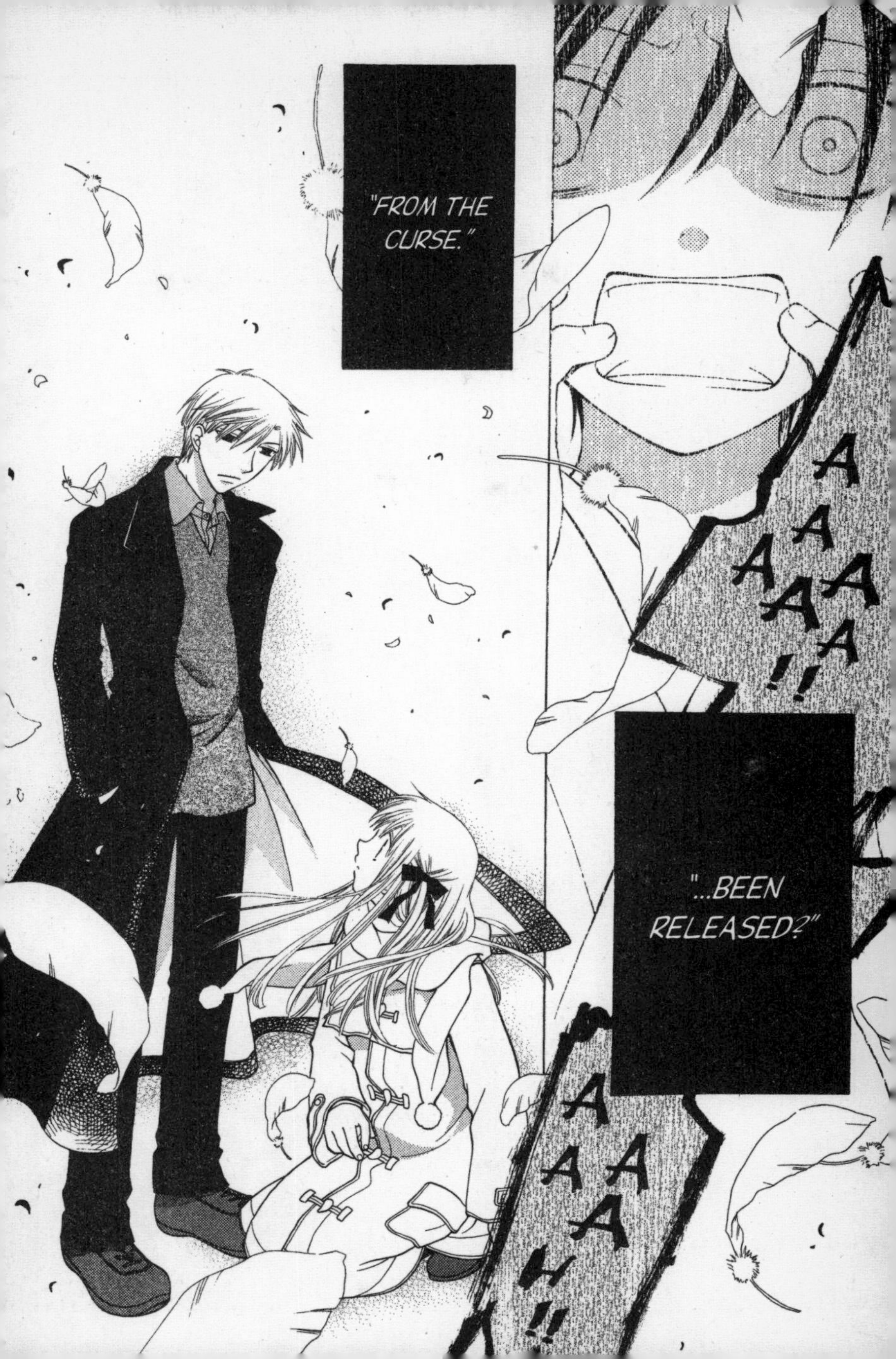
AAAAAAA!!
"...BEEN RELEASED?"
AAAAAH!!
"FROM THE CURSE."

Chapter 97

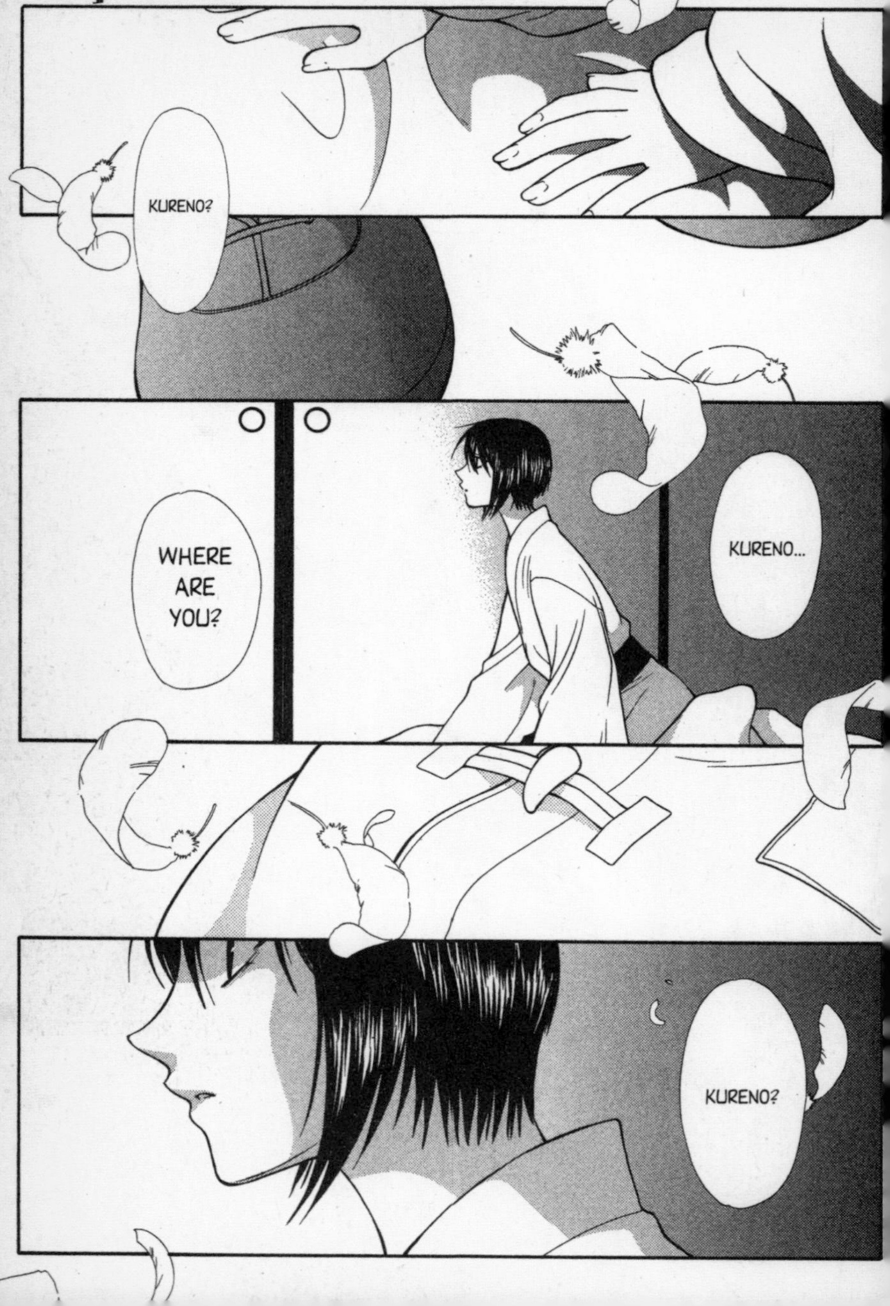
KURENO?
KURENO...
WHERE ARE YOU?
KURENO?

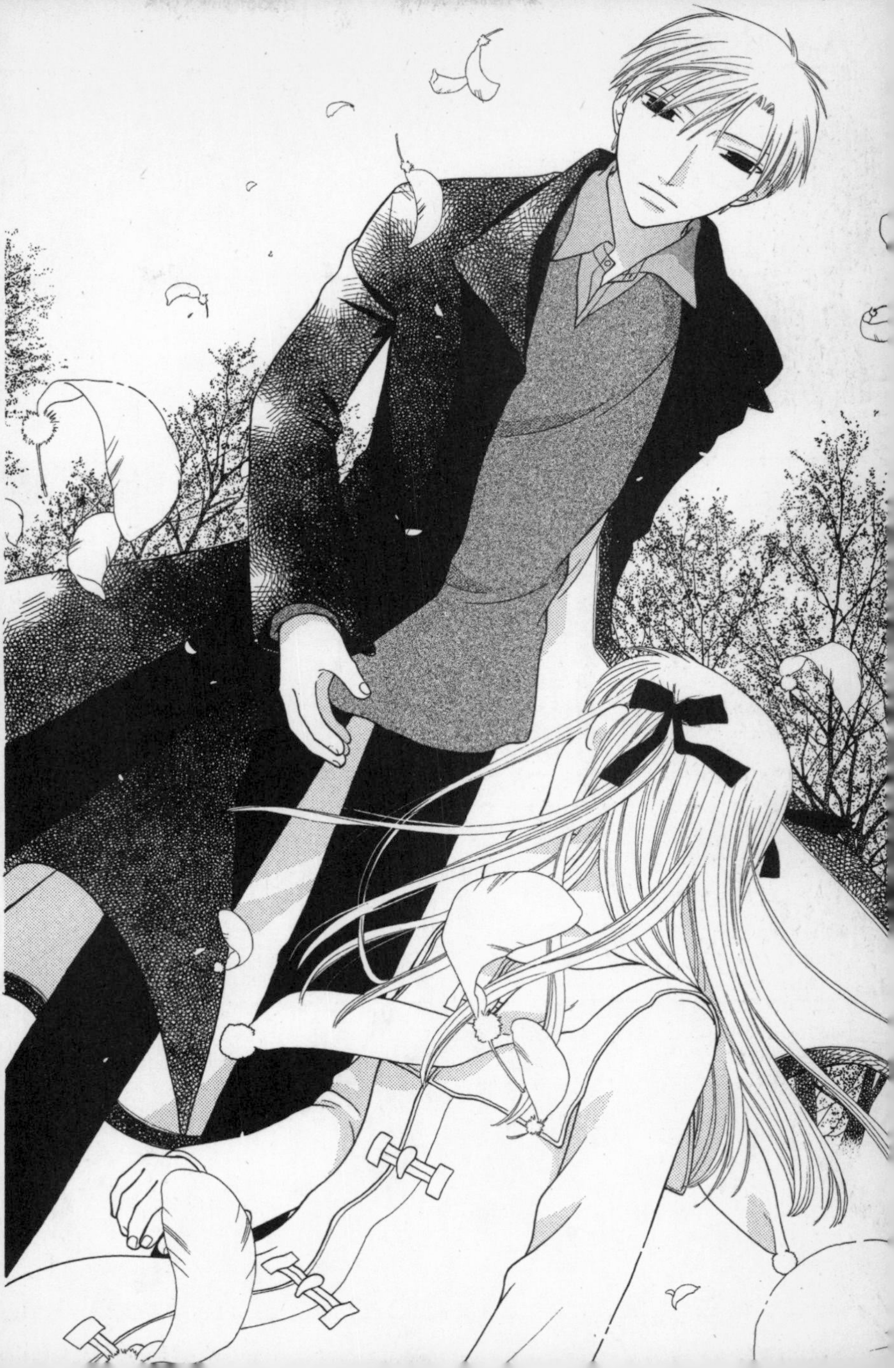

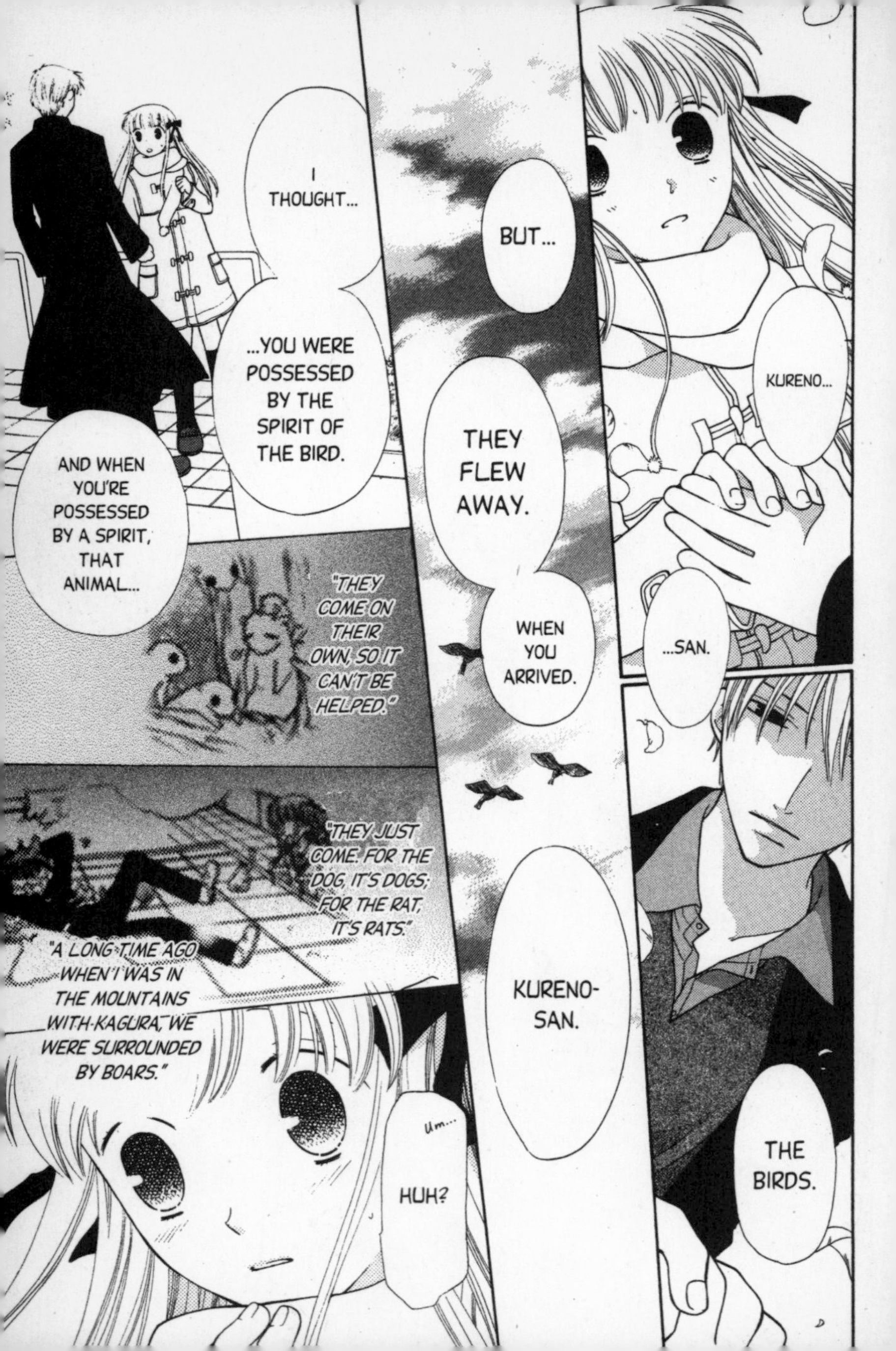
KURENO...
...SAN.
THE BIRDS.
BUT...
THEY FLEW AWAY.
WHEN YOU ARRIVED.
KURENO-SAN.
I THOUGHT...
...YOU WERE POSSESSED BY THE SPIRIT OF THE BIRD.
AND WHEN YOU'RE POSSESSED BY A SPIRIT, THAT ANIMAL...
"THEY COME ON THEIR OWN, SO IT CAN'T BE HELPED."
"THEY JUST COME. FOR THE DOG, IT'S DOGS; FOR THE RAT, IT'S RATS."
"A LONG TIME AGO WHEN I WAS IN THE MOUNTAINS WITH KAGURA, WE WERE SURROUNDED BY BOARS."
Um...
HUH?

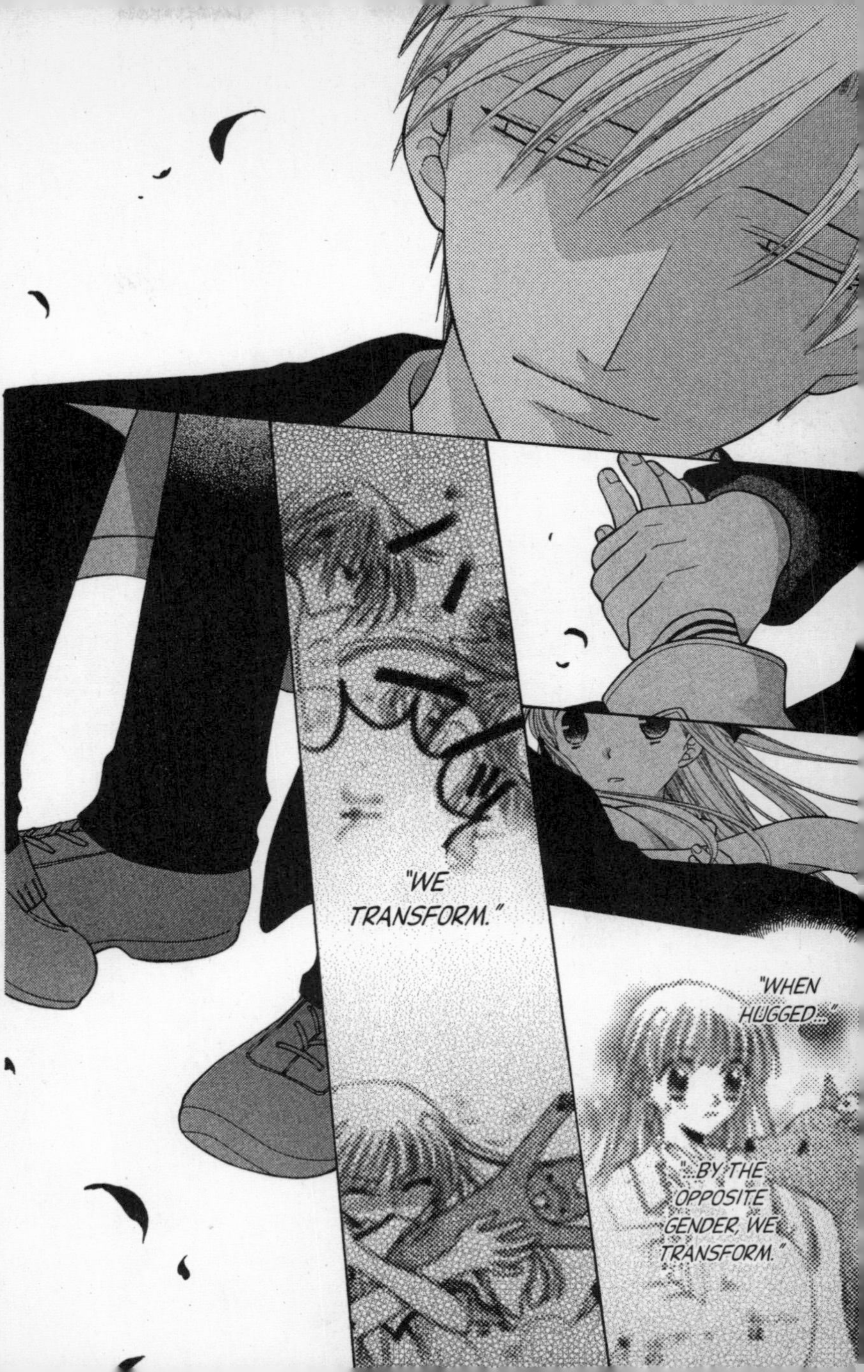
"WHEN HUGGED..."
"...BY THE OPPOSITE GENDER, WE TRANSFORM."
"WE TRANSFORM."

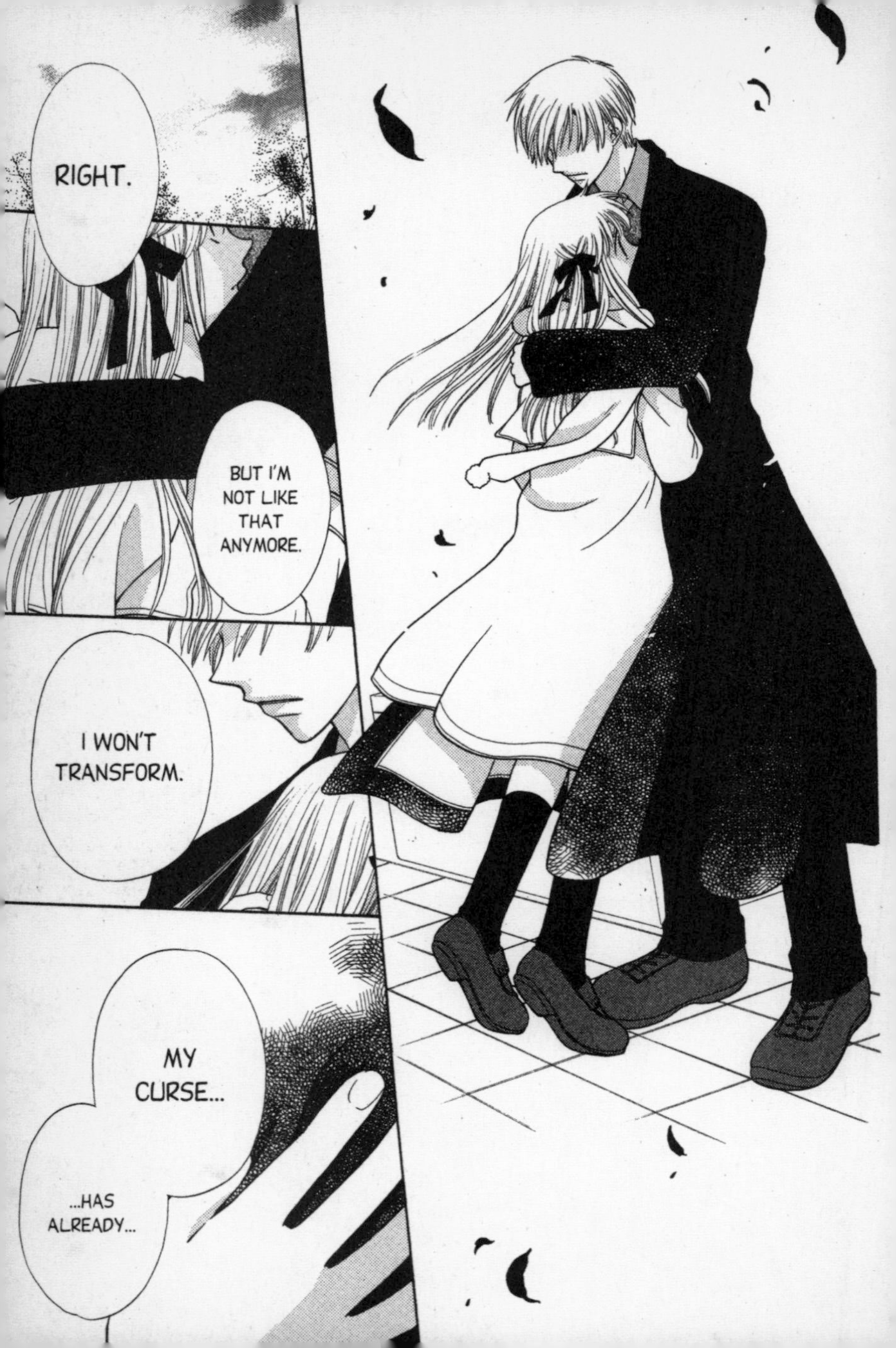
RIGHT.
BUT I'M NOT LIKE THAT ANYMORE.
I WON'T TRANSFORM.
MY CURSE...
...HAS ALREADY...

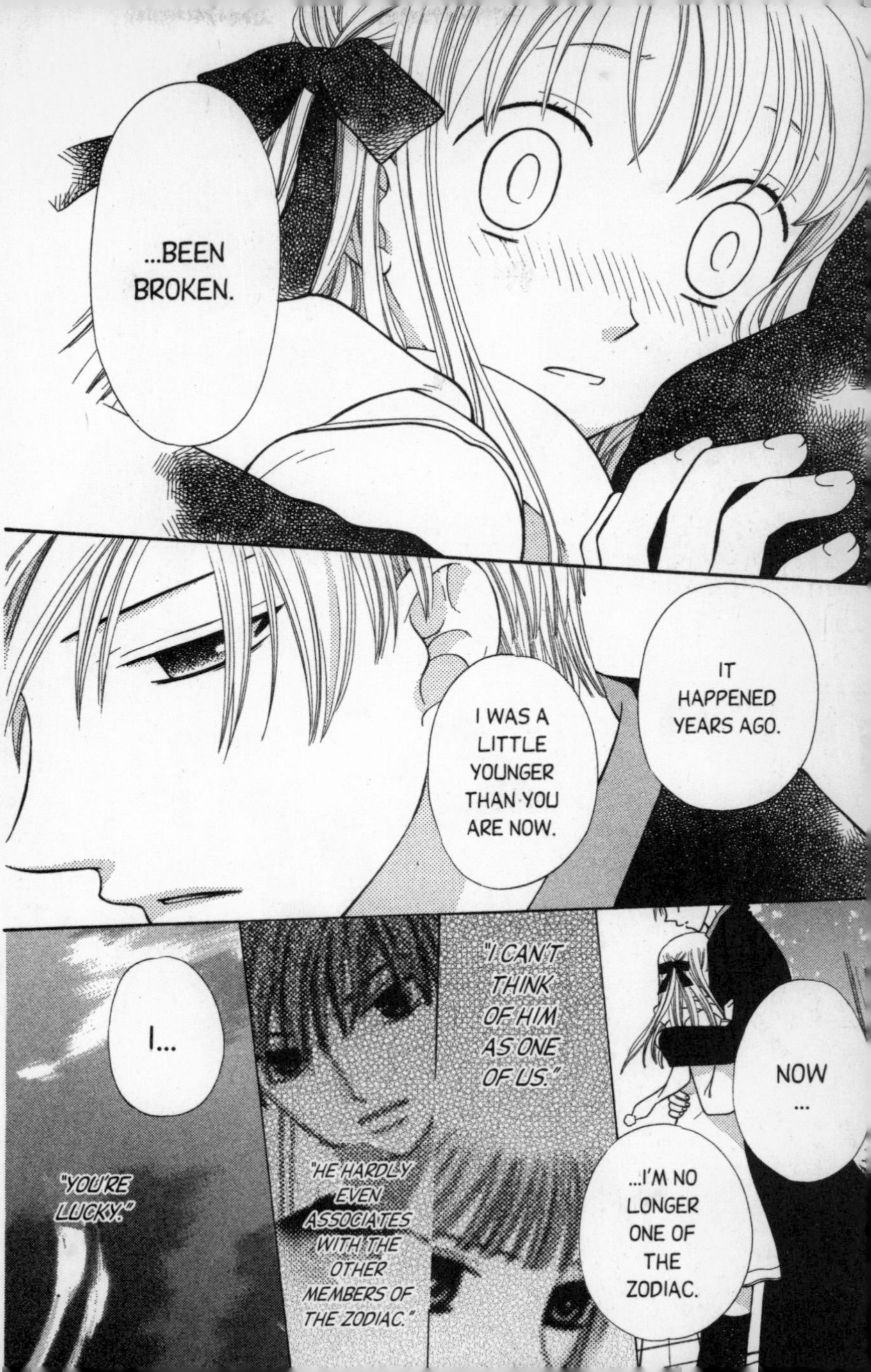
...BEEN BROKEN.
IT HAPPENED YEARS AGO.
I WAS A LITTLE YOUNGER THAN YOU ARE NOW.
NOW ...
...I'M NO LONGER ONE OF THE ZODIAC.
"I CAN'T THINK OF HIM AS ONE OF US."
"HE HARDLY EVEN ASSOCIATES WITH THE OTHER MEMBERS OF THE ZODIAC."
I...
"YOU'RE LUCKY."

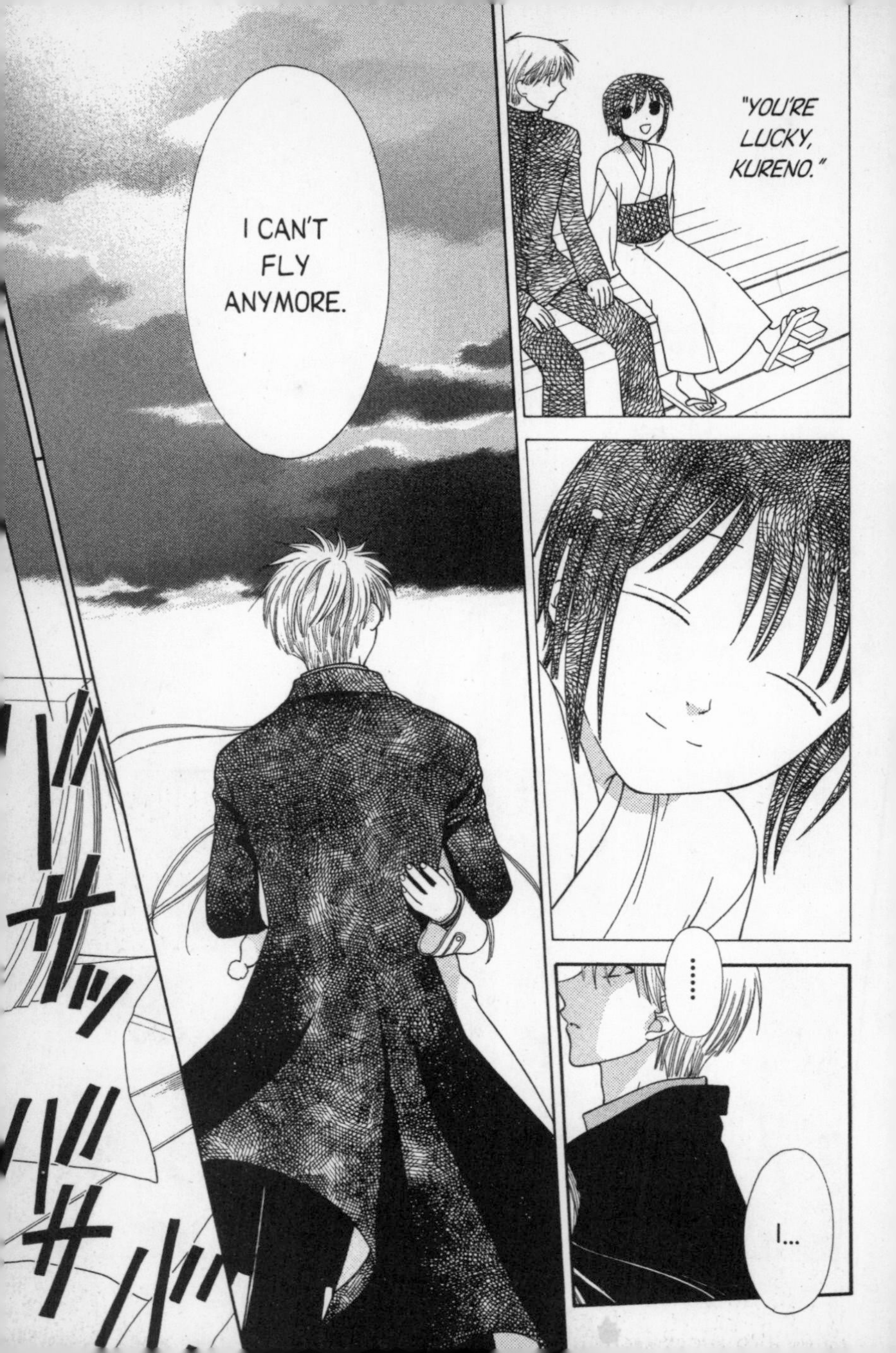
"YOU'RE LUCKY, KURENO."
......
I...
I CAN'T FLY ANYMORE.

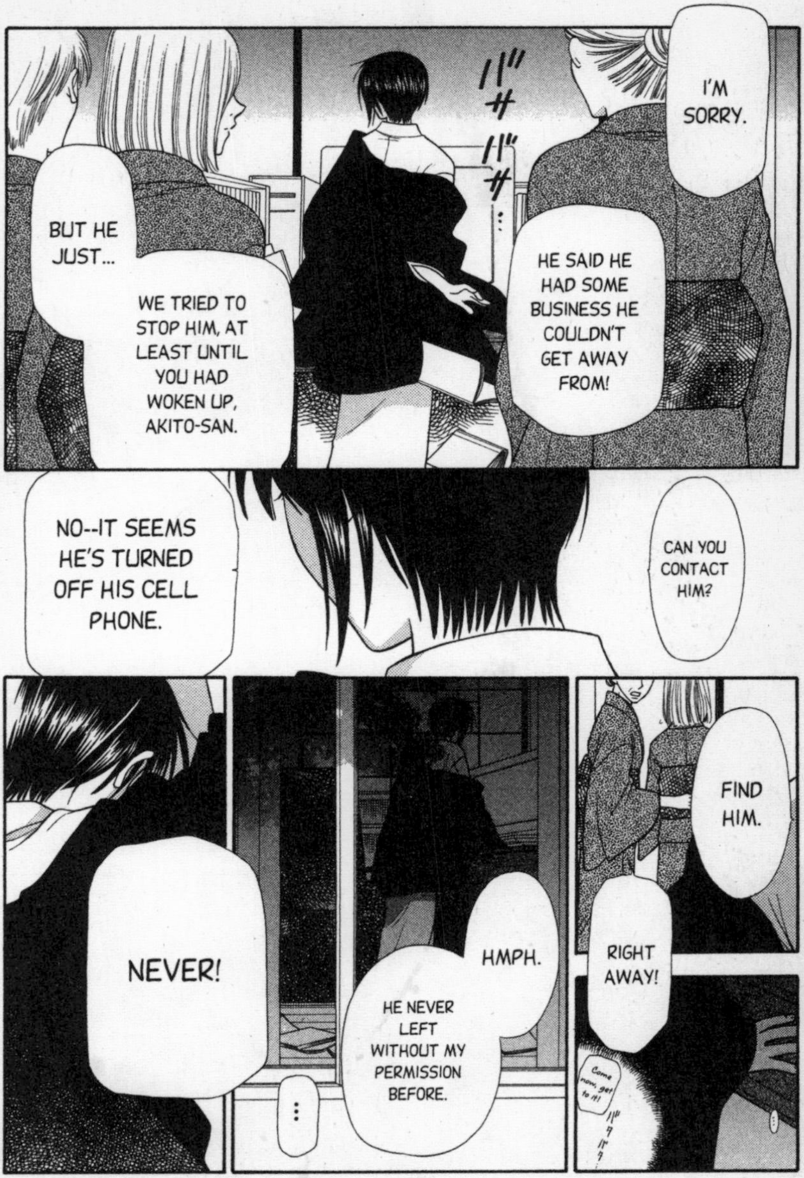
I'M SORRY.
HE SAID HE HAD SOME BUSINESS HE COULDN'T GET AWAY FROM!
BUT HE JUST...
WE TRIED TO STOP HIM, AT LEAST UNTIL YOU HAD WOKEN UP, AKITO-SAN.
CAN YOU CONTACT HIM?
NO--IT SEEMS HE'S TURNED OFF HIS CELL PHONE.
FIND HIM.
RIGHT AWAY!
Come now, get to it!
...
HMPH.
HE NEVER LEFT WITHOUT MY PERMISSION BEFORE.
...
NEVER!

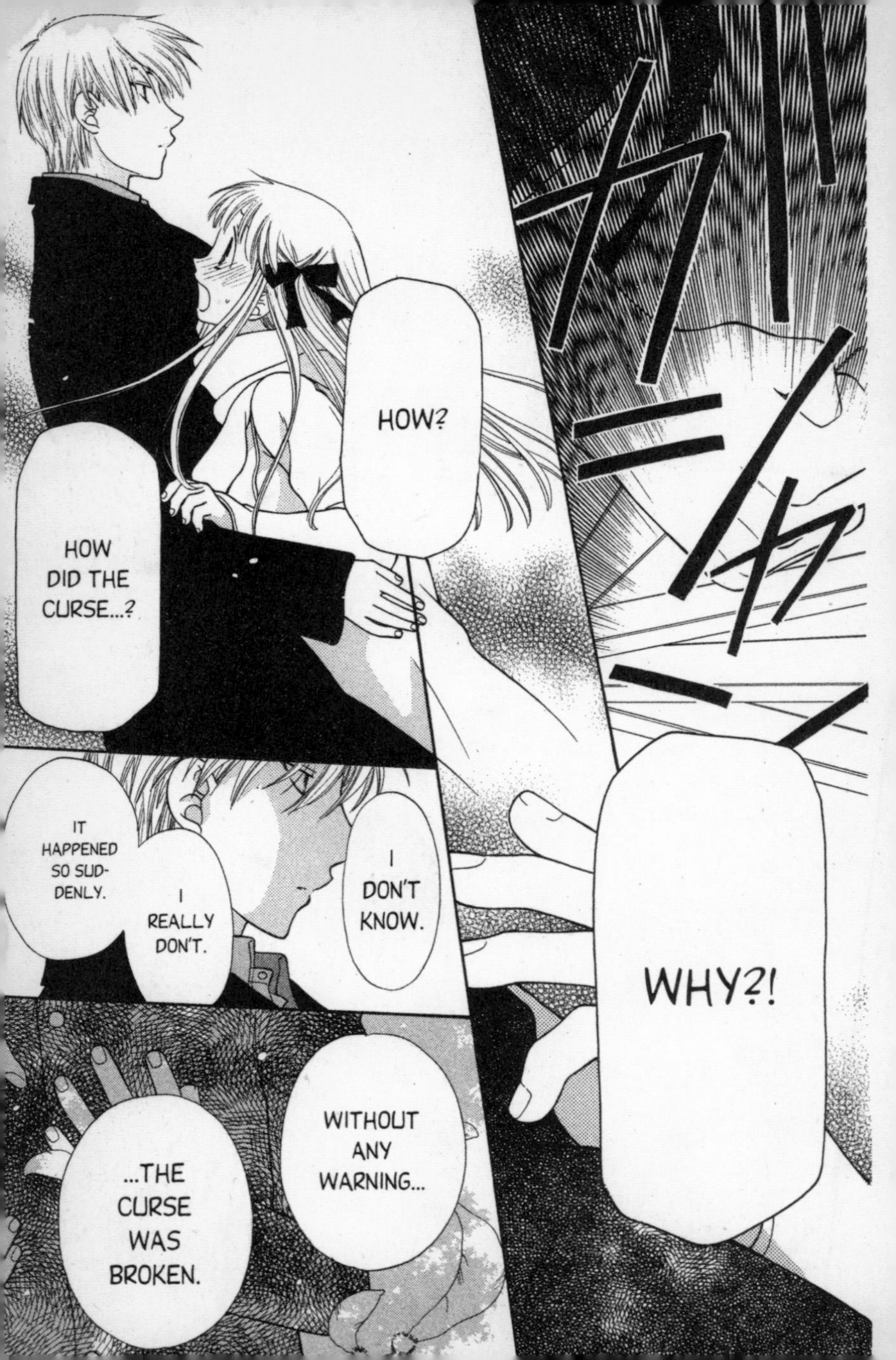
WHY?!
HOW?
HOW DID THE CURSE...?
I DON'T KNOW.
I REALLY DON'T.
IT HAPPENED SO SUD-DENLY.
WITHOUT ANY WARNING...
...THE CURSE WAS BROKEN.

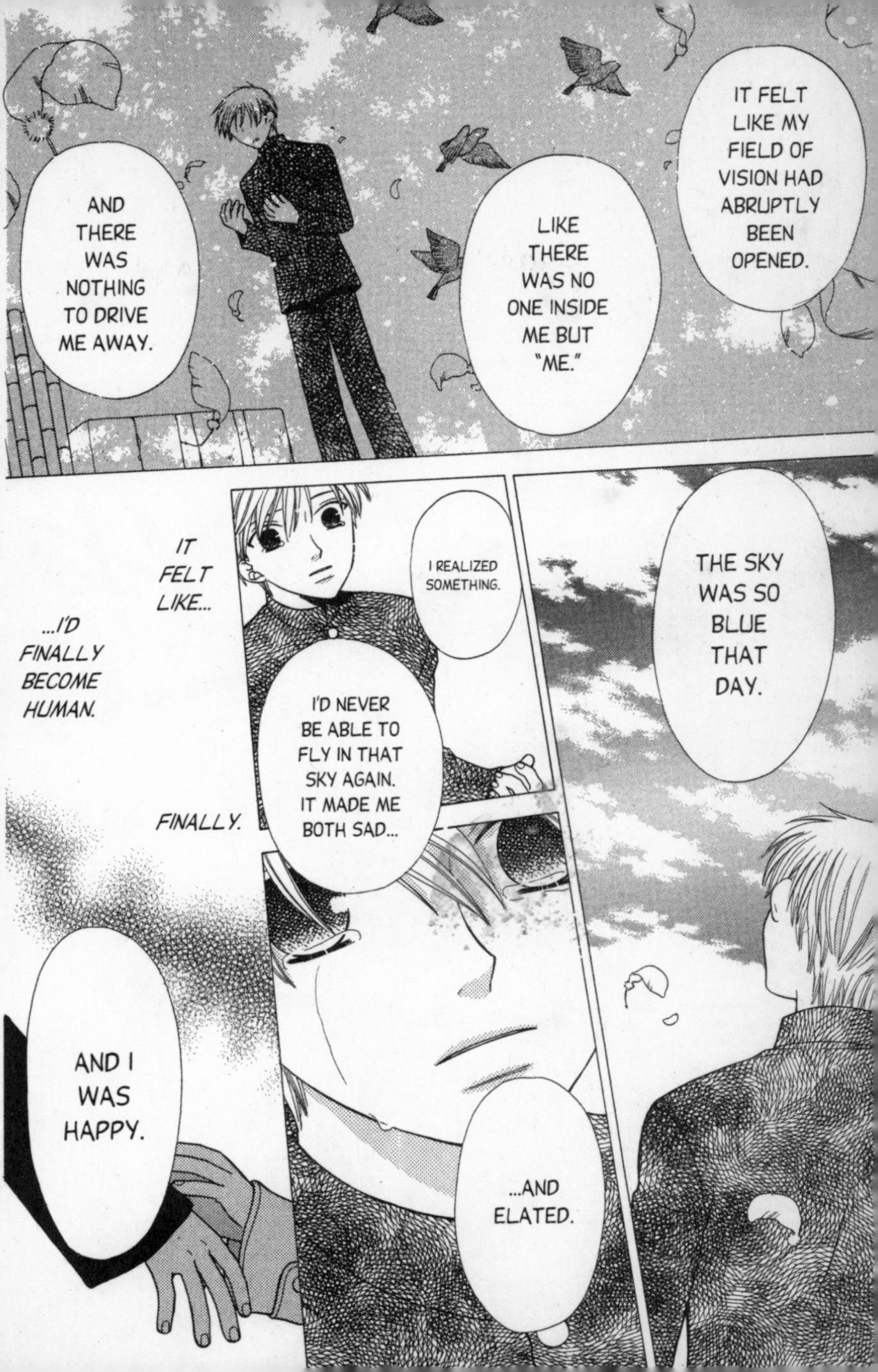
IT FELT LIKE MY FIELD OF VISION HAD ABRUPTLY BEEN OPENED.
LIKE THERE WAS NO ONE INSIDE ME BUT "ME."
AND THERE WAS NOTHING TO DRIVE ME AWAY.
THE SKY WAS SO BLUE THAT DAY.
I REALIZED SOMETHING.
I'D NEVER BE ABLE TO FLY IN THAT SKY AGAIN. IT MADE ME BOTH SAD...
...AND ELATED.
IT FELT LIKE...
...I'D FINALLY BECOME HUMAN.
FINALLY.
AND I WAS HAPPY.

At first, maybe people didn't really know the word "waves," because I got asked what it means a lot.

Hana-chan.

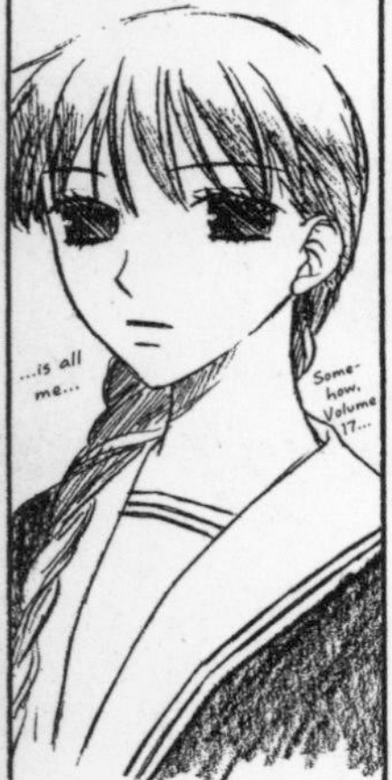
Somehow, Volume 17...
...is all me...

- With her father, mother, grandmother, and younger brother (Megumi), Hana-chan has a family of five.
- I think I've mentioned everything about Hana-chan in the story, so there's not really anything to add.
- She likes shojo manga and shojo novels more (?) than you'd expect.
- After the sleepover, she made sure to buy "Summer-Colored Sigh" and read it again.
- Her admiration for Shishou is strong.
- But I wonder if my thinking they'd make a good couple is just my blind love for them as their creator (laugh).

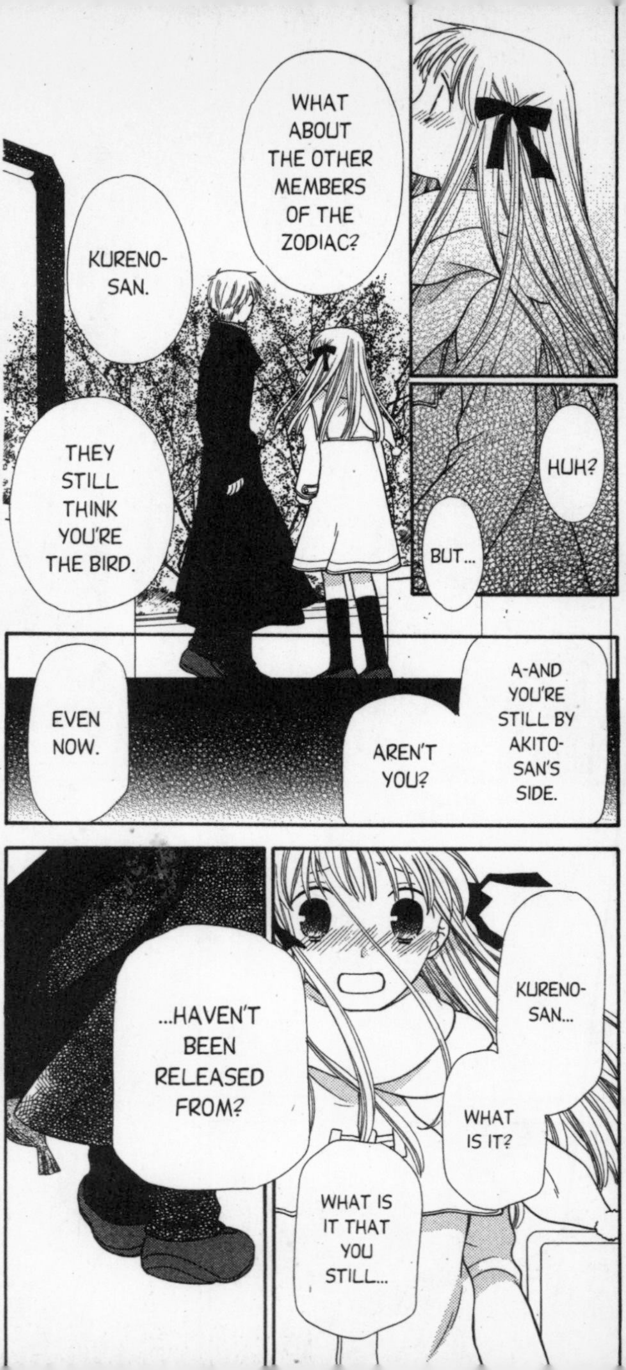
WHAT ABOUT THE OTHER MEMBERS OF THE ZODIAC?
HUH?
BUT...
KURENO-SAN.
THEY STILL THINK YOU'RE THE BIRD.
A-AND YOU'RE STILL BY AKITO-SAN'S SIDE.
AREN'T YOU?
EVEN NOW.
KURENO-SAN...
WHAT IS IT?
WHAT IS IT THAT YOU STILL...
...HAVEN'T BEEN RELEASED FROM?

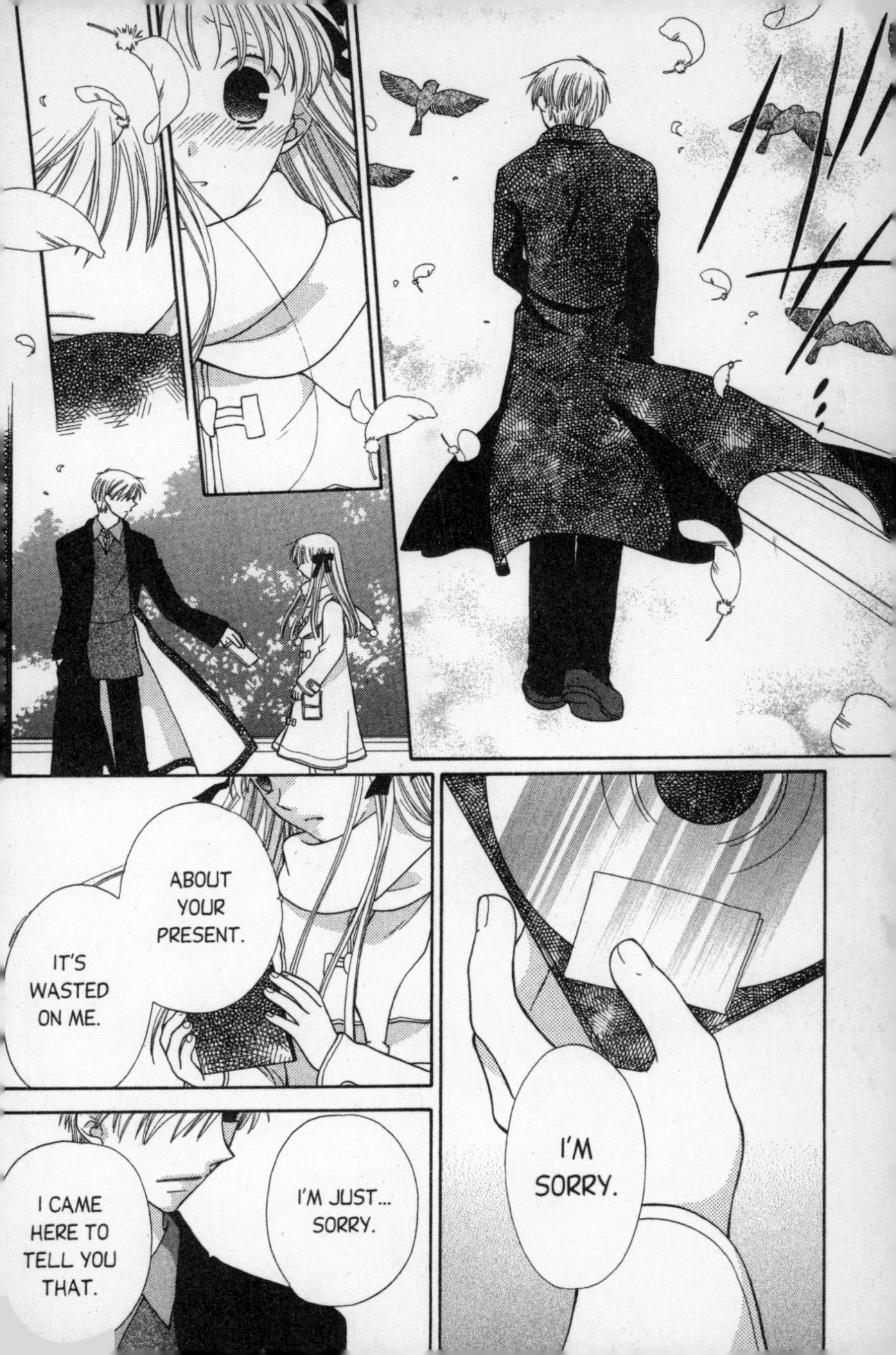
I'M SORRY.
ABOUT YOUR PRESENT.
IT'S WASTED ON ME.
I'M JUST... SORRY.
I CAME HERE TO TELL YOU THAT.

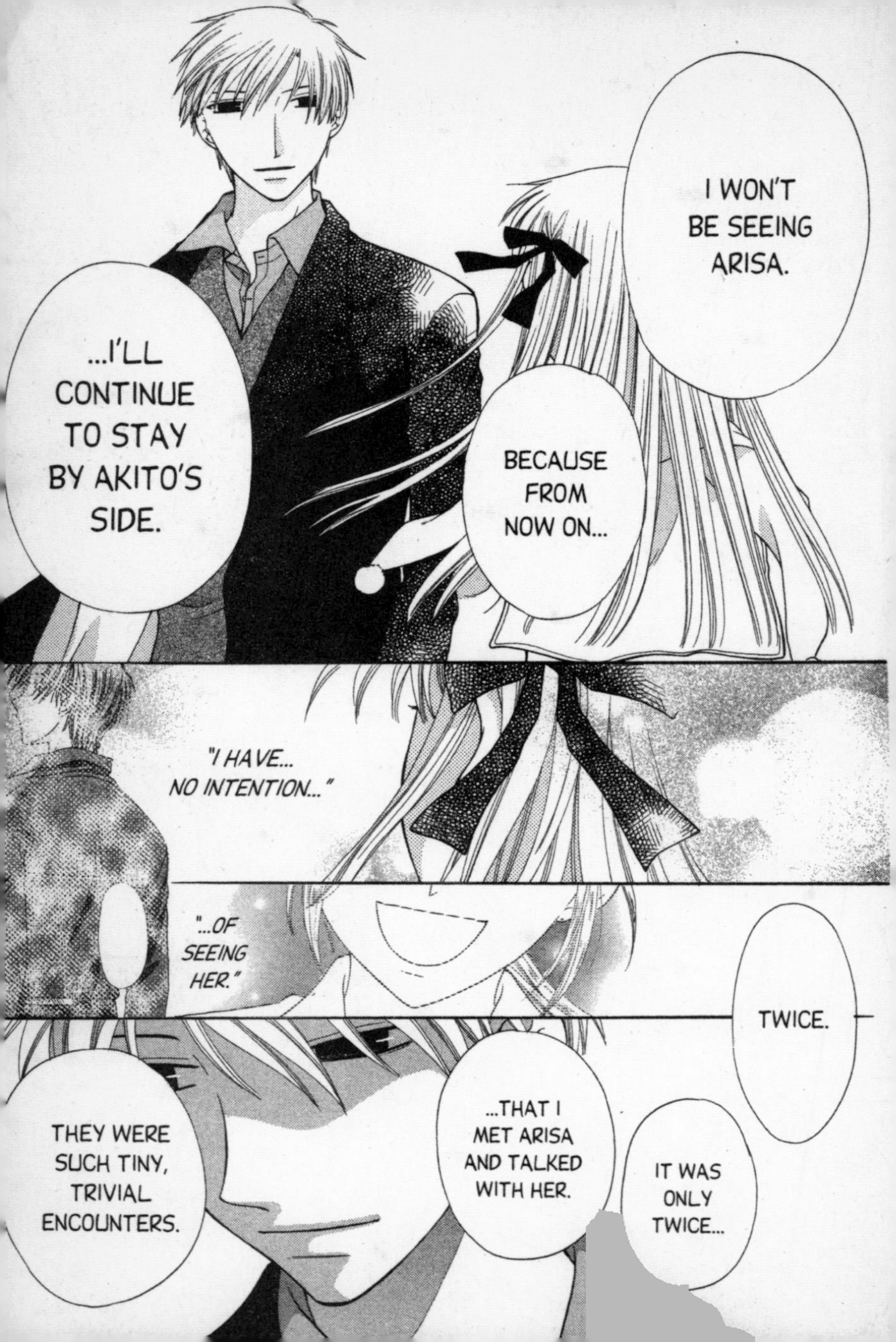
I WON'T BE SEEING ARISA.
BECAUSE FROM NOW ON...
...I'LL CONTINUE TO STAY BY AKITO'S SIDE.
"I HAVE... NO INTENTION..."
"...OF SEEING HER."
TWICE.
IT WAS ONLY TWICE...
...THAT I MET ARISA AND TALKED WITH HER.
THEY WERE SUCH TINY, TRIVIAL ENCOUNTERS.

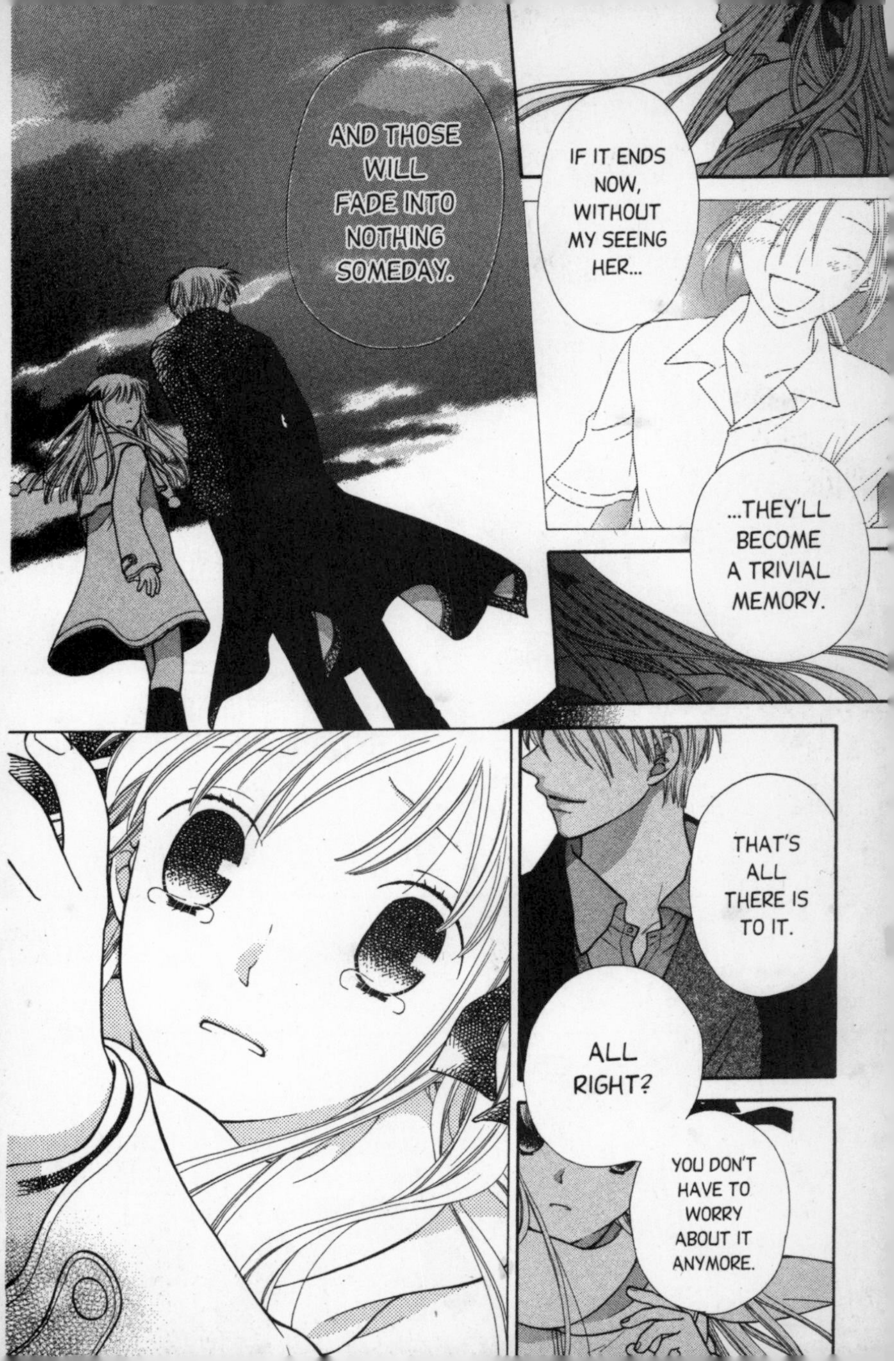
IF IT ENDS NOW, WITHOUT MY SEEING HER...
...THEY'LL BECOME A TRIVIAL MEMORY.
AND THOSE WILL FADE INTO NOTHING SOMEDAY.
THAT'S ALL THERE IS TO IT.
ALL RIGHT?
YOU DON'T HAVE TO WORRY ABOUT IT ANYMORE.

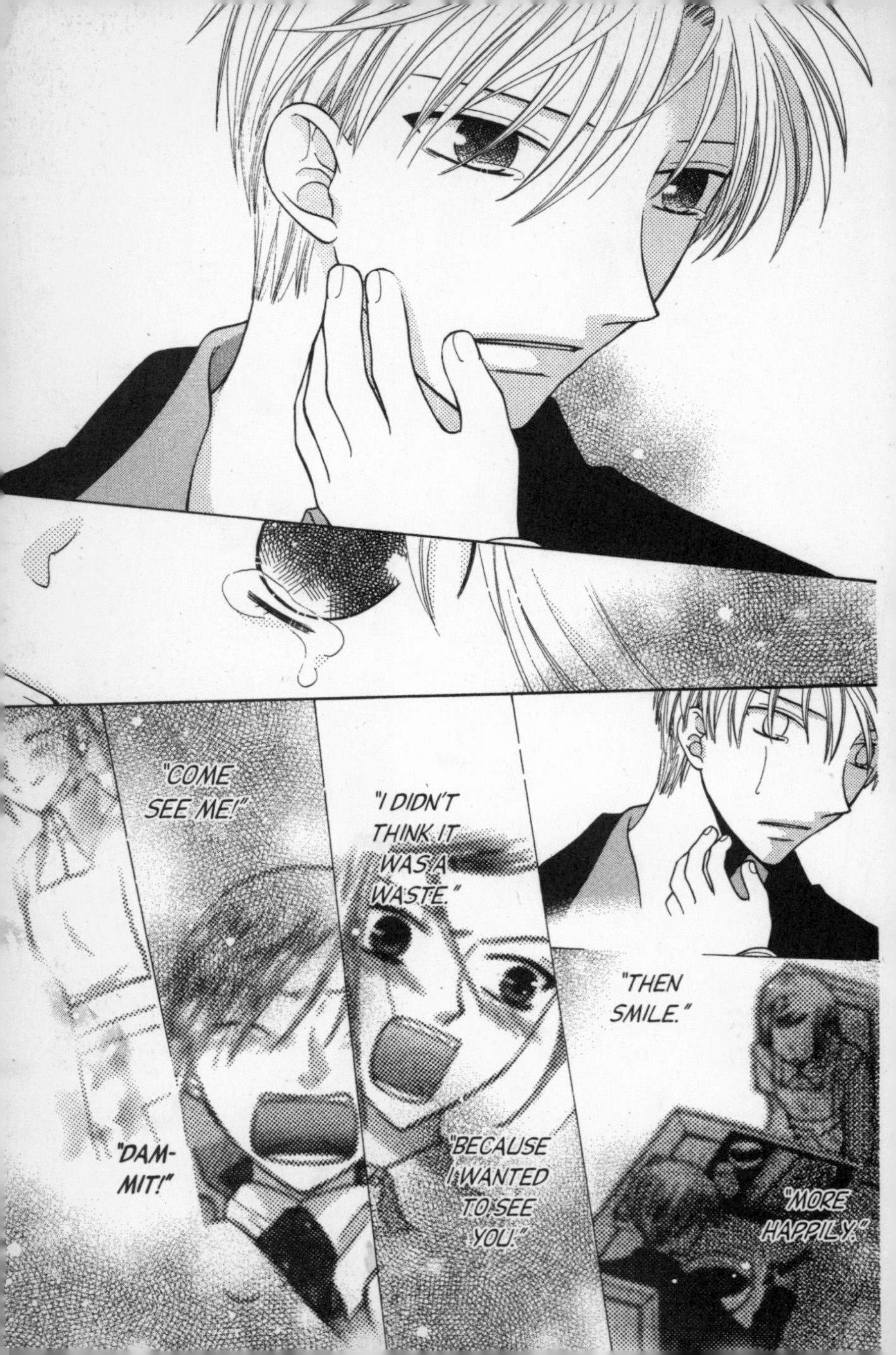
"THEN SMILE."
"MORE HAPPILY."
"I DIDN'T THINK IT WAS A WASTE."
"BECAUSE I WANTED TO SEE YOU."
"COME SEE ME!"
"DAM-MIT!"

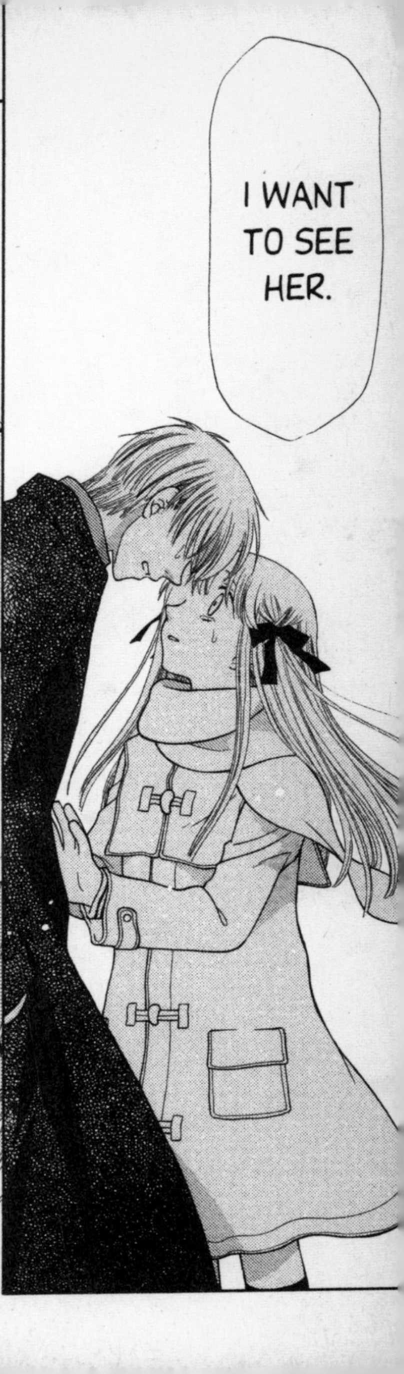
I WANT TO SEE HER.
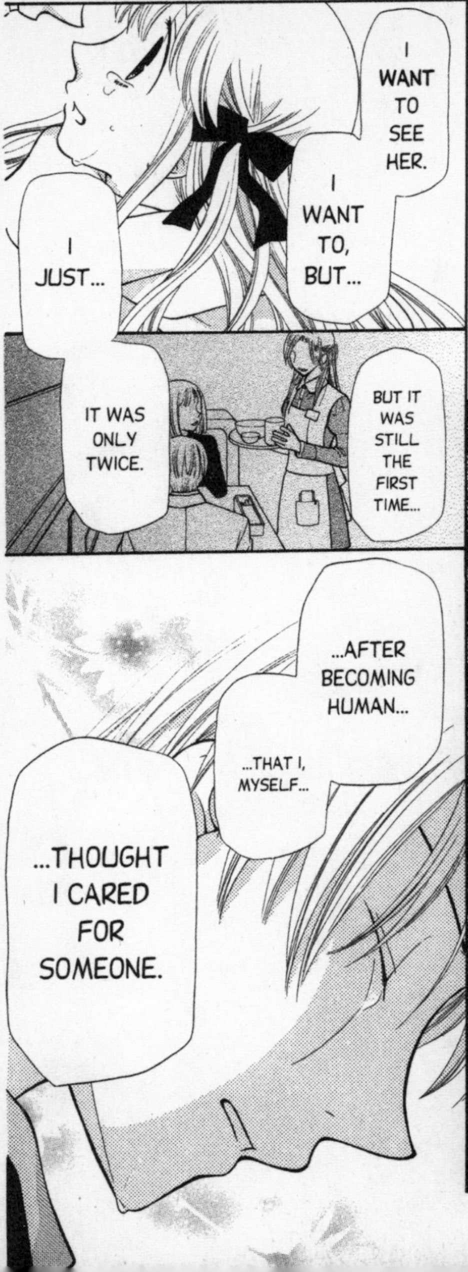
I WANT TO SEE HER.
I WANT TO, BUT...
I JUST...
IT WAS ONLY TWICE.
BUT IT WAS STILL THE FIRST TIME...
...AFTER BECOMING HUMAN...
...THAT I, MYSELF...
...THOUGHT I CARED FOR SOMEONE.

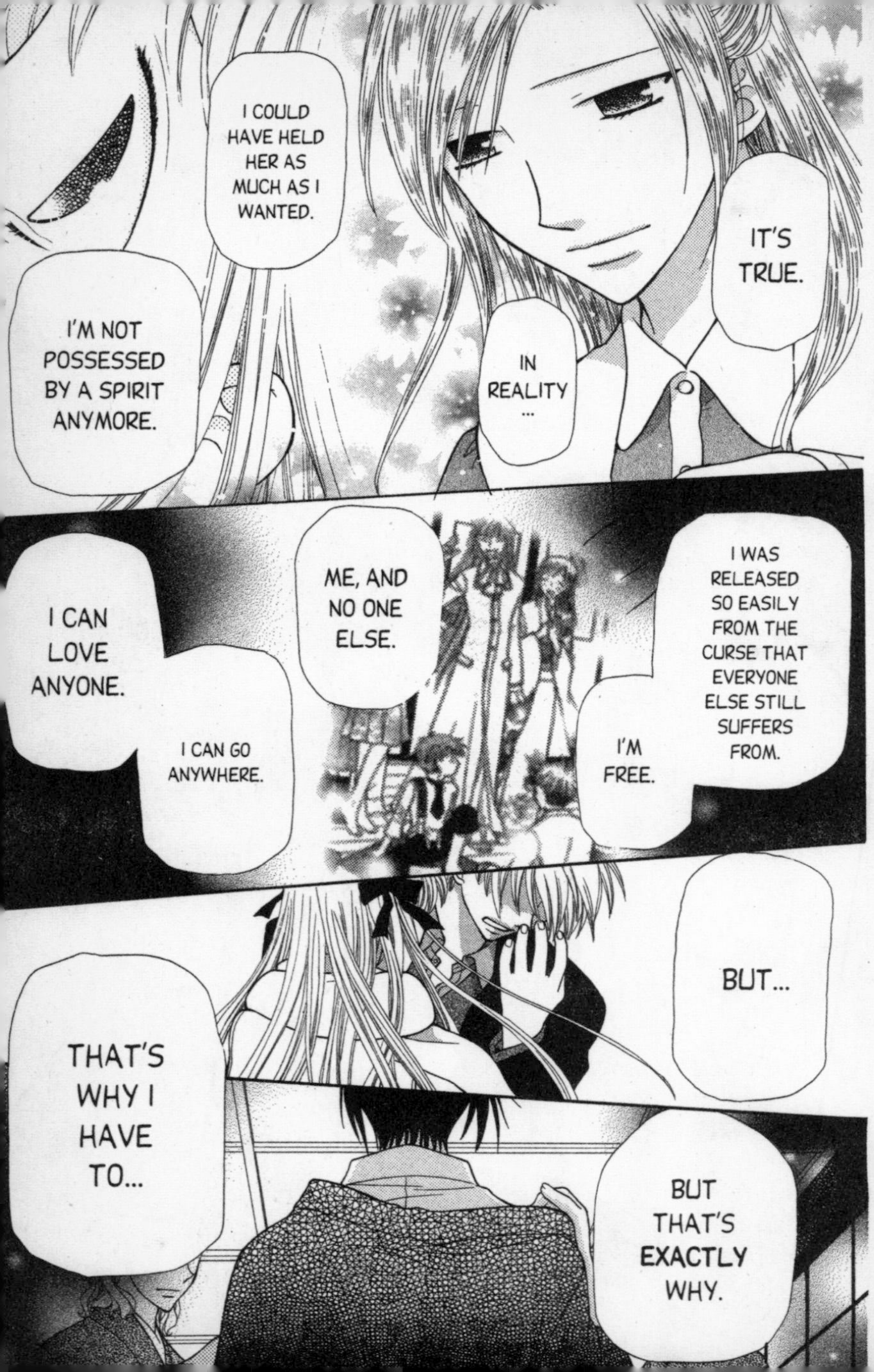
IT'S TRUE.
IN REALITY...
I COULD HAVE HELD HER AS MUCH AS I WANTED.
I'M NOT POSSESSED BY A SPIRIT ANYMORE.
I WAS RELEASED SO EASILY FROM THE CURSE THAT EVERYONE ELSE STILL SUFFERS FROM.
I'M FREE.
ME, AND NO ONE ELSE.
I CAN LOVE ANYONE.
I CAN GO ANYWHERE.
BUT...
BUT THAT'S EXACTLY WHY.
THAT'S WHY I HAVE TO...

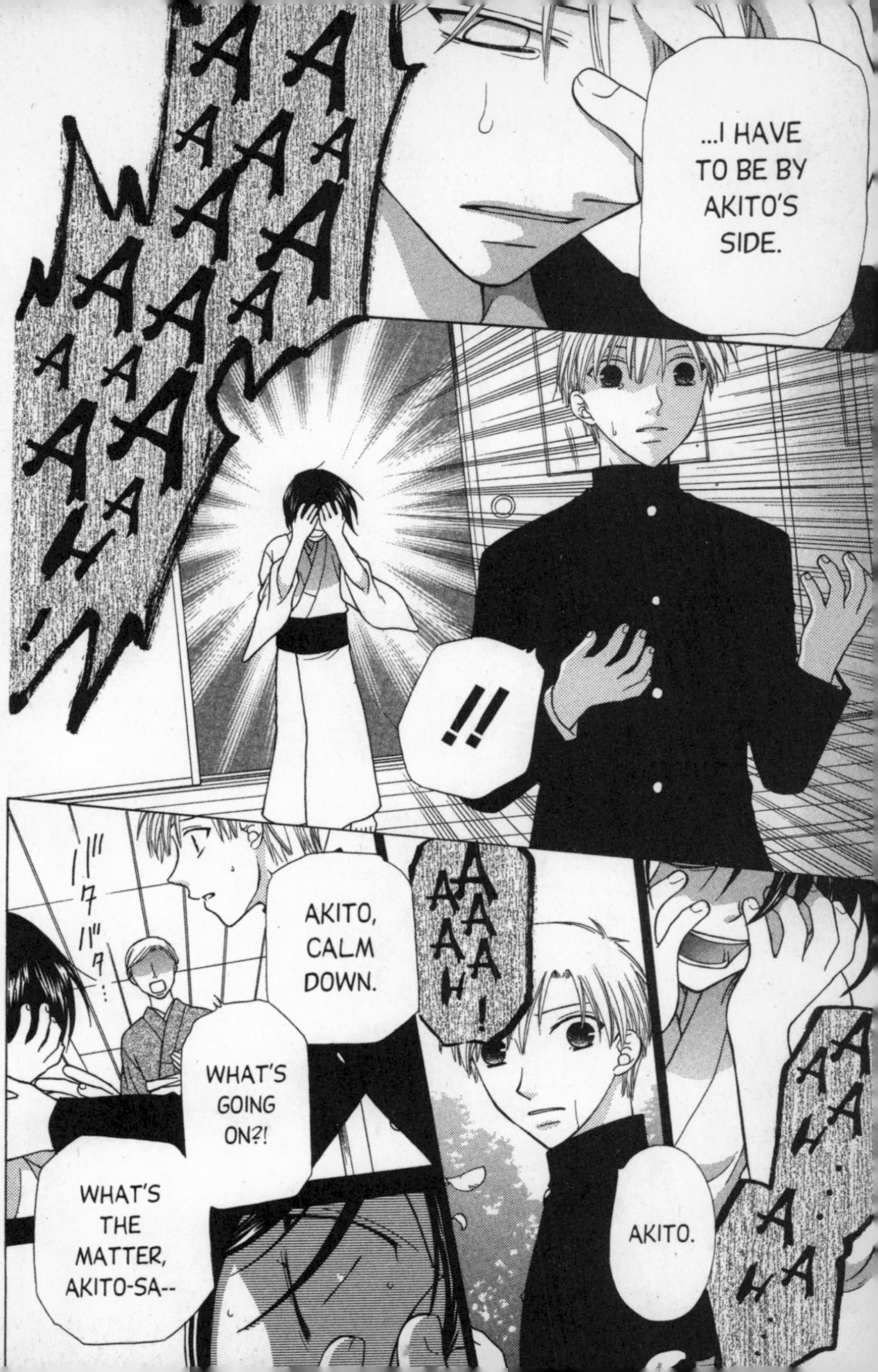
...I HAVE TO BE BY AKITO'S SIDE.
WAAAAAAAAAAAAAAH!
!!
AAAHAAHAAA
AKITO.
AAAAAH!
AKITO, CALM DOWN.
バタバタ…
WHAT'S GOING ON?!
WHAT'S THE MATTER, AKITO-SA--

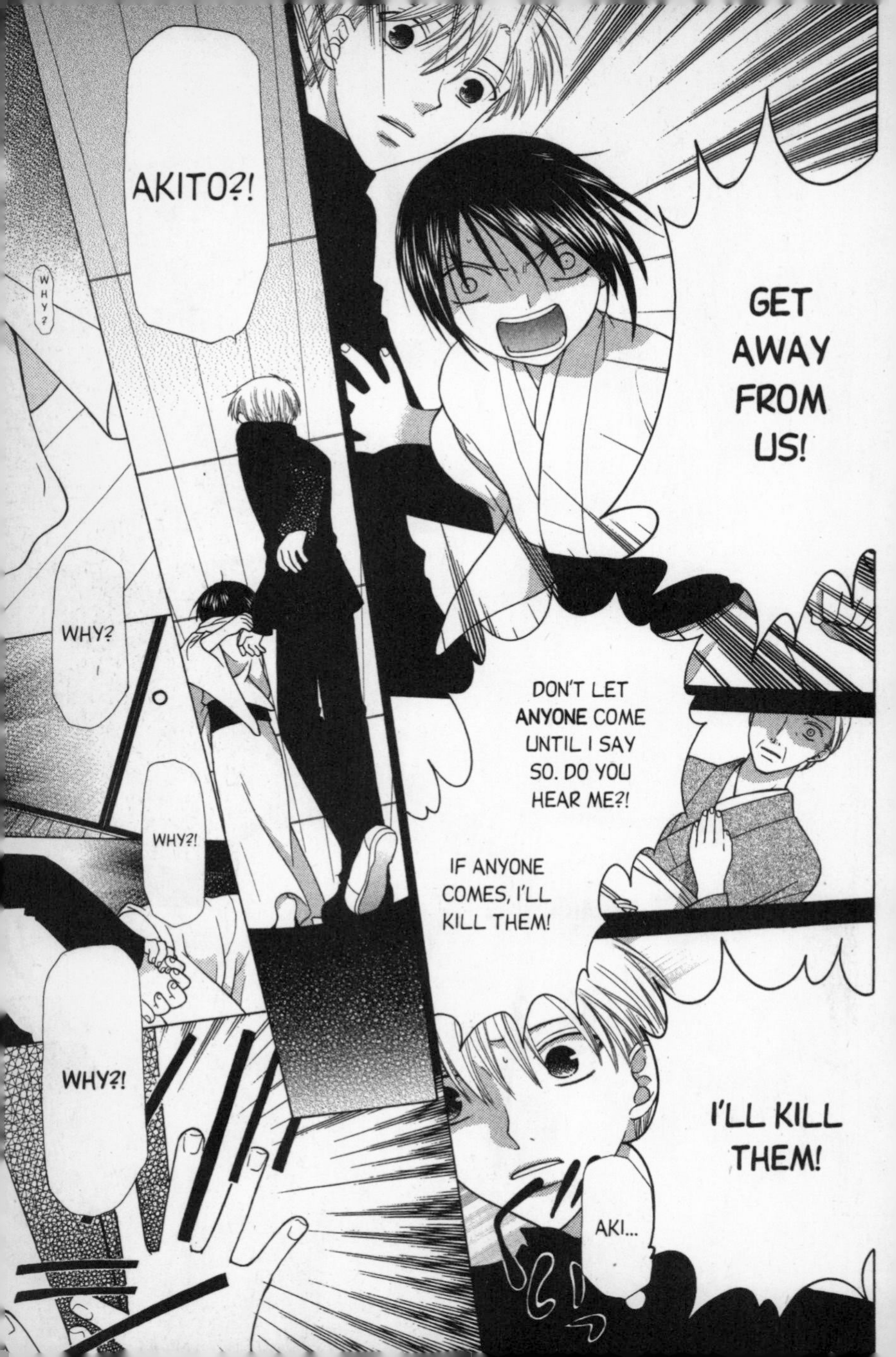
GET AWAY FROM US!
DON'T LET ANYONE COME UNTIL I SAY SO. DO YOU HEAR ME?!
IF ANYONE COMES, I'LL KILL THEM!
I'LL KILL THEM!
AKI...
AKITO?!
WHY?
WHY?
WHY?!
WHY?!

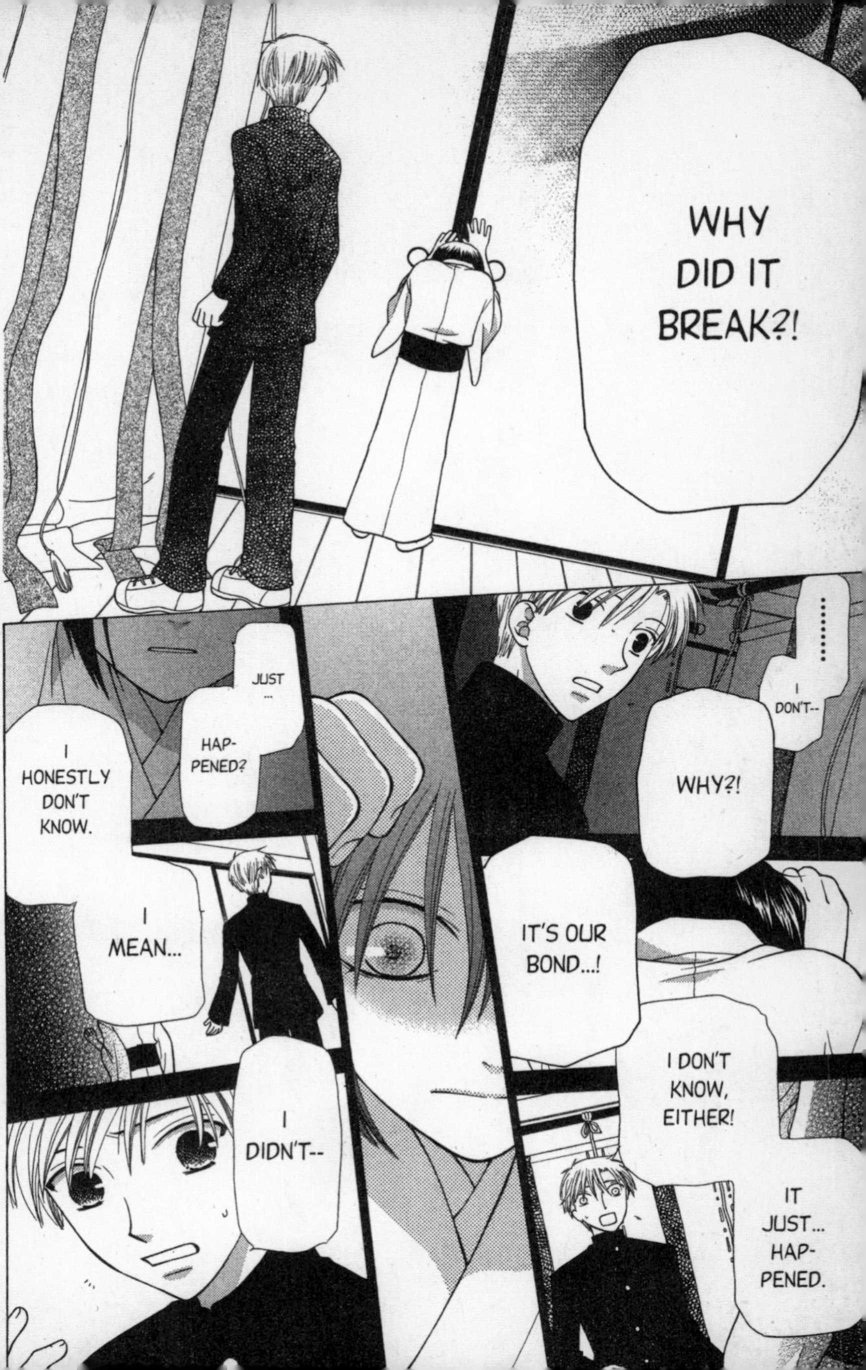
WHY DID IT BREAK?!
......
I DON'T--
WHY?!
IT'S OUR BOND...!
I DON'T KNOW, EITHER!
IT JUST... HAP-PENED.
JUST ... HAP-PENED?
I HONESTLY DON'T KNOW.
I MEAN...
I DIDN'T--

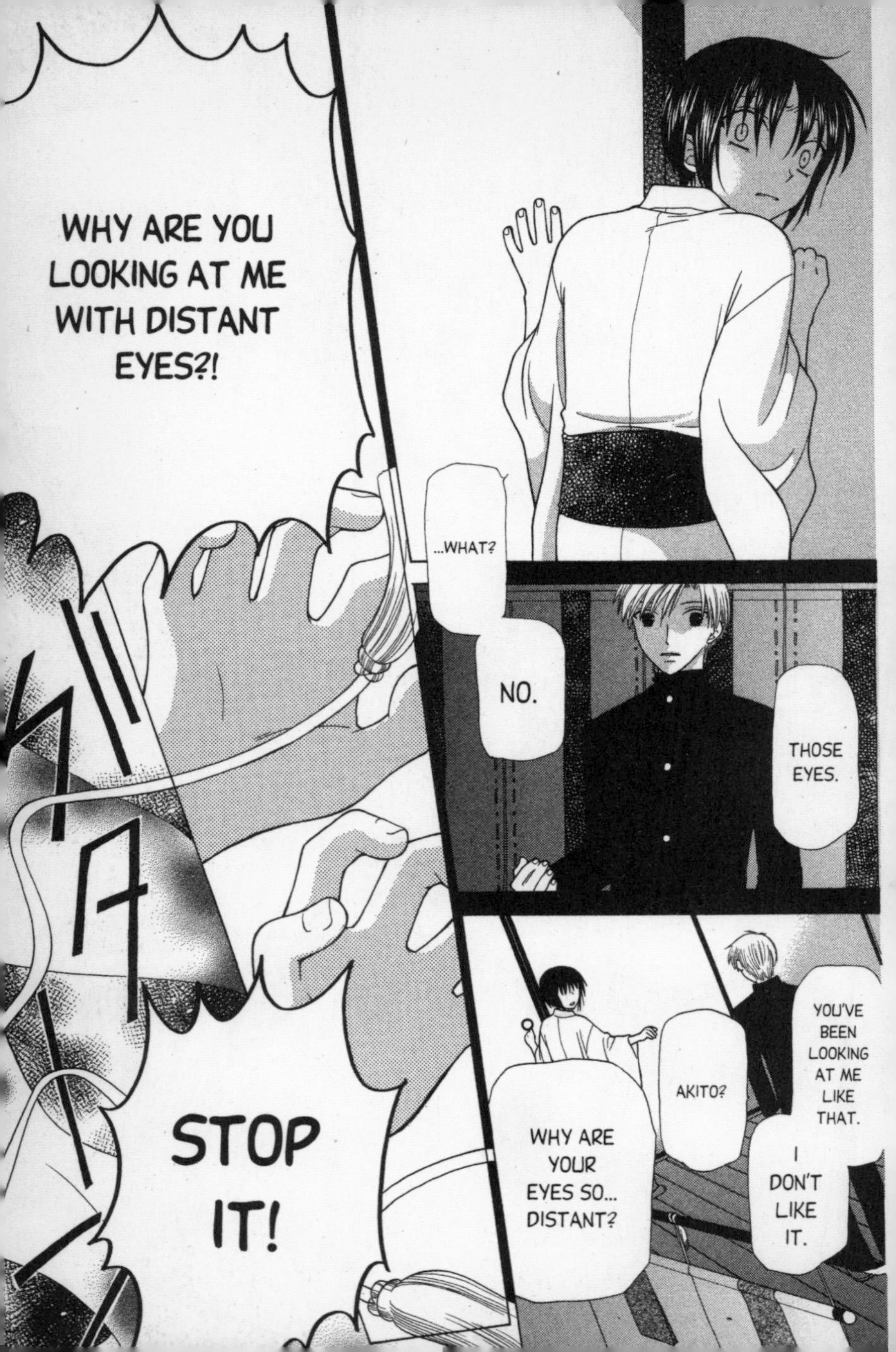
...WHAT?
NO.
THOSE EYES.
YOU'VE BEEN LOOKING AT ME LIKE THAT.
I DON'T LIKE IT.
AKITO?
WHY ARE YOUR EYES SO... DISTANT?
WHY ARE YOU LOOKING AT ME WITH DISTANT EYES?!
STOP IT!

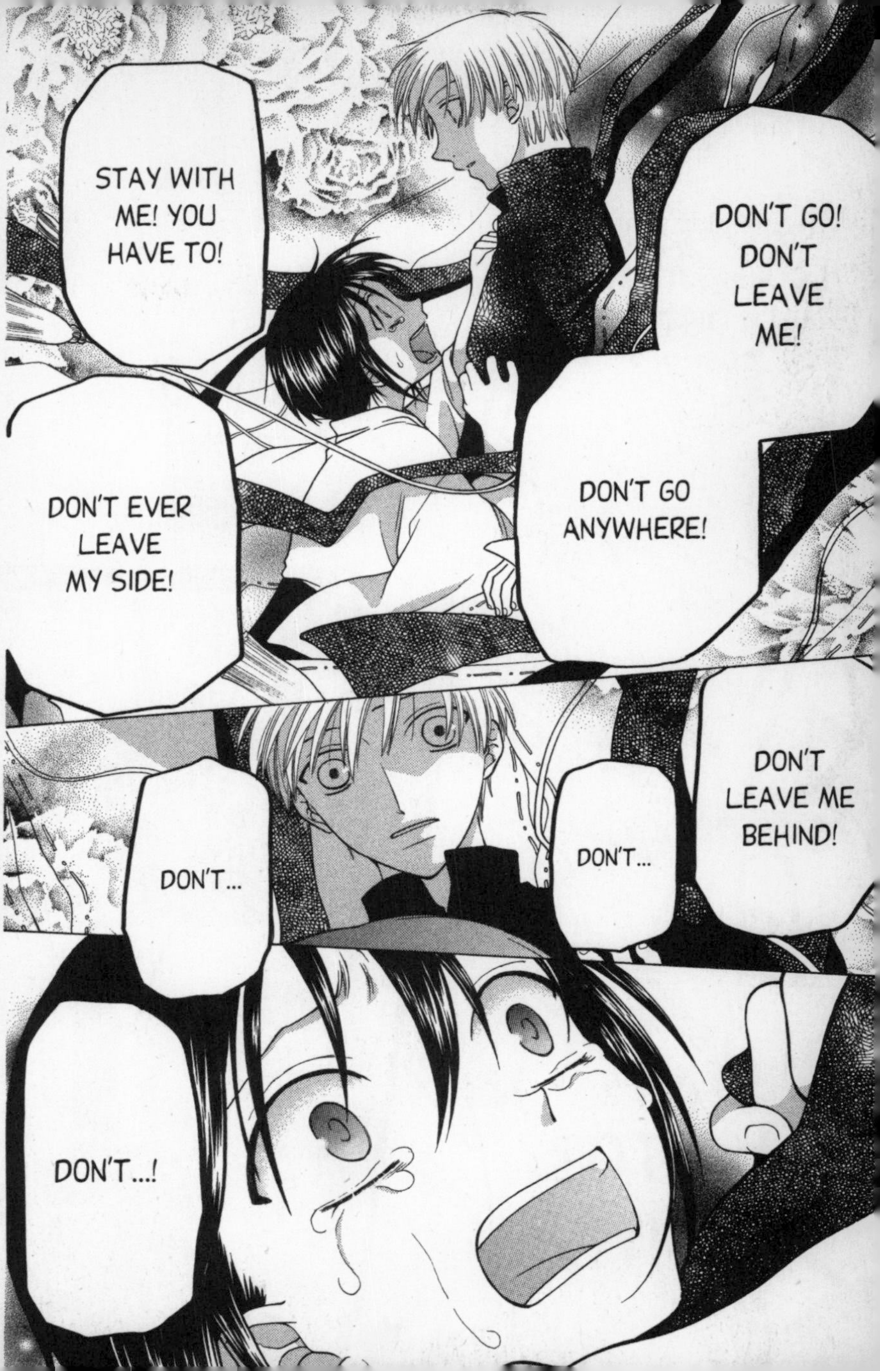
DON'T GO! DON'T LEAVE ME!
STAY WITH ME! YOU HAVE TO!
DON'T GO ANYWHERE!
DON'T EVER LEAVE MY SIDE!
DON'T LEAVE ME BEHIND!
DON'T...
DON'T...
DON'T...!

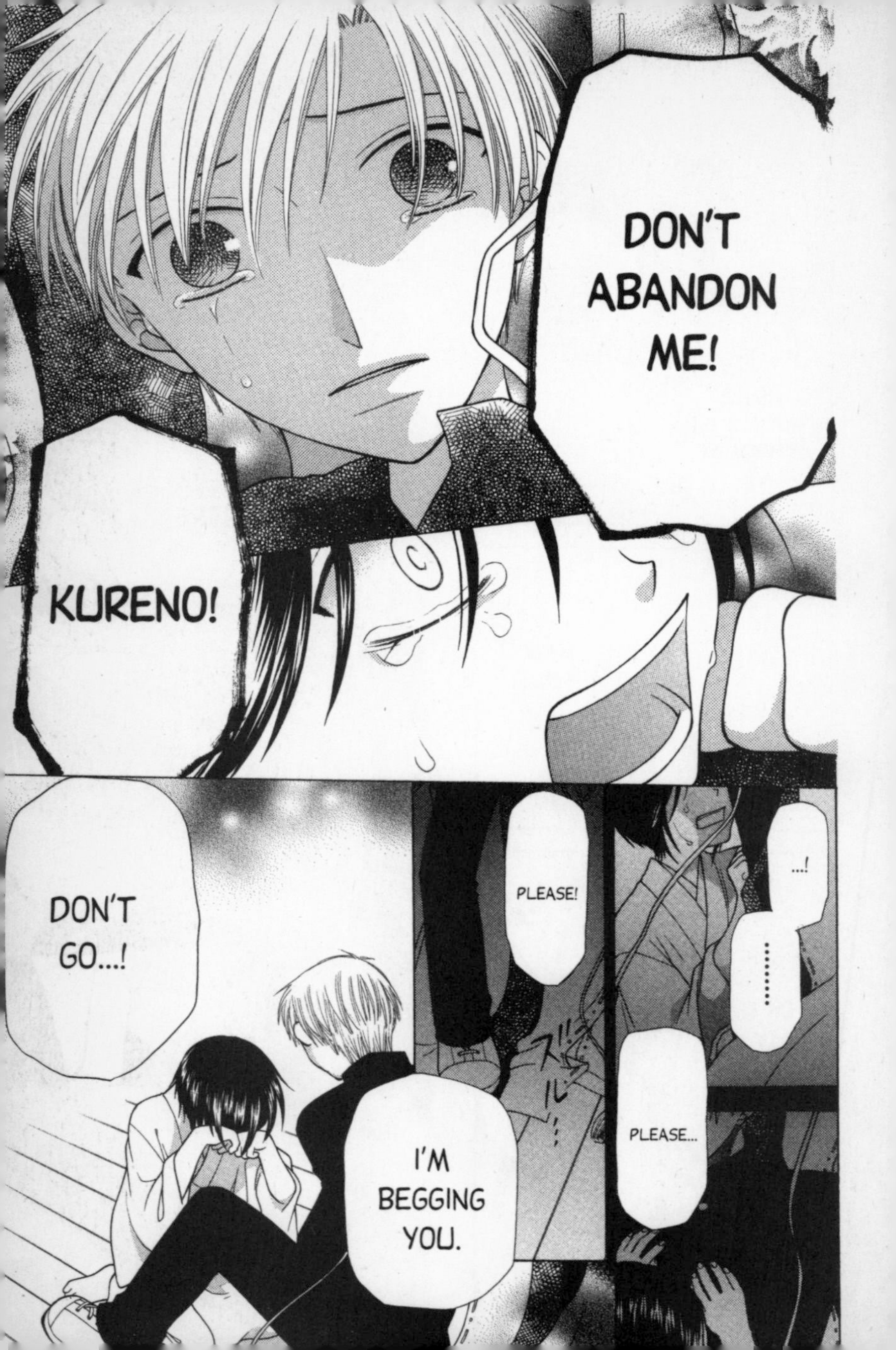
DON'T ABANDON ME!
KURENO!
...!
....
PLEASE...
PLEASE!
DON'T GO...!
I'M BEGGING YOU.

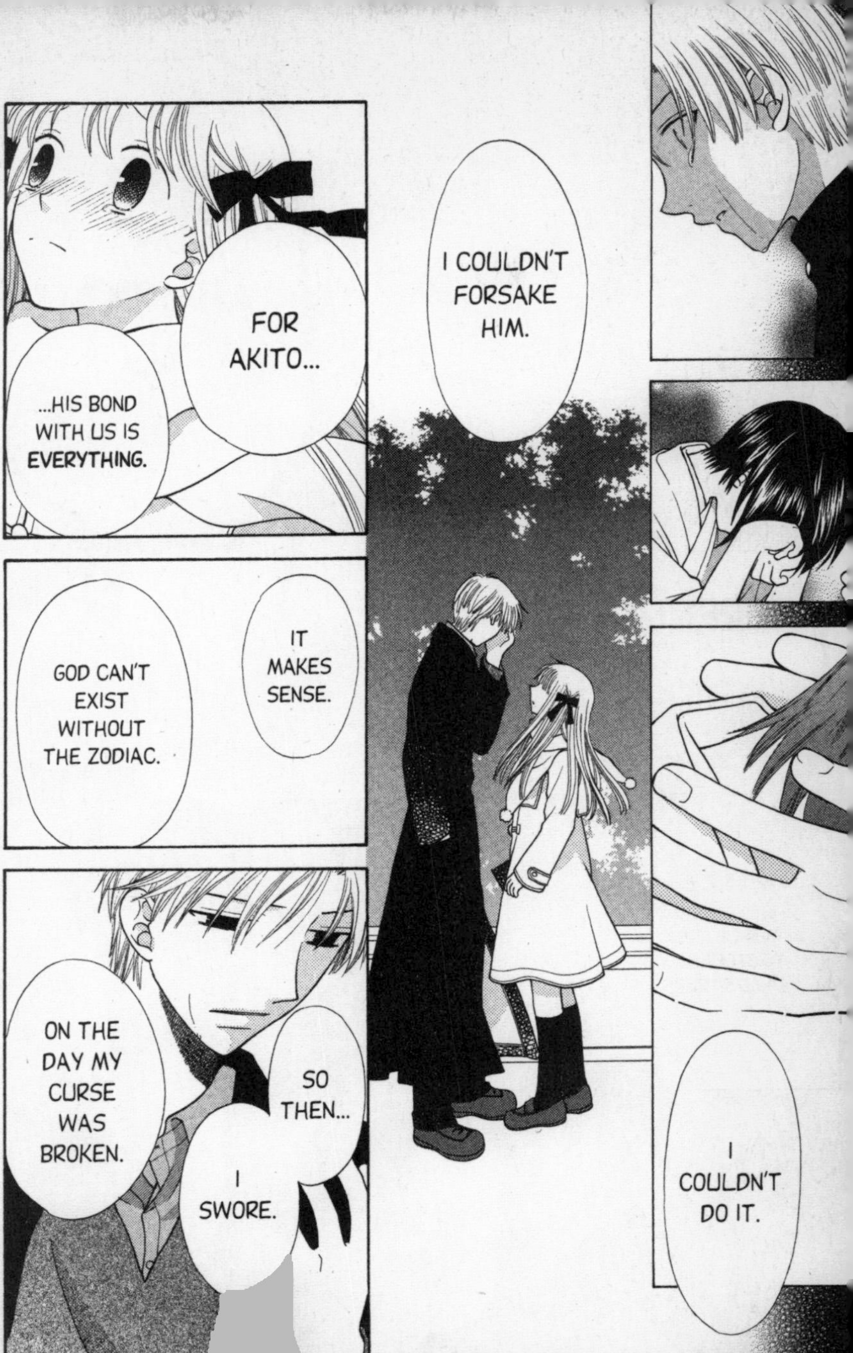
I COULDN'T DO IT.
I COULDN'T FORSAKE HIM.
FOR AKITO...
...HIS BOND WITH US IS EVERYTHING.
IT MAKES SENSE.
GOD CAN'T EXIST WITHOUT THE ZODIAC.
SO THEN...
I SWORE.
ON THE DAY MY CURSE WAS BROKEN.

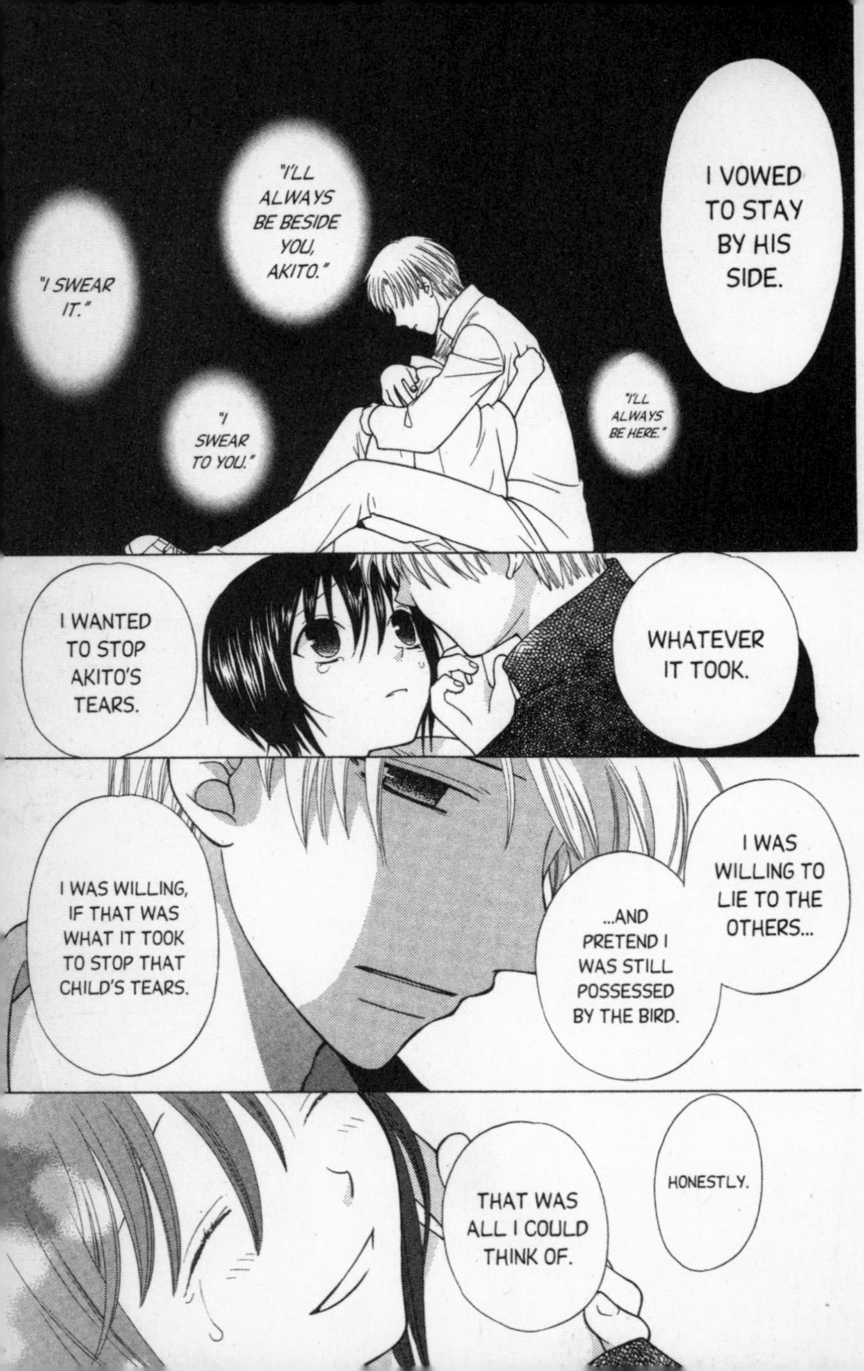

I VOWED TO STAY BY HIS SIDE.
"I'LL ALWAYS BE BESIDE YOU, AKITO."
"I'LL ALWAYS BE HERE."
"I SWEAR IT."
"I SWEAR TO YOU."
WHATEVER IT TOOK.
I WANTED TO STOP AKITO'S TEARS.
I WAS WILLING TO LIE TO THE OTHERS...
...AND PRETEND I WAS STILL POSSESSED BY THE BIRD.
I WAS WILLING, IF THAT WAS WHAT IT TOOK TO STOP THAT CHILD'S TEARS.
HONESTLY.
THAT WAS ALL I COULD THINK OF.

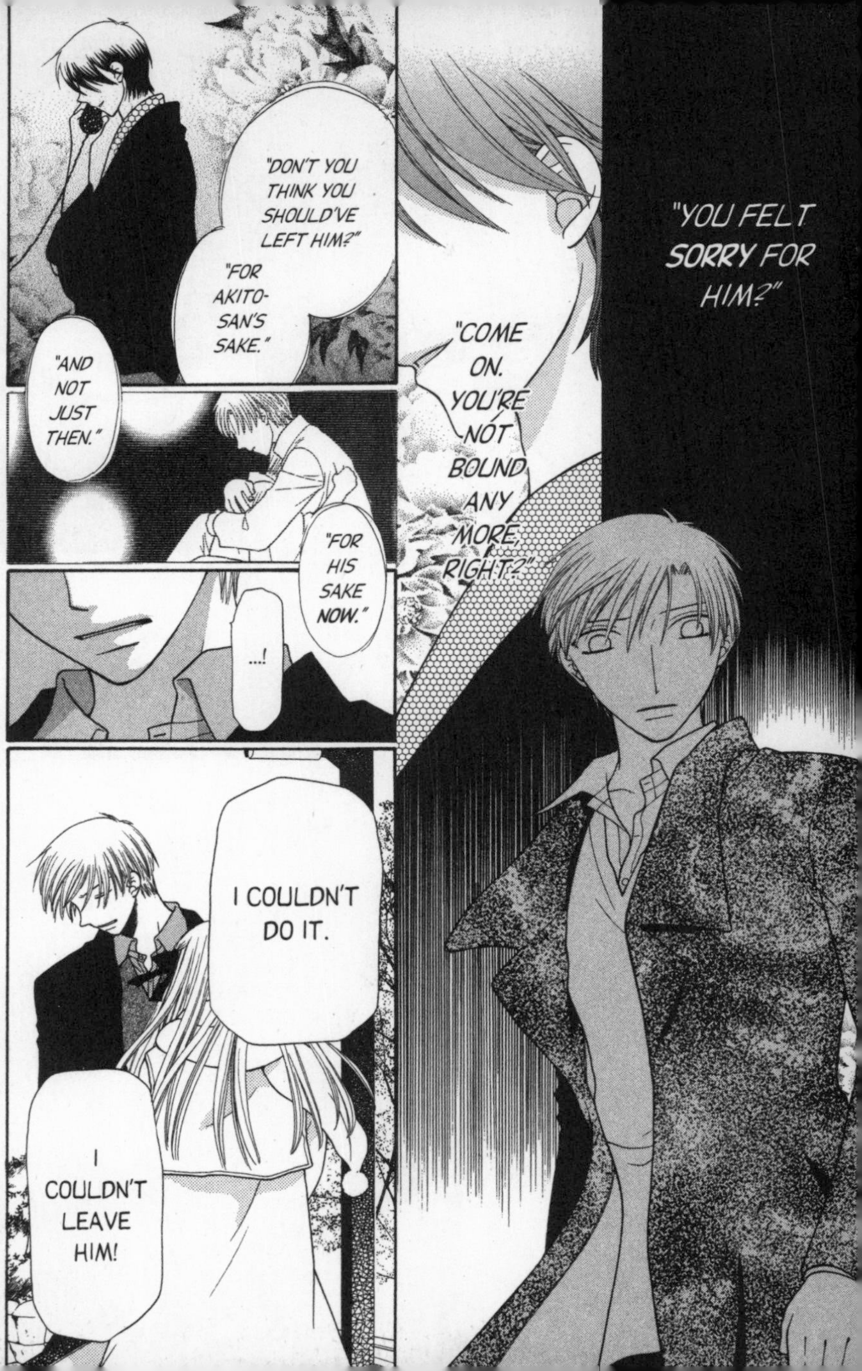
"YOU FELT SORRY FOR HIM?"
"COME ON. YOU'RE NOT BOUND ANY MORE, RIGHT?"
"DON'T YOU THINK YOU SHOULD'VE LEFT HIM?"
"FOR AKITO-SAN'S SAKE."
"AND NOT JUST THEN."
"FOR HIS SAKE NOW."
...!
I COULDN'T DO IT.
I COULDN'T LEAVE HIM!

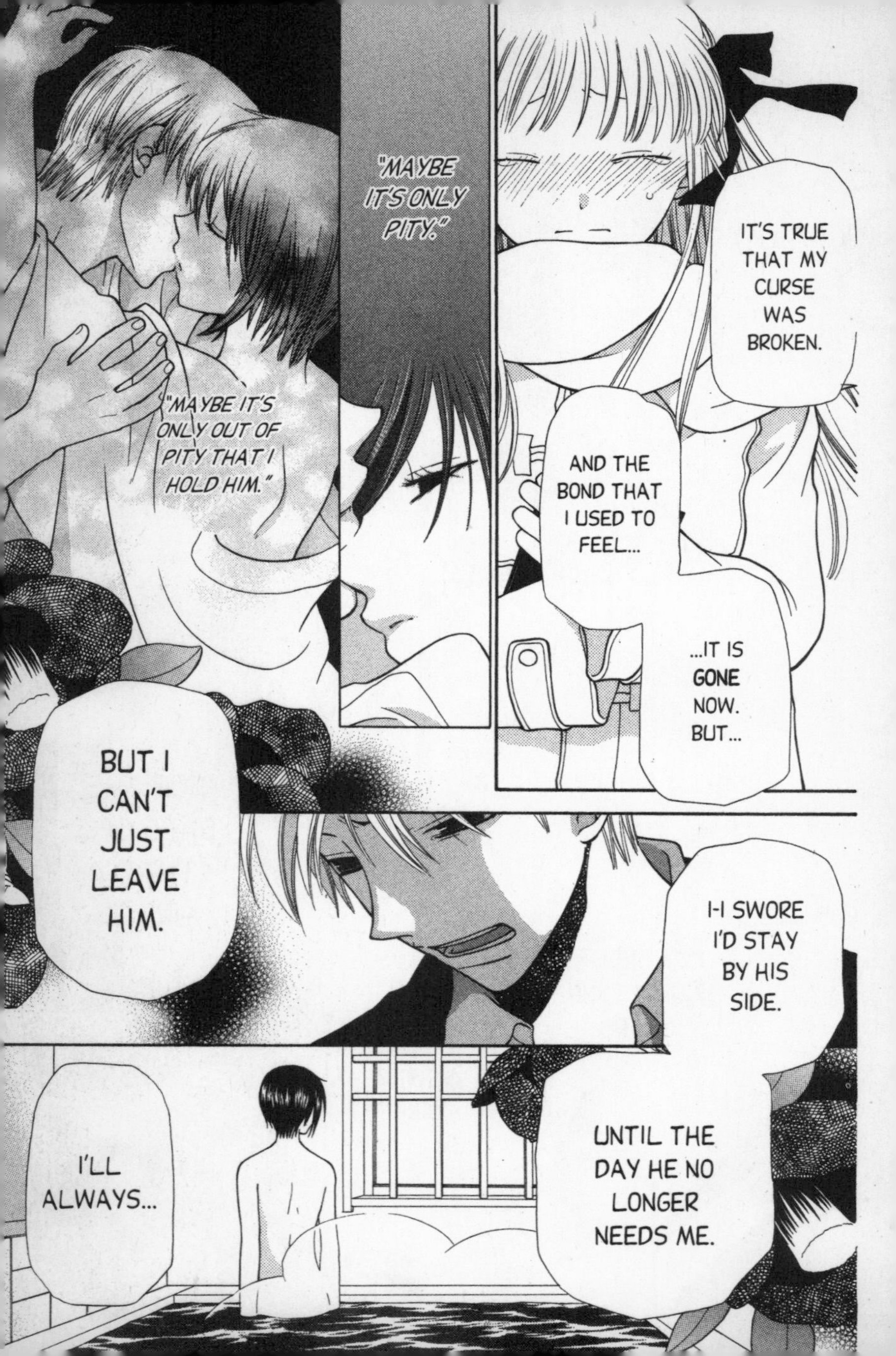
IT'S TRUE THAT MY CURSE WAS BROKEN.
AND THE BOND THAT I USED TO FEEL...
...IT IS GONE NOW. BUT...
"MAYBE IT'S ONLY PITY."
"MAYBE IT'S ONLY OUT OF PITY THAT I HOLD HIM."
BUT I CAN'T JUST LEAVE HIM.
I-I SWORE I'D STAY BY HIS SIDE.
UNTIL THE DAY HE NO LONGER NEEDS ME.
I'LL ALWAYS...

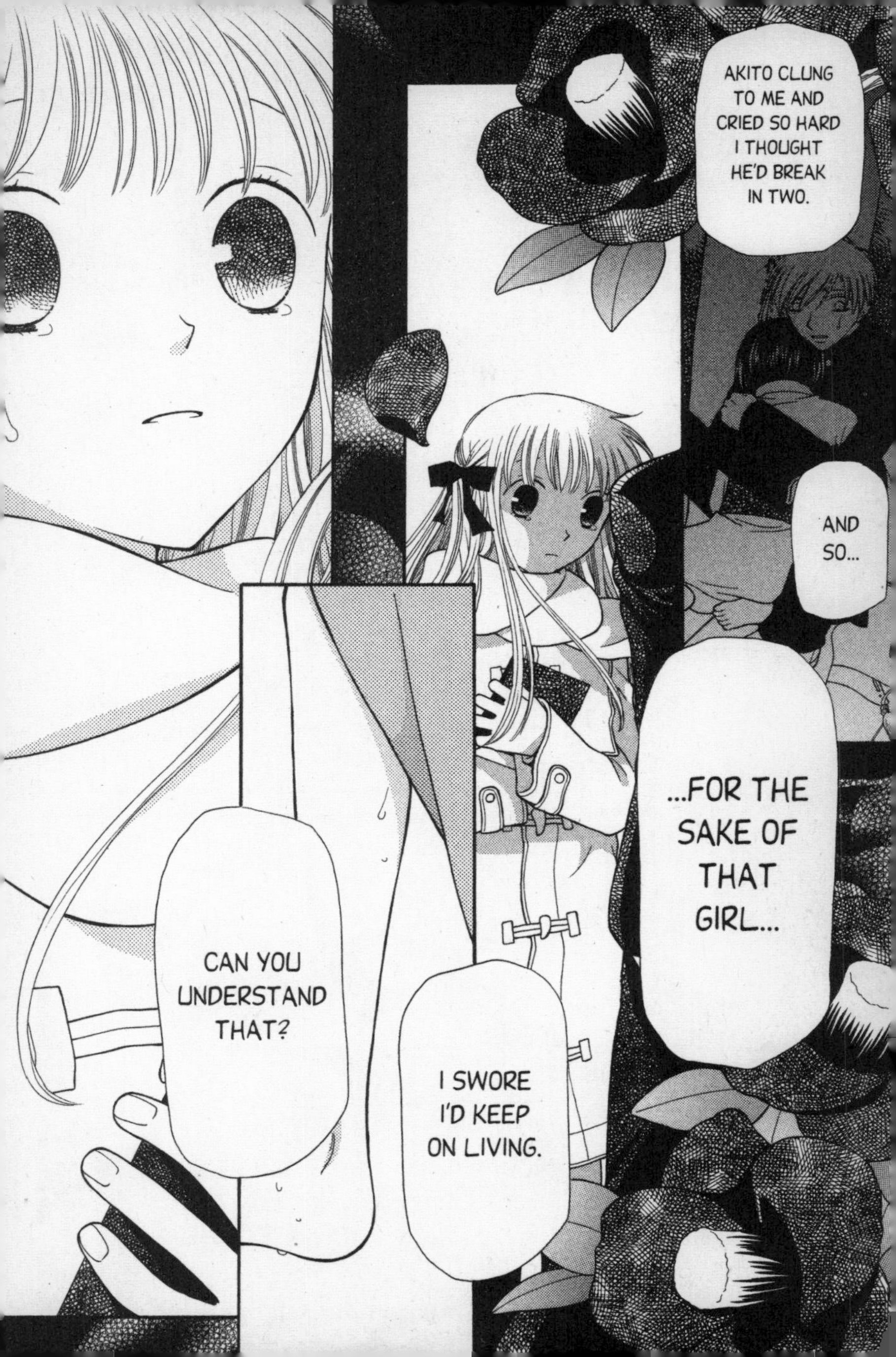
AKITO CLUNG TO ME AND CRIED SO HARD I THOUGHT HE'D BREAK IN TWO.
AND SO...
...FOR THE SAKE OF THAT GIRL...
I SWORE I'D KEEP ON LIVING.
CAN YOU UNDERSTAND THAT?

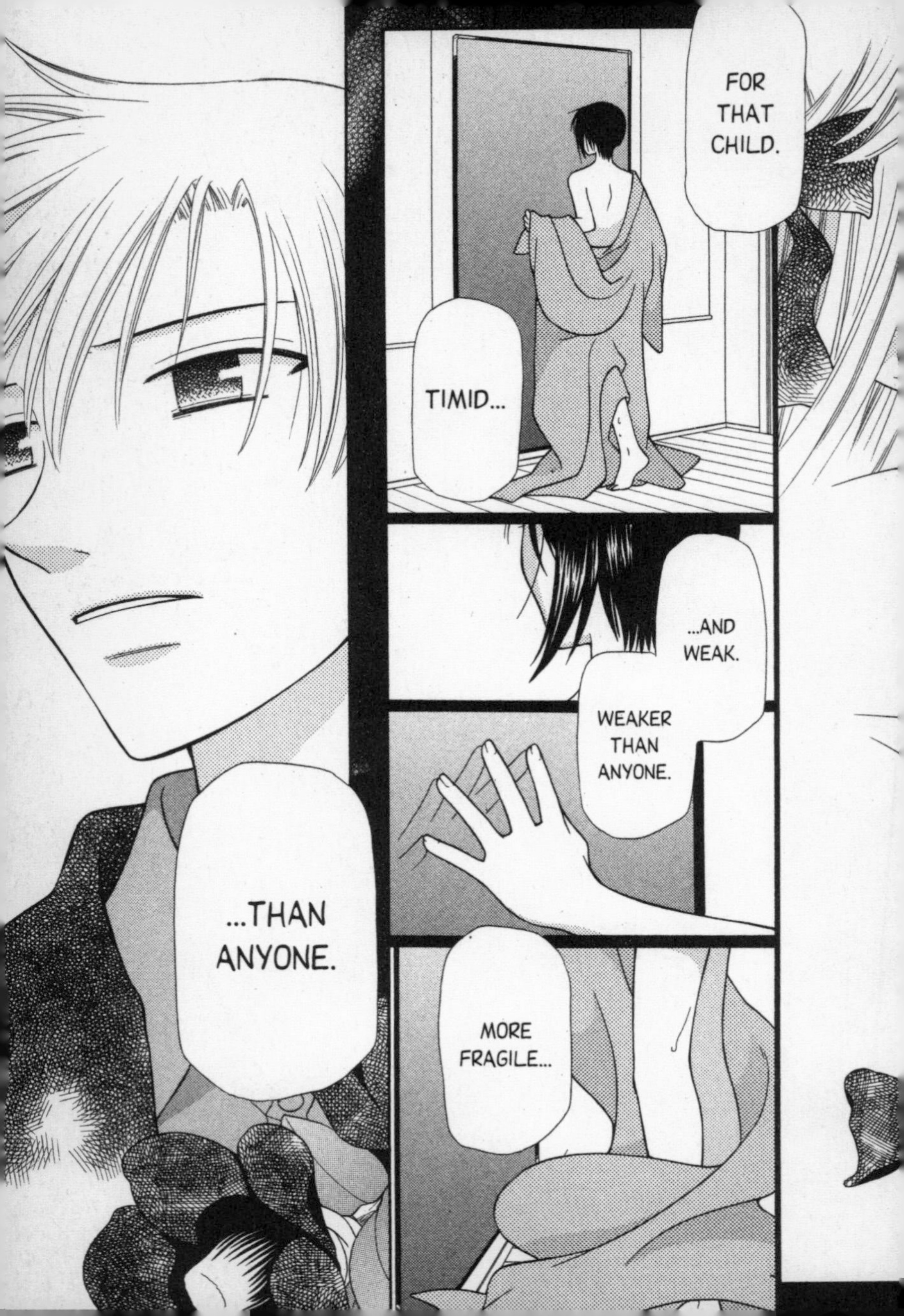
FOR THAT CHILD.
TIMID...
...AND WEAK.
WEAKER THAN ANYONE.
MORE FRAGILE...
...THAN ANYONE.

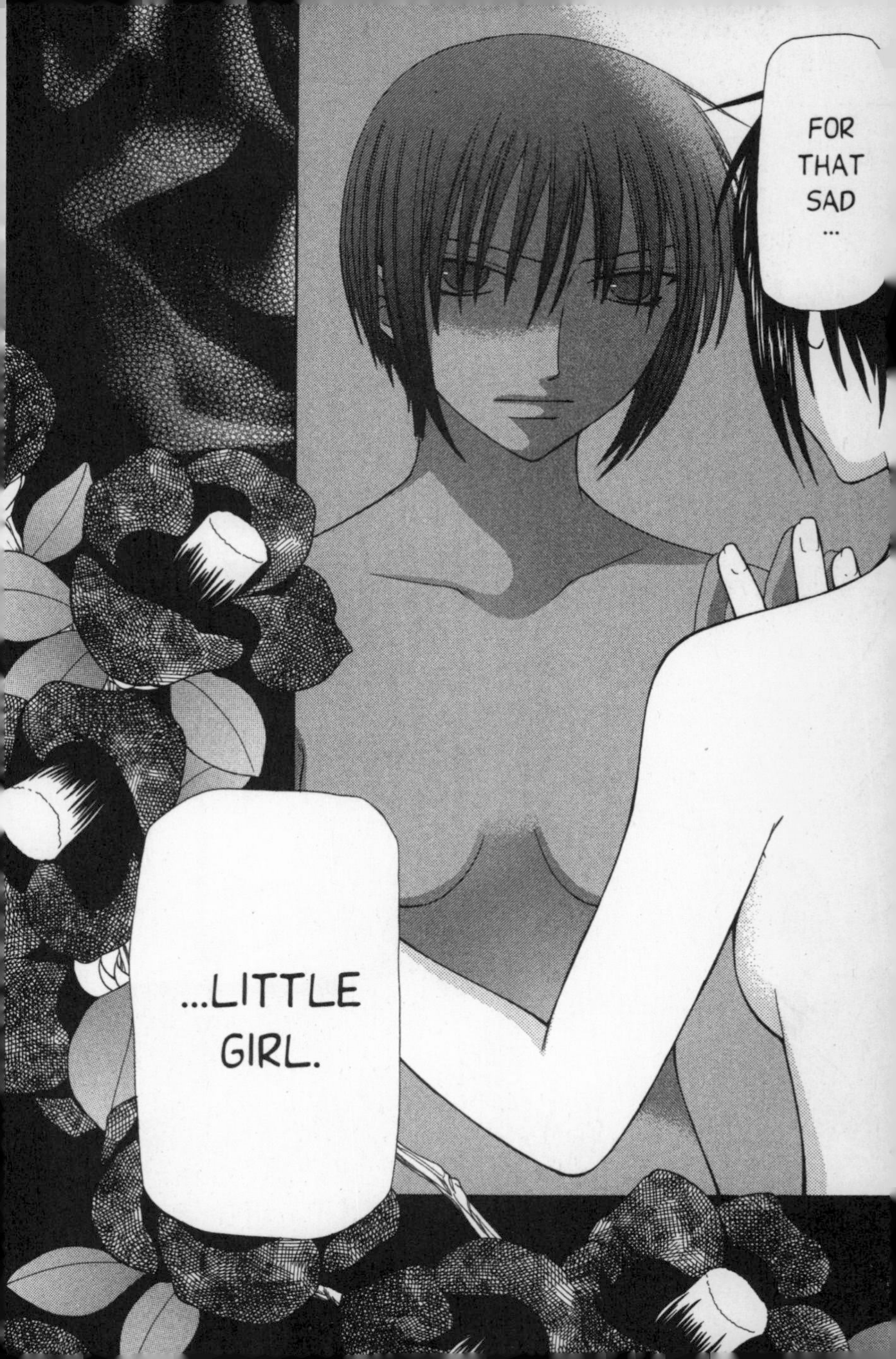
FOR THAT SAD ...
...LITTLE GIRL.

Chapter 98

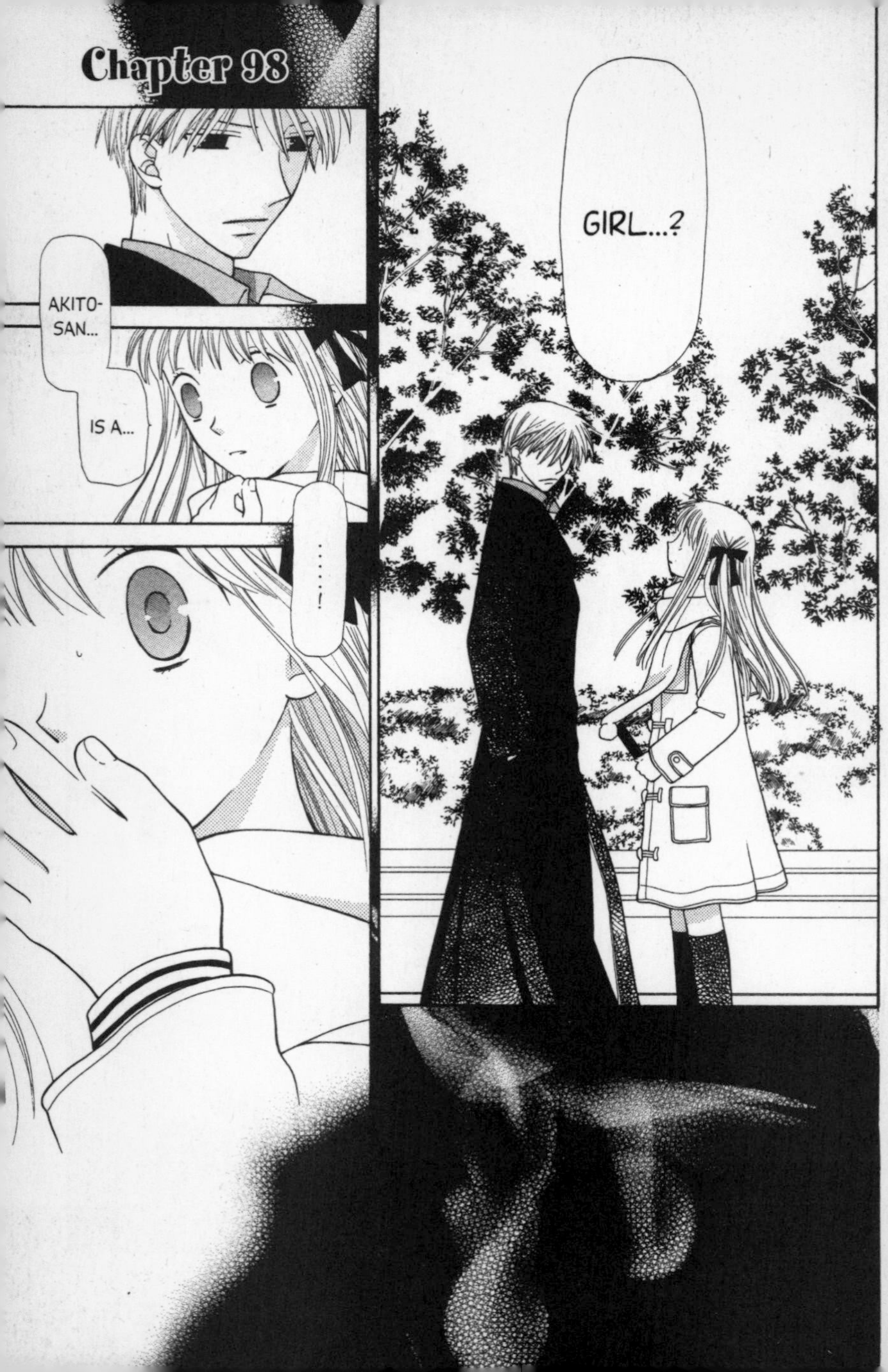
GIRL...?
AKITO-SAN...
IS A...
......!

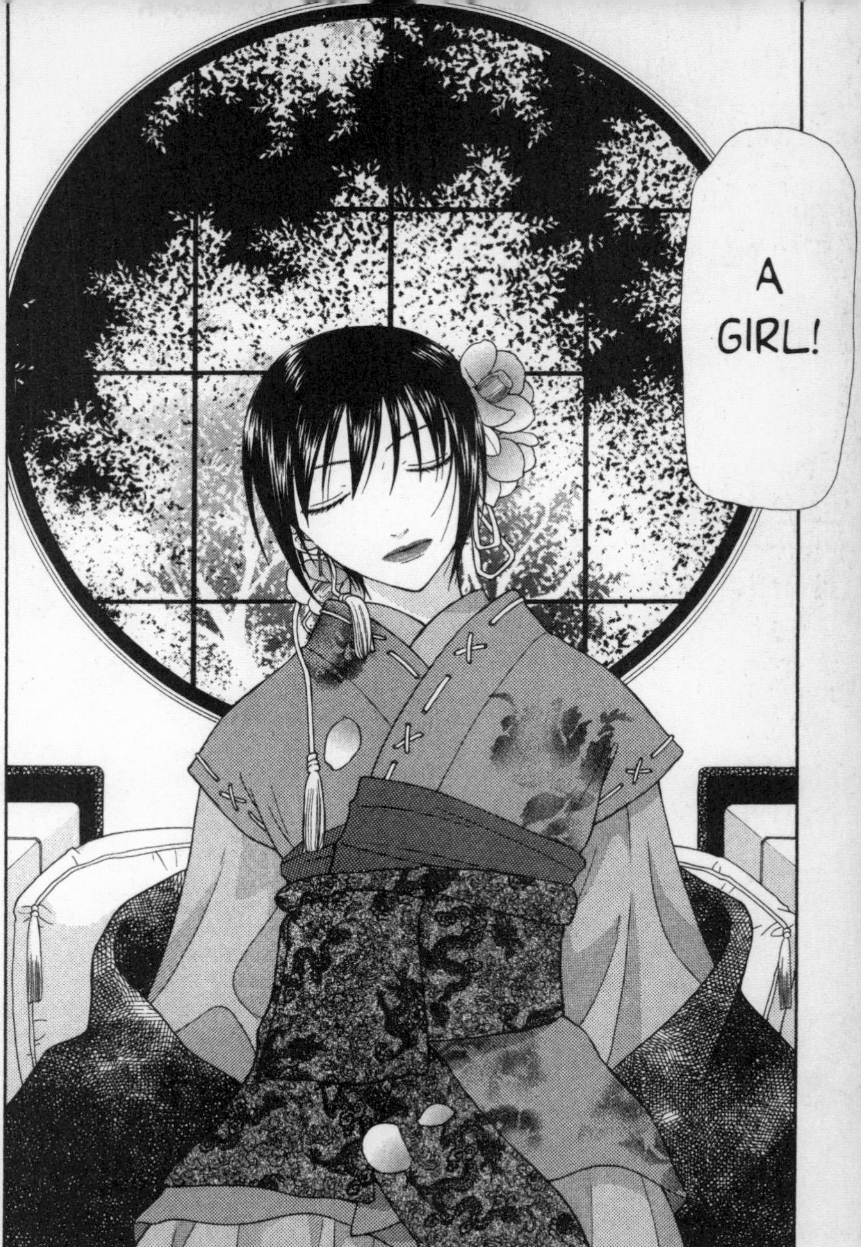
A GIRL!

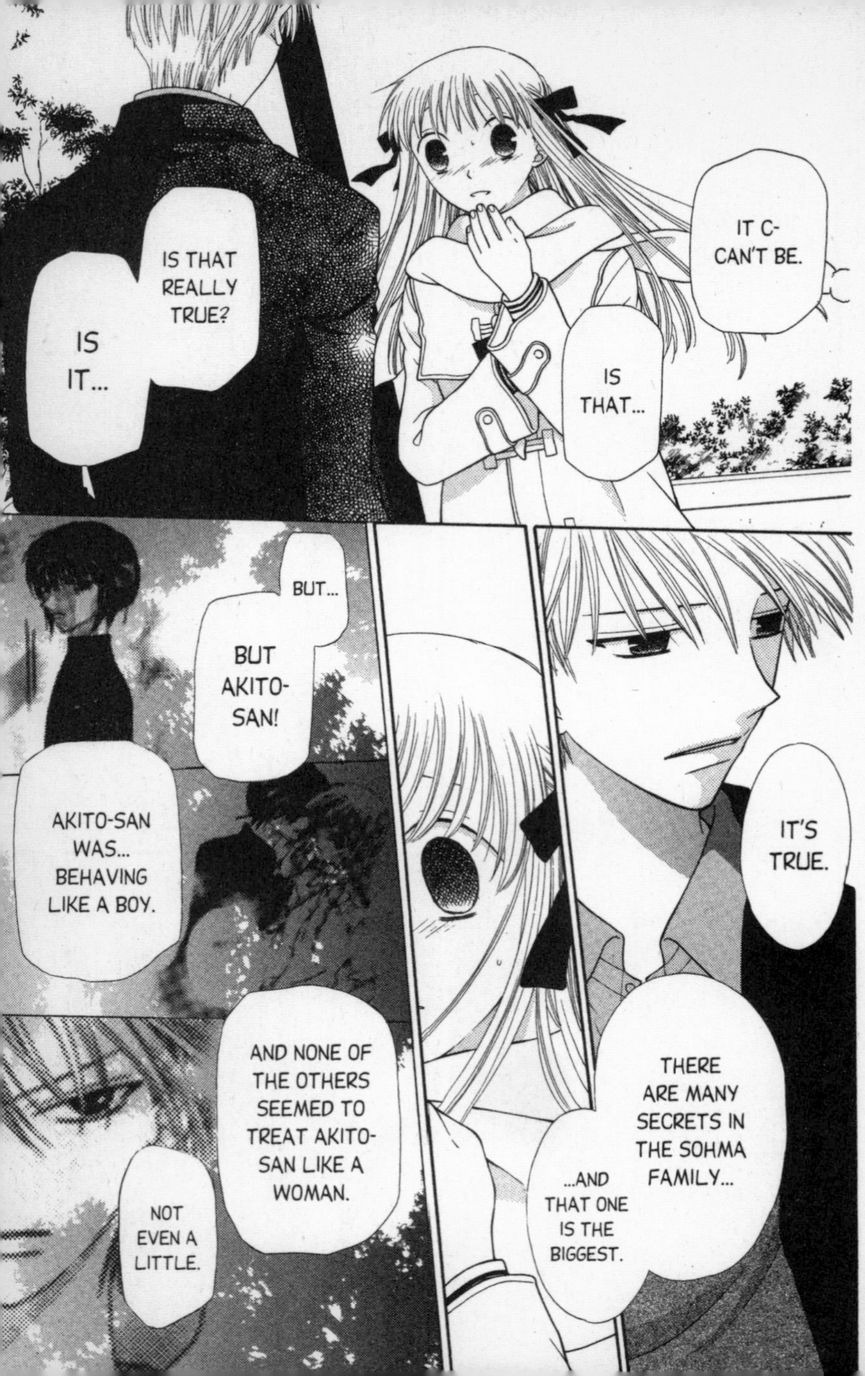
IT C- CAN'T BE.
IS THAT...
IS THAT REALLY TRUE?
IS IT...
IT'S TRUE.
THERE ARE MANY SECRETS IN THE SOHMA FAMILY...
...AND THAT ONE IS THE BIGGEST.
BUT...
BUT AKITO-SAN!
AKITO-SAN WAS... BEHAVING LIKE A BOY.
AND NONE OF THE OTHERS SEEMED TO TREAT AKITO-SAN LIKE A WOMAN.
NOT EVEN A LITTLE.

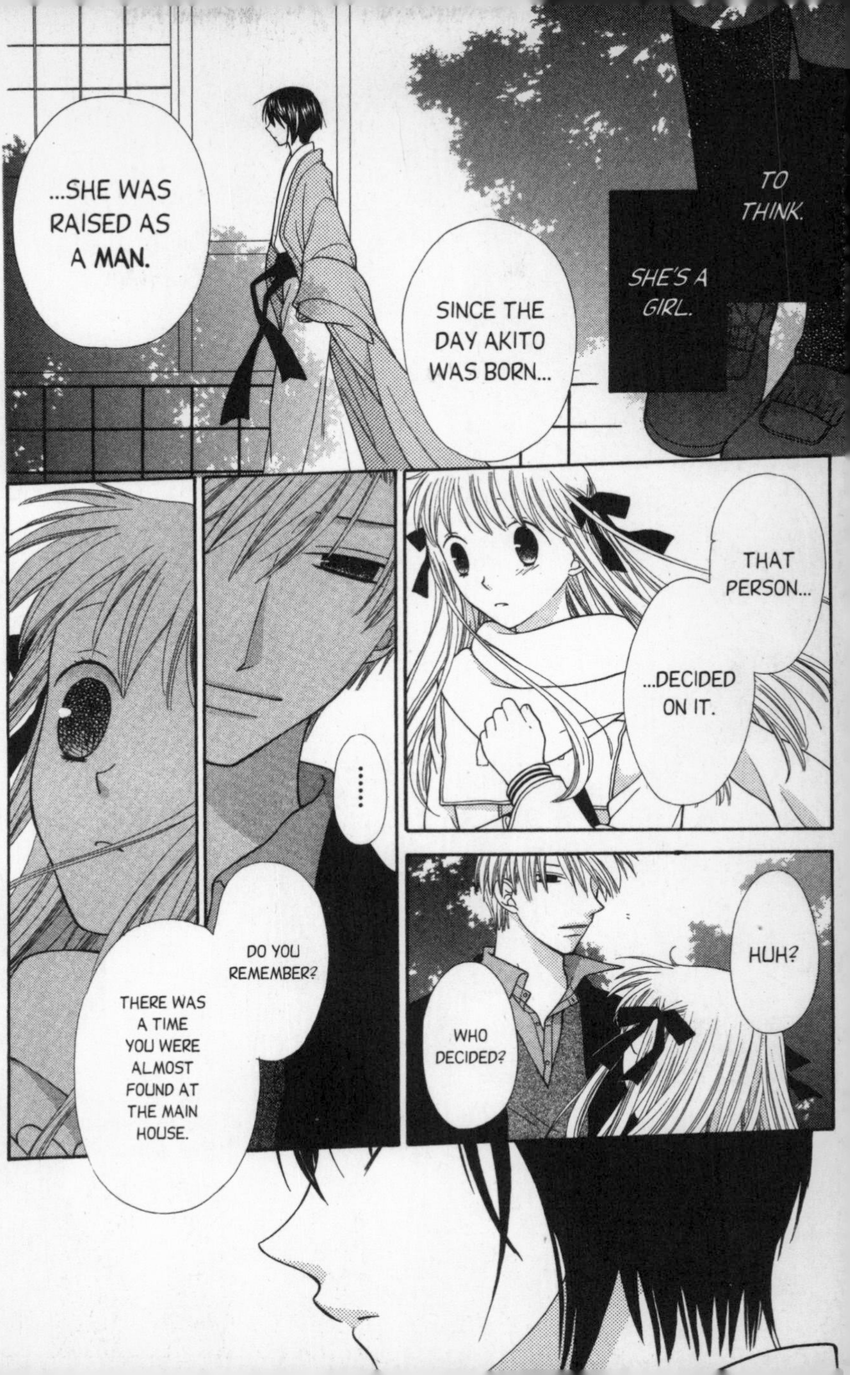
TO THINK.
SHE'S A GIRL.
SINCE THE DAY AKITO WAS BORN...
...SHE WAS RAISED AS A MAN.
THAT PERSON...
...DECIDED ON IT.
HUH?
WHO DECIDED?
......
DO YOU REMEMBER?
THERE WAS A TIME YOU WERE ALMOST FOUND AT THE MAIN HOUSE.

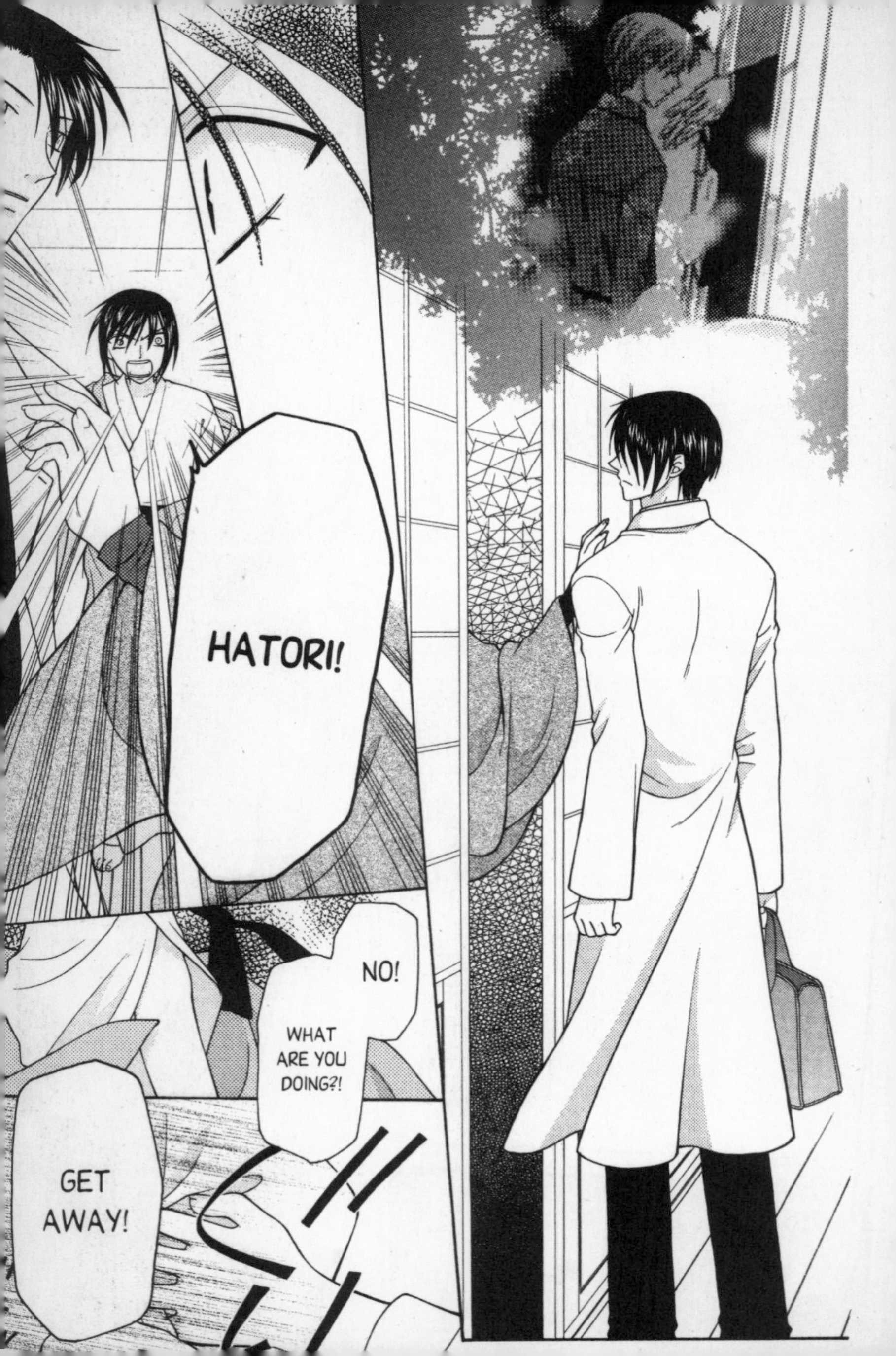
HATORI!
NO!
WHAT ARE YOU DOING?!
GET AWAY!

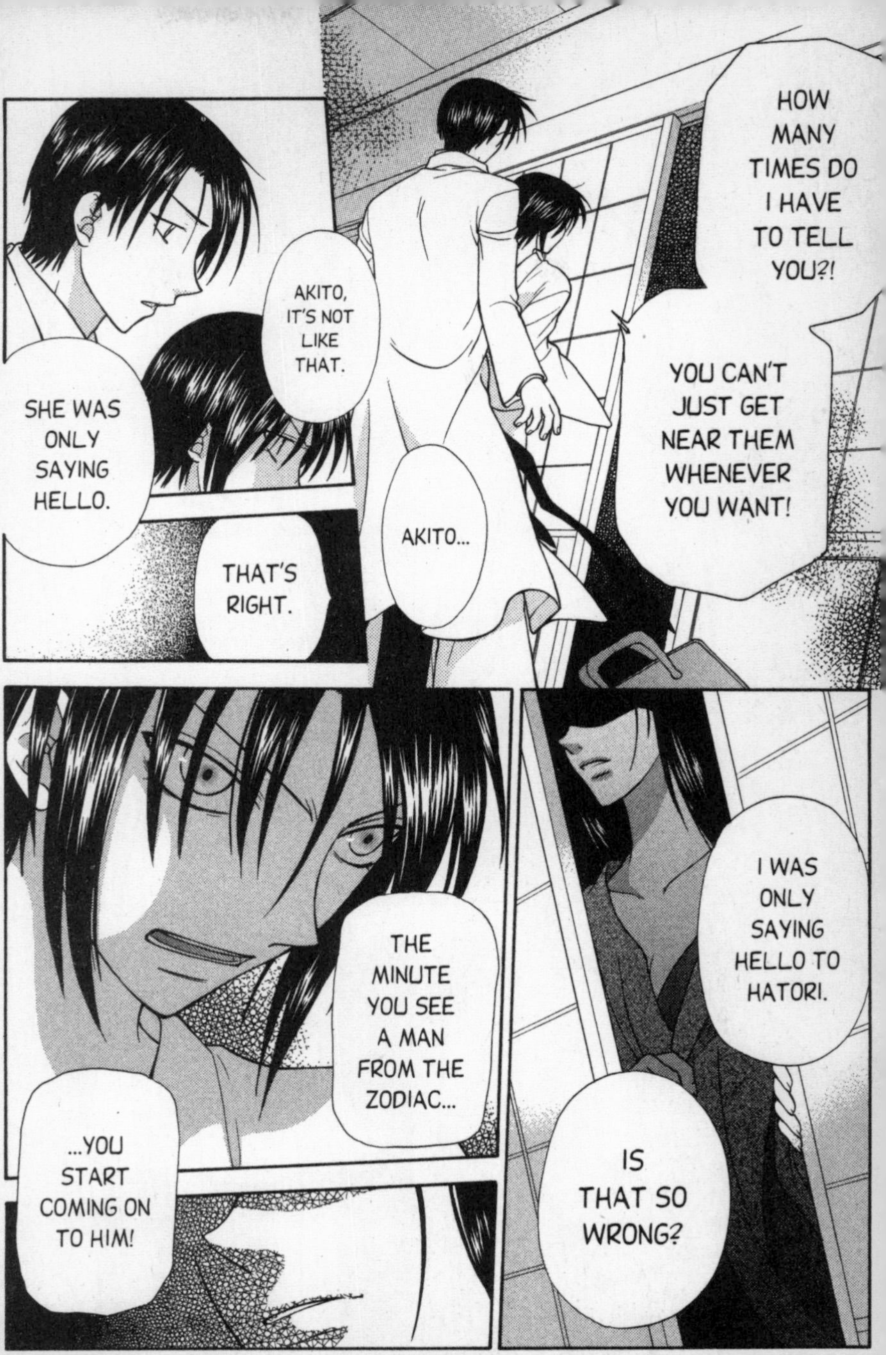
HOW MANY TIMES DO I HAVE TO TELL YOU?!
YOU CAN'T JUST GET NEAR THEM WHENEVER YOU WANT!
AKITO...
AKITO, IT'S NOT LIKE THAT.
SHE WAS ONLY SAYING HELLO.
THAT'S RIGHT.
I WAS ONLY SAYING HELLO TO HATORI.
IS THAT SO WRONG?
THE MINUTE YOU SEE A MAN FROM THE ZODIAC...
...YOU START COMING ON TO HIM!

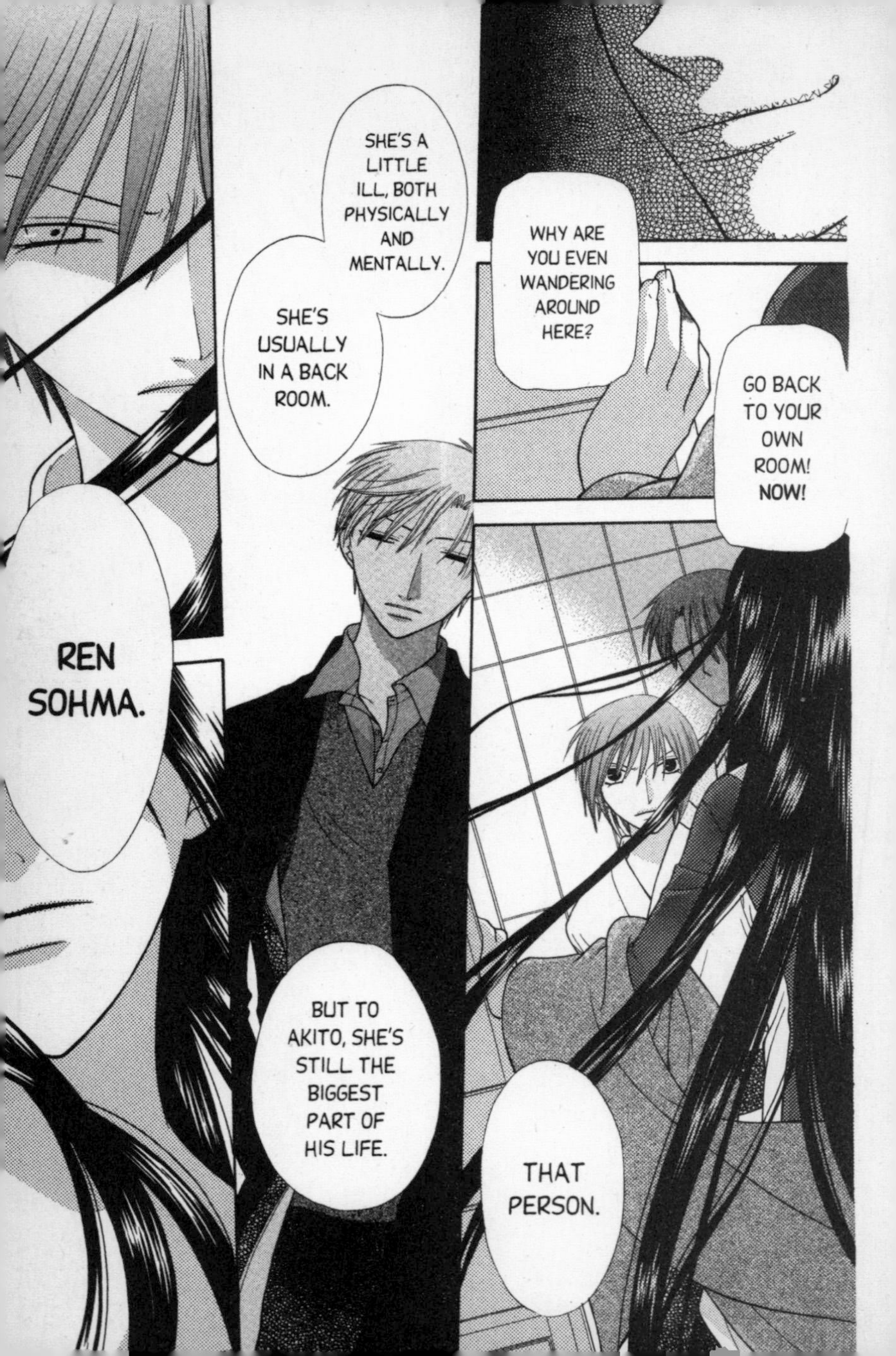
WHY ARE YOU EVEN WANDERING AROUND HERE?
GO BACK TO YOUR OWN ROOM! NOW!
THAT PERSON.
SHE'S A LITTLE ILL, BOTH PHYSICALLY AND MENTALLY.
SHE'S USUALLY IN A BACK ROOM.
BUT TO AKITO, SHE'S STILL THE BIGGEST PART OF HIS LIFE.
REN SOHMA.

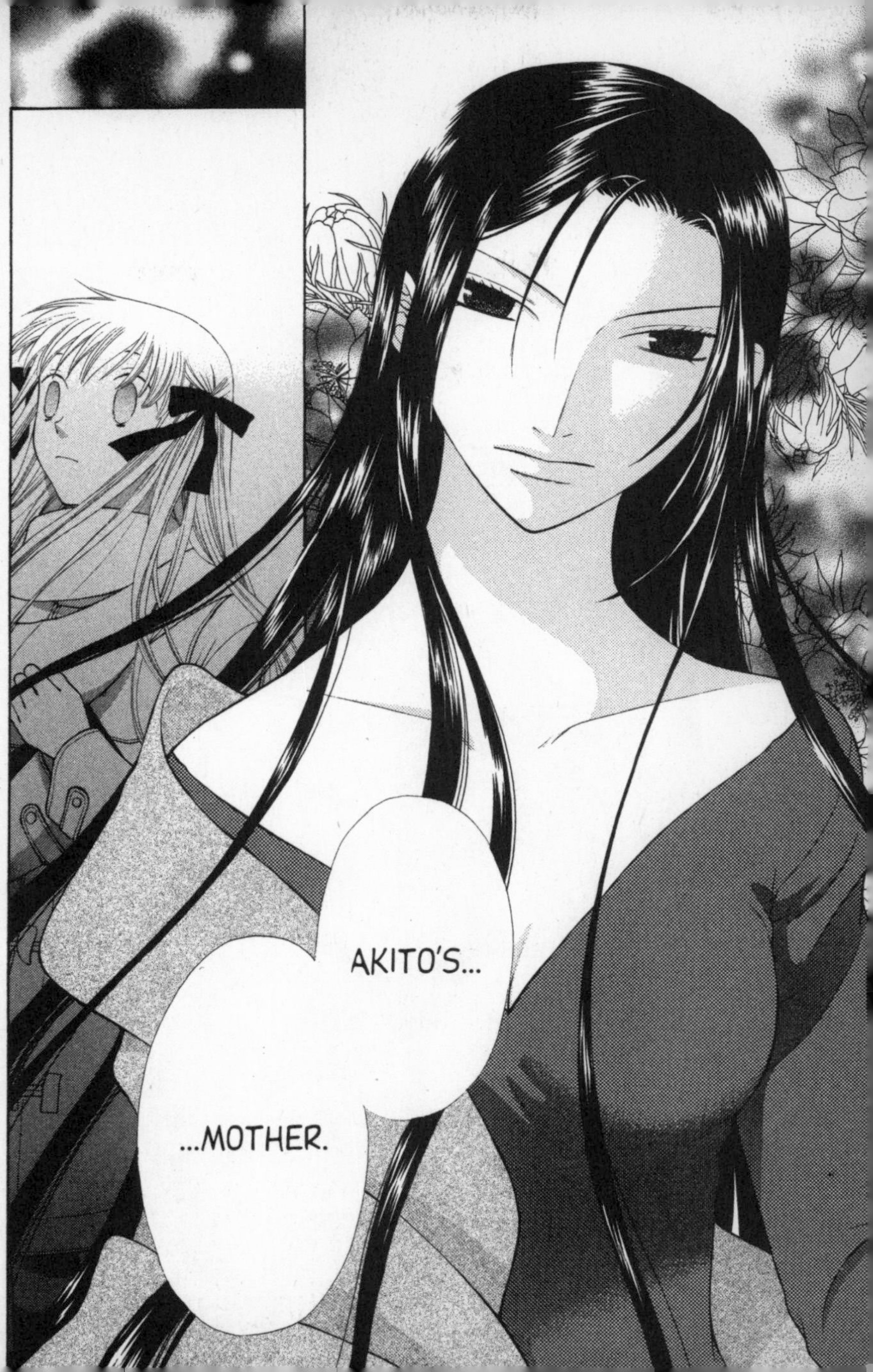
AKITO'S...
...MOTHER.

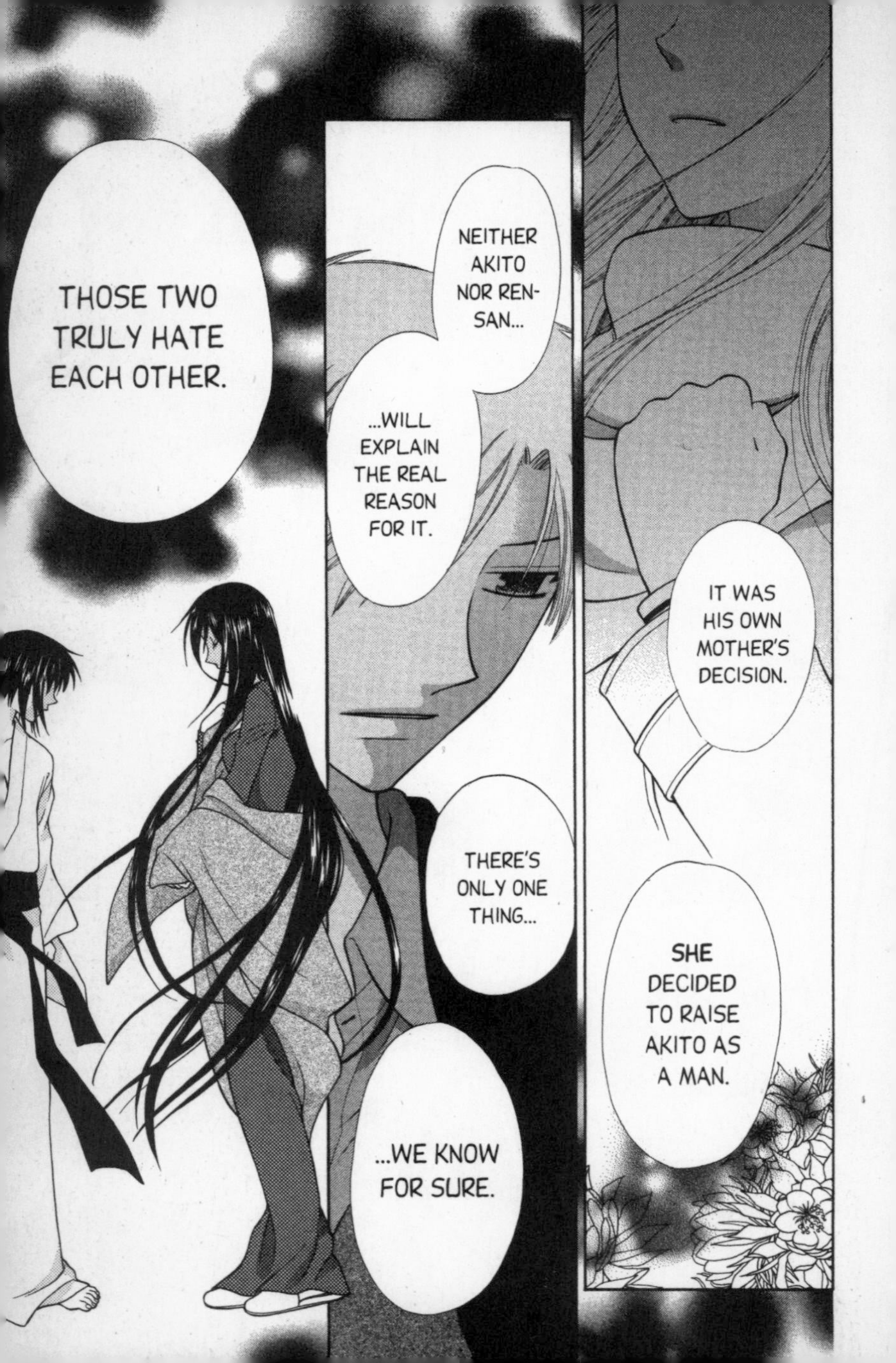
IT WAS HIS OWN MOTHER'S DECISION.
SHE DECIDED TO RAISE AKITO AS A MAN.
NEITHER AKITO NOR REN-SAN...
...WILL EXPLAIN THE REAL REASON FOR IT.
THERE'S ONLY ONE THING...
...WE KNOW FOR SURE.
THOSE TWO TRULY HATE EACH OTHER.

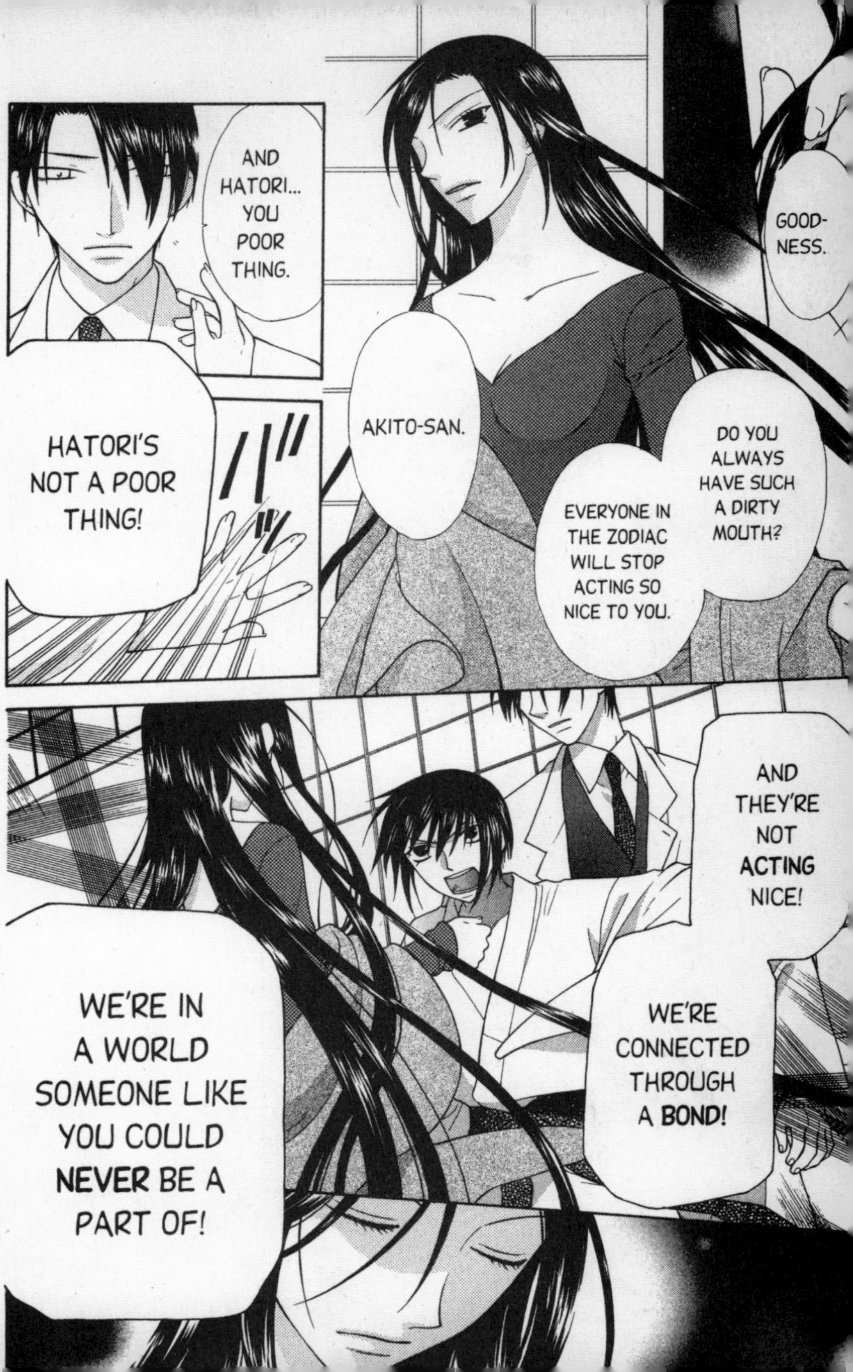
GOOD-NESS.
AKITO-SAN.
DO YOU ALWAYS HAVE SUCH A DIRTY MOUTH?
EVERYONE IN THE ZODIAC WILL STOP ACTING SO NICE TO YOU.
AND HATORI... YOU POOR THING.
HATORI'S NOT A POOR THING!
AND THEY'RE NOT **ACTING** NICE!
WE'RE CONNECTED THROUGH A **BOND**!
WE'RE IN A WORLD SOMEONE LIKE YOU COULD **NEVER** BE A PART OF!

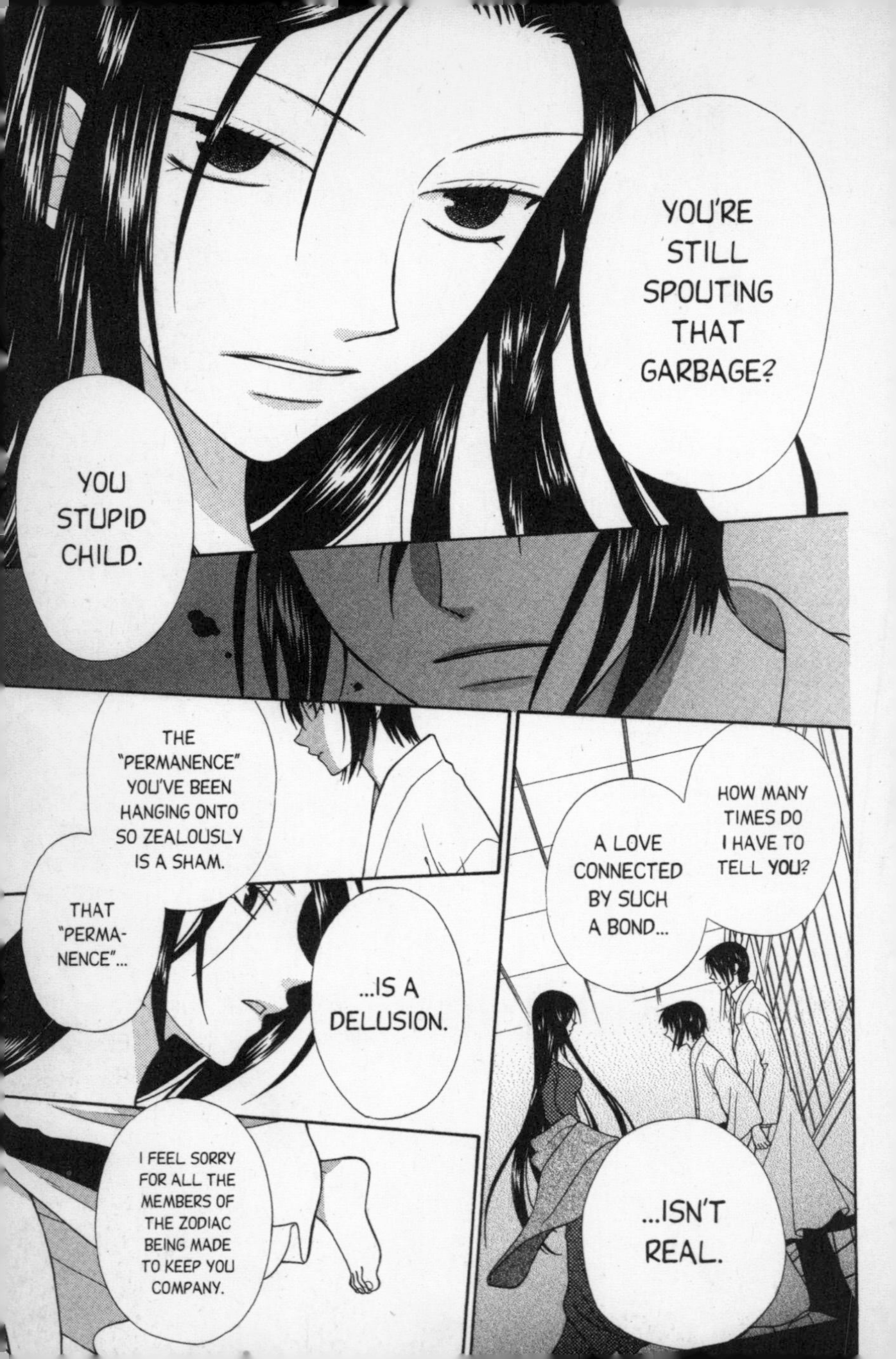
YOU'RE STILL SPOUTING THAT GARBAGE?
YOU STUPID CHILD.
HOW MANY TIMES DO I HAVE TO TELL YOU?
A LOVE CONNECTED BY SUCH A BOND...
...ISN'T REAL.
THE "PERMANENCE" YOU'VE BEEN HANGING ONTO SO ZEALOUSLY IS A SHAM.
THAT "PERMA-NENCE"...
...IS A DELUSION.
I FEEL SORRY FOR ALL THE MEMBERS OF THE ZODIAC BEING MADE TO KEEP YOU COMPANY.

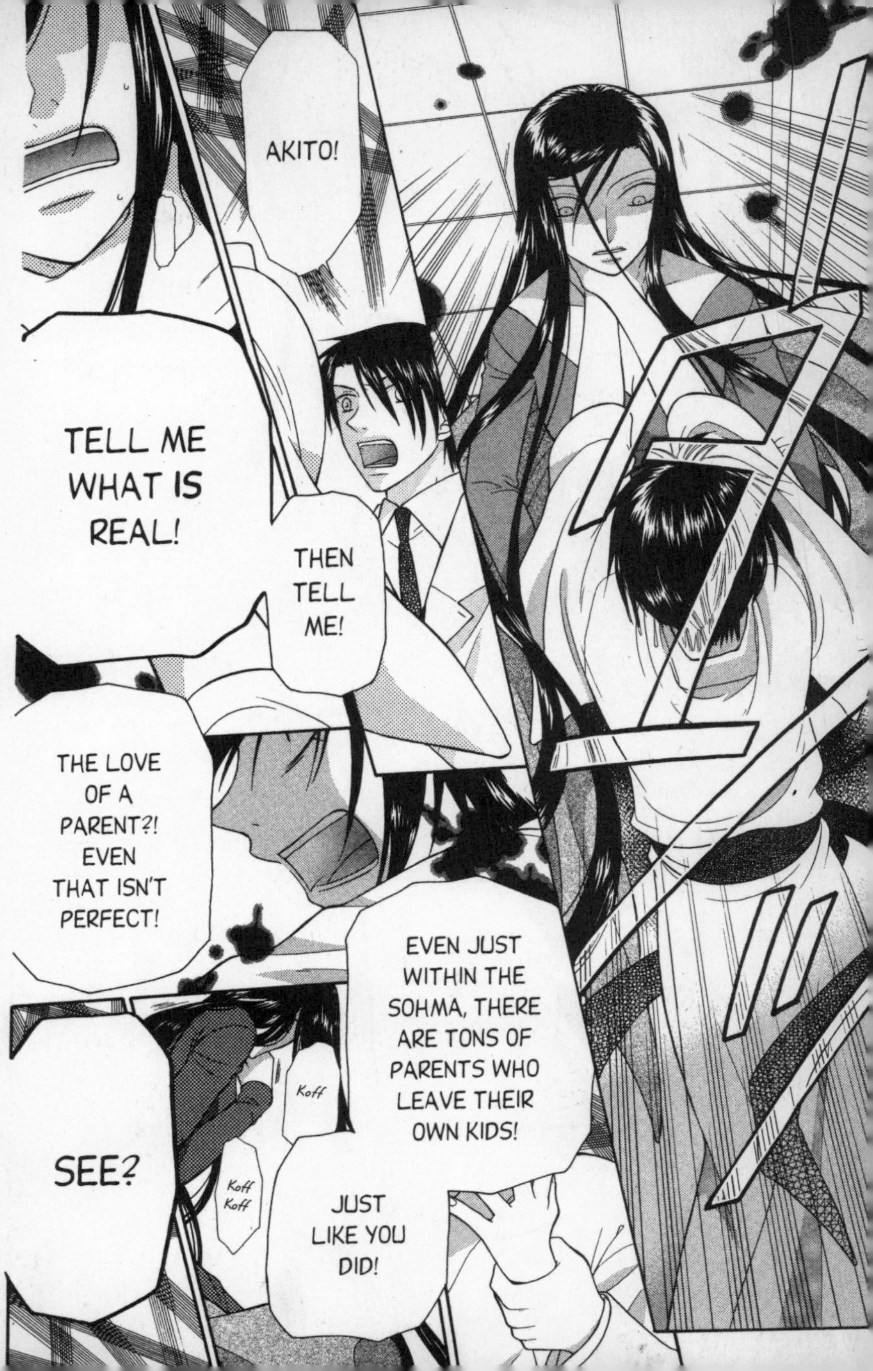

AKITO!
TELL ME WHAT IS REAL!
THEN TELL ME!
THE LOVE OF A PARENT?! EVEN THAT ISN'T PERFECT!
EVEN JUST WITHIN THE SOHMA, THERE ARE TONS OF PARENTS WHO LEAVE THEIR OWN KIDS!
JUST LIKE YOU DID!
Koff
Koff Koff
SEE?

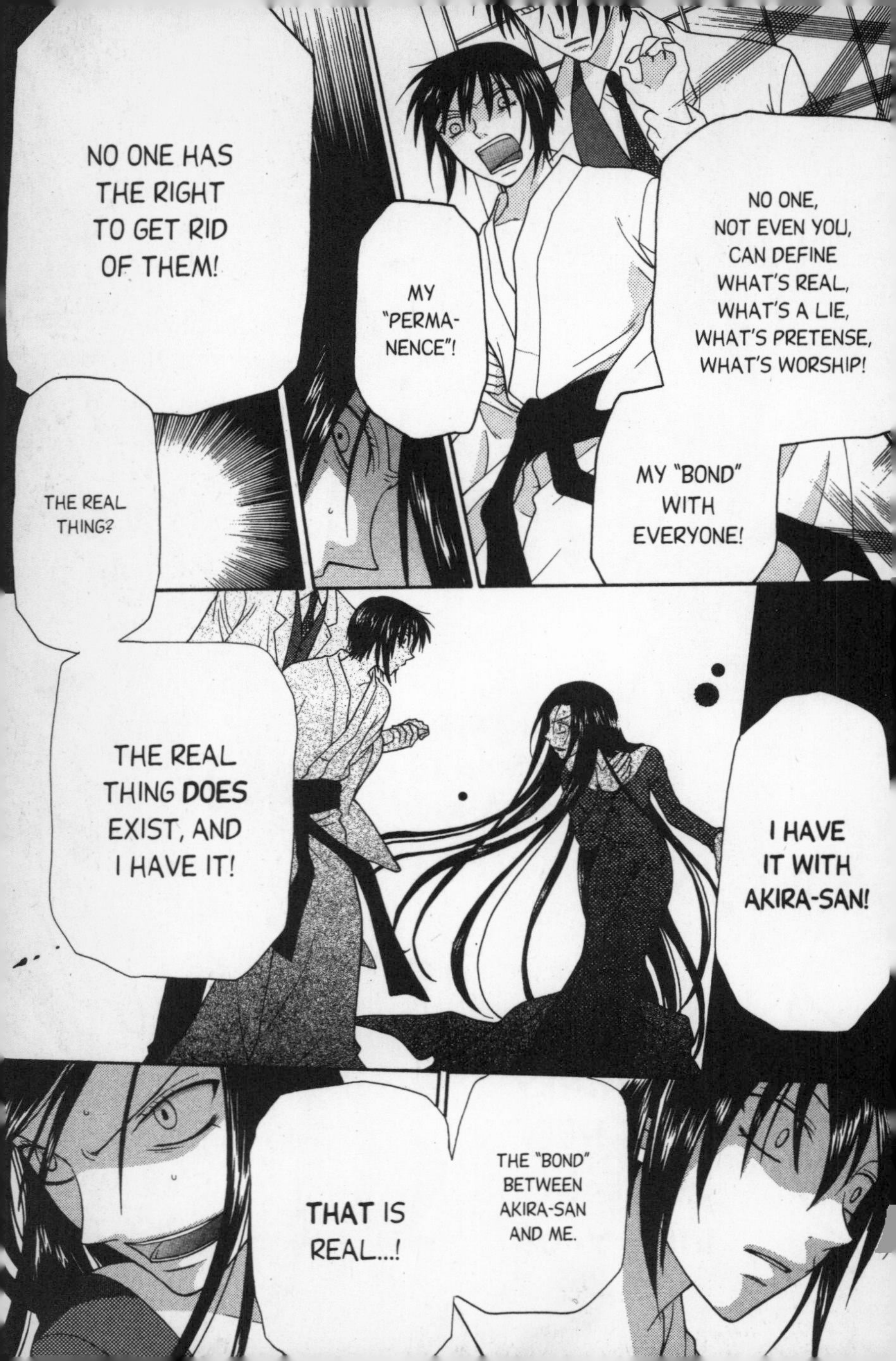
NO ONE, NOT EVEN YOU, CAN DEFINE WHAT'S REAL, WHAT'S A LIE, WHAT'S PRETENSE, WHAT'S WORSHIP!
MY "BOND" WITH EVERYONE!
MY "PERMANENCE"!
NO ONE HAS THE RIGHT TO GET RID OF THEM!
THE REAL THING?
THE REAL THING **DOES** EXIST, AND I HAVE IT!
I HAVE IT WITH AKIRA-SAN!
THE "BOND" BETWEEN AKIRA-SAN AND ME.
THAT IS REAL...!

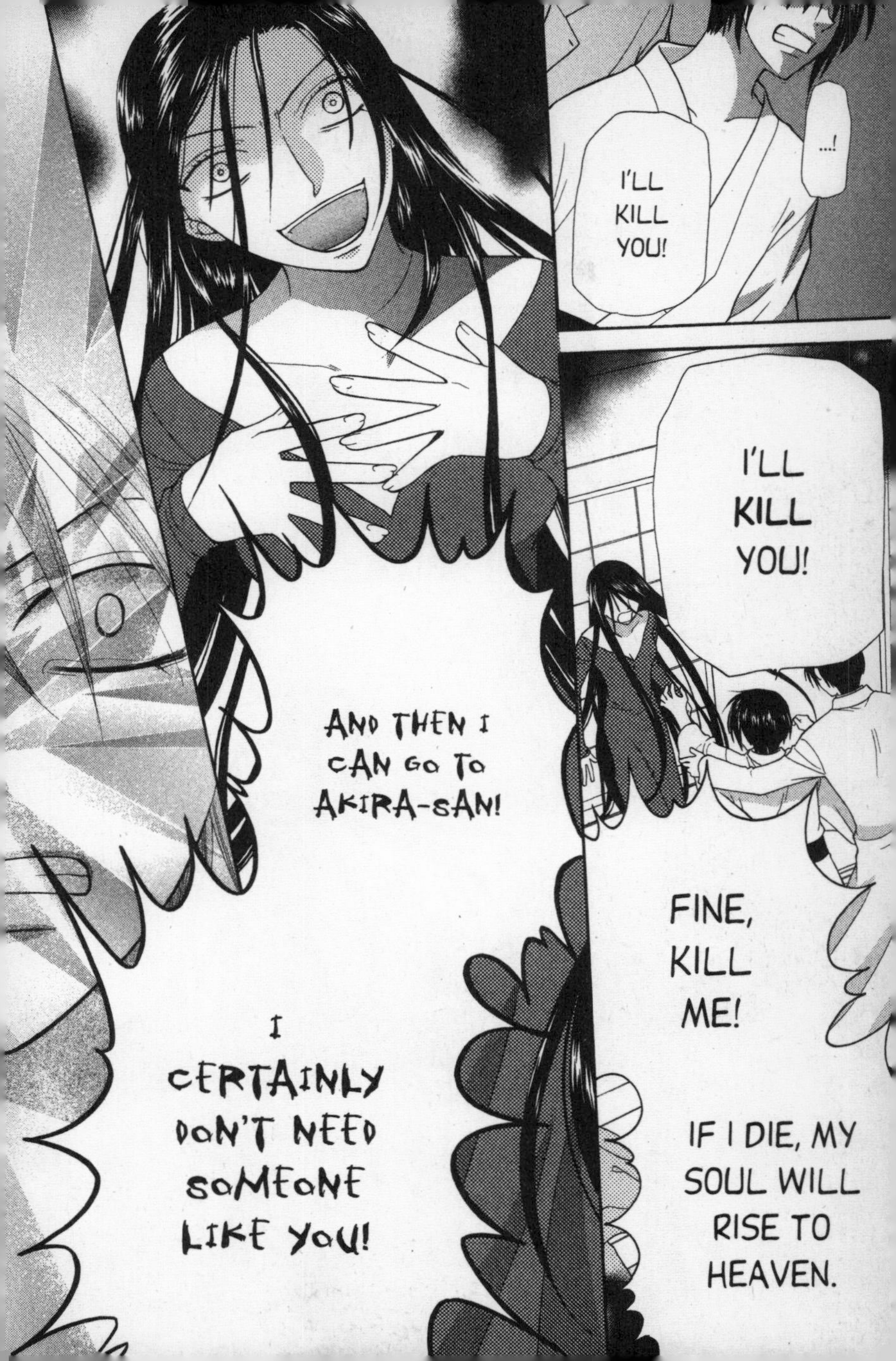
...!
I'LL KILL YOU!
I'LL KILL YOU!
FINE, KILL ME!
IF I DIE, MY SOUL WILL RISE TO HEAVEN.
AND THEN I CAN GO TO AKIRA-SAN!
I CERTAINLY DON'T NEED SOMEONE LIKE YOU!

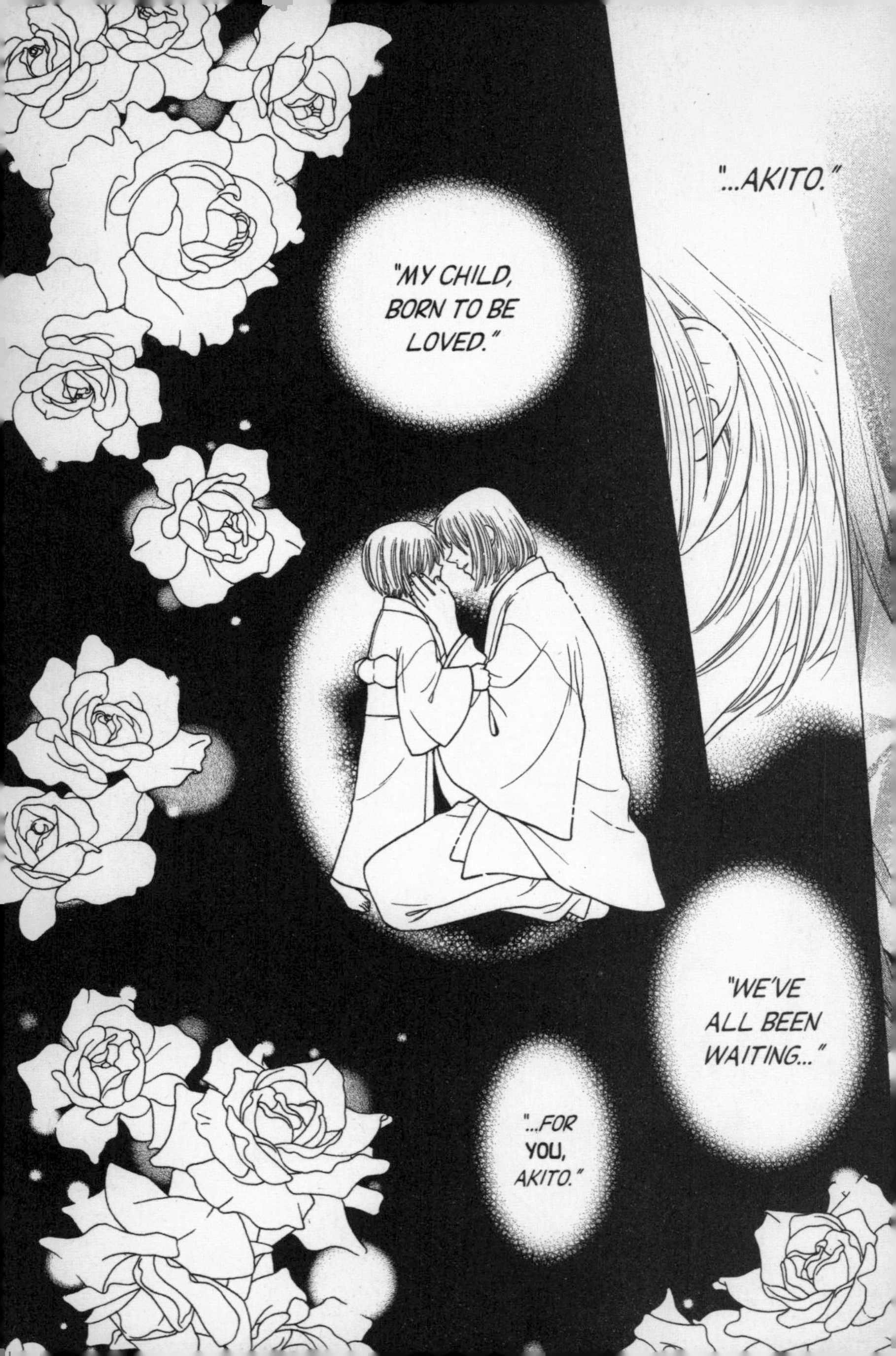
"...AKITO."
"MY CHILD, BORN TO BE LOVED."
"WE'VE ALL BEEN WAITING..."
"...FOR YOU, AKITO."

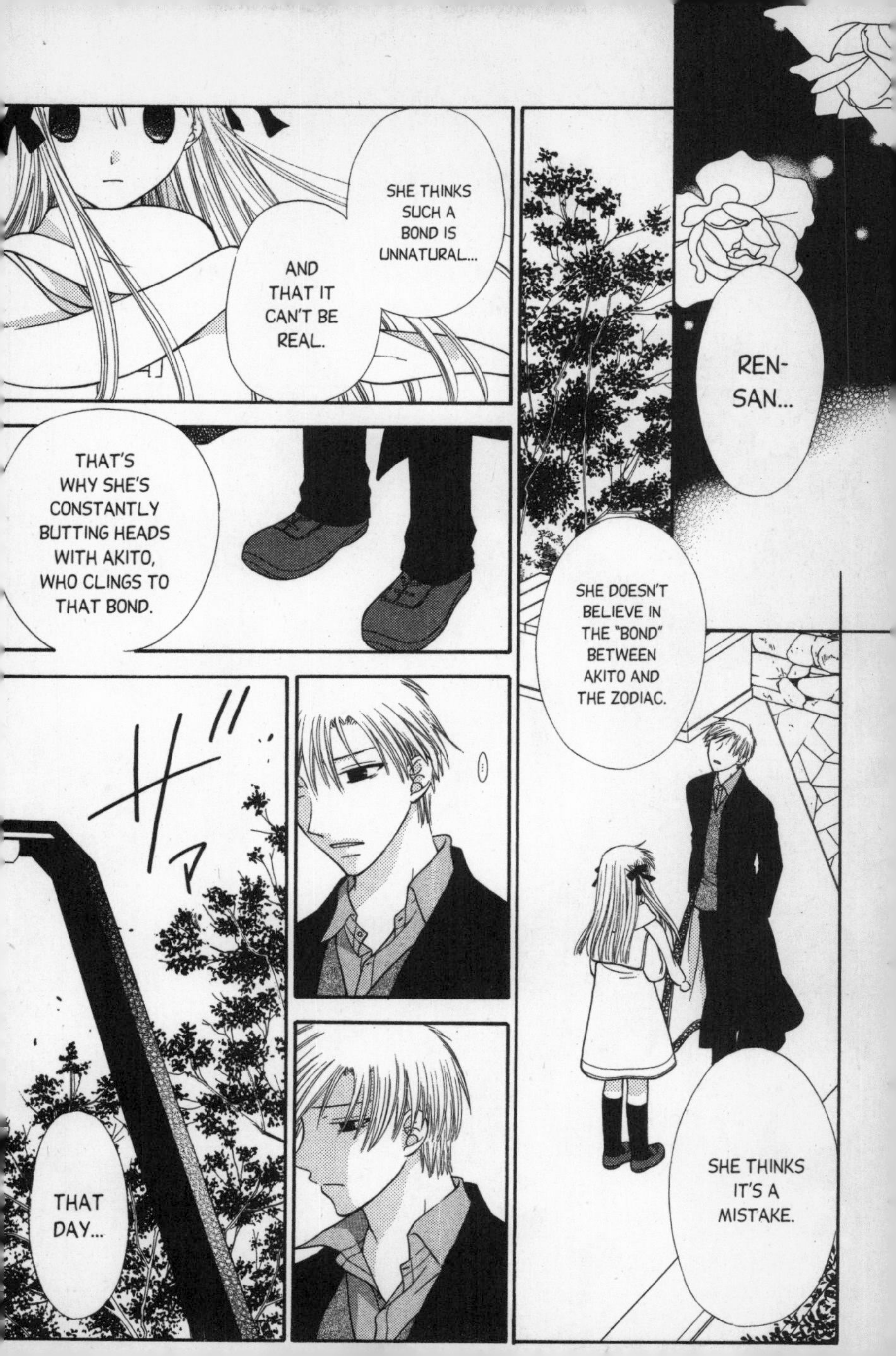

REN-SAN...
SHE DOESN'T BELIEVE IN THE "BOND" BETWEEN AKITO AND THE ZODIAC.
SHE THINKS IT'S A MISTAKE.
SHE THINKS SUCH A BOND IS UNNATURAL...
AND THAT IT CAN'T BE REAL.
THAT'S WHY SHE'S CONSTANTLY BUTTING HEADS WITH AKITO, WHO CLINGS TO THAT BOND.
...
THAT DAY...

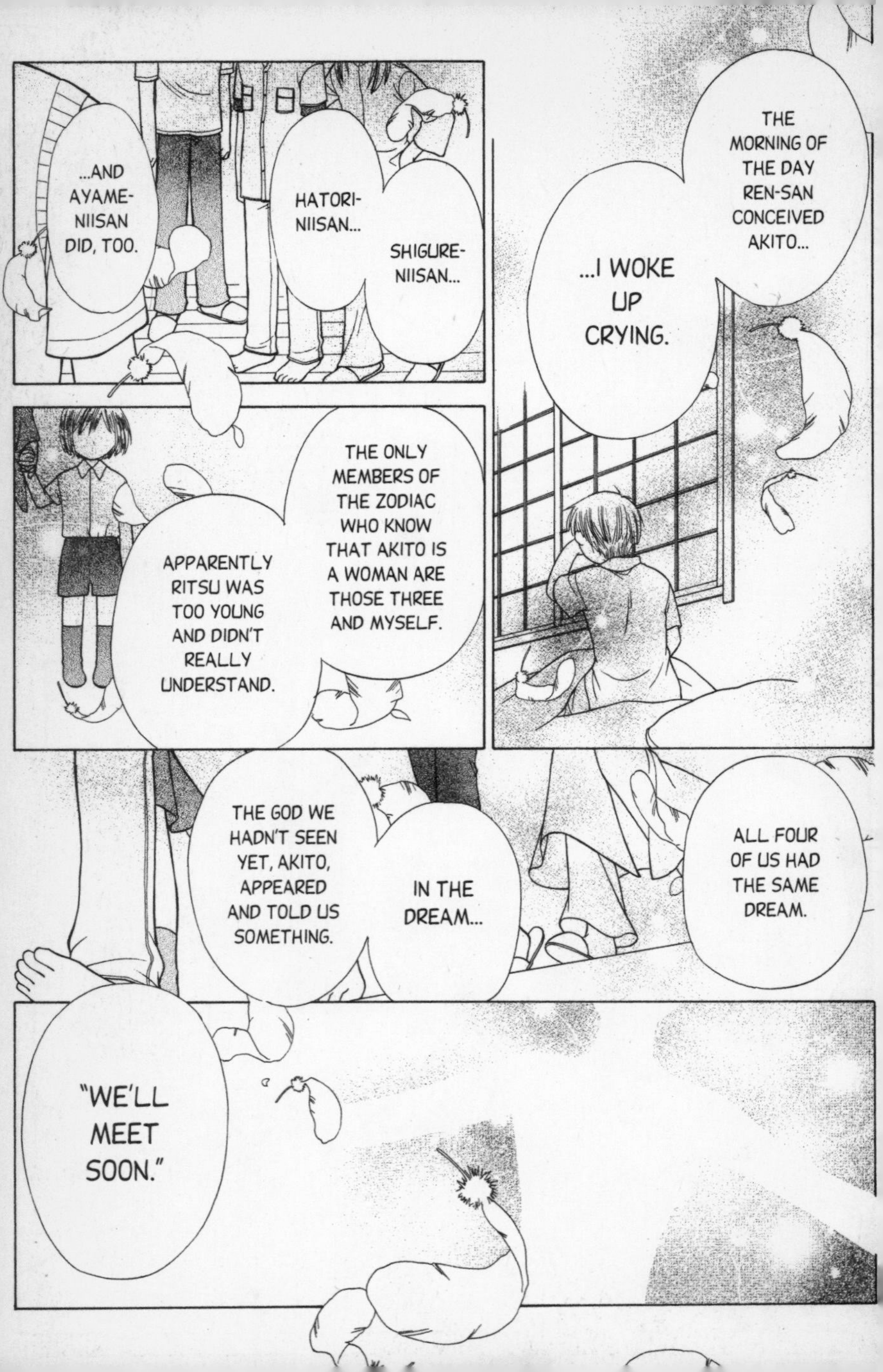
THE MORNING OF THE DAY REN-SAN CONCEIVED AKITO...
...I WOKE UP CRYING.
SHIGURE-NIISAN...
HATORI-NIISAN...
...AND AYAME-NIISAN DID, TOO.
THE ONLY MEMBERS OF THE ZODIAC WHO KNOW THAT AKITO IS A WOMAN ARE THOSE THREE AND MYSELF.
APPARENTLY RITSU WAS TOO YOUNG AND DIDN'T REALLY UNDERSTAND.
ALL FOUR OF US HAD THE SAME DREAM.
IN THE DREAM...
THE GOD WE HADN'T SEEN YET, AKITO, APPEARED AND TOLD US SOMETHING.
"WE'LL MEET SOON."

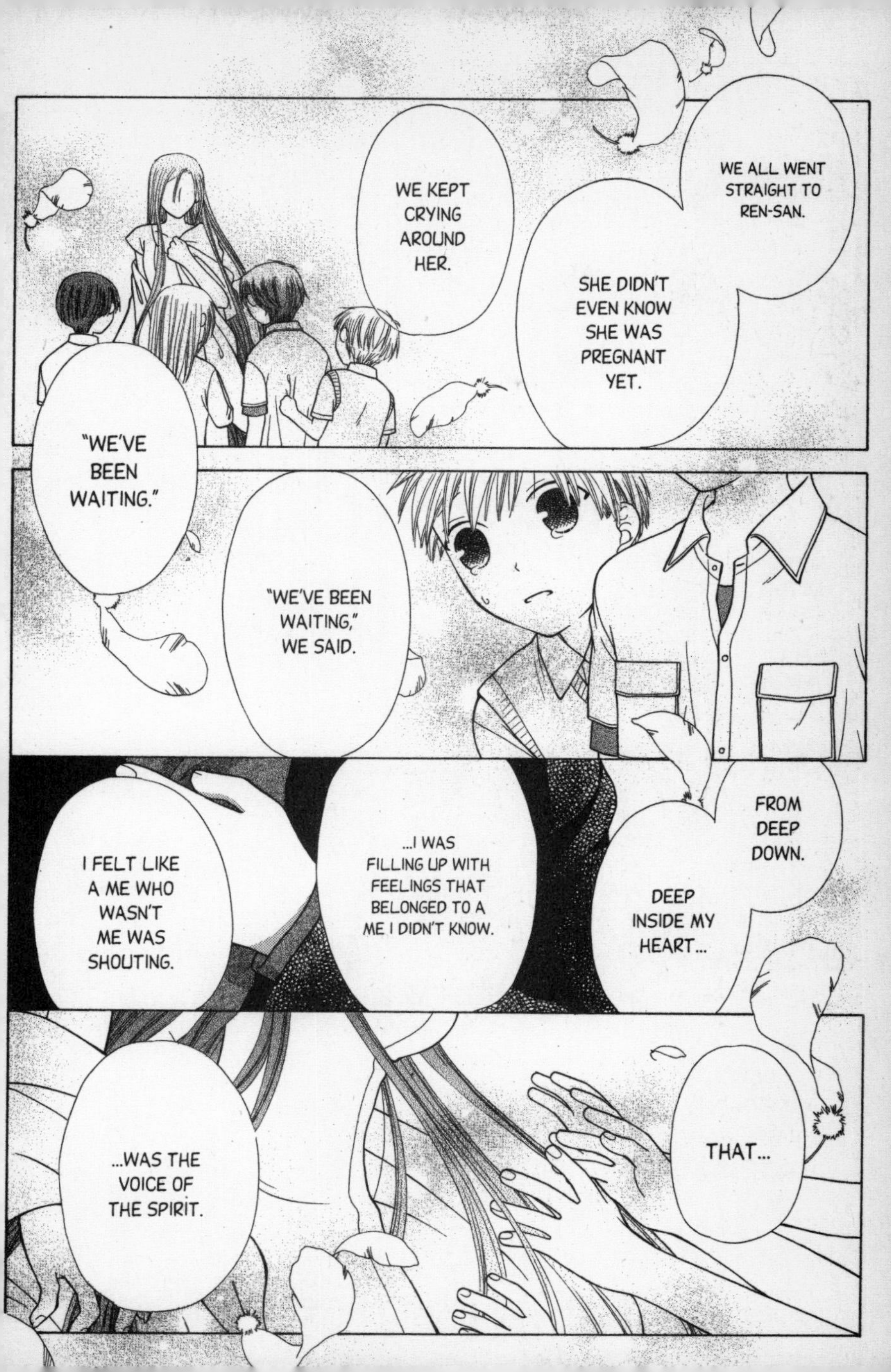
WE ALL WENT STRAIGHT TO REN-SAN.
SHE DIDN'T EVEN KNOW SHE WAS PREGNANT YET.
WE KEPT CRYING AROUND HER.
"WE'VE BEEN WAITING."
"WE'VE BEEN WAITING," WE SAID.
FROM DEEP DOWN.
DEEP INSIDE MY HEART...
...I WAS FILLING UP WITH FEELINGS THAT BELONGED TO A ME I DIDN'T KNOW.
I FELT LIKE A ME WHO WASN'T ME WAS SHOUTING.
THAT...
...WAS THE VOICE OF THE SPIRIT.

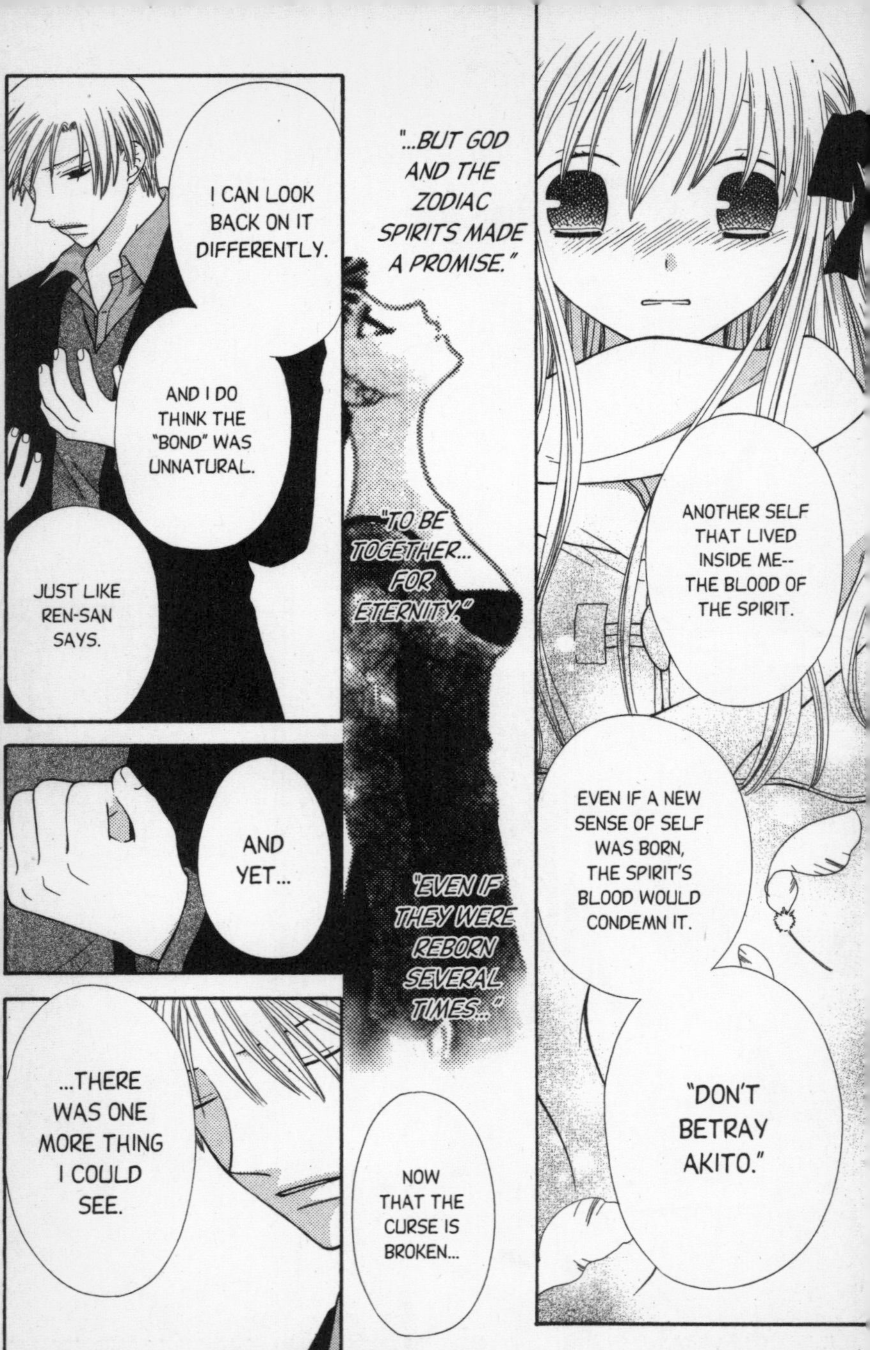
ANOTHER SELF THAT LIVED INSIDE ME-- THE BLOOD OF THE SPIRIT.
EVEN IF A NEW SENSE OF SELF WAS BORN, THE SPIRIT'S BLOOD WOULD CONDEMN IT.
"DON'T BETRAY AKITO."
"...BUT GOD AND THE ZODIAC SPIRITS MADE A PROMISE."
"TO BE TOGETHER... FOR ETERNITY."
"EVEN IF THEY WERE REBORN SEVERAL TIMES..."
NOW THAT THE CURSE IS BROKEN...
I CAN LOOK BACK ON IT DIFFERENTLY.
AND I DO THINK THE "BOND" WAS UNNATURAL.
JUST LIKE REN-SAN SAYS.
AND YET...
...THERE WAS ONE MORE THING I COULD SEE.

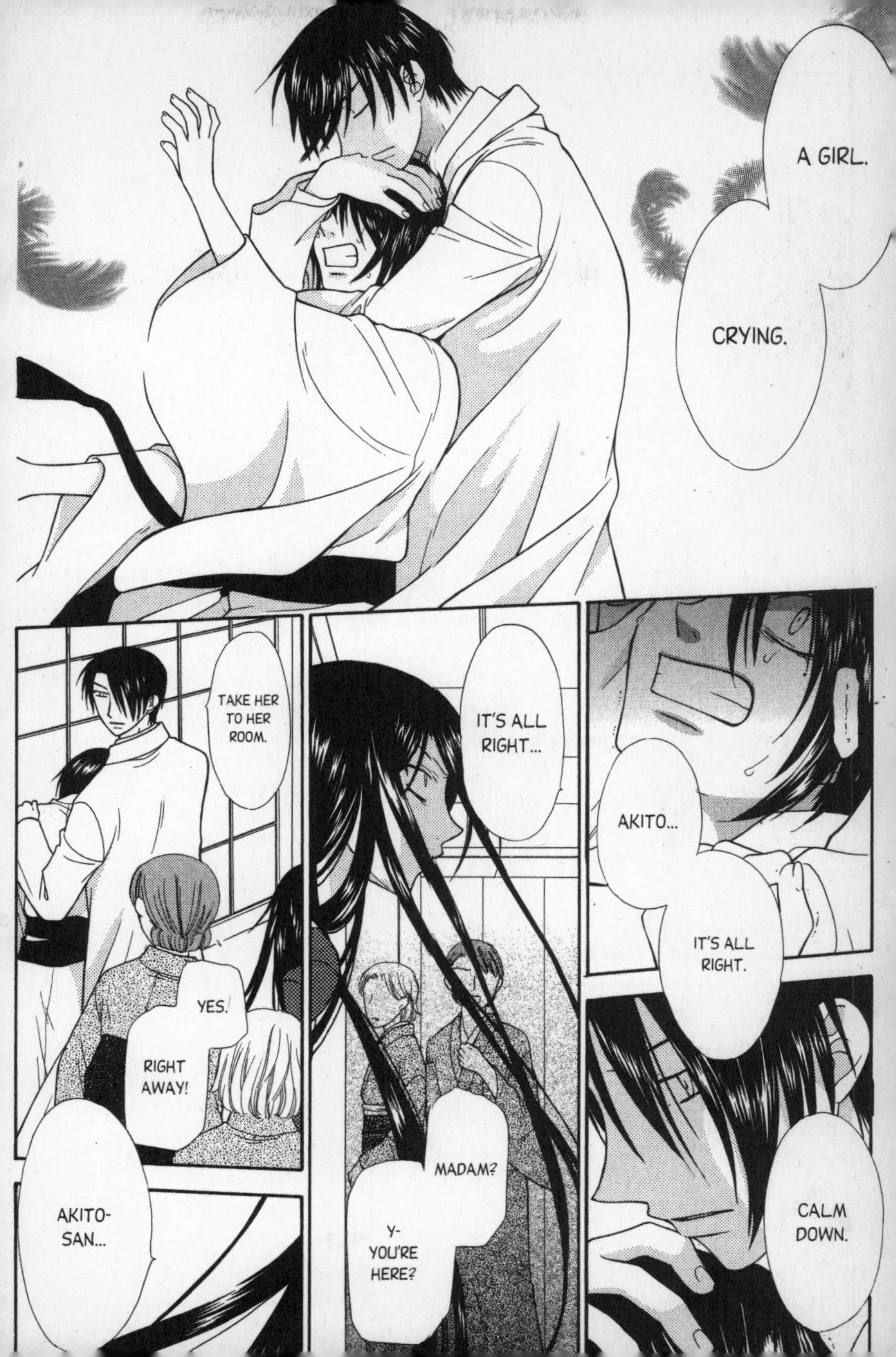
A GIRL.
CRYING.
AKITO...
IT'S ALL RIGHT.
CALM DOWN.
IT'S ALL RIGHT...
MADAM?
Y- YOU'RE HERE?
TAKE HER TO HER ROOM.
YES.
RIGHT AWAY!
AKITO-SAN...

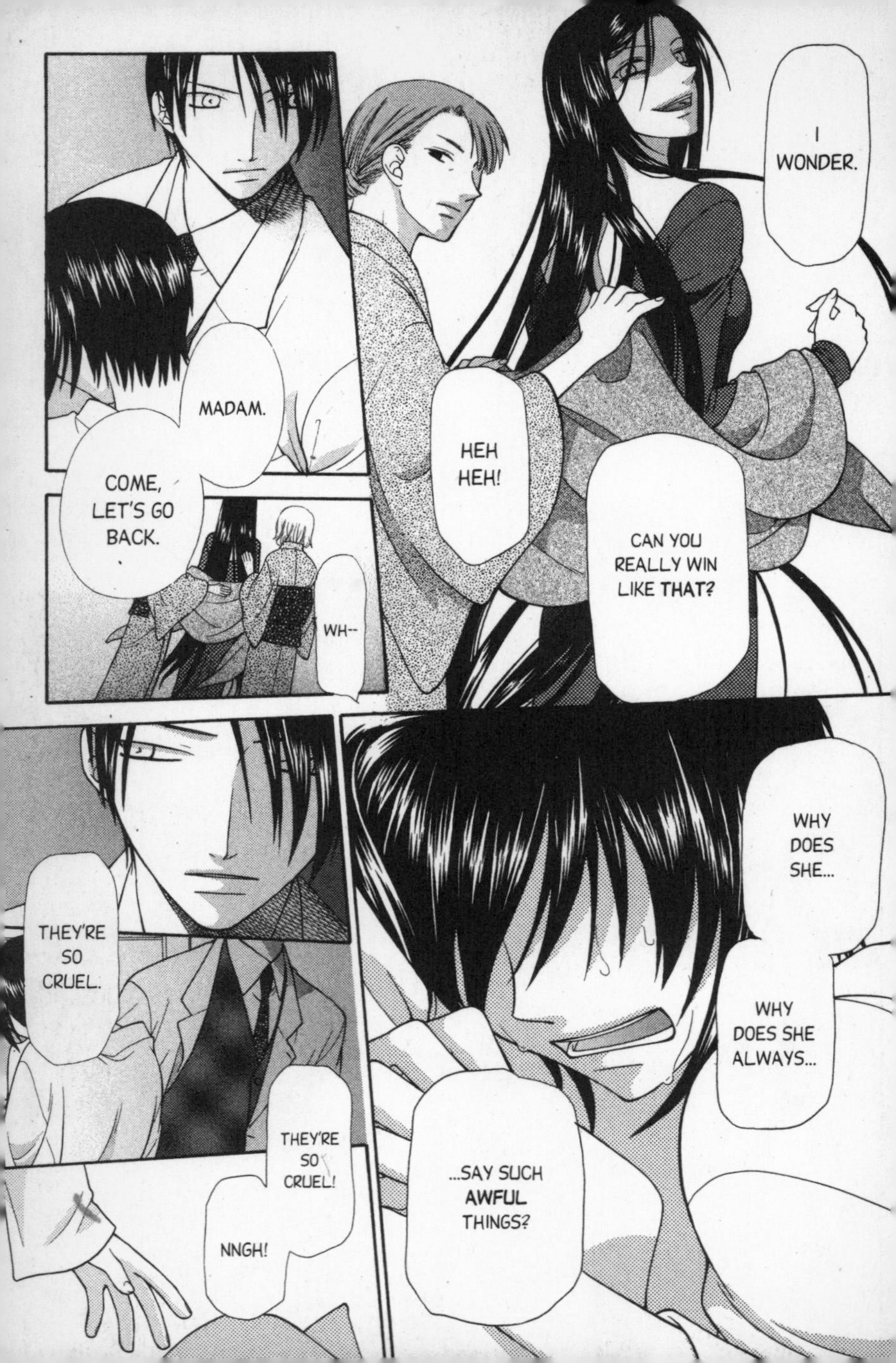
I WONDER.
CAN YOU REALLY WIN LIKE THAT?
HEH HEH!
MADAM.
COME, LET'S GO BACK.
WH--
WHY DOES SHE...
WHY DOES SHE ALWAYS...
...SAY SUCH AWFUL THINGS?
THEY'RE SO CRUEL.
THEY'RE SO CRUEL!
NNGH!

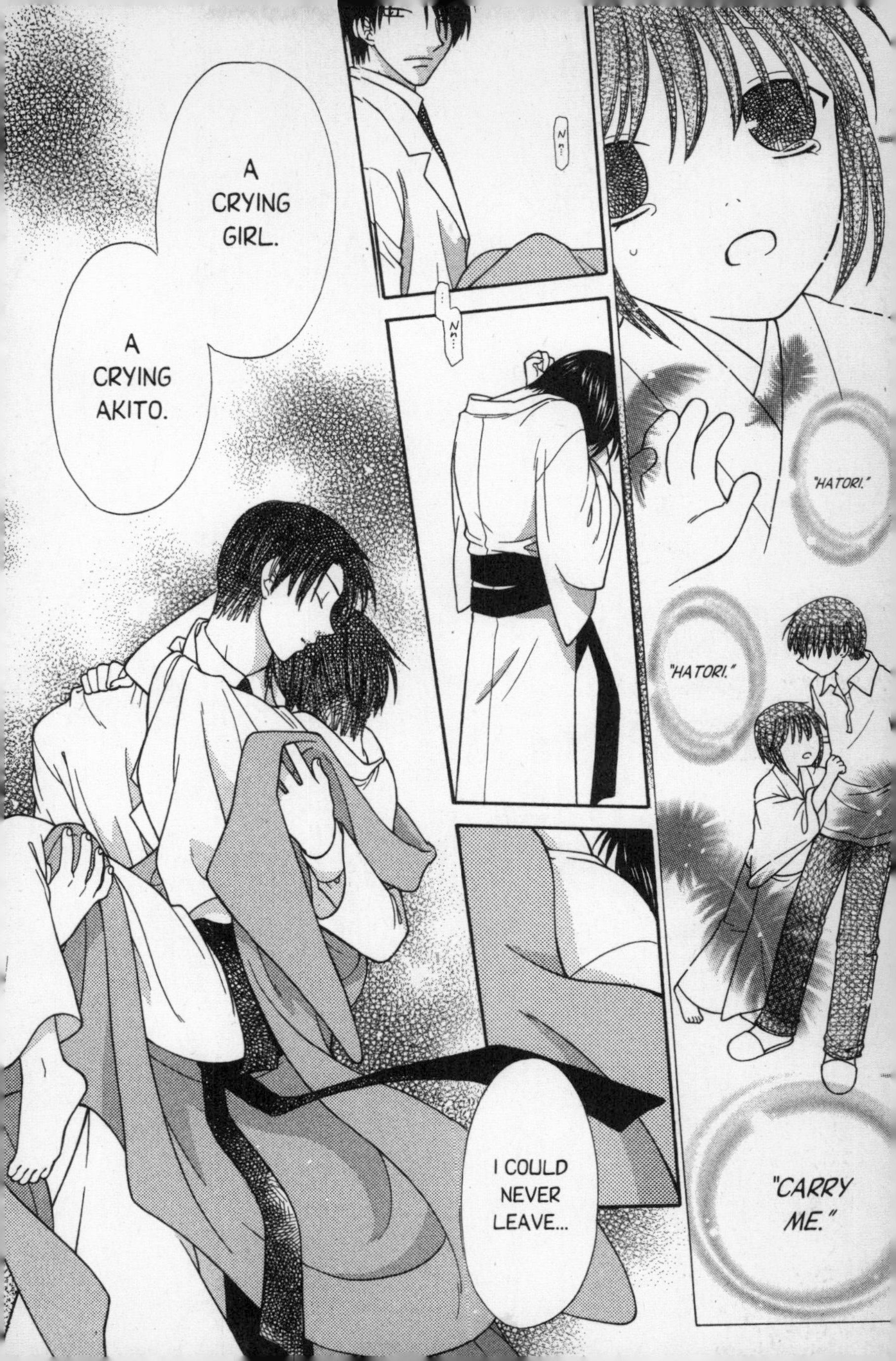
"HATORI."
"HATORI."
"CARRY ME."
Nn...
... Nn...
A CRYING GIRL.
A CRYING AKITO.
I COULD NEVER LEAVE...

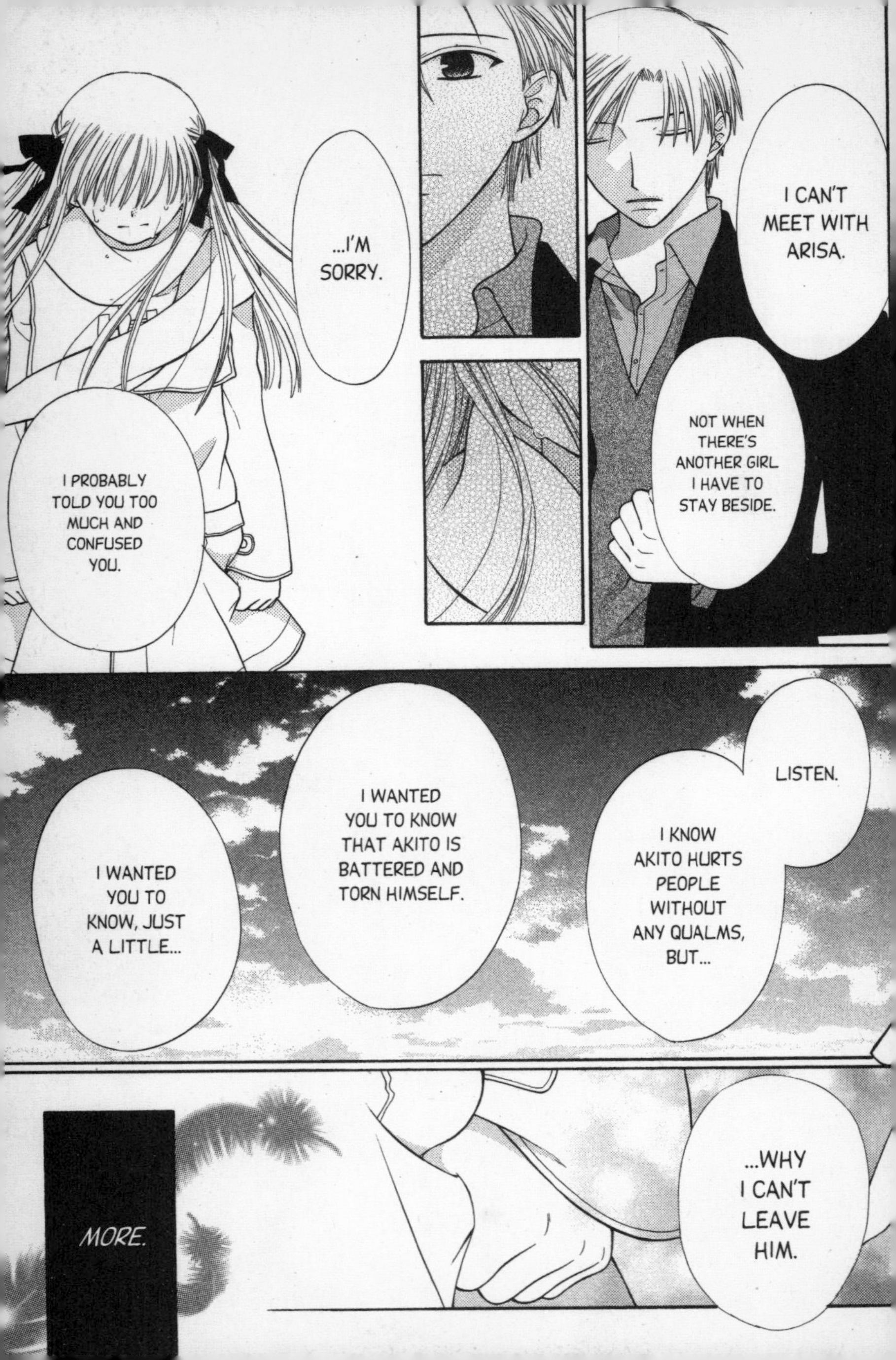
I CAN'T MEET WITH ARISA.
NOT WHEN THERE'S ANOTHER GIRL I HAVE TO STAY BESIDE.
...I'M SORRY.
I PROBABLY TOLD YOU TOO MUCH AND CONFUSED YOU.
LISTEN.
I KNOW AKITO HURTS PEOPLE WITHOUT ANY QUALMS, BUT...
I WANTED YOU TO KNOW THAT AKITO IS BATTERED AND TORN HIMSELF.
I WANTED YOU TO KNOW, JUST A LITTLE...
...WHY I CAN'T LEAVE HIM.
MORE.

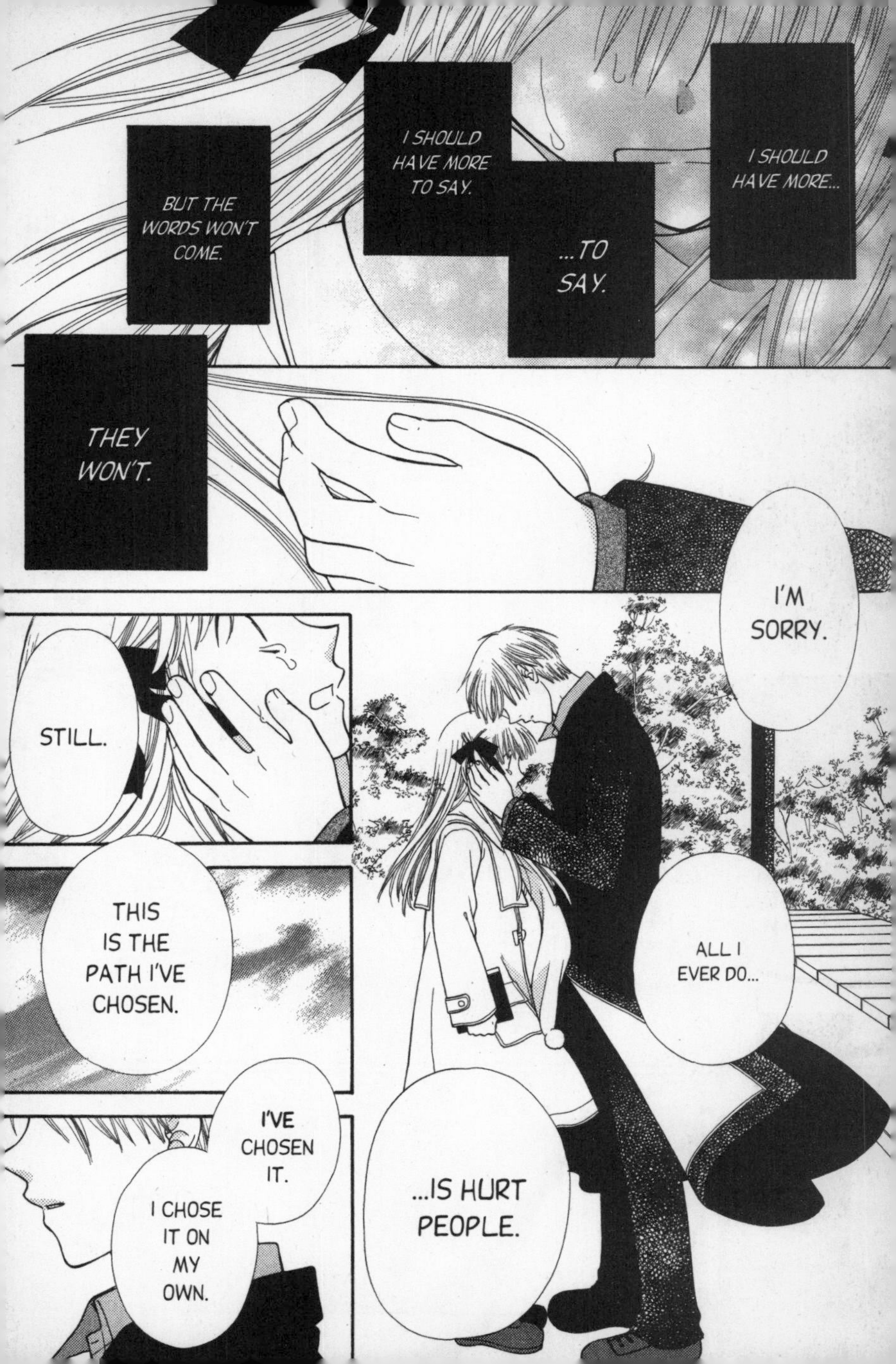
I SHOULD HAVE MORE...
...TO SAY.
I SHOULD HAVE MORE TO SAY.
BUT THE WORDS WON'T COME.
THEY WON'T.
I'M SORRY.
ALL I EVER DO...
...IS HURT PEOPLE.
STILL.
THIS IS THE PATH I'VE CHOSEN.
I'VE CHOSEN IT.
I CHOSE IT ON MY OWN.

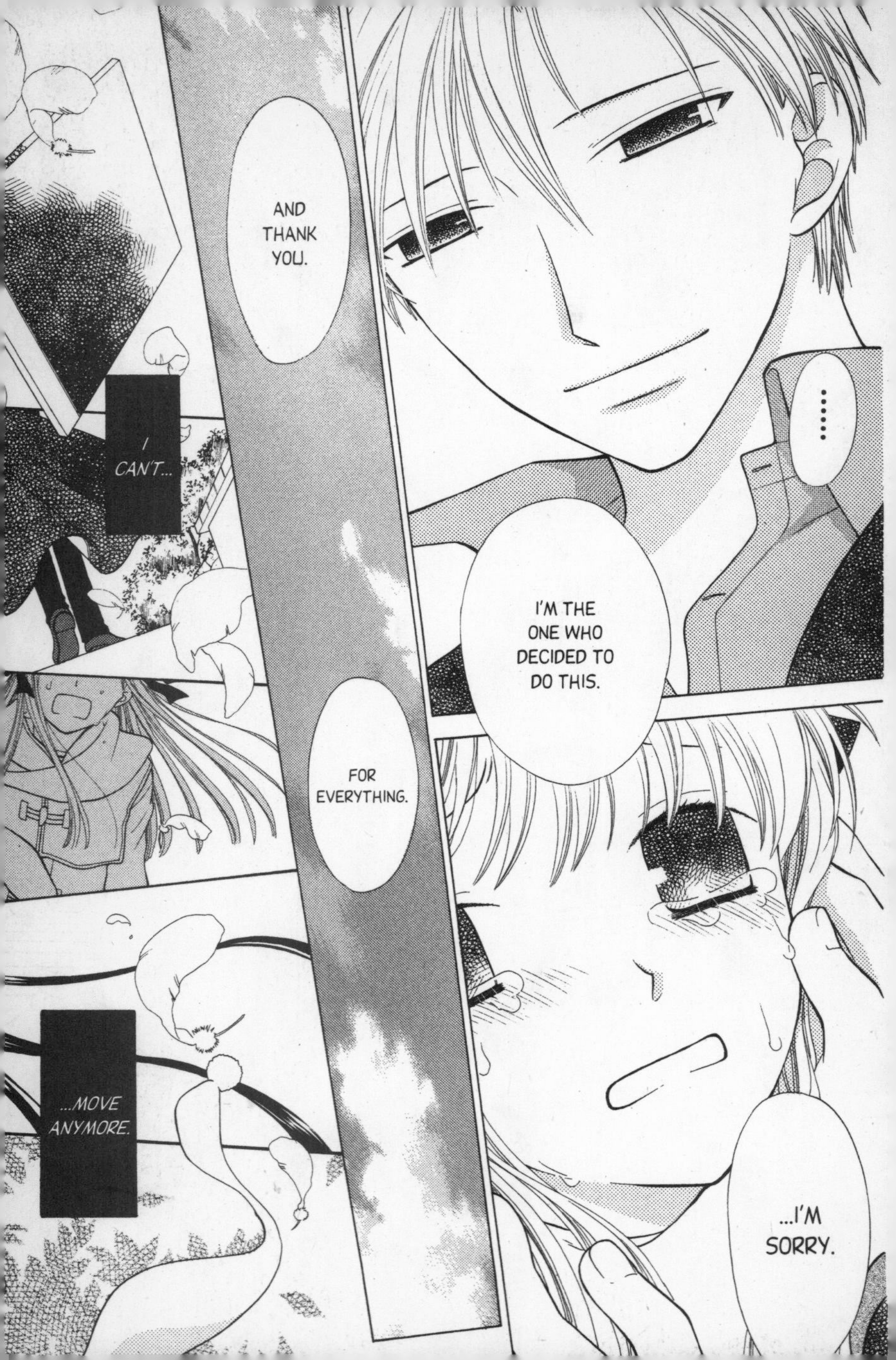
......
I'M THE ONE WHO DECIDED TO DO THIS.
AND THANK YOU.
FOR EVERYTHING.
...I'M SORRY.
I CAN'T...
...MOVE ANYMORE.

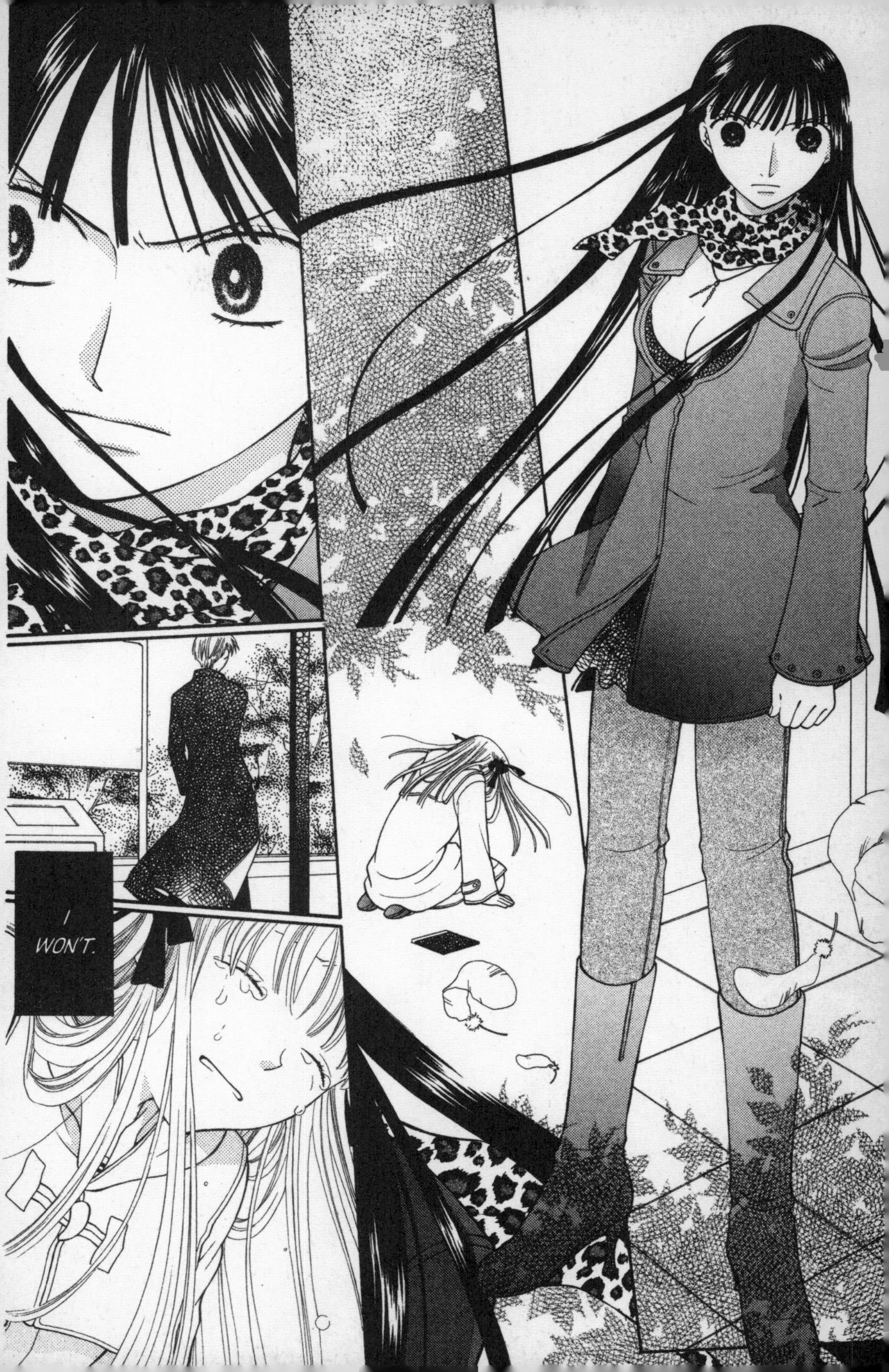
I WON'T.

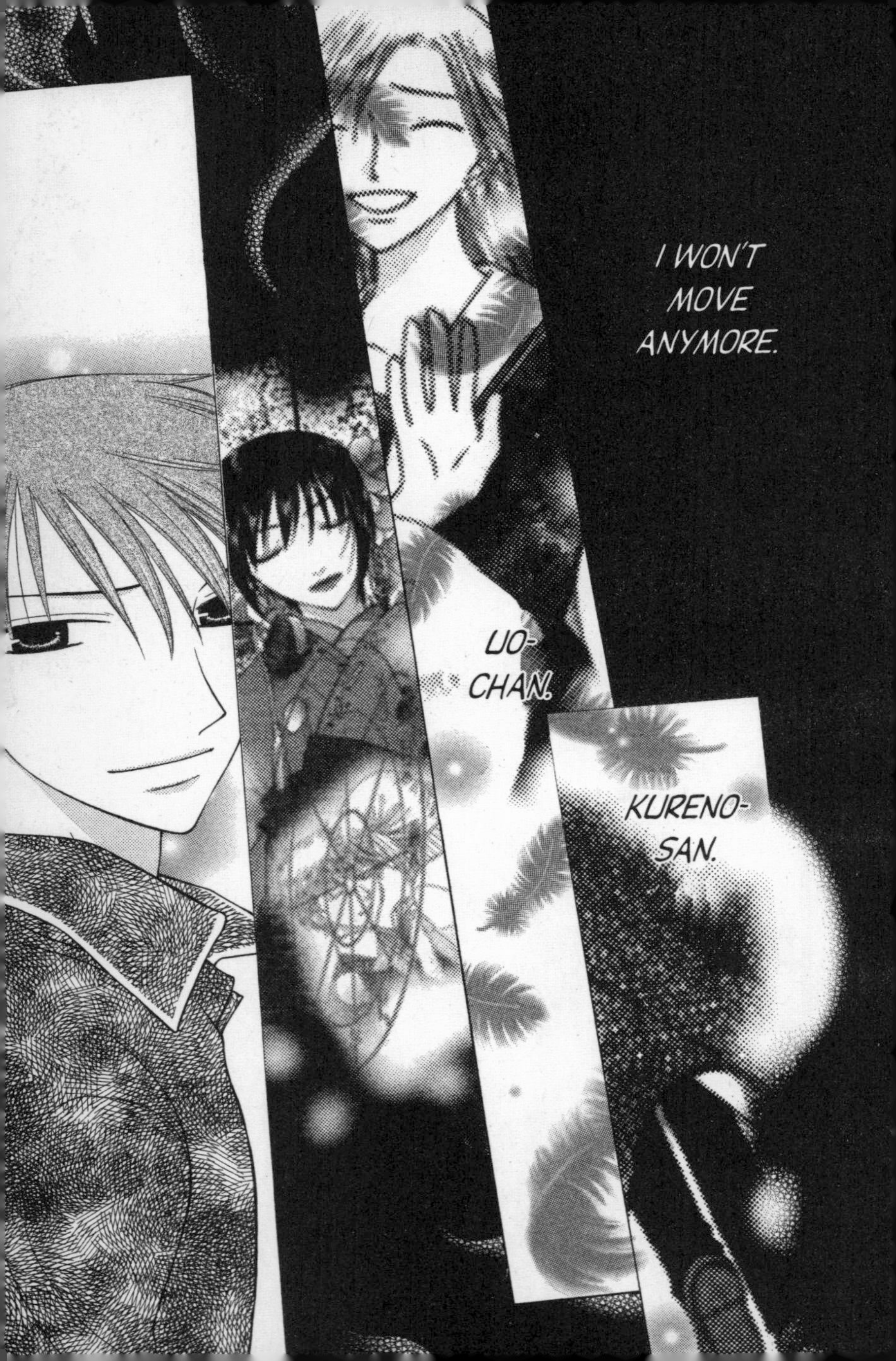
I WON'T MOVE ANYMORE.
KURENO-SAN.
UO-CHAN.

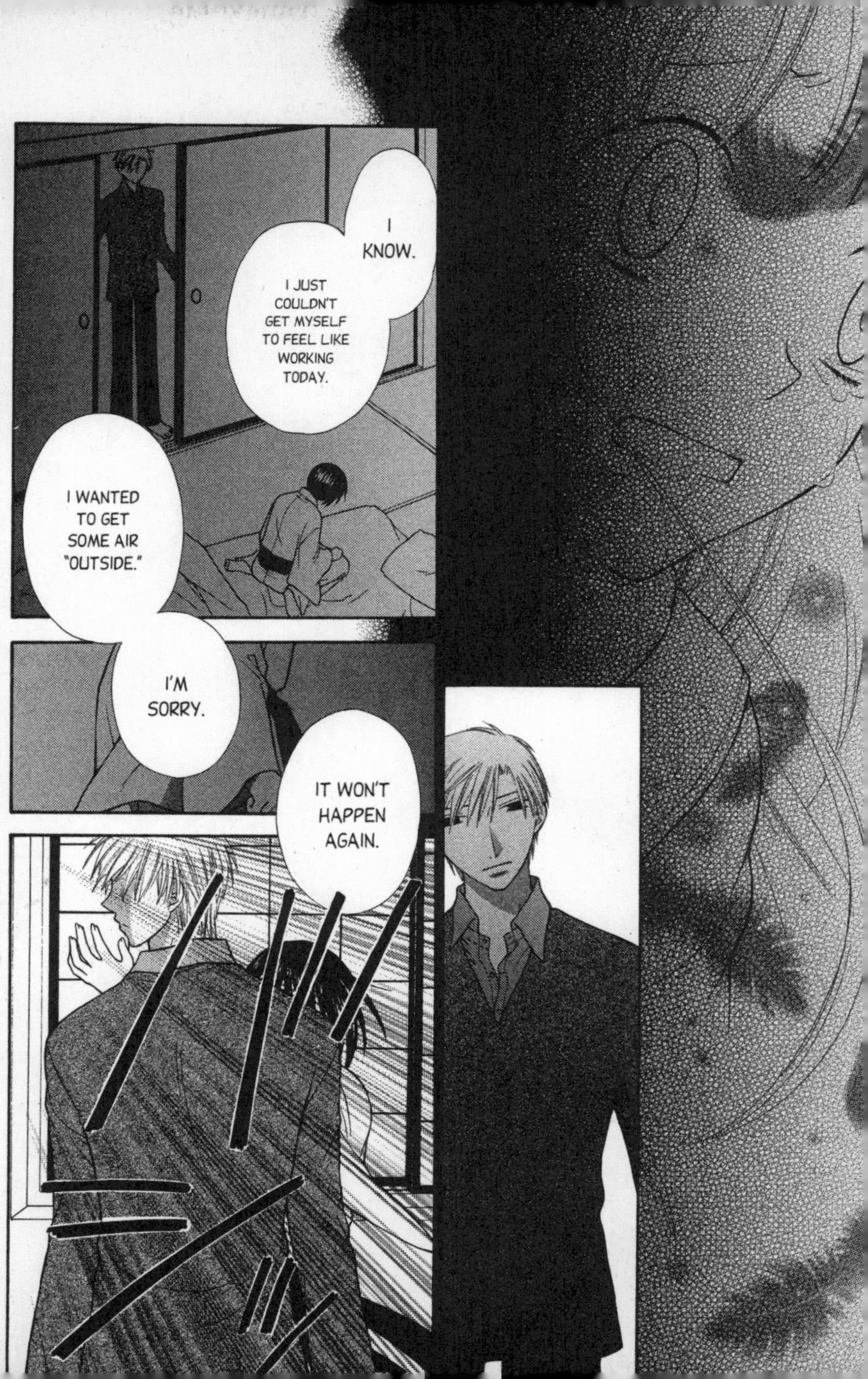
I KNOW.
I JUST COULDN'T GET MYSELF TO FEEL LIKE WORKING TODAY.
I WANTED TO GET SOME AIR "OUTSIDE."
I'M SORRY.
IT WON'T HAPPEN AGAIN.

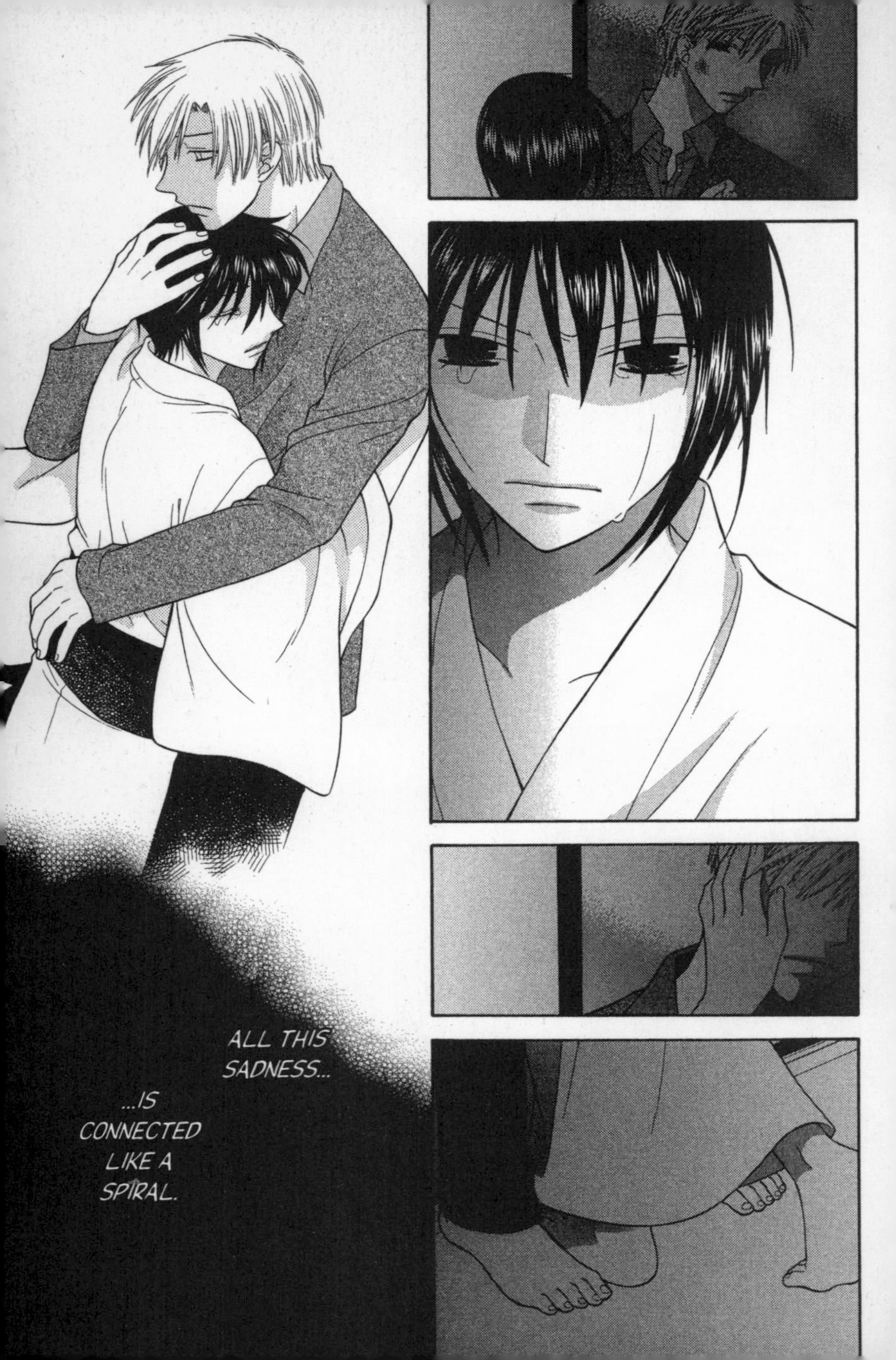
ALL THIS SADNESS...
...IS CONNECTED LIKE A SPIRAL.

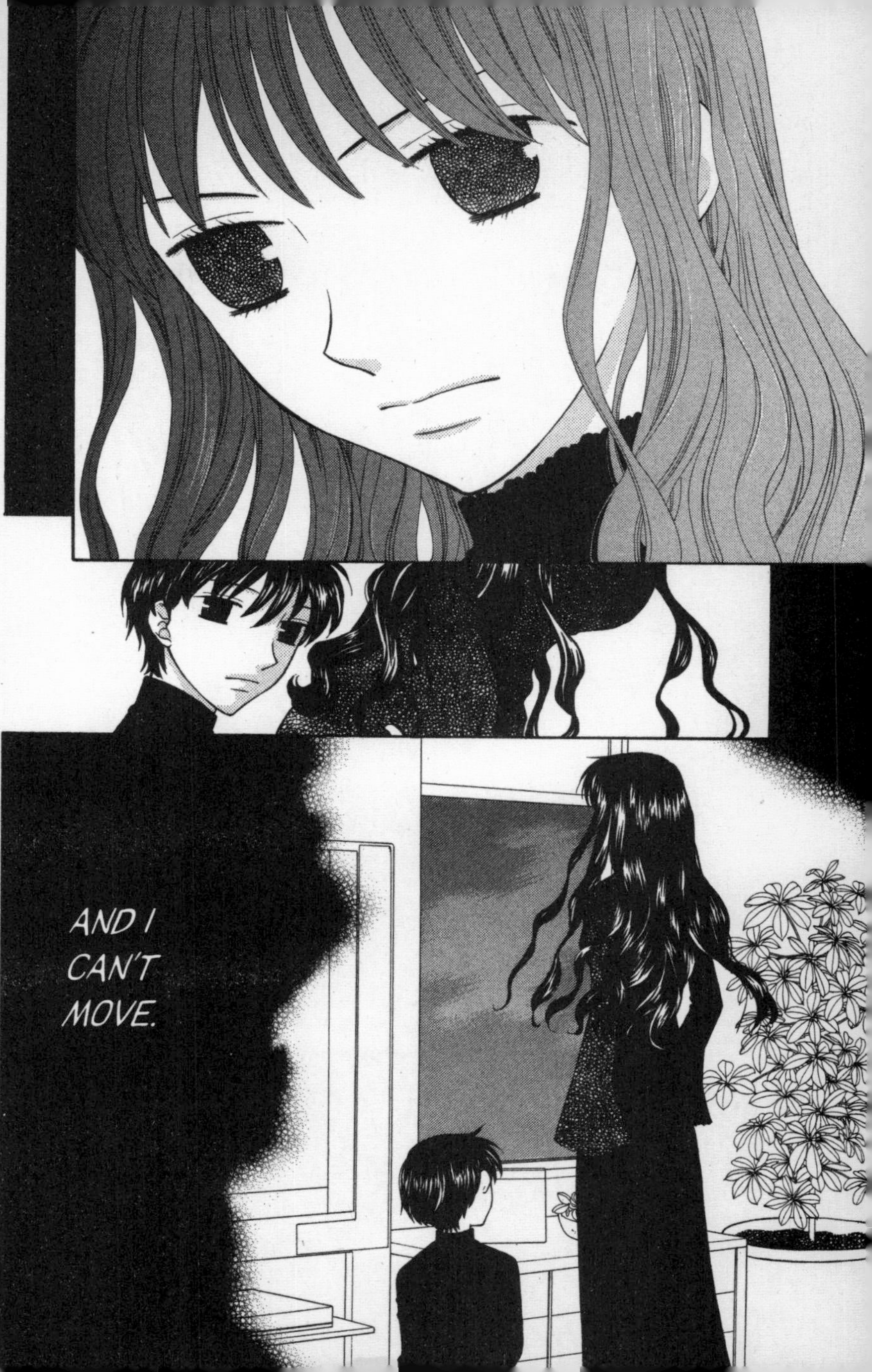
AND I
CAN'T
MOVE.

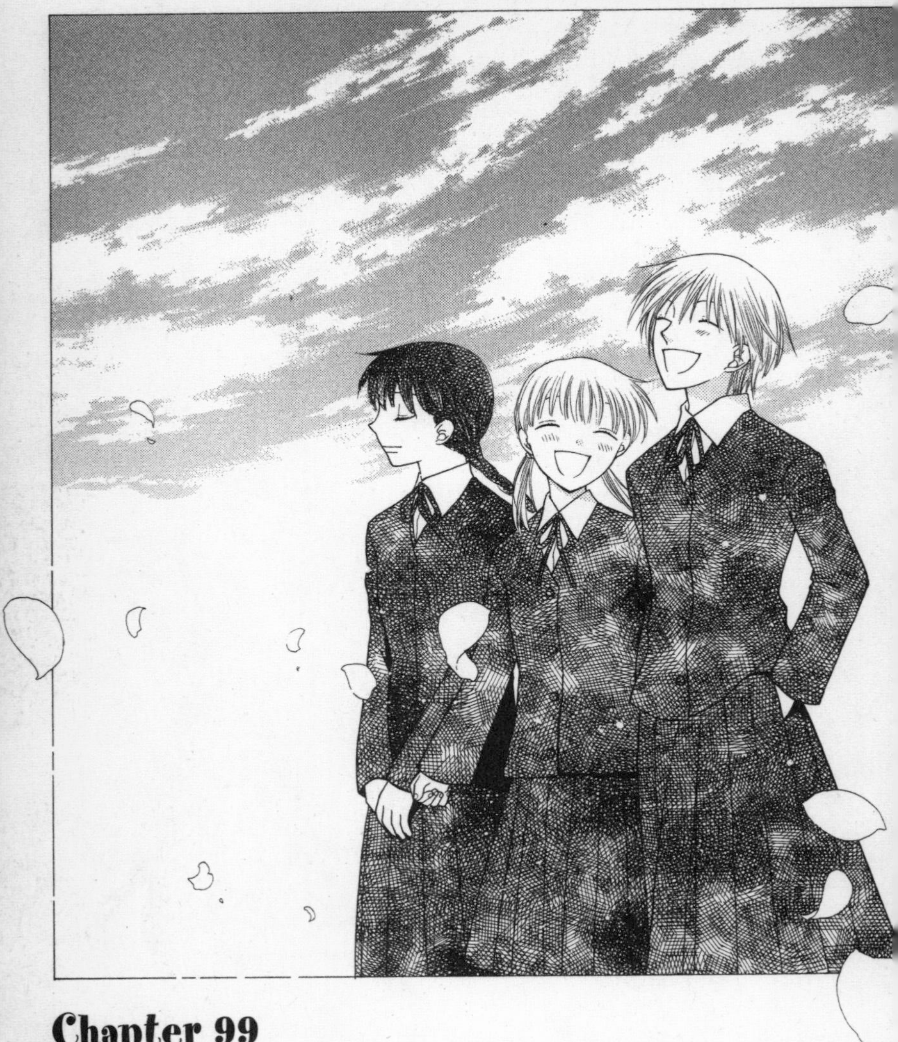

Chapter 99

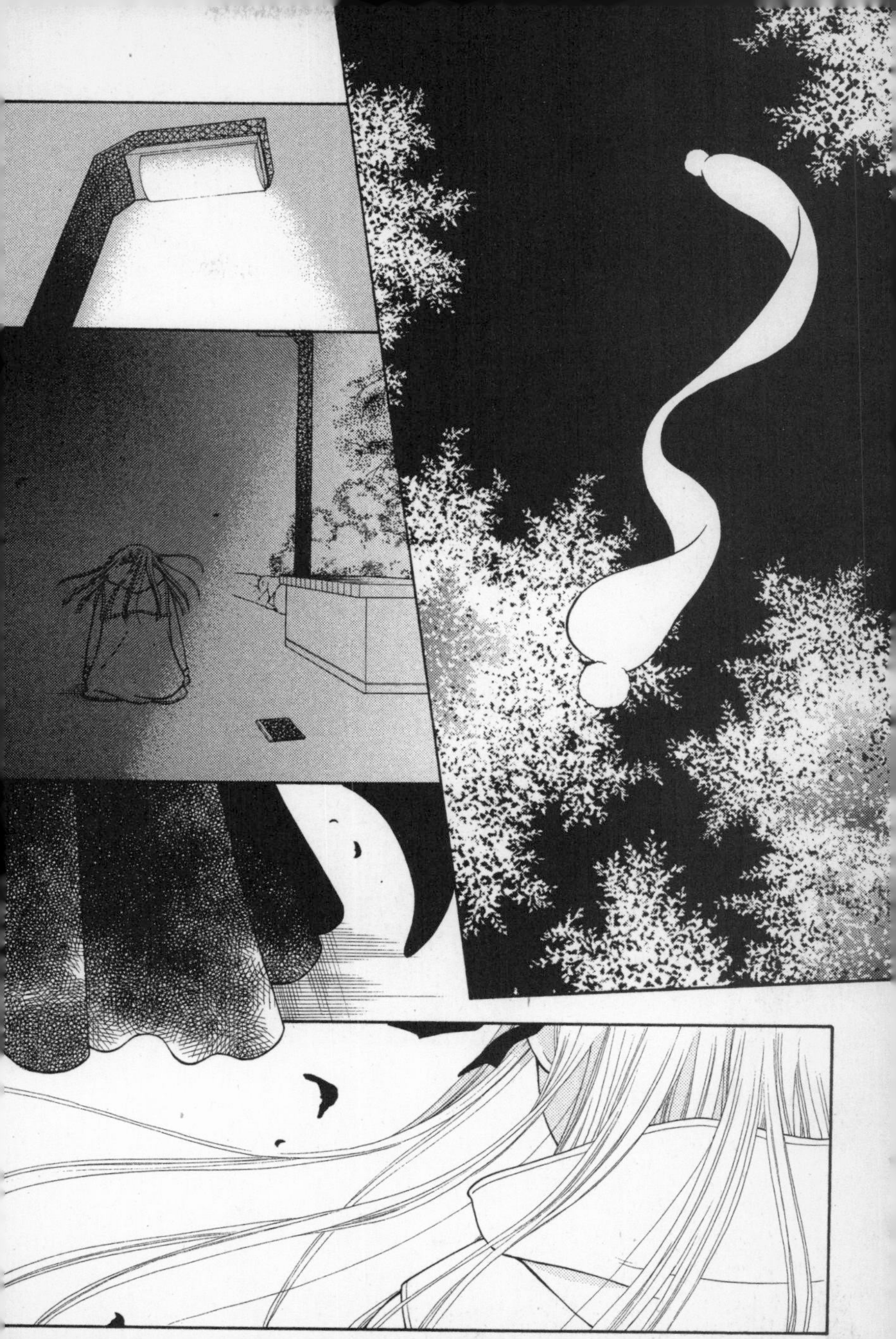

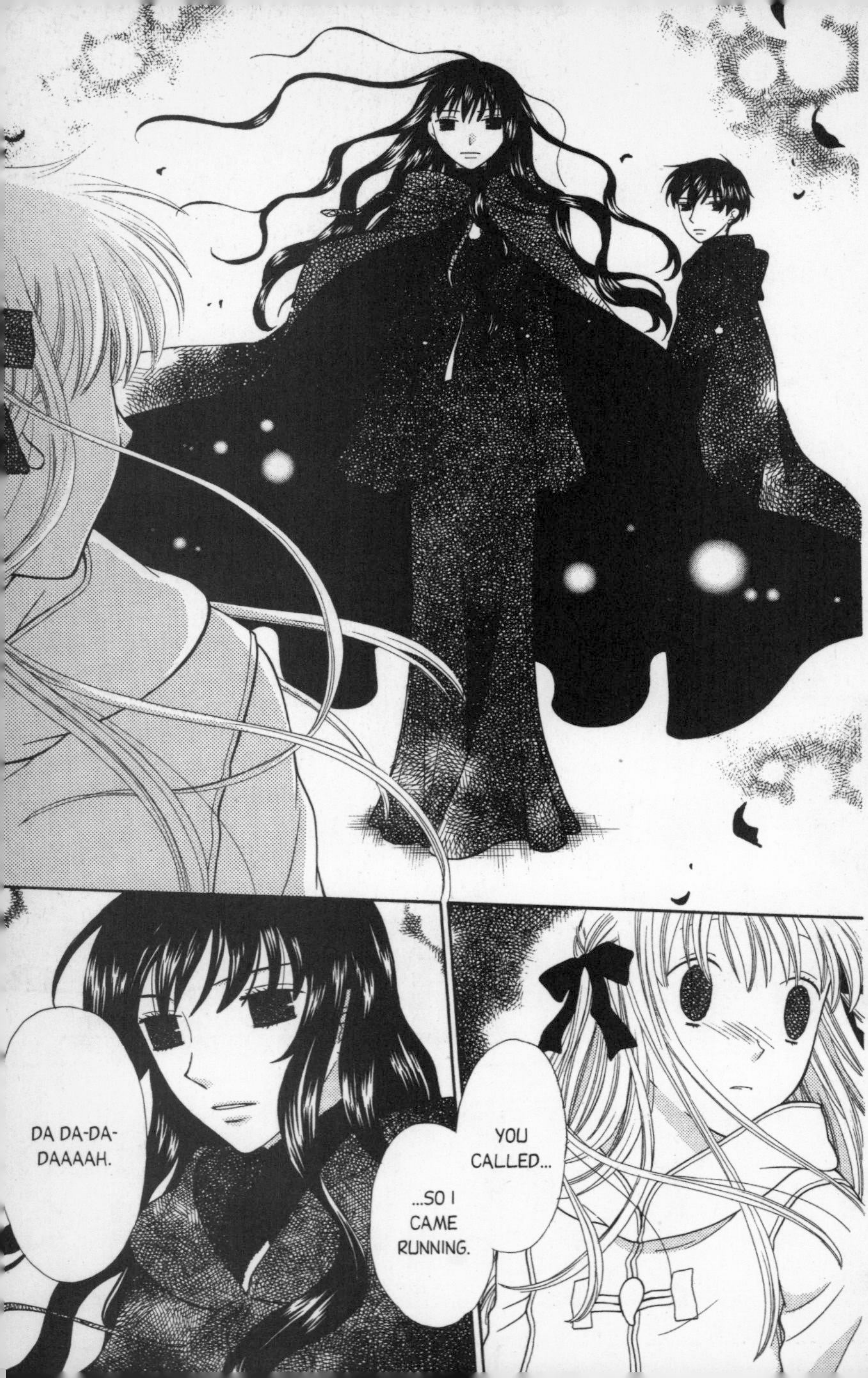
YOU CALLED...
...SO I CAME RUNNING.
DA DA-DA-DAAAAH.

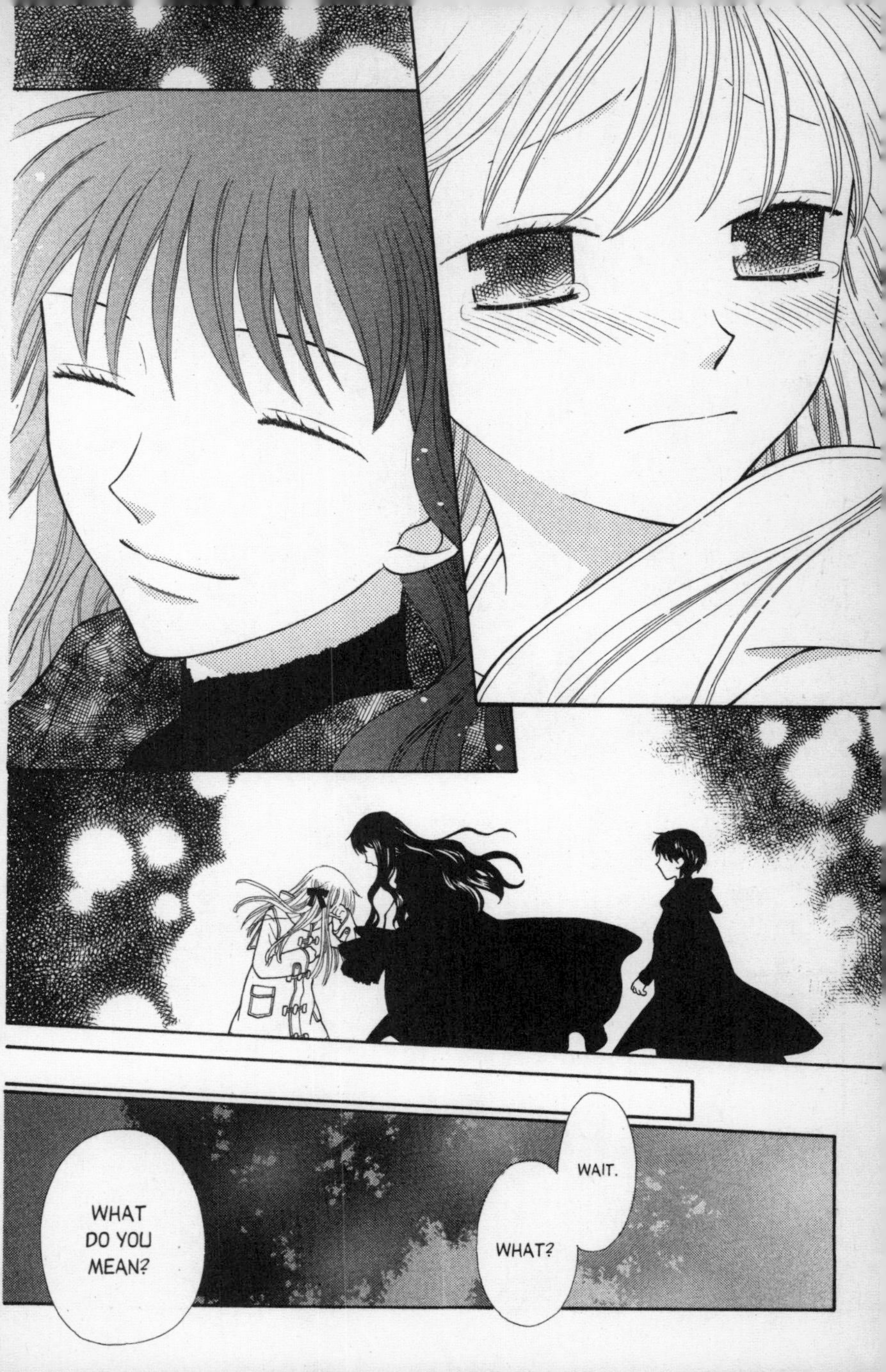
WAIT.
WHAT?
WHAT DO YOU MEAN?

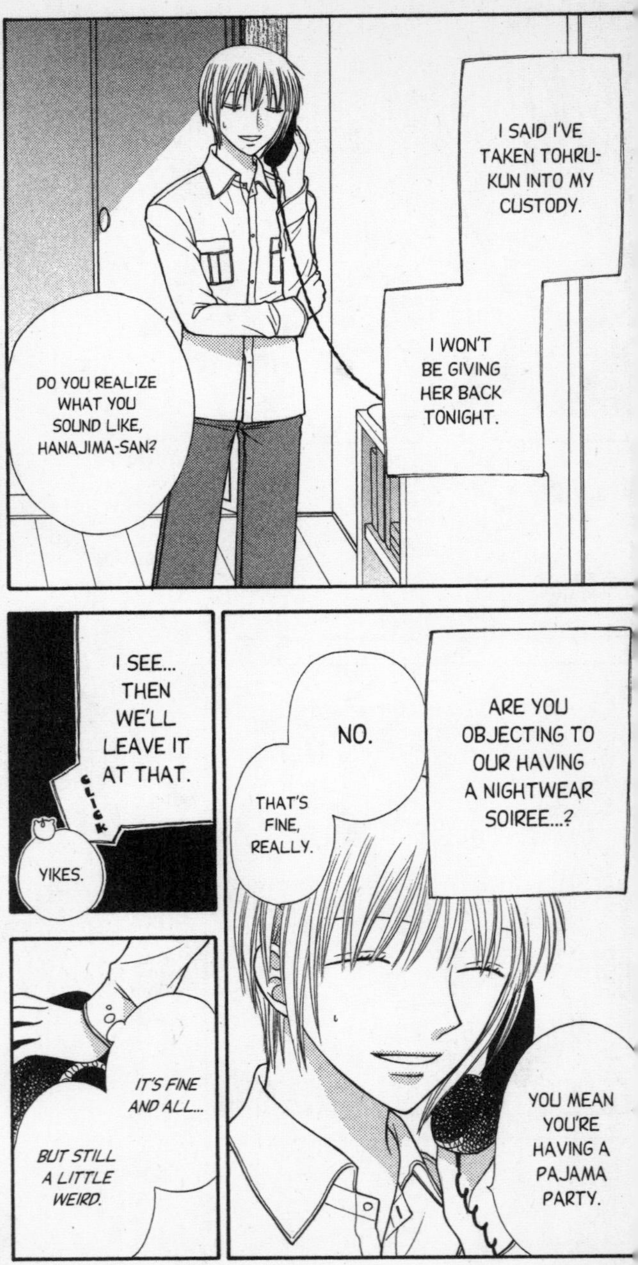
I SAID I'VE TAKEN TOHRU-KUN INTO MY CUSTODY.
I WON'T BE GIVING HER BACK TONIGHT.
DO YOU REALIZE WHAT YOU SOUND LIKE, HANAJIMA-SAN?
ARE YOU OBJECTING TO OUR HAVING A NIGHTWEAR SOIREE...?
NO.
THAT'S FINE, REALLY.
YOU MEAN YOU'RE HAVING A PAJAMA PARTY.
I SEE... THEN WE'LL LEAVE IT AT THAT.
CLICK
YIKES.
IT'S FINE AND ALL...
BUT STILL A LITTLE WEIRD.

Regarding this girl, letters usually tell me "I like her, but I wouldn't want her as a friend."

Kimi.

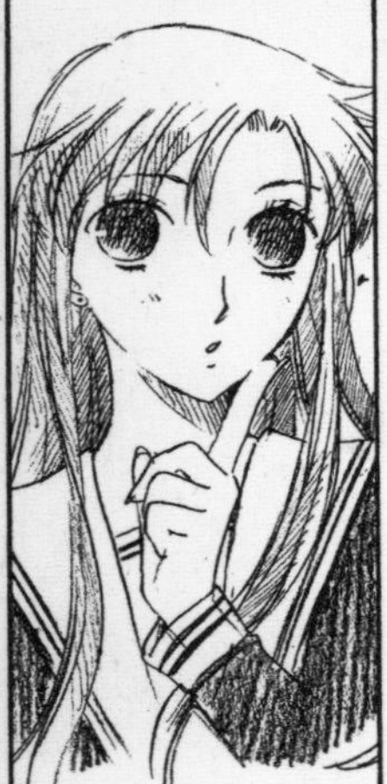

- With her father and mother, Kimi is in a family of three.
- Her father is elite, so she grew up in a fairly affluent home.
- When creating Kimi, my top priority was to make a girl who had absolutely no connection with "the Sohma family or emotional pain."
- But I get the feeling that she's uselessly lively.
- And my editor told me, "You like drawing girls like this, don't you?"
- In Chapter 66, when Kakeru said, "But really, she's just--" I got a letter asking if the end to that sentence was "an okama." That's a reader with a good memory (laugh).

Why an okama? Isn't an okama a drag queen?

← To be continued

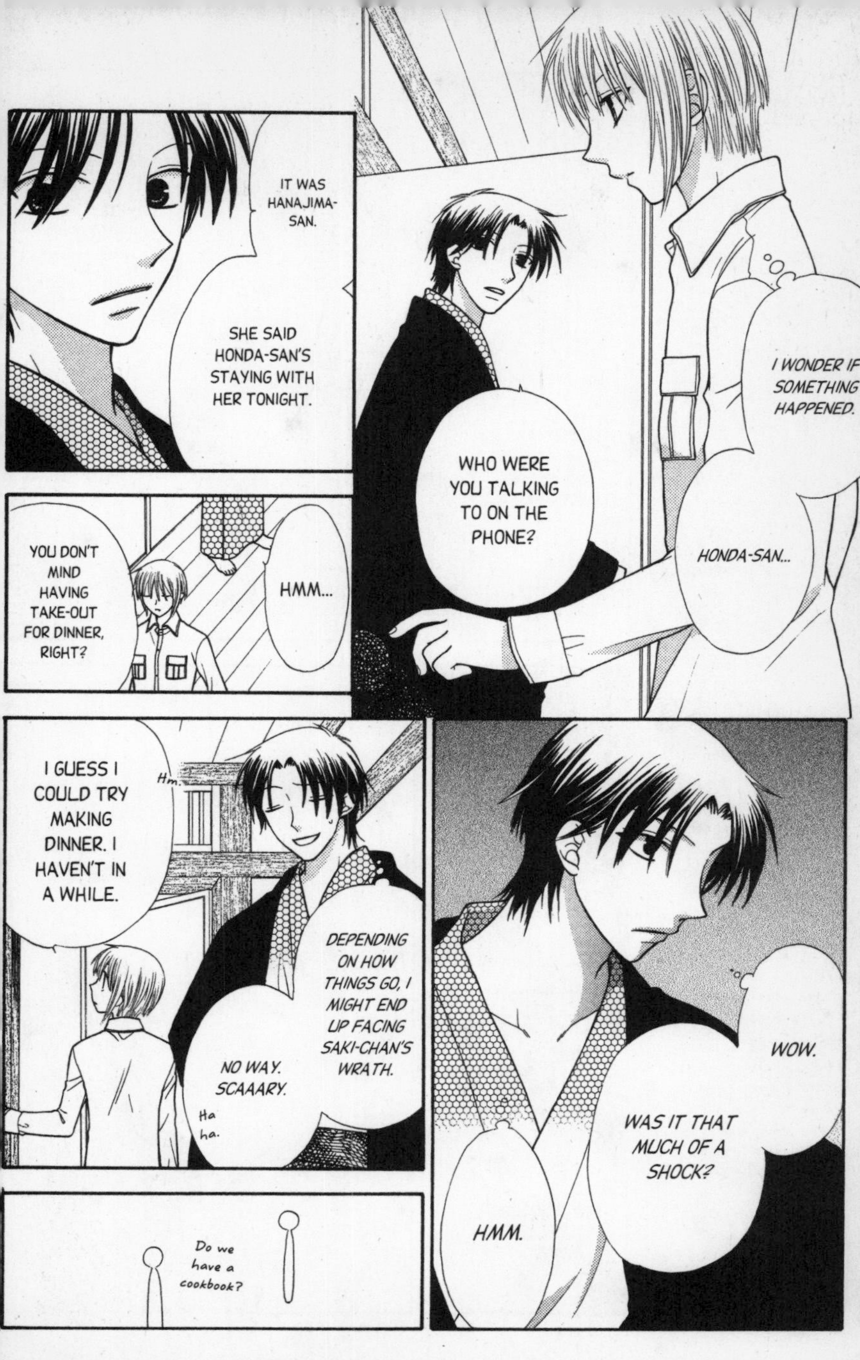
I WONDER IF SOMETHING HAPPENED.
HONDA-SAN...
WHO WERE YOU TALKING TO ON THE PHONE?
IT WAS HANAJIMA-SAN.
SHE SAID HONDA-SAN'S STAYING WITH HER TONIGHT.
HMM...
YOU DON'T MIND HAVING TAKE-OUT FOR DINNER, RIGHT?
WOW.
WAS IT THAT MUCH OF A SHOCK?
HMM.
I GUESS I COULD TRY MAKING DINNER. I HAVEN'T IN A WHILE.
Hm.
DEPENDING ON HOW THINGS GO, I MIGHT END UP FACING SAKI-CHAN'S WRATH.
NO WAY. SCAAARY.
Ha ha.
Do we have a cookbook?

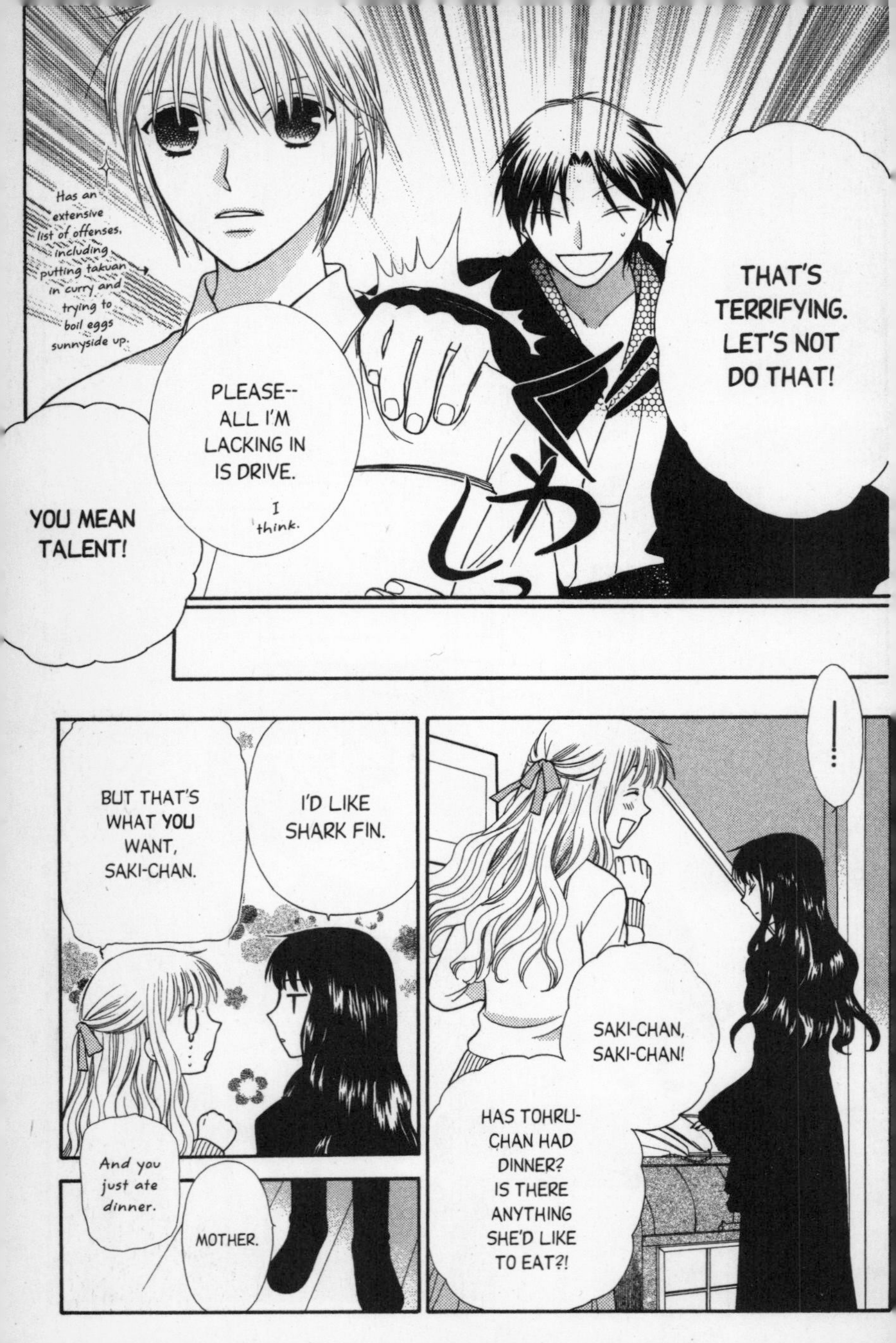
THAT'S TERRIFYING. LET'S NOT DO THAT!
Has an extensive list of offenses, including putting takuan in curry and trying to boil eggs sunnyside up.
PLEASE-- ALL I'M LACKING IN IS DRIVE.
I think.
YOU MEAN TALENT!
!...
SAKI-CHAN, SAKI-CHAN!
HAS TOHRU-CHAN HAD DINNER? IS THERE ANYTHING SHE'D LIKE TO EAT?!
I'D LIKE SHARK FIN.
BUT THAT'S WHAT YOU WANT, SAKI-CHAN.
MOTHER.
And you just ate dinner.

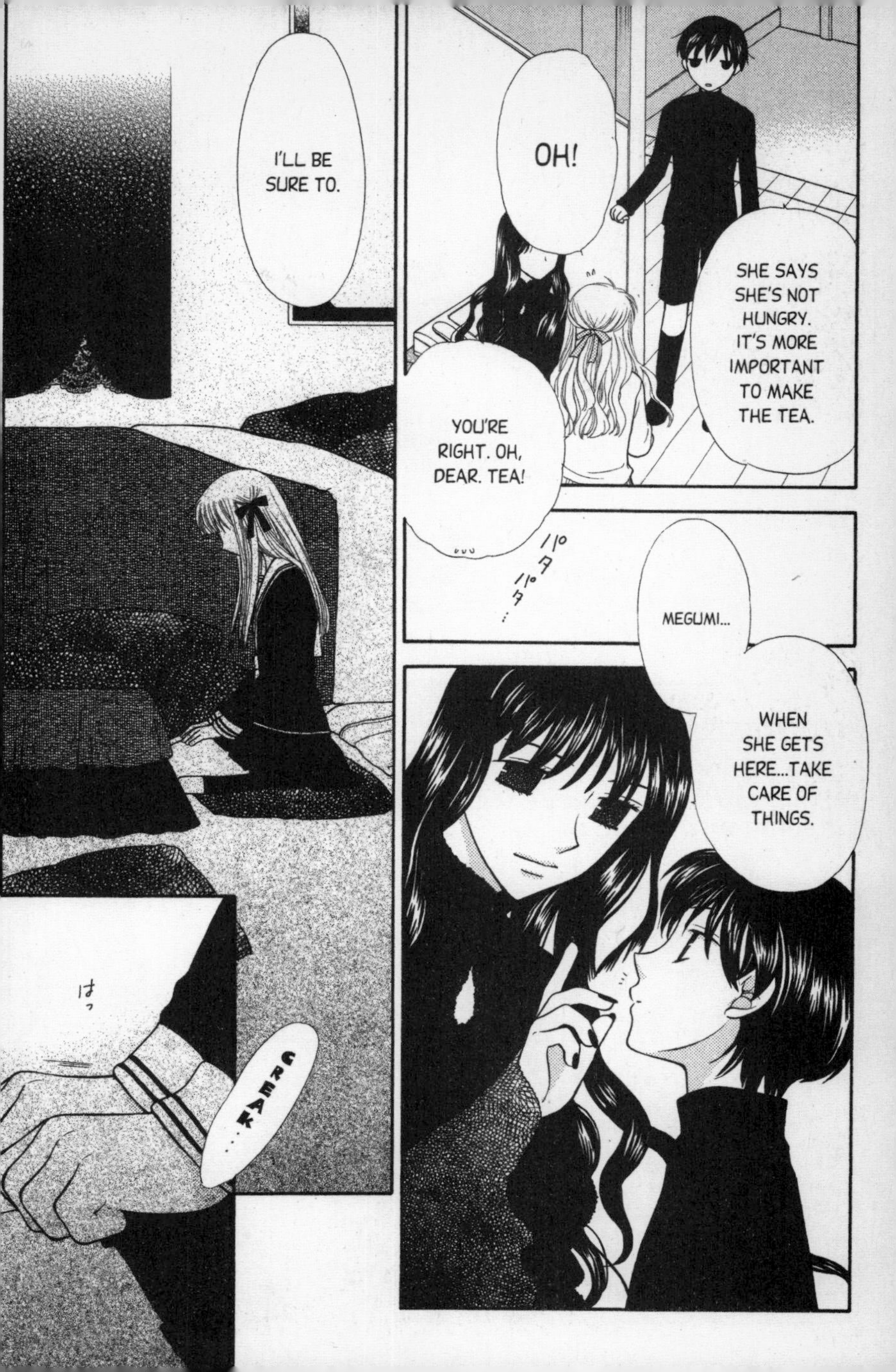
OH!
SHE SAYS SHE'S NOT HUNGRY. IT'S MORE IMPORTANT TO MAKE THE TEA.
YOU'RE RIGHT. OH, DEAR. TEA!
パタパタ…
MEGUMI...
WHEN SHE GETS HERE...TAKE CARE OF THINGS.
I'LL BE SURE TO.
はっ
CREAK...

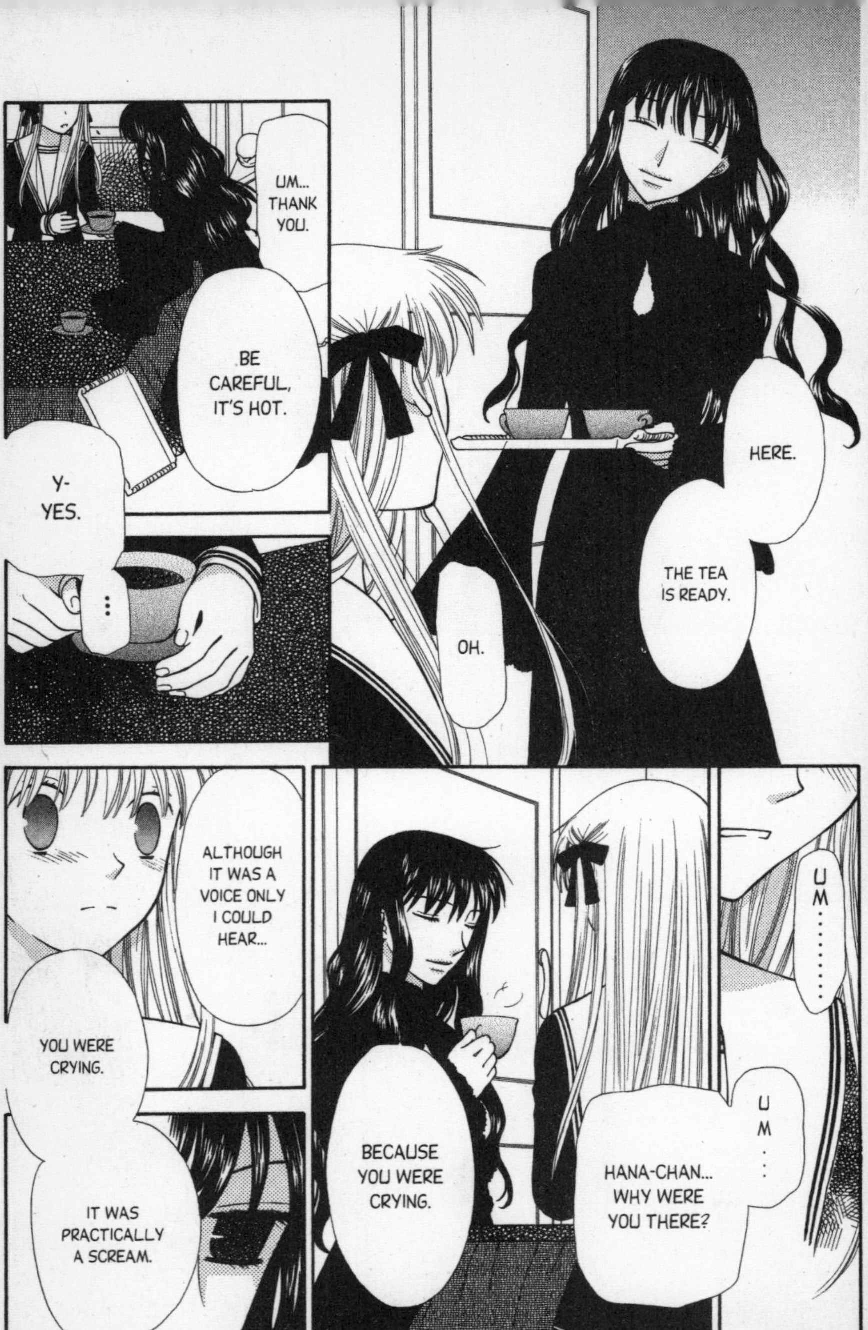
HERE.
THE TEA IS READY.
OH.
UM... THANK YOU.
BE CAREFUL, IT'S HOT.
Y- YES.
...
UM.........
UM...
HANA-CHAN... WHY WERE YOU THERE?
BECAUSE YOU WERE CRYING.
ALTHOUGH IT WAS A VOICE ONLY I COULD HEAR...
YOU WERE CRYING.
IT WAS PRACTICALLY A SCREAM.

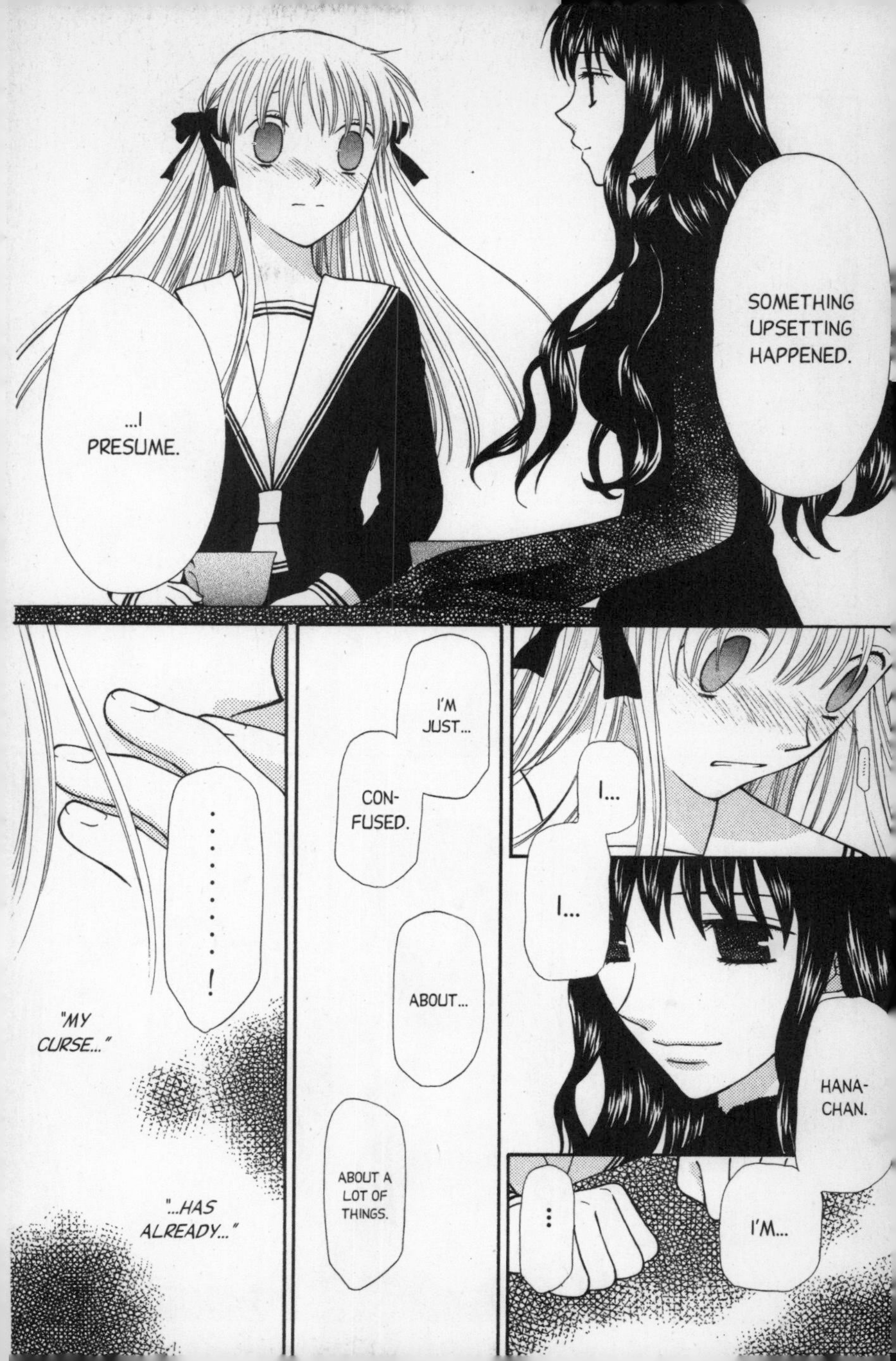
SOMETHING UPSETTING HAPPENED.
...I PRESUME.
...
I...
I...
HANA-CHAN.
I'M...
...
I'M JUST...
CON-FUSED.
ABOUT...
ABOUT A LOT OF THINGS.
.........!
"MY CURSE..."
"...HAS ALREADY..."

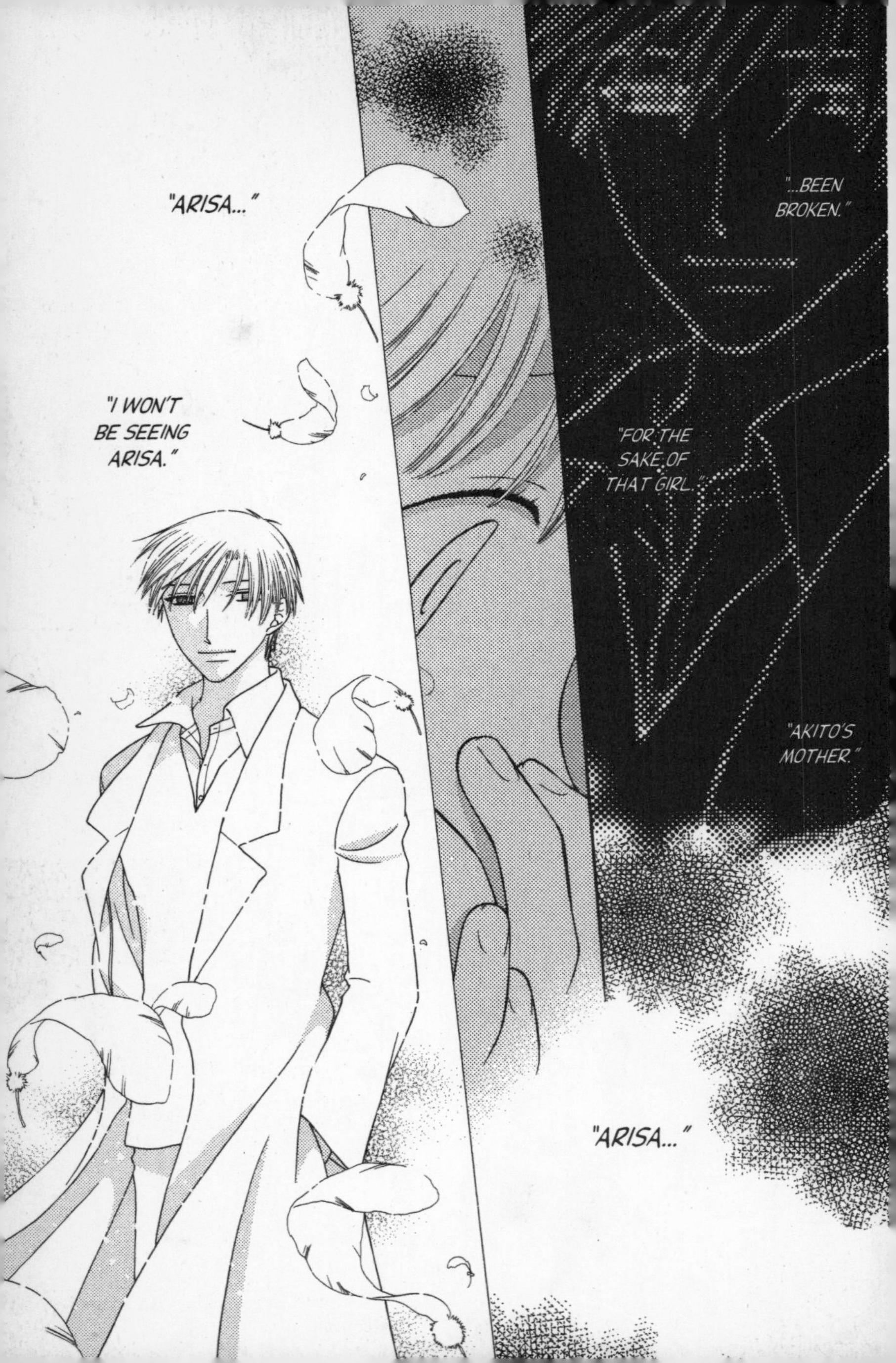
"...BEEN BROKEN."
"FOR THE SAKE OF THAT GIRL."
"AKITO'S MOTHER."
"ARISA..."
"ARISA..."
"I WON'T BE SEEING ARISA."

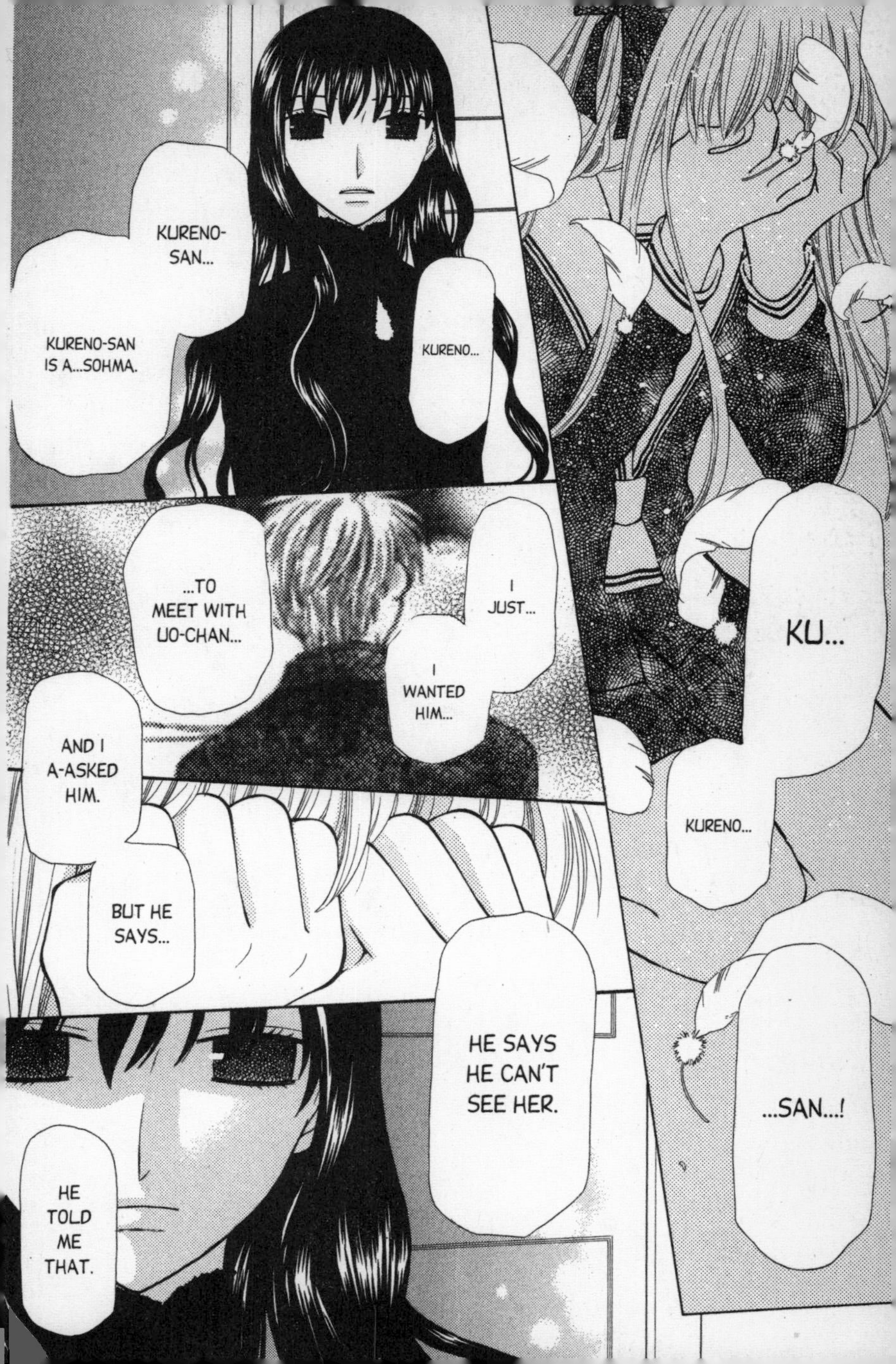
KU...
KURENO...
...SAN...!
KURENO...
KURENO-SAN...
KURENO-SAN IS A...SOHMA.
I JUST...
I WANTED HIM...
...TO MEET WITH UO-CHAN...
AND I A-ASKED HIM.
BUT HE SAYS...
HE SAYS HE CAN'T SEE HER.
HE TOLD ME THAT.

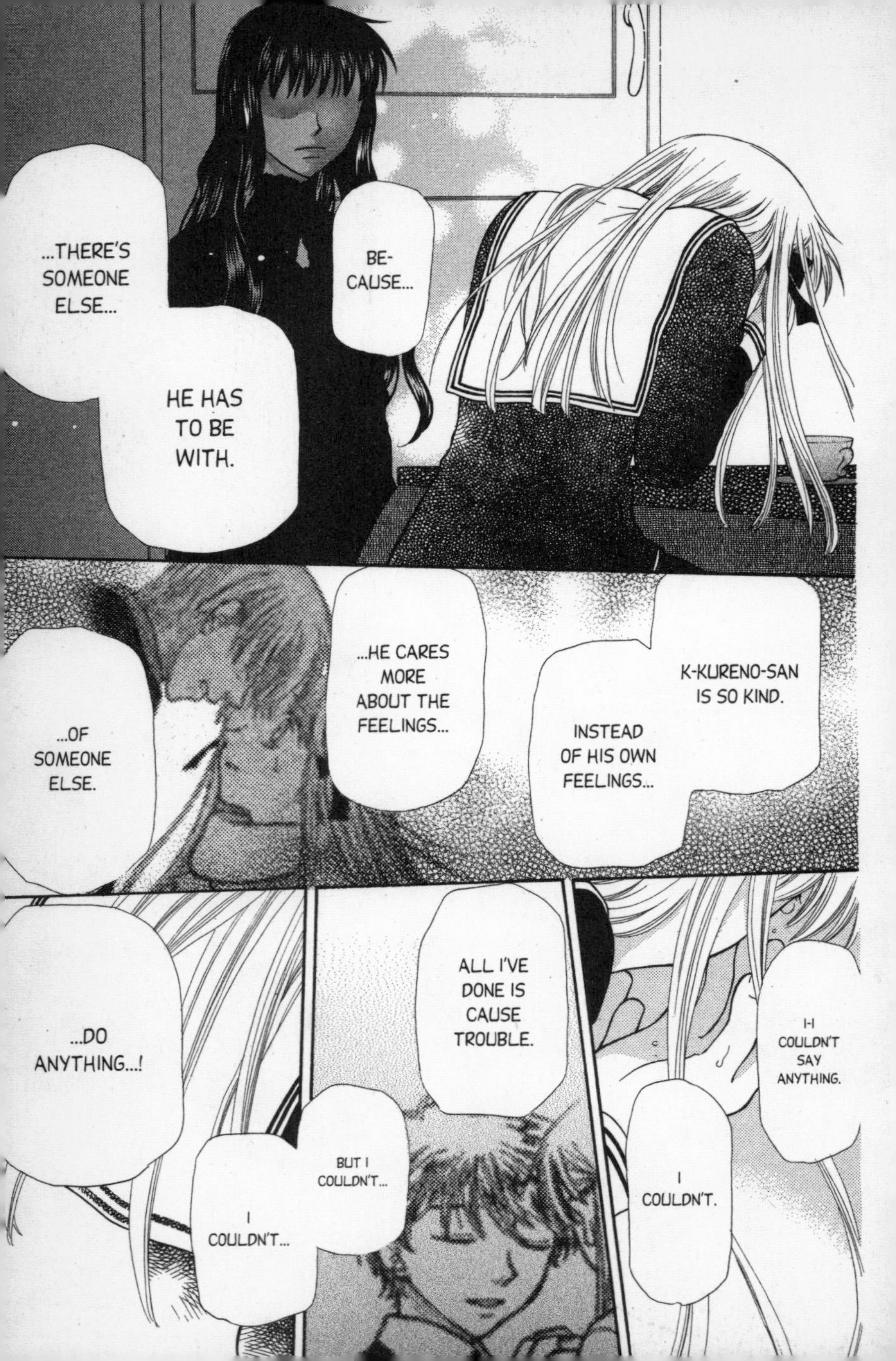
BE-CAUSE...
...THERE'S SOMEONE ELSE...
HE HAS TO BE WITH.
K-KURENO-SAN IS SO KIND.
INSTEAD OF HIS OWN FEELINGS...
...HE CARES MORE ABOUT THE FEELINGS...
...OF SOMEONE ELSE.
I-I COULDN'T SAY ANYTHING.
I COULDN'T.
ALL I'VE DONE IS CAUSE TROUBLE.
BUT I COULDN'T...
I COULDN'T...
...DO ANYTHING...!

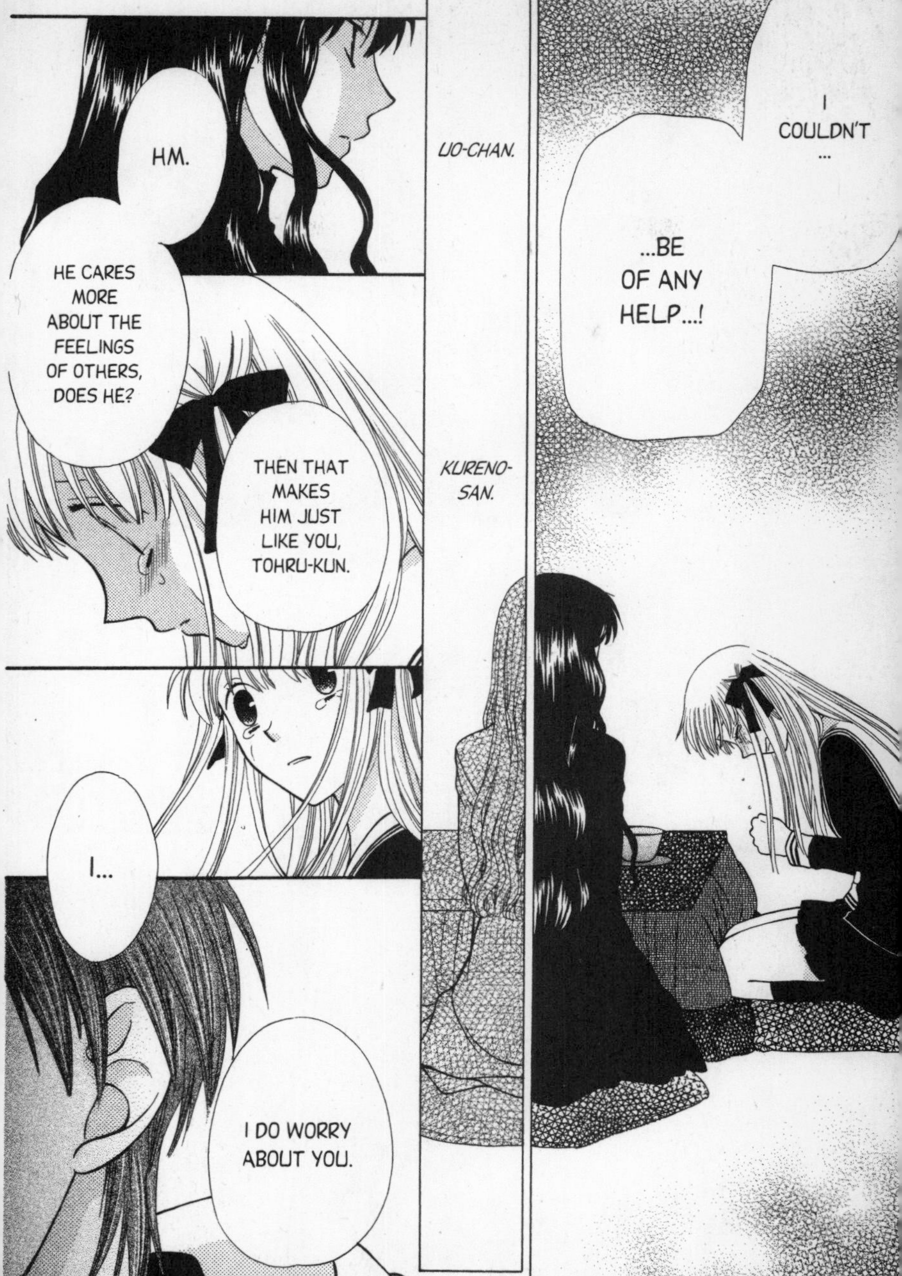
I COULDN'T ...
...BE OF ANY HELP...!
UO-CHAN.
KURENO-SAN.
HM.
HE CARES MORE ABOUT THE FEELINGS OF OTHERS, DOES HE?
THEN THAT MAKES HIM JUST LIKE YOU, TOHRU-KUN.
I...
I DO WORRY ABOUT YOU.

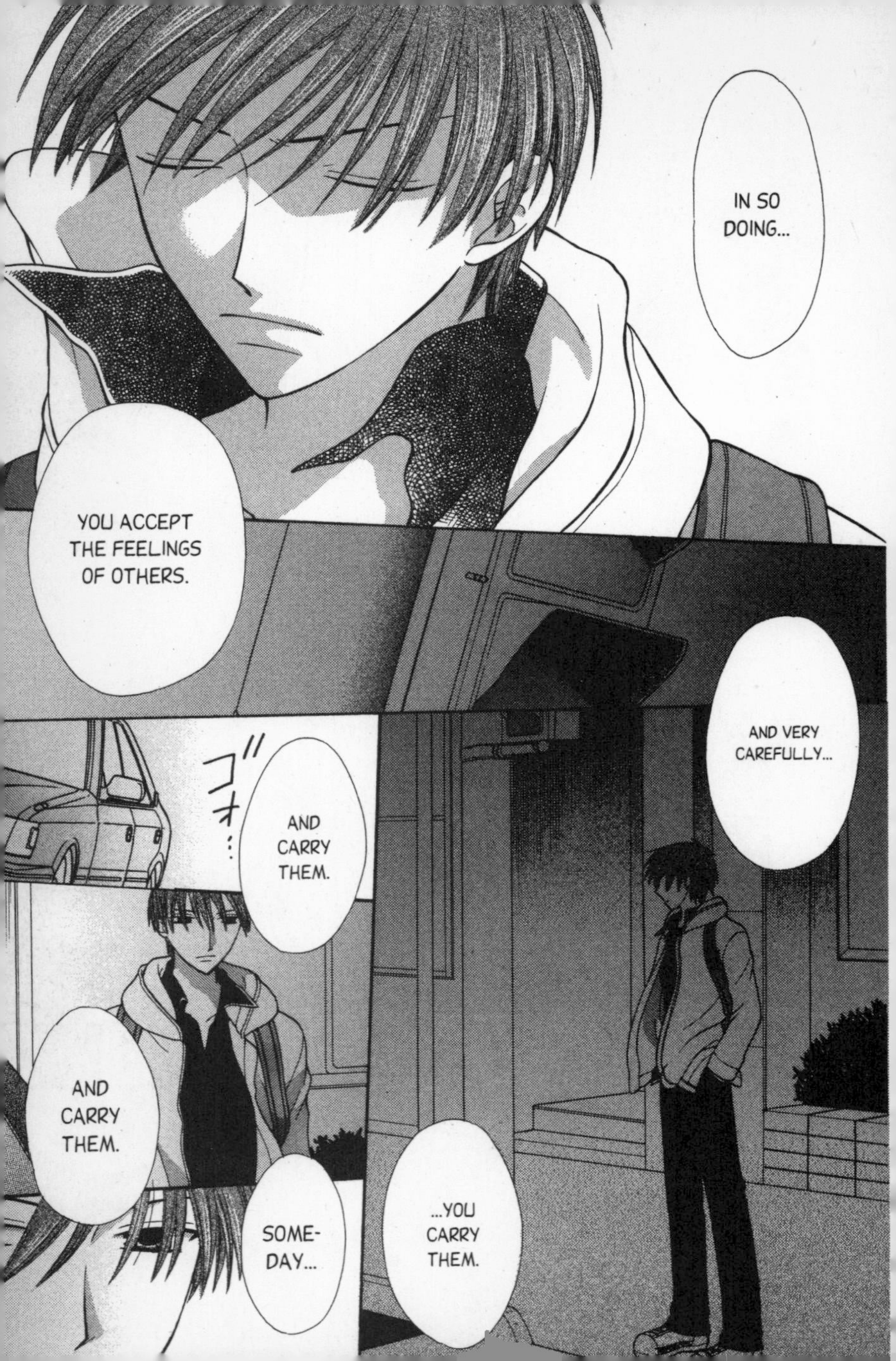
IN SO DOING...
YOU ACCEPT THE FEELINGS OF OTHERS.
AND VERY CAREFULLY...
...YOU CARRY THEM.
ゴォ…
AND CARRY THEM.
AND CARRY THEM.
SOME-DAY...

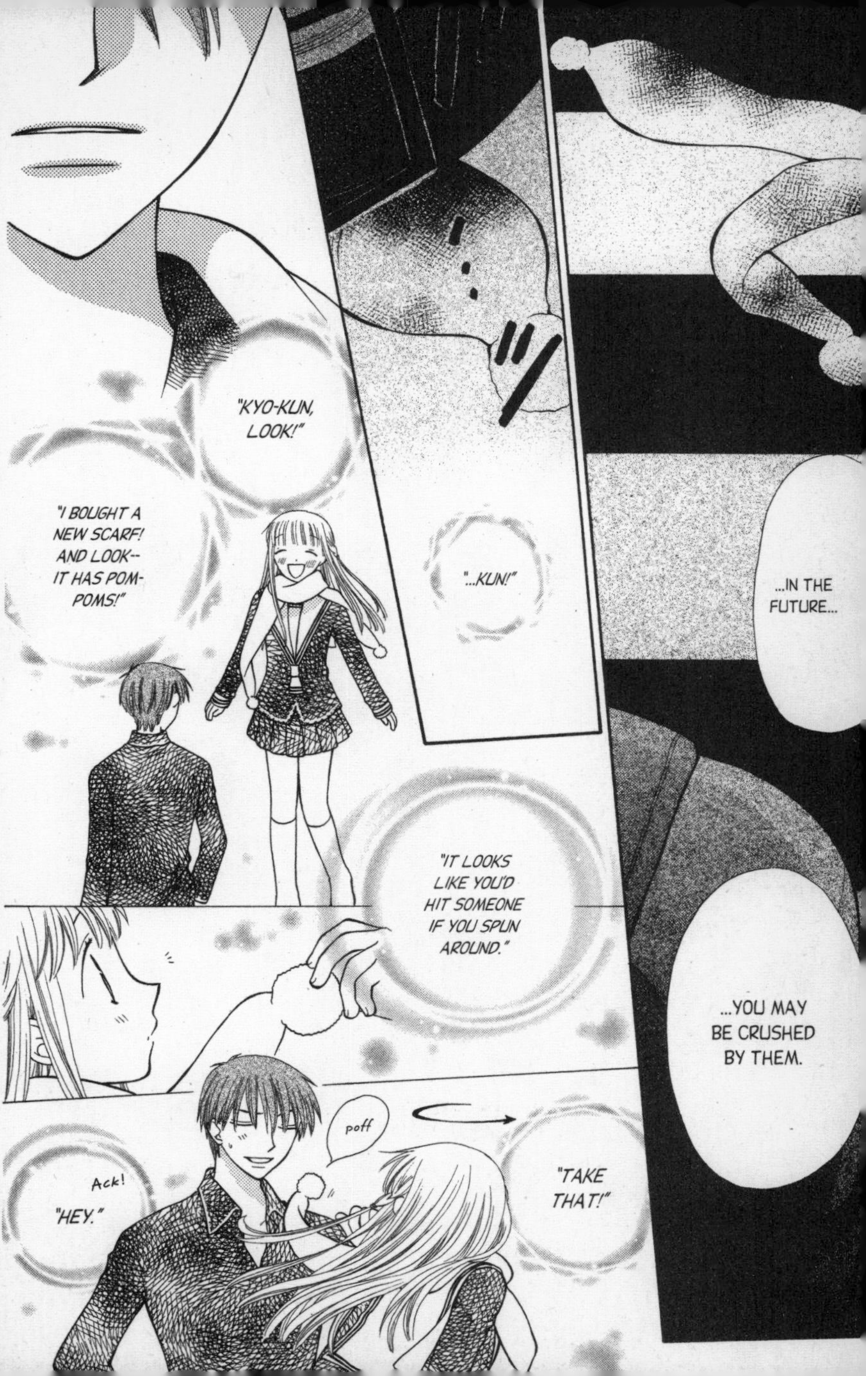
...IN THE FUTURE...
...YOU MAY BE CRUSHED BY THEM.
"...KUN!"
"KYO-KUN, LOOK!"
"I BOUGHT A NEW SCARF! AND LOOK-- IT HAS POM-POMS!"
"IT LOOKS LIKE YOU'D HIT SOMEONE IF YOU SPUN AROUND."
"TAKE THAT!"
poff
Ack!
"HEY."

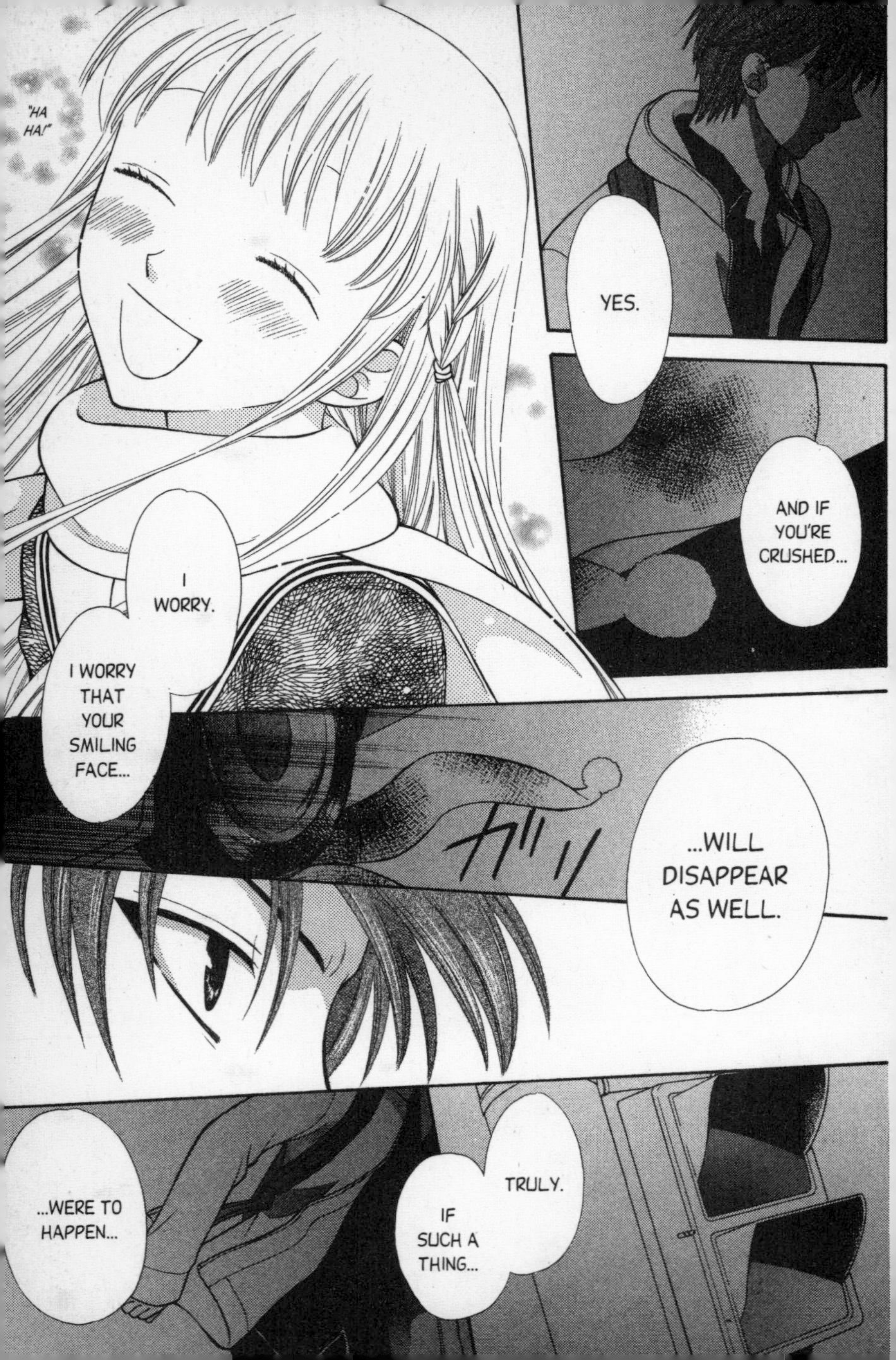
YES.
AND IF YOU'RE CRUSHED...
"HA HA!"
I WORRY.
I WORRY THAT YOUR SMILING FACE...
...WILL DISAPPEAR AS WELL.
TRULY.
IF SUCH A THING...
...WERE TO HAPPEN...

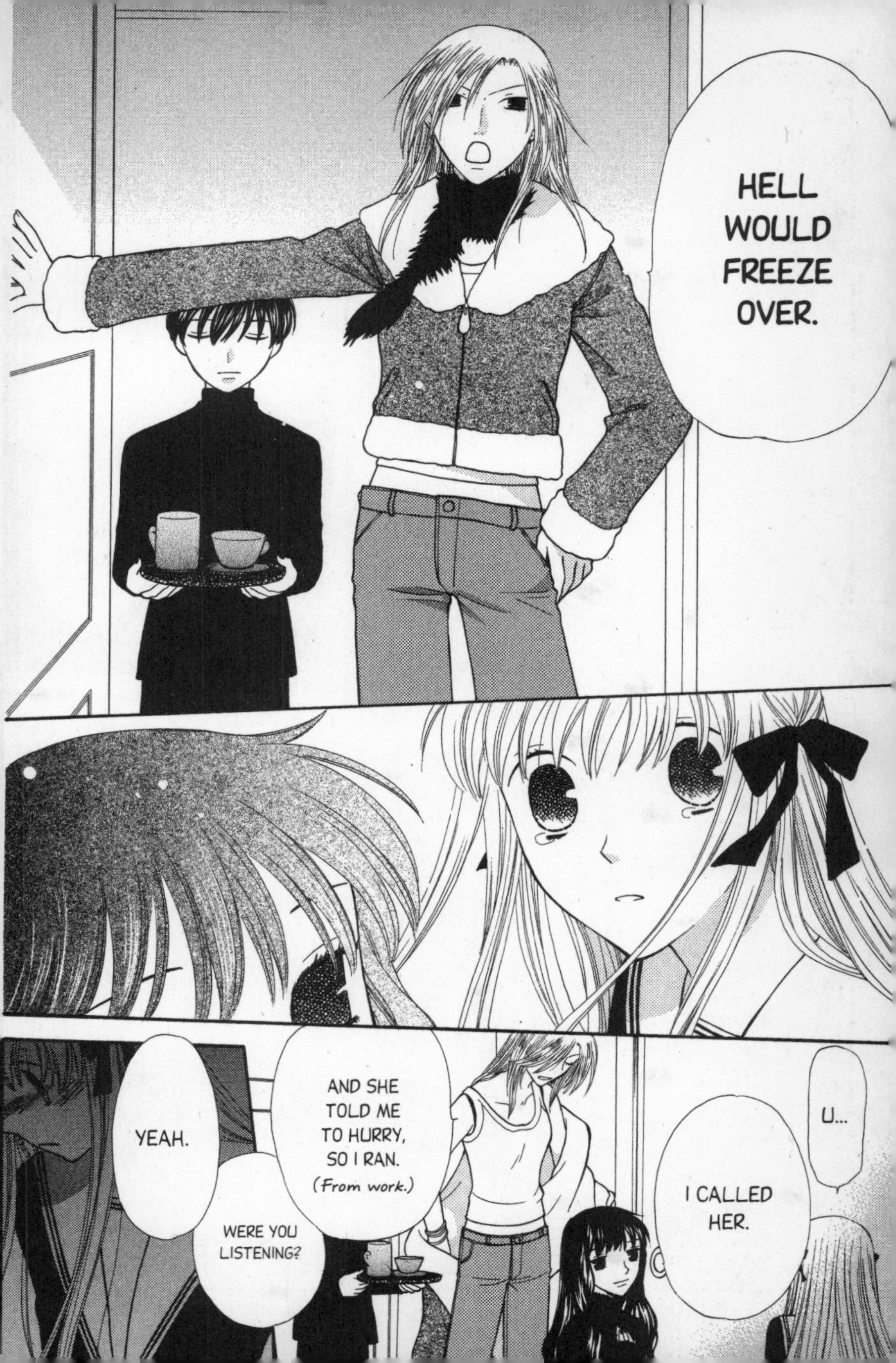
HELL WOULD FREEZE OVER.
U...
I CALLED HER.
AND SHE TOLD ME TO HURRY, SO I RAN.
(From work.)
WERE YOU LISTENING?
YEAH.

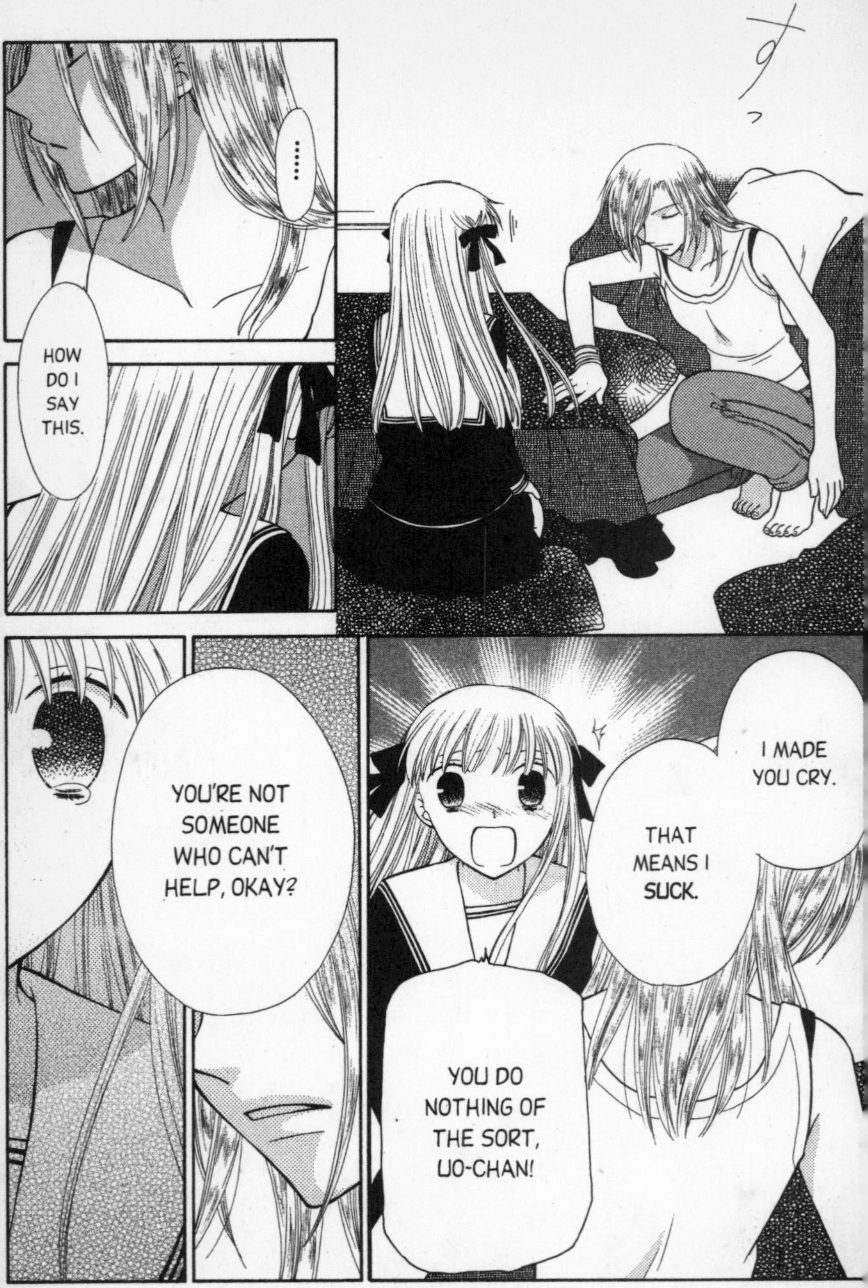
すっ
……
HOW DO I SAY THIS.
I MADE YOU CRY.
THAT MEANS I SUCK.
YOU DO NOTHING OF THE SORT, UO-CHAN!
YOU'RE NOT SOMEONE WHO CAN'T HELP, OKAY?

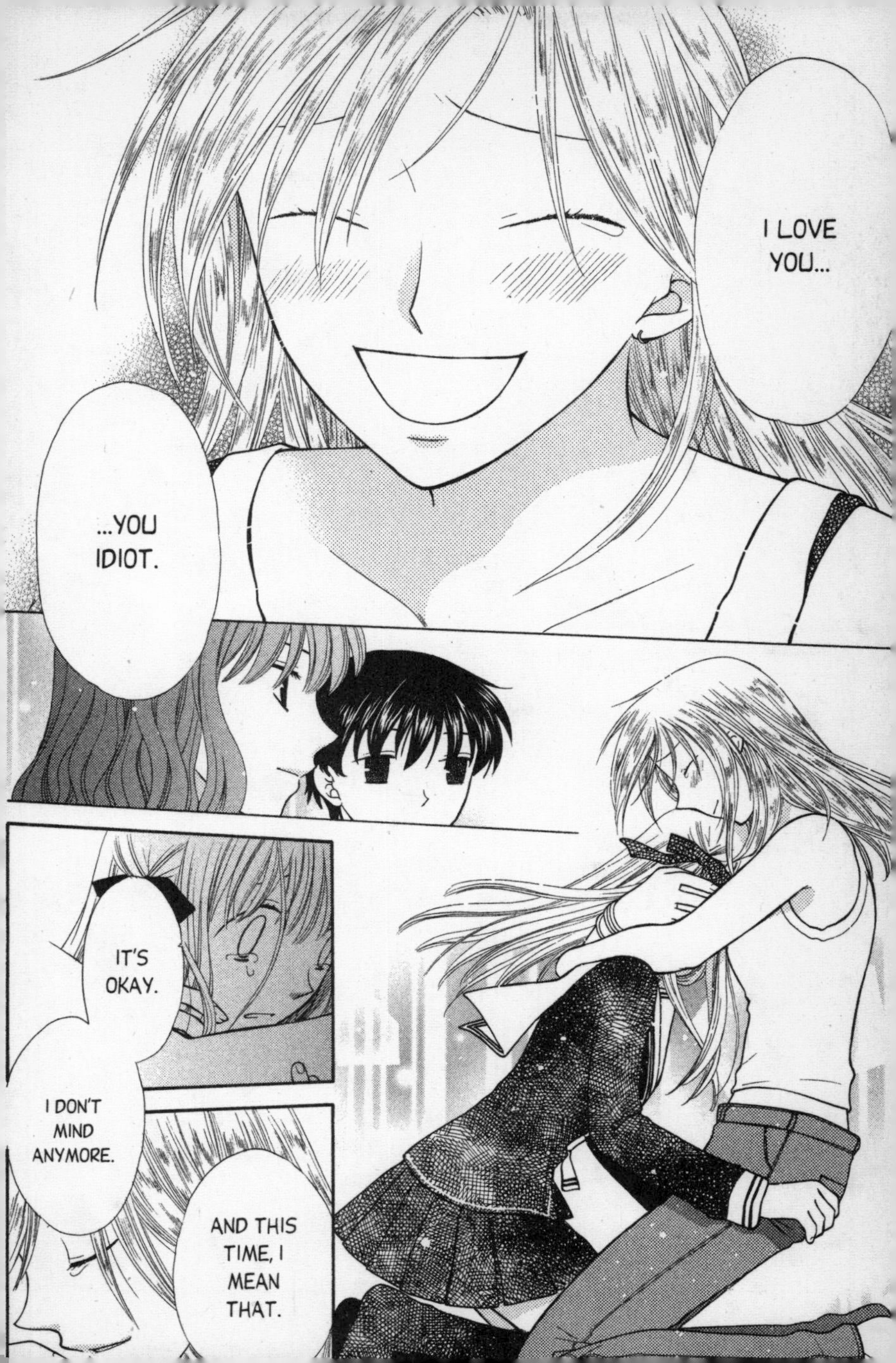
I LOVE YOU...
...YOU IDIOT.
IT'S OKAY.
I DON'T MIND ANYMORE.
AND THIS TIME, I MEAN THAT.

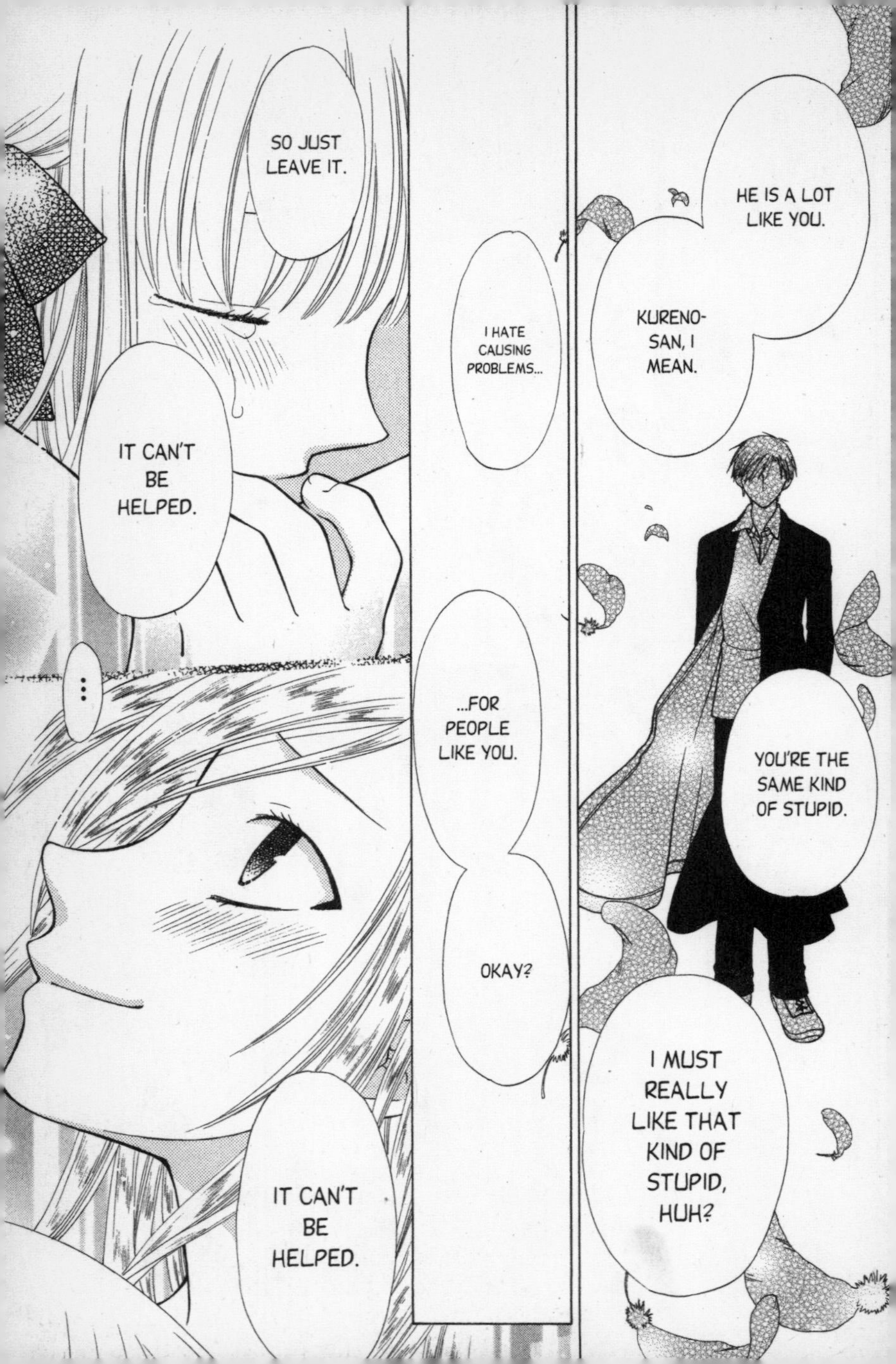
HE IS A LOT LIKE YOU.
KURENO-SAN, I MEAN.
YOU'RE THE SAME KIND OF STUPID.
I MUST REALLY LIKE THAT KIND OF STUPID, HUH?
I HATE CAUSING PROBLEMS...
...FOR PEOPLE LIKE YOU.
OKAY?
SO JUST LEAVE IT.
IT CAN'T BE HELPED.
...
IT CAN'T BE HELPED.

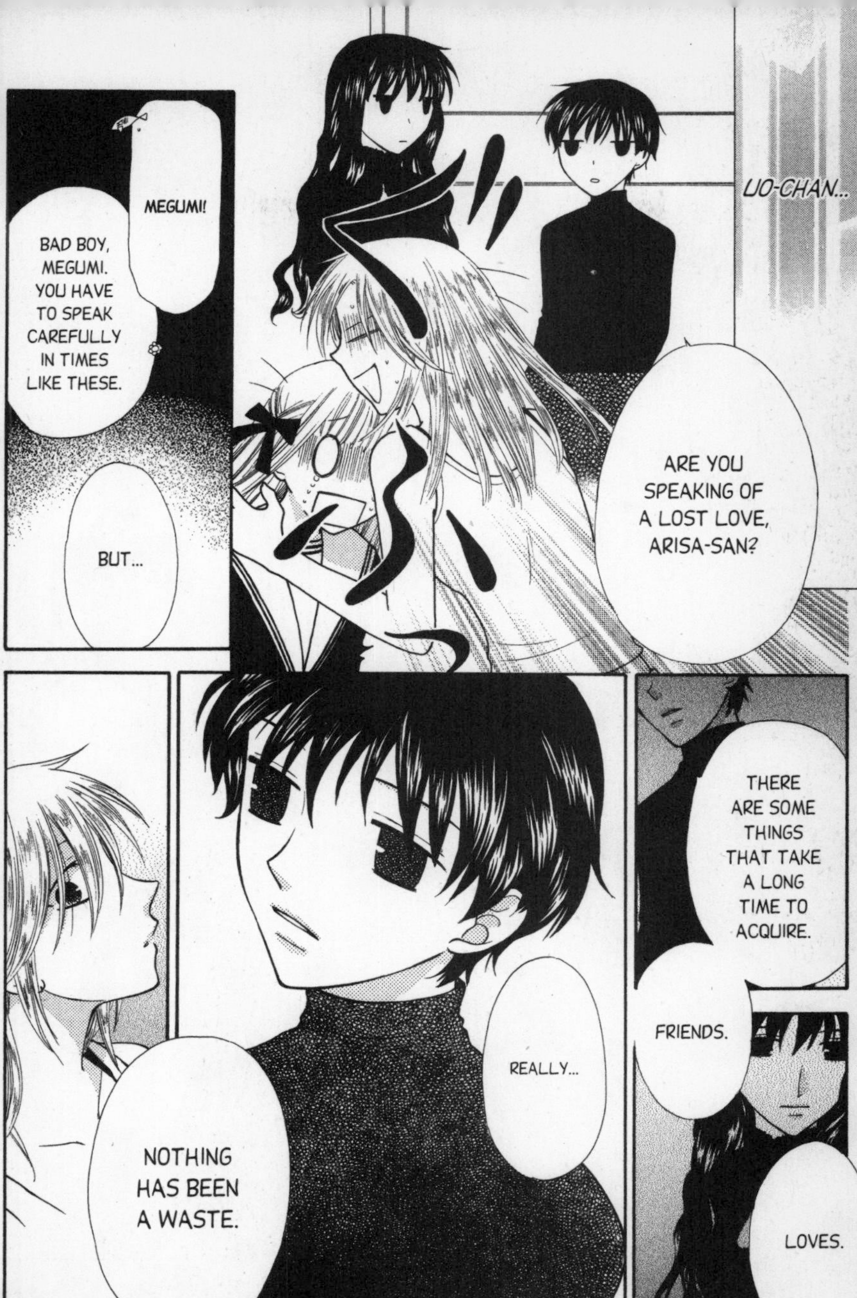

UO-CHAN...
ARE YOU SPEAKING OF A LOST LOVE, ARISA-SAN?
MEGUMI!
BAD BOY, MEGUMI. YOU HAVE TO SPEAK CAREFULLY IN TIMES LIKE THESE.
BUT...
THERE ARE SOME THINGS THAT TAKE A LONG TIME TO ACQUIRE.
FRIENDS.
LOVES.
REALLY...
NOTHING HAS BEEN A WASTE.

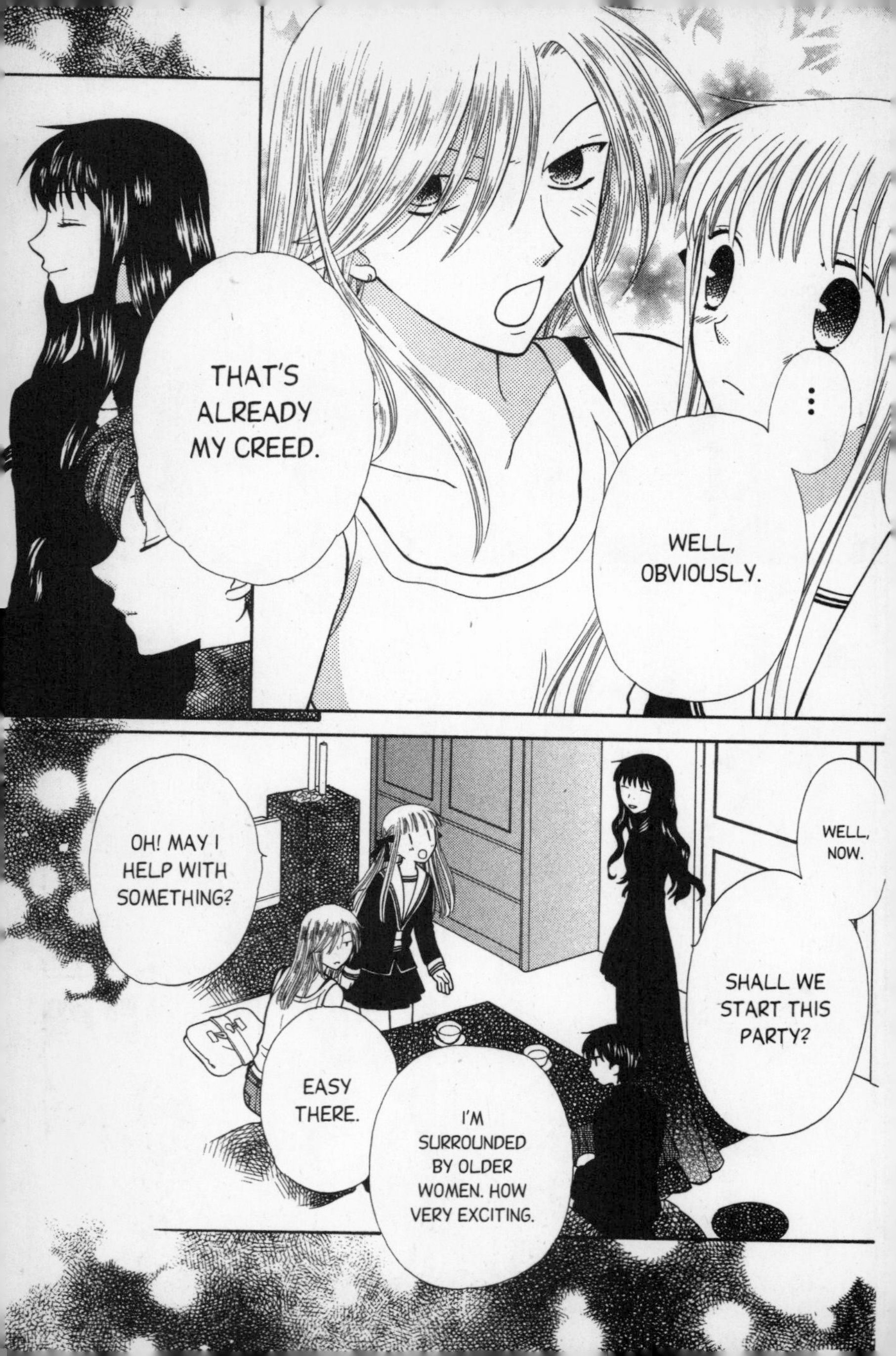
...
WELL, OBVIOUSLY.
THAT'S ALREADY MY CREED.
WELL, NOW.
SHALL WE START THIS PARTY?
OH! MAY I HELP WITH SOMETHING?
I'M SURROUNDED BY OLDER WOMEN. HOW VERY EXCITING.
EASY THERE.

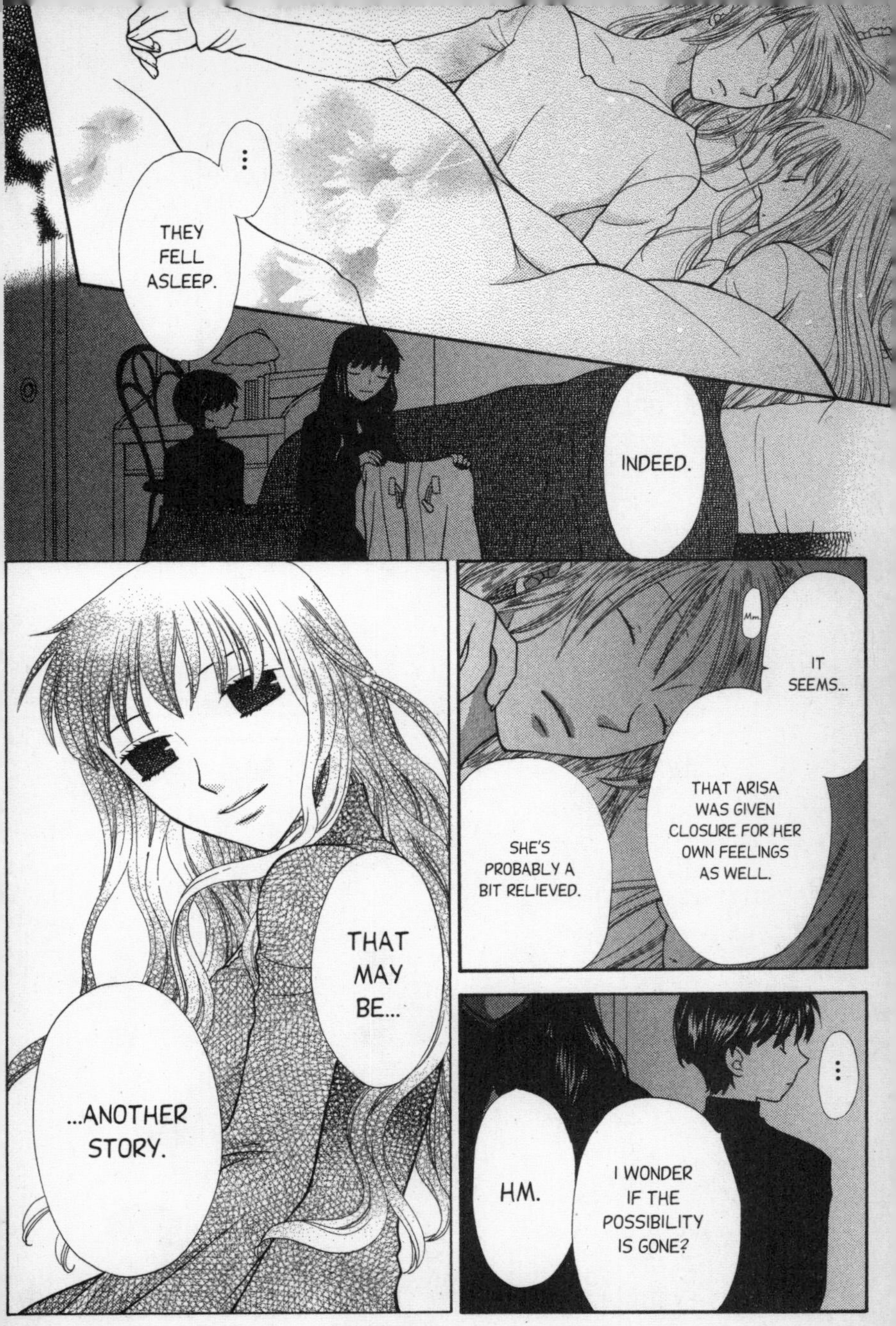
...
THEY FELL ASLEEP.
INDEED.
Mm.
IT SEEMS...
THAT ARISA WAS GIVEN CLOSURE FOR HER OWN FEELINGS AS WELL.
SHE'S PROBABLY A BIT RELIEVED.
...
I WONDER IF THE POSSIBILITY IS GONE?
HM.
THAT MAY BE...
...ANOTHER STORY.

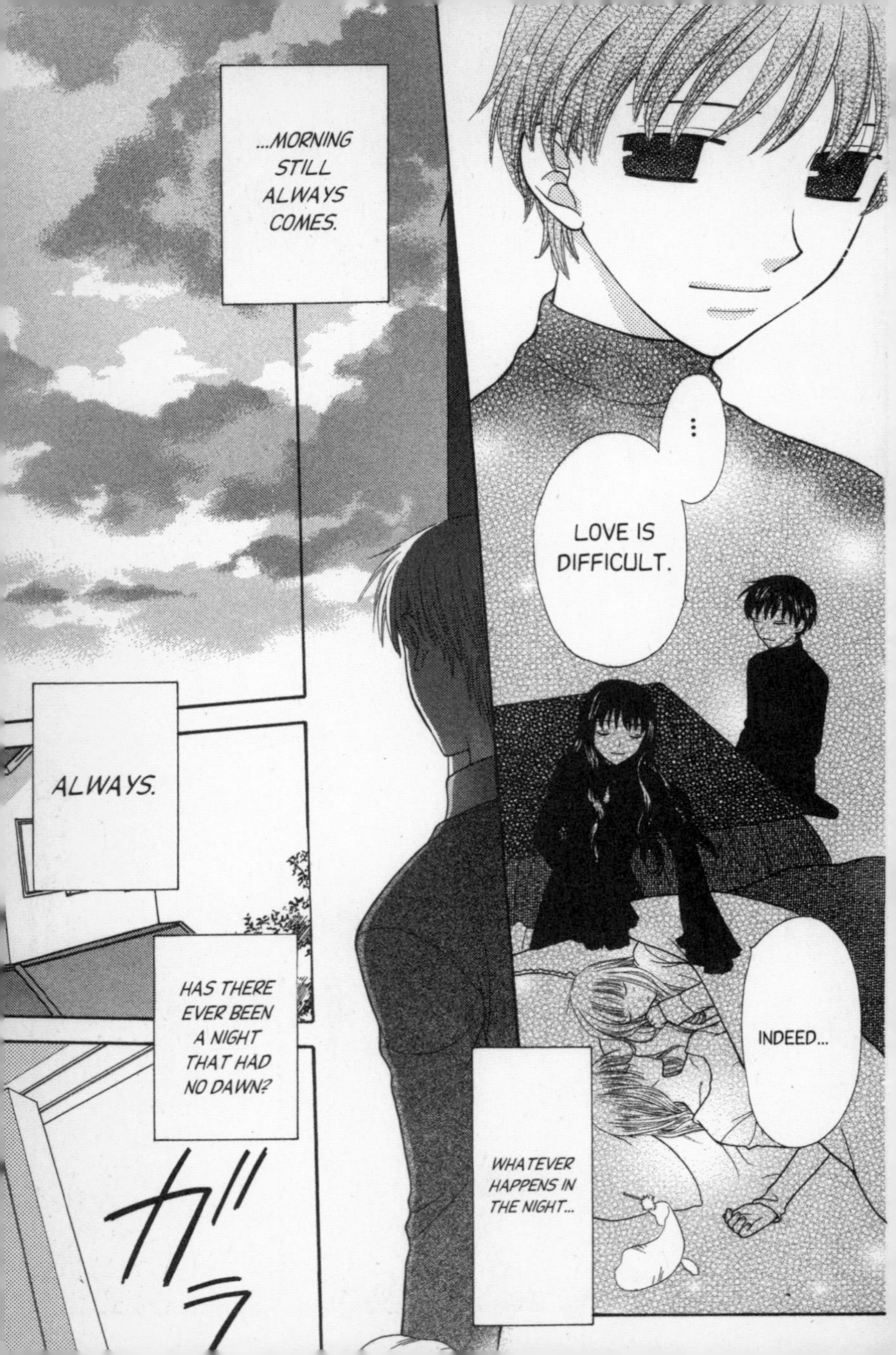
...
LOVE IS DIFFICULT.
INDEED...
WHATEVER HAPPENS IN THE NIGHT...
...MORNING STILL ALWAYS COMES.
ALWAYS.
HAS THERE EVER BEEN A NIGHT THAT HAD NO DAWN?
ガラ

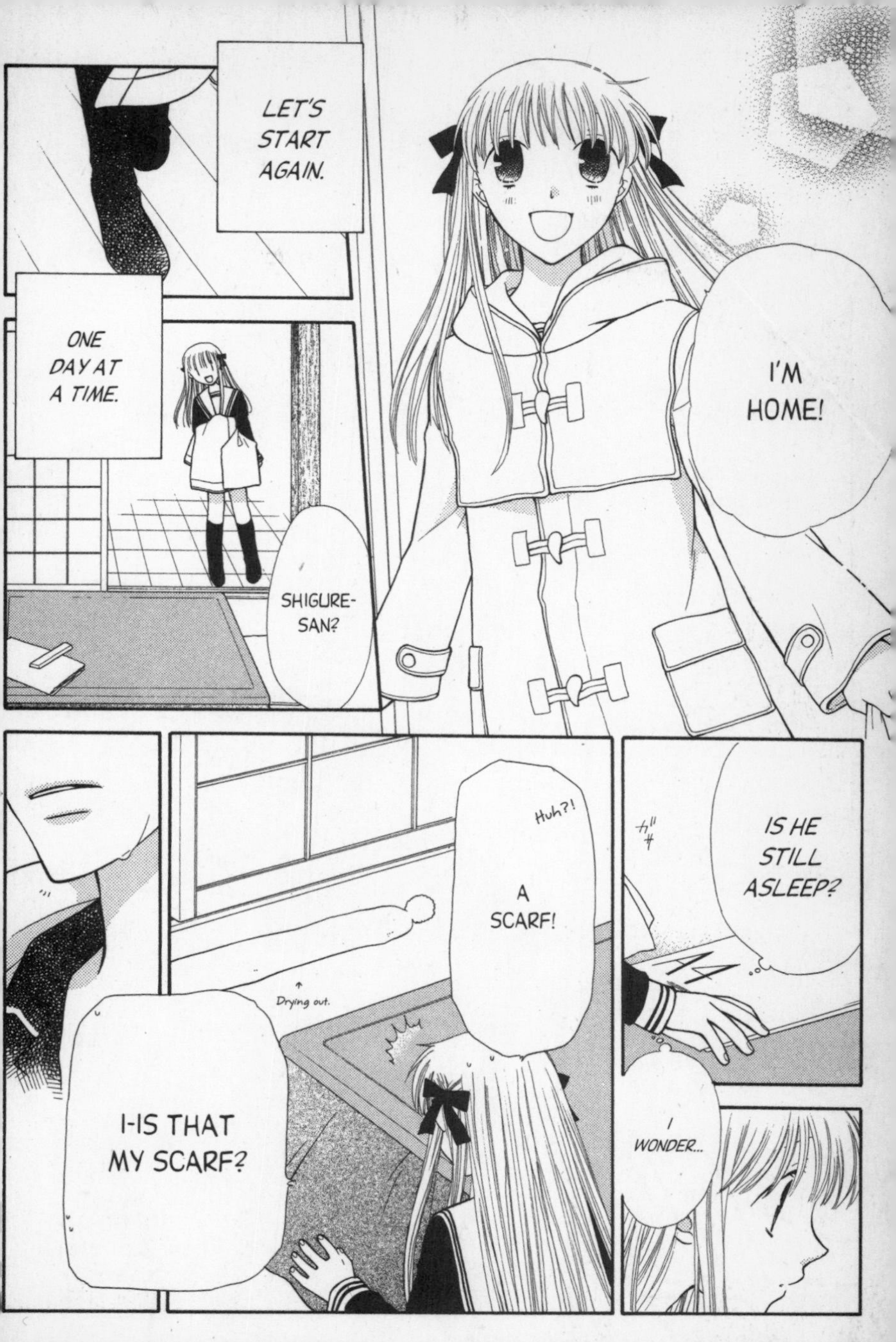
I'M HOME!
LET'S START AGAIN.
ONE DAY AT A TIME.
SHIGURE-SAN?
IS HE STILL ASLEEP?
I WONDER...
Huh?!
A SCARF!
Drying out.
I-IS THAT MY SCARF?

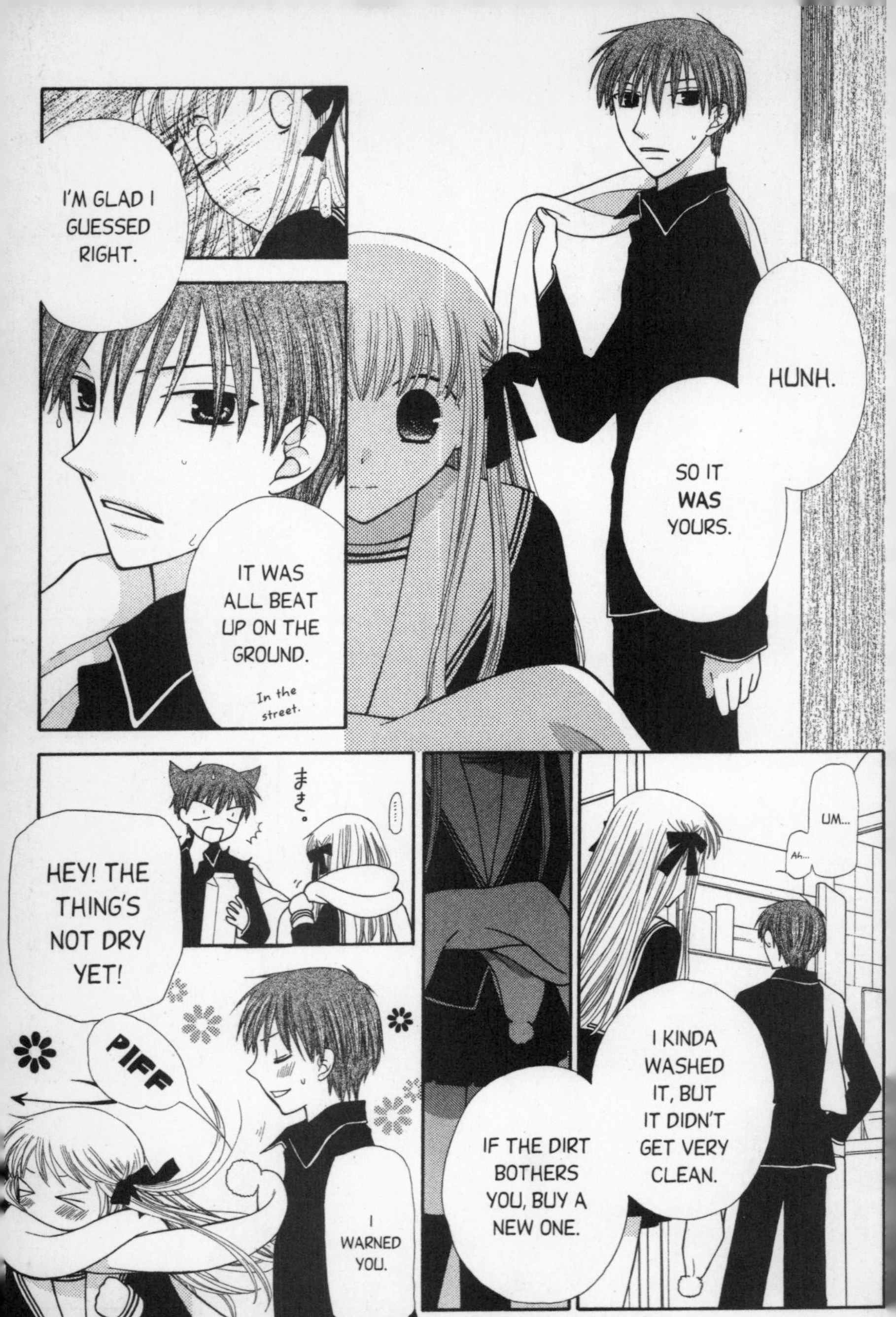
HUNH.
SO IT WAS YOURS.
I'M GLAD I GUESSED RIGHT.
IT WAS ALL BEAT UP ON THE GROUND.
In the street.
UM...
Ah...
I KINDA WASHED IT, BUT IT DIDN'T GET VERY CLEAN.
IF THE DIRT BOTHERS YOU, BUY A NEW ONE.
まき。
......
HEY! THE THING'S NOT DRY YET!
PIFF
I WARNED YOU.

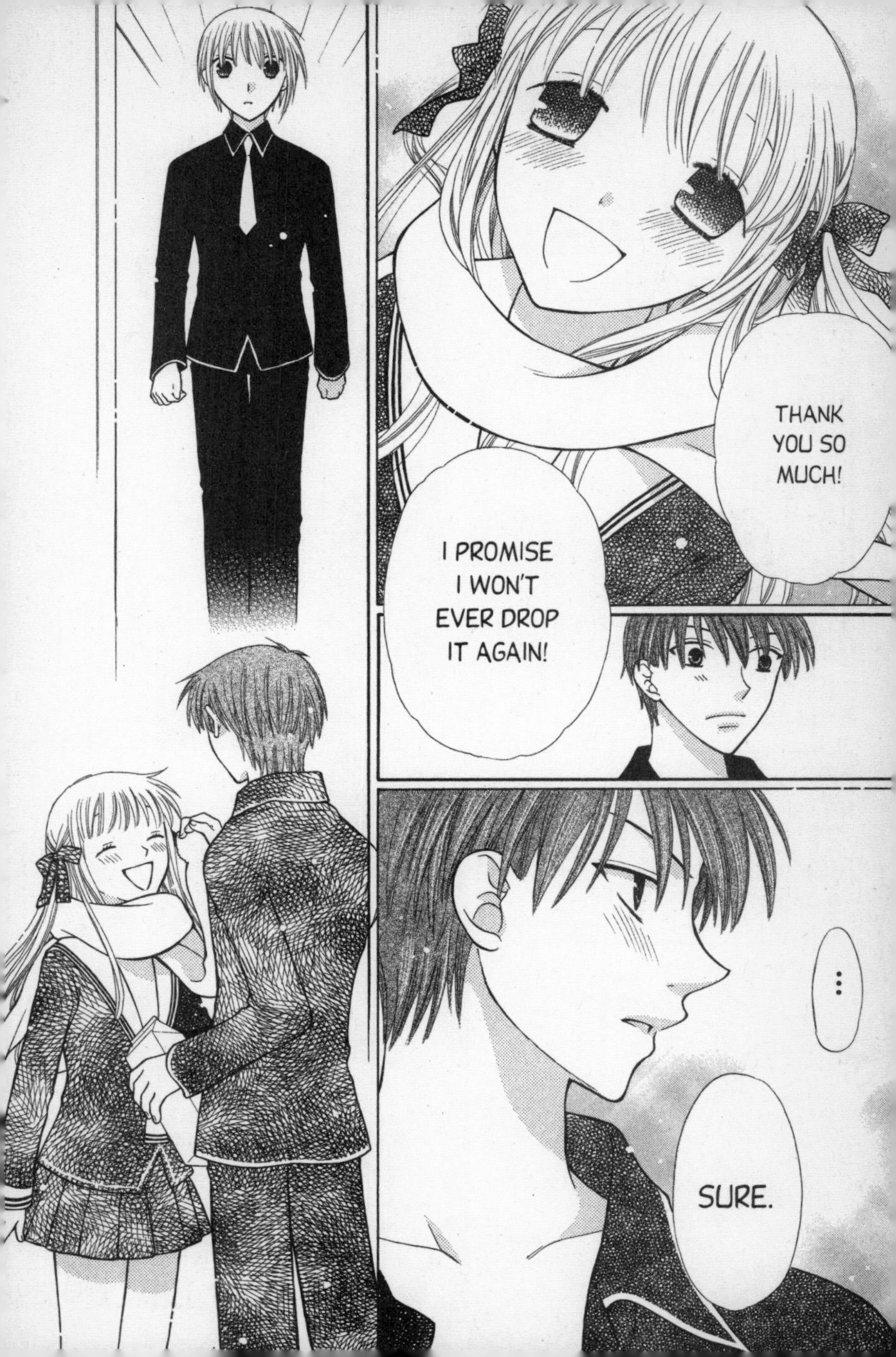
THANK YOU SO MUCH!
I PROMISE I WON'T EVER DROP IT AGAIN!
...
SURE.

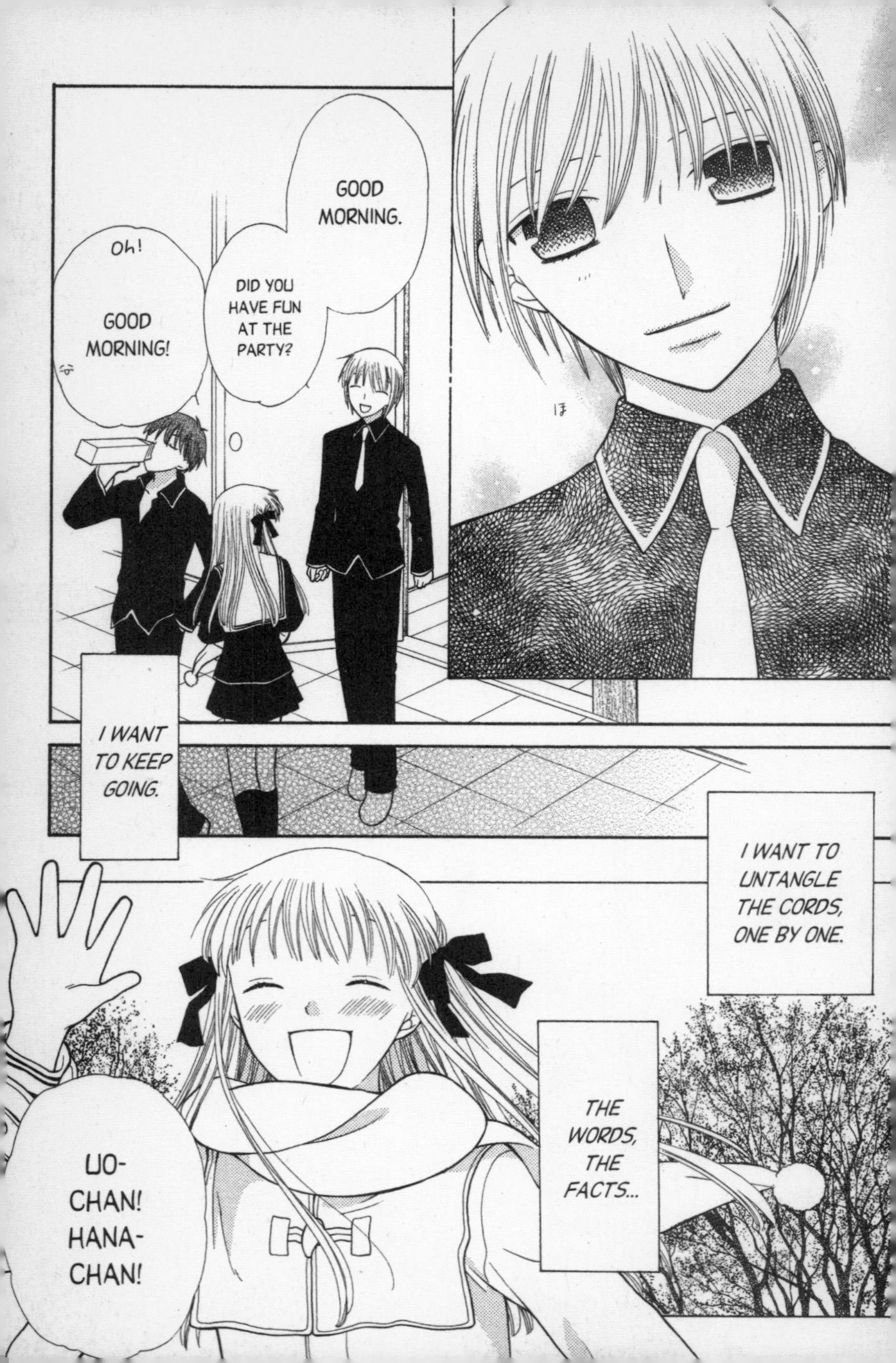
ほ
GOOD MORNING.
DID YOU HAVE FUN AT THE PARTY?
Oh!
GOOD MORNING!
I WANT TO KEEP GOING.
I WANT TO UNTANGLE THE CORDS, ONE BY ONE.
THE WORDS, THE FACTS...
UO-CHAN! HANA-CHAN!

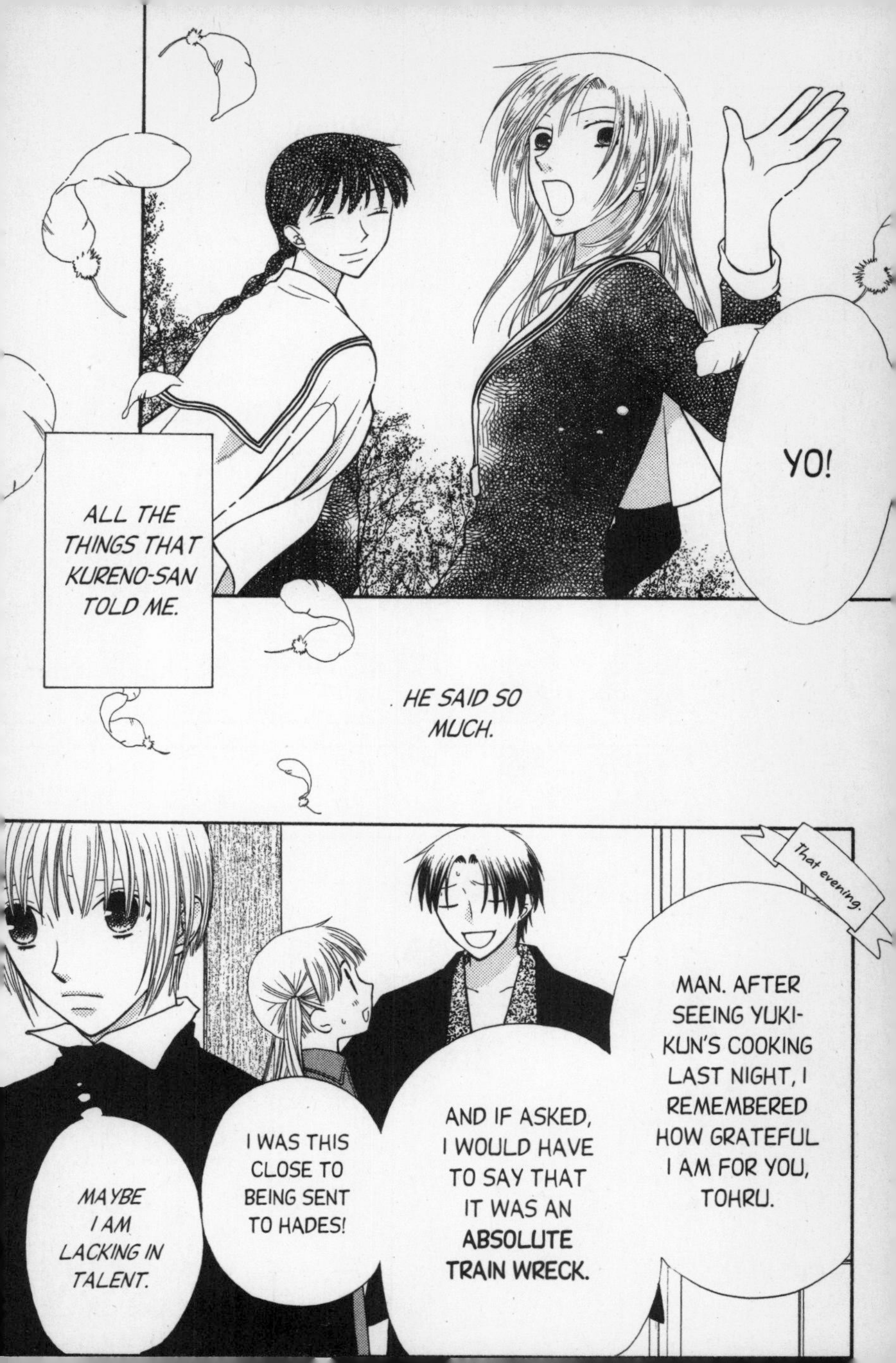

YO!
ALL THE THINGS THAT KURENO-SAN TOLD ME.
HE SAID SO MUCH.
That evening.
MAN. AFTER SEEING YUKI-KUN'S COOKING LAST NIGHT, I REMEMBERED HOW GRATEFUL I AM FOR YOU, TOHRU.
AND IF ASKED, I WOULD HAVE TO SAY THAT IT WAS AN ABSOLUTE TRAIN WRECK.
I WAS THIS CLOSE TO BEING SENT TO HADES!
MAYBE I AM LACKING IN TALENT.

Filler Sketch

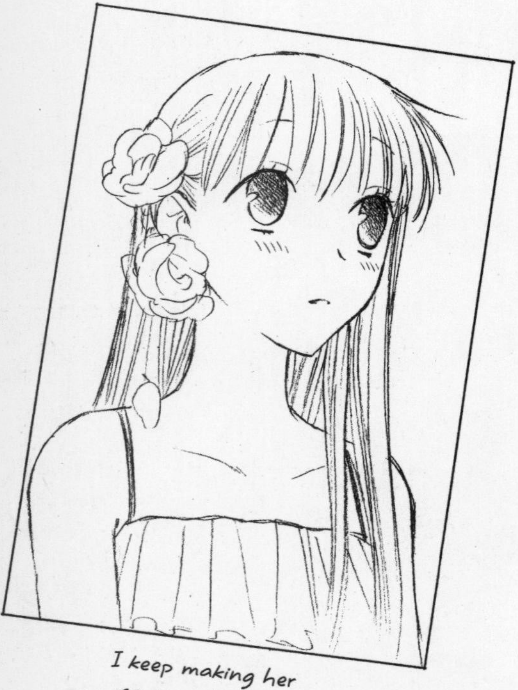

I keep making her cause problems...

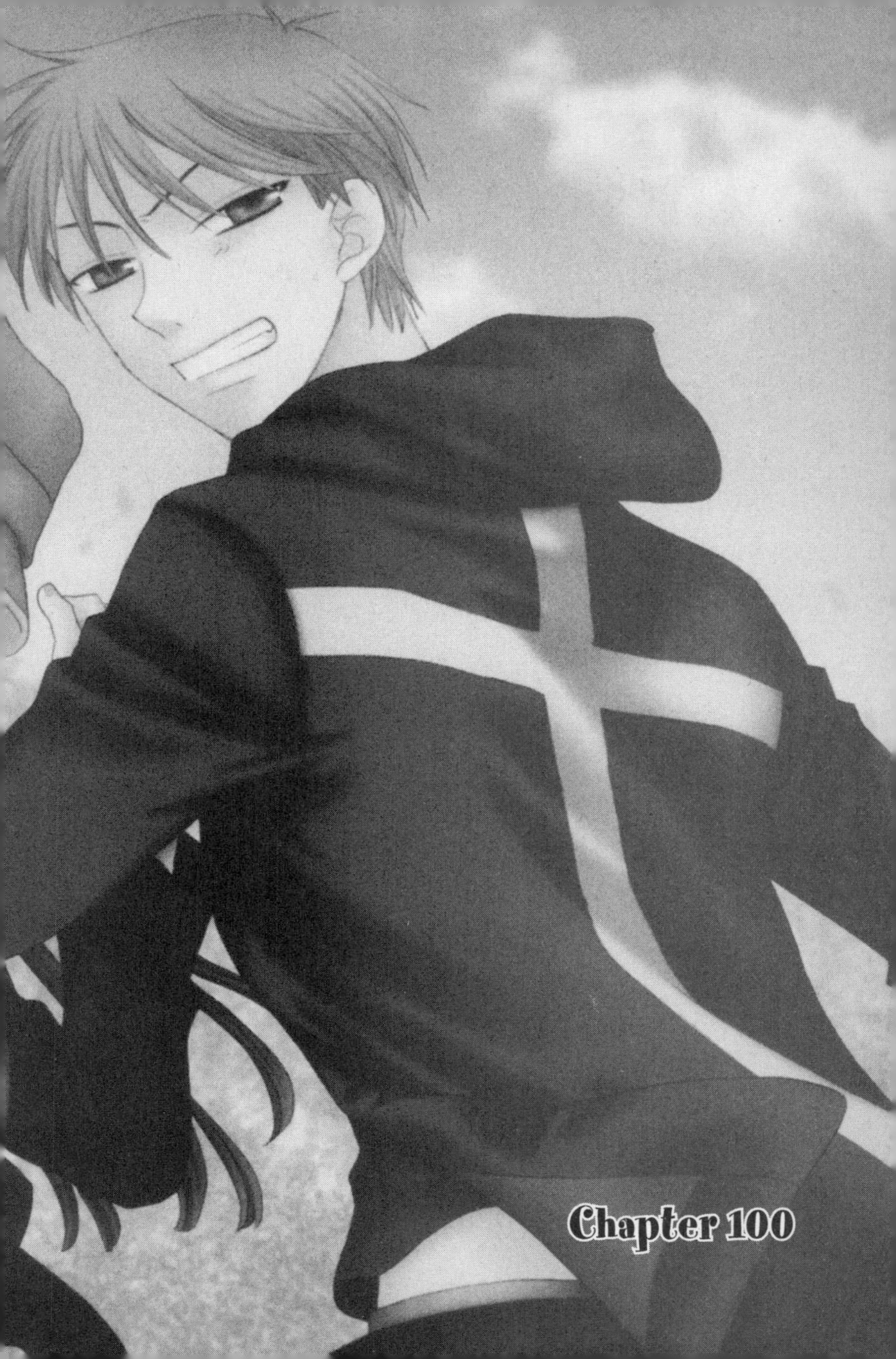
Chapter 100

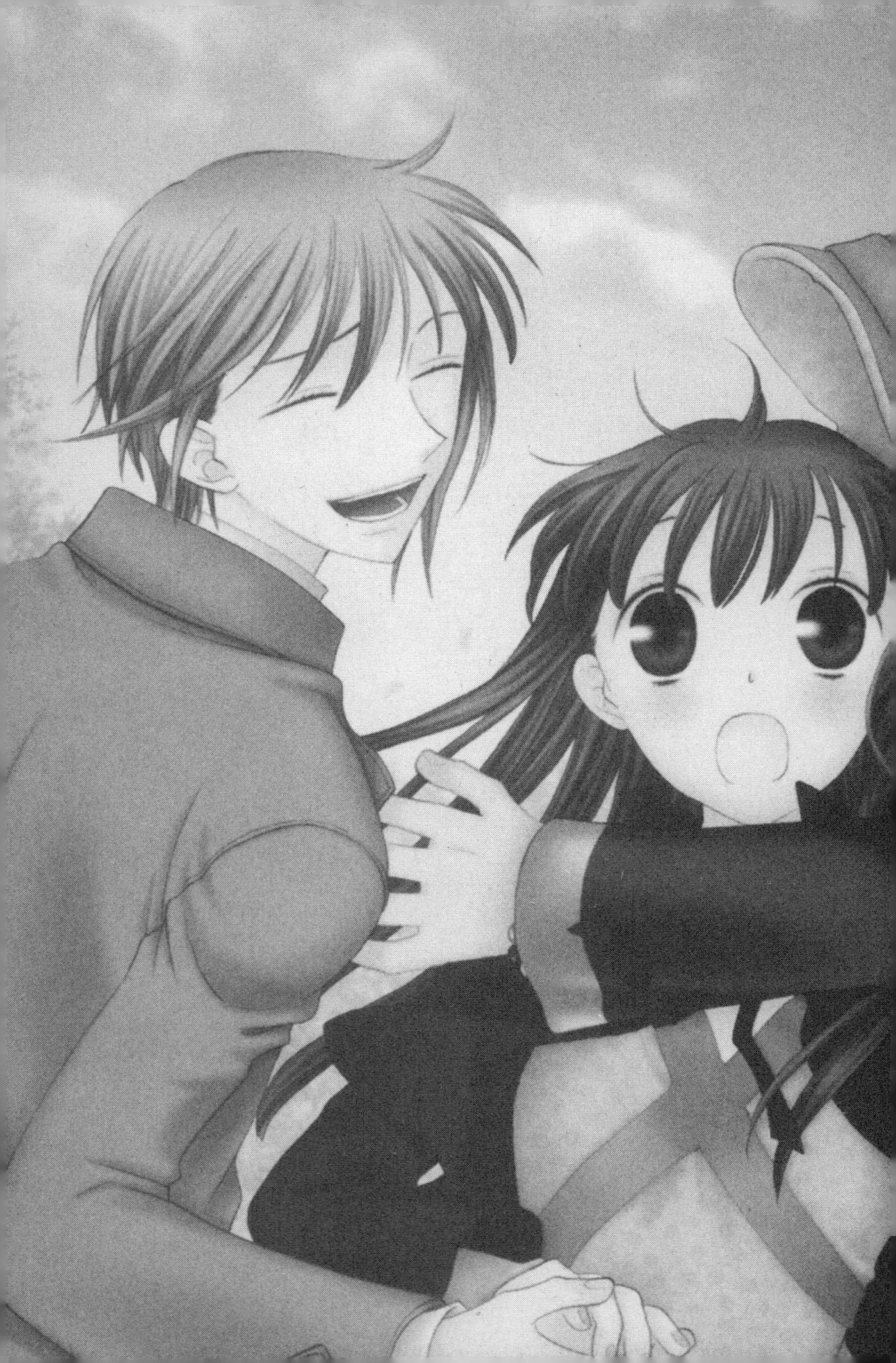

Filler Sketch

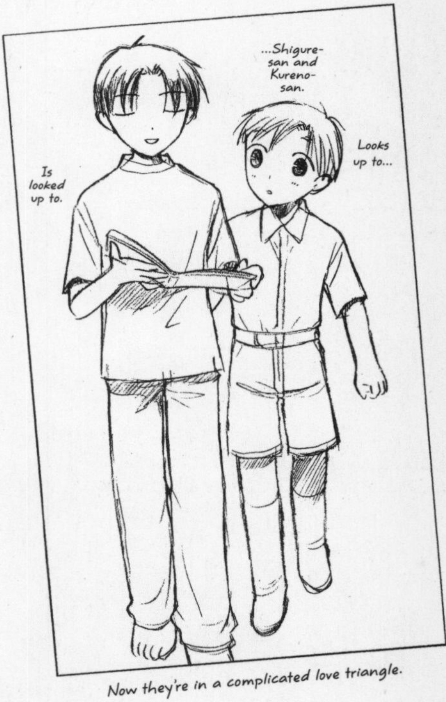
...Shigure-san and Kureno-san.
Looks up to...
Is looked up to.

Now they're in a complicated love triangle.

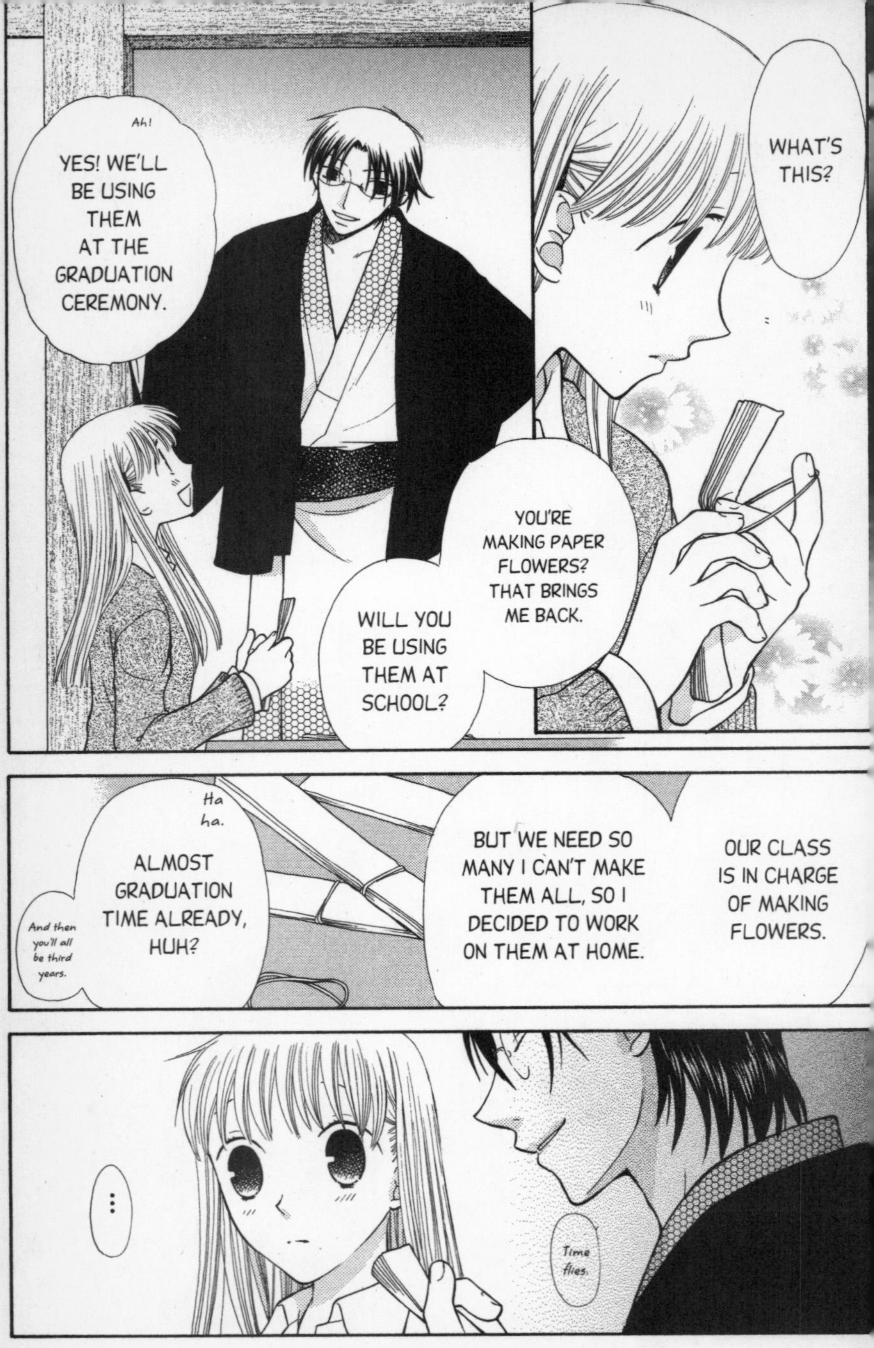

WHAT'S THIS?
YOU'RE MAKING PAPER FLOWERS? THAT BRINGS ME BACK.
WILL YOU BE USING THEM AT SCHOOL?
Ah!
YES! WE'LL BE USING THEM AT THE GRADUATION CEREMONY.
OUR CLASS IS IN CHARGE OF MAKING FLOWERS.
BUT WE NEED SO MANY I CAN'T MAKE THEM ALL, SO I DECIDED TO WORK ON THEM AT HOME.
Ha ha.
ALMOST GRADUATION TIME ALREADY, HUH?
And then you'll all be third years.
Time flies.
...

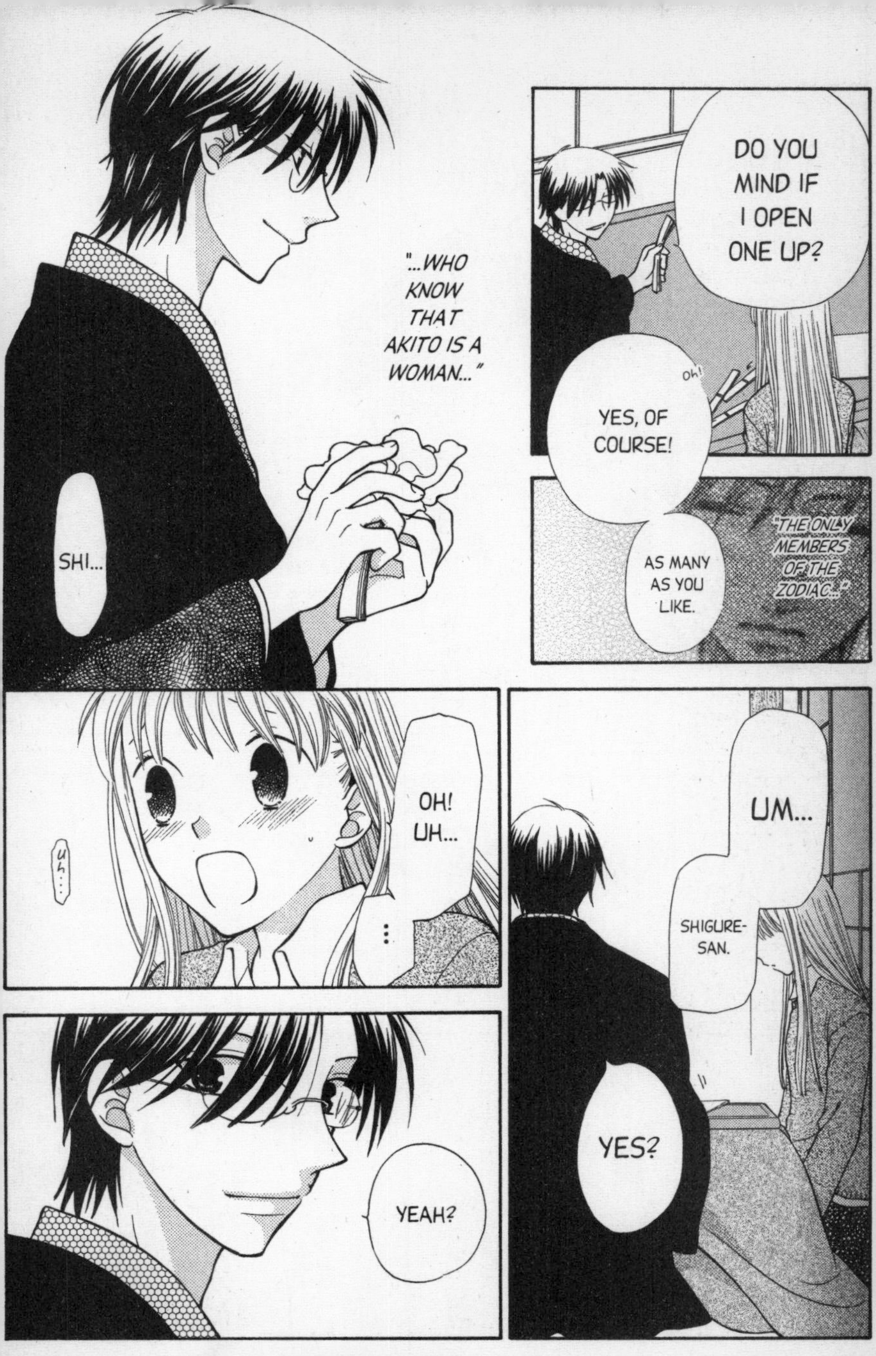

DO YOU MIND IF I OPEN ONE UP?
Oh!
YES, OF COURSE!
"THE ONLY MEMBERS OF THE ZODIAC..."
AS MANY AS YOU LIKE.
"...WHO KNOW THAT AKITO IS A WOMAN..."
SHI...
UM...
SHIGURE-SAN.
YES?
OH! UH...
uh...
...
YEAH?

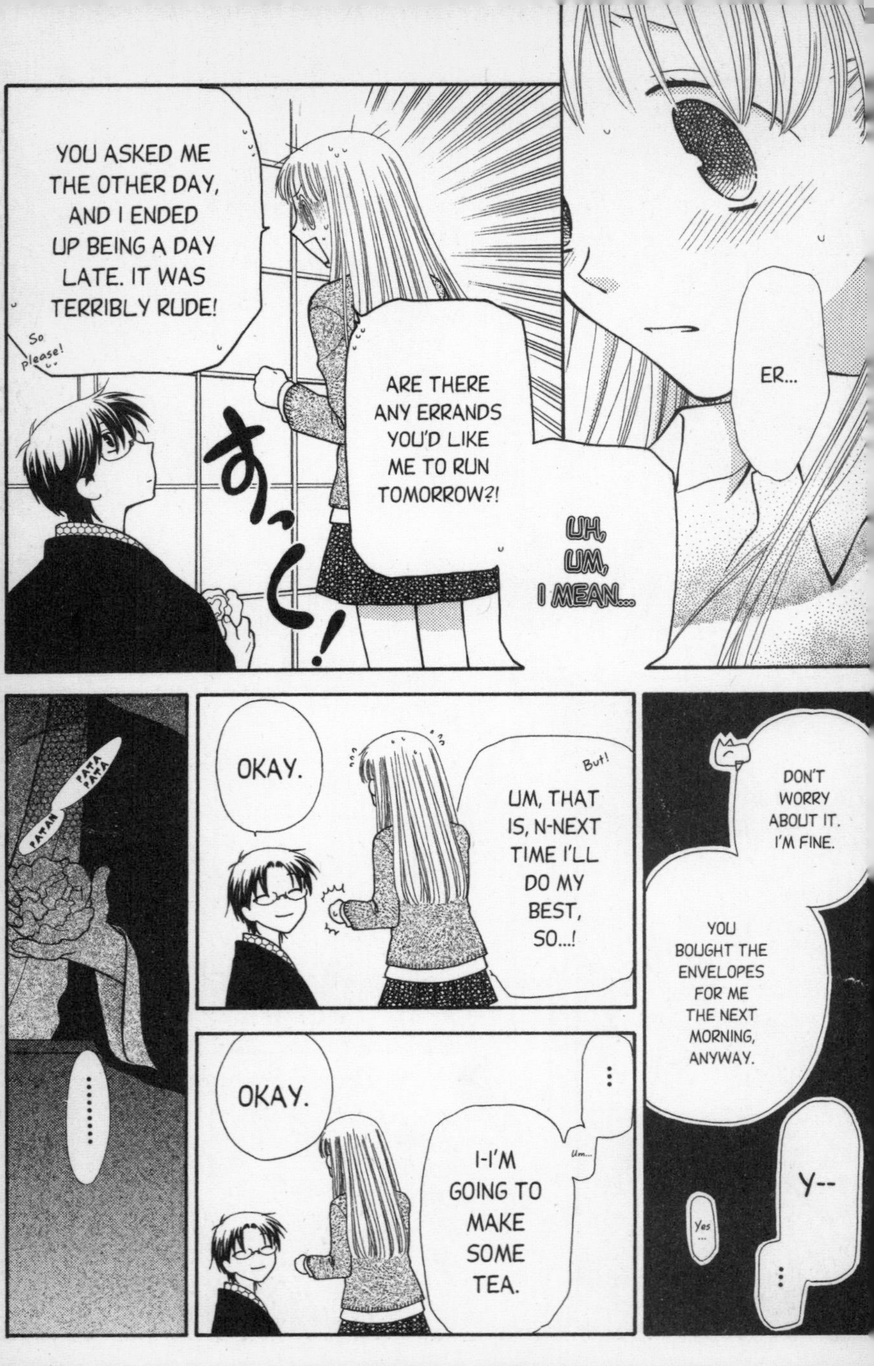
ER...
UH, UM, I MEAN...
ARE THERE ANY ERRANDS YOU'D LIKE ME TO RUN TOMORROW?!
すっく!
YOU ASKED ME THE OTHER DAY, AND I ENDED UP BEING A DAY LATE. IT WAS TERRIBLY RUDE!
So please!
DON'T WORRY ABOUT IT. I'M FINE.
YOU BOUGHT THE ENVELOPES FOR ME THE NEXT MORNING, ANYWAY.
Y--
...
Yes...
But!
UM, THAT IS, N-NEXT TIME I'LL DO MY BEST, SO...!
OKAY.
...
Um...
I-I'M GOING TO MAKE SOME TEA.
OKAY.
PATA PATA
PATAN
....

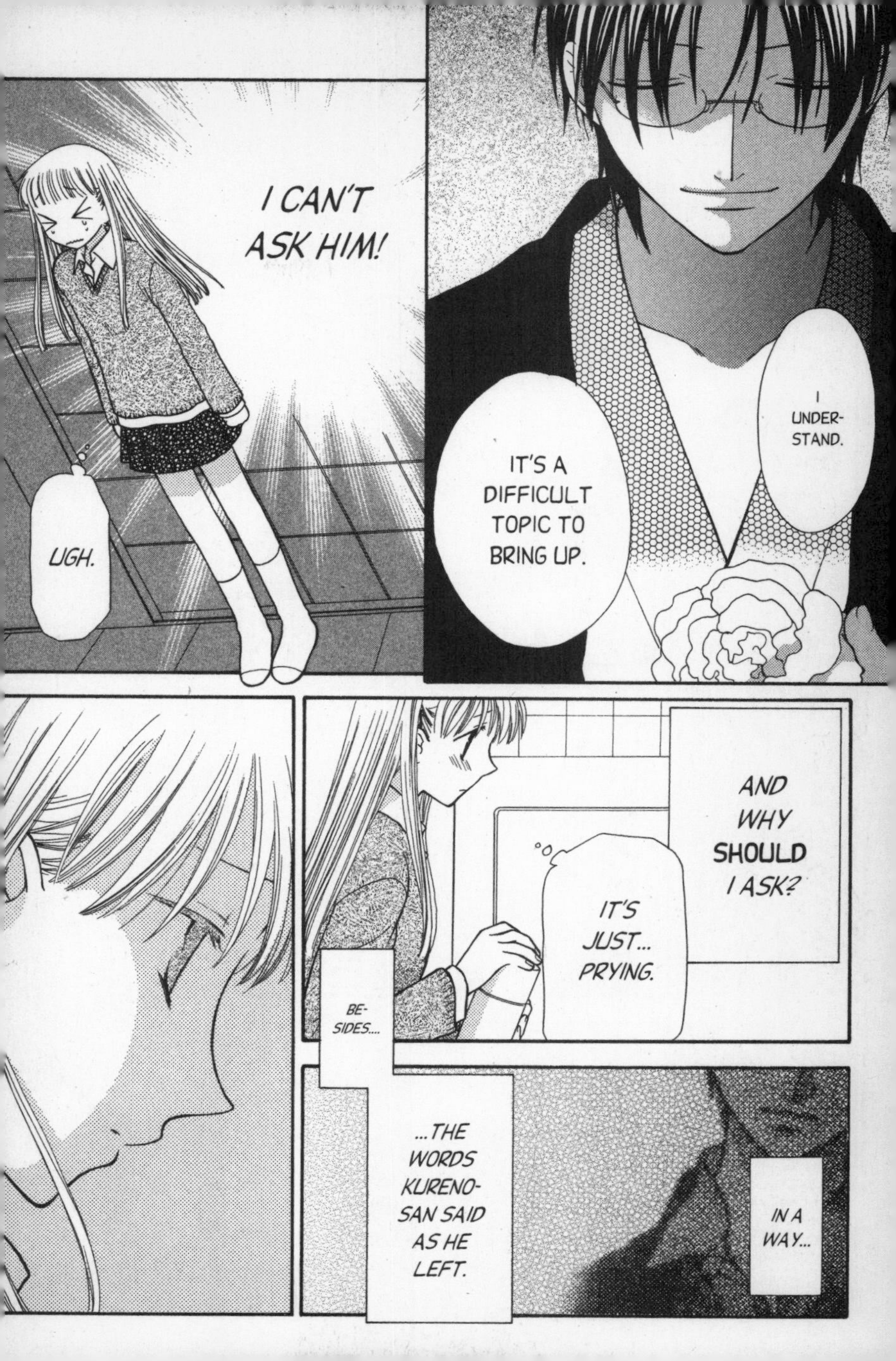
I UNDERSTAND.
IT'S A DIFFICULT TOPIC TO BRING UP.
I CAN'T ASK HIM!
UGH.
AND WHY SHOULD I ASK?
IT'S JUST... PRYING.
BESIDES....
...THE WORDS KURENO-SAN SAID AS HE LEFT.
IN A WAY...

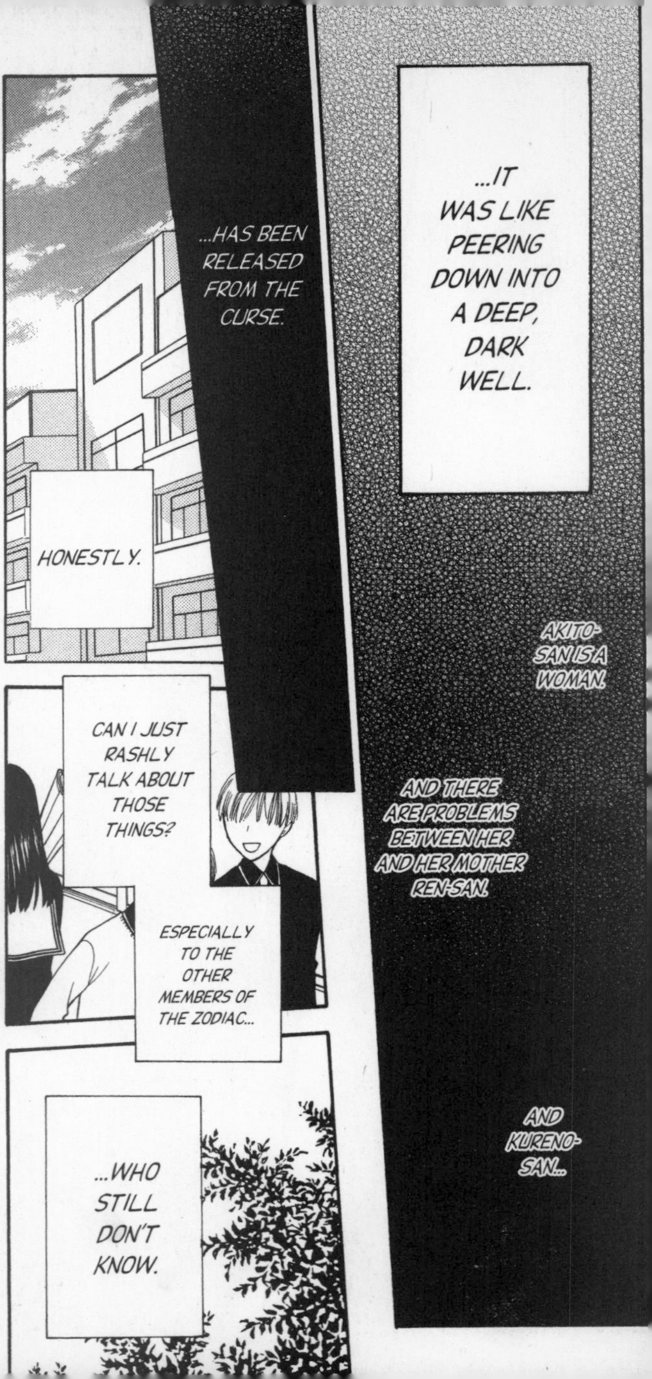
...IT WAS LIKE PEERING DOWN INTO A DEEP, DARK WELL.
AKITO-SAN IS A WOMAN.
AND THERE ARE PROBLEMS BETWEEN HER AND HER MOTHER REN-SAN.
AND KURENO-SAN...
...HAS BEEN RELEASED FROM THE CURSE.
HONESTLY.
CAN I JUST RASHLY TALK ABOUT THOSE THINGS?
ESPECIALLY TO THE OTHER MEMBERS OF THE ZODIAC...
...WHO STILL DON'T KNOW.

Continued →

- Kimi-chan really thinks that all the men around her love her from the bottom of their hearts, all the women around her are there to make her look better by contrast, and that if they all like her, she can go out with as many people as she wants. She considers that permissible. It's nice that Kimi-chan is so honest with herself (laugh)!

- I hope you can always be like that.

It's all right; I'm sure she will.

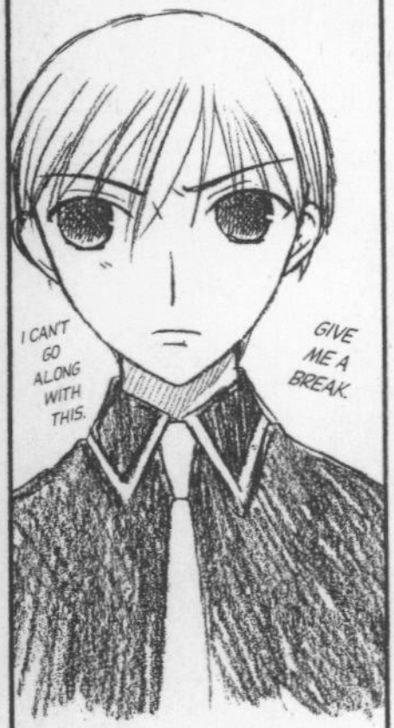
GIVE ME A BREAK.
I CAN'T GO ALONG WITH THIS.

- Come to think of it, I don't think I've ever drawn this guy smiling...

Naohito.

- With his father, mother, eldest sister (full-fledged member of society), and next older sister (college student), Nao-chan has a family of five.

← To be continued

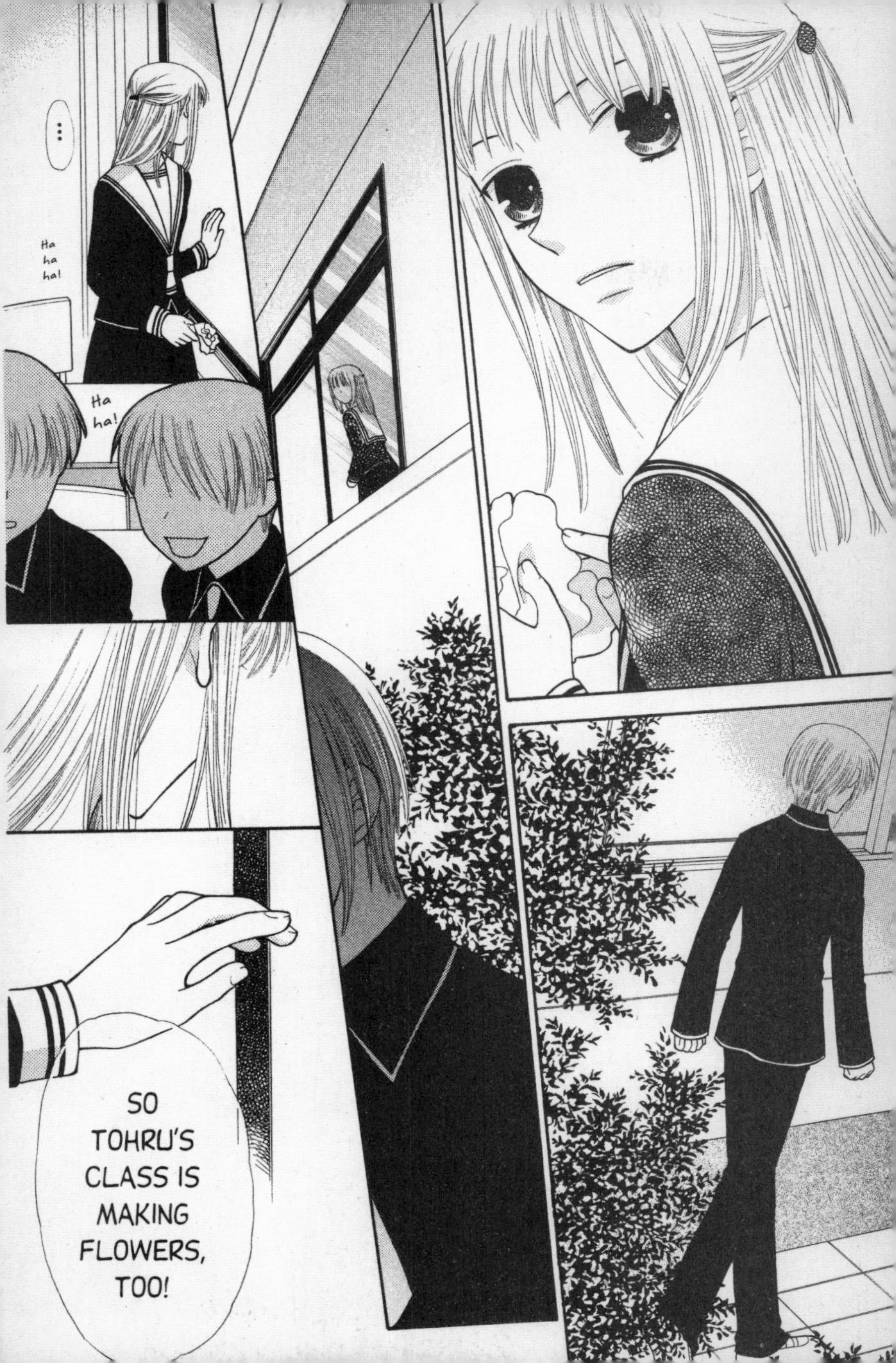
...
Ha ha ha!
Ha ha!
SO TOHRU'S CLASS IS MAKING FLOWERS, TOO!

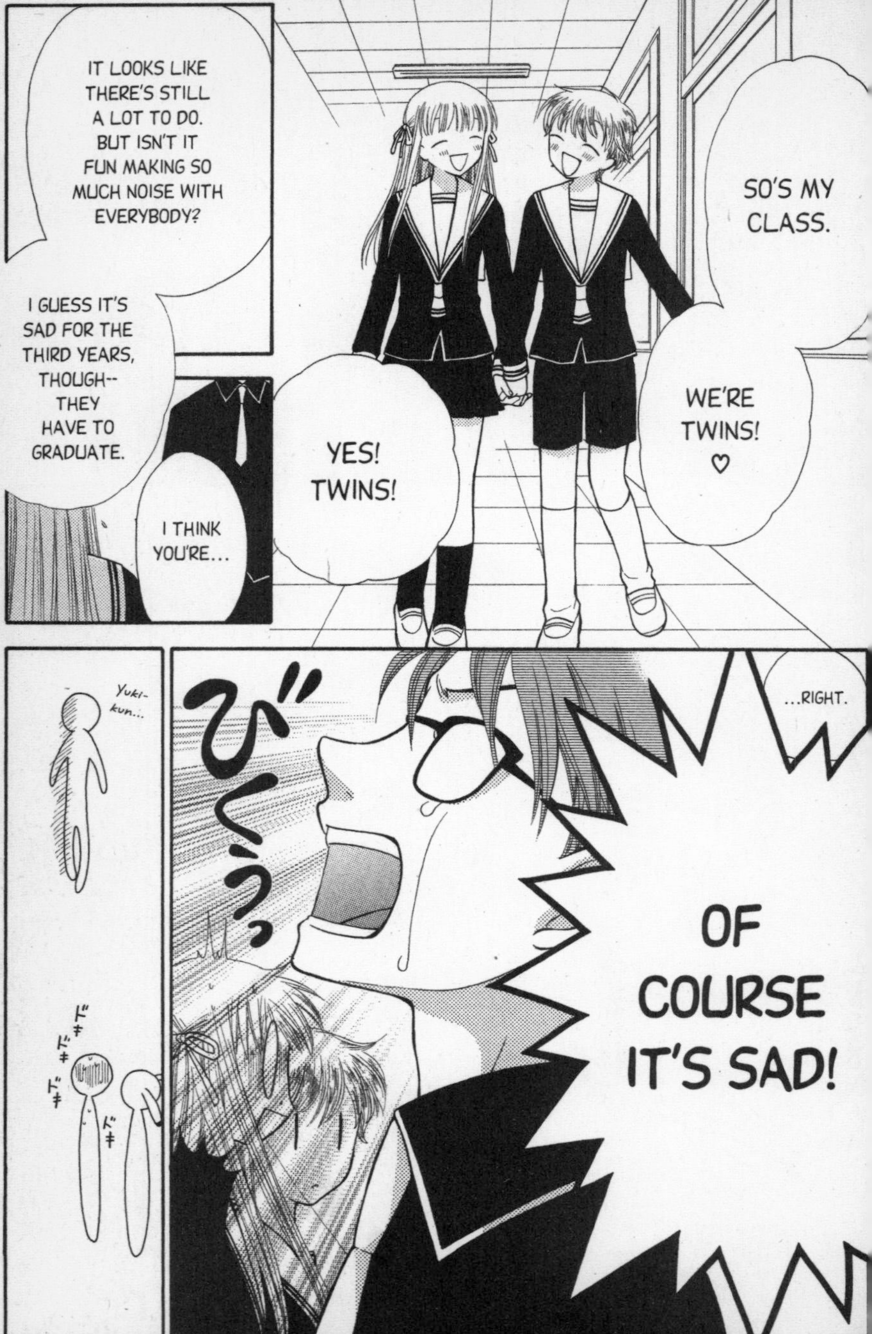
SO'S MY CLASS.
WE'RE TWINS! ♡
YES! TWINS!
IT LOOKS LIKE THERE'S STILL A LOT TO DO. BUT ISN'T IT FUN MAKING SO MUCH NOISE WITH EVERYBODY?
I GUESS IT'S SAD FOR THE THIRD YEARS, THOUGH-- THEY HAVE TO GRADUATE.
I THINK YOU'RE...
...RIGHT.
びくぅっ
OF COURSE IT'S SAD!
Yuki-kun...
ドキ ドキ
ドキ ドキ

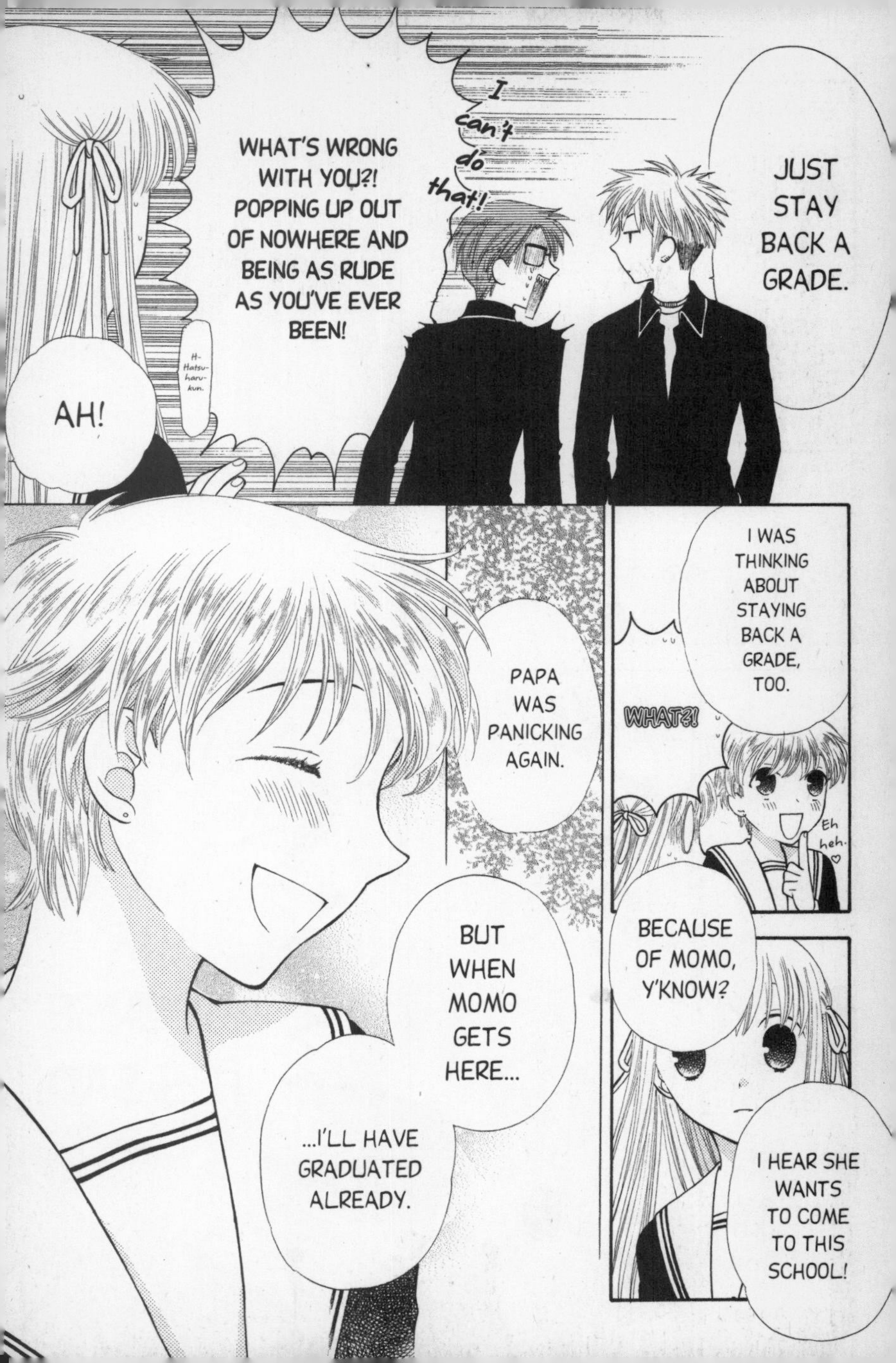
JUST STAY BACK A GRADE.
I can't do that!
WHAT'S WRONG WITH YOU?! POPPING UP OUT OF NOWHERE AND BEING AS RUDE AS YOU'VE EVER BEEN!
H-Hatsuharu-kun.
AH!
I WAS THINKING ABOUT STAYING BACK A GRADE, TOO.
WHAT?!
Eh heh.
BECAUSE OF MOMO, Y'KNOW?
I HEAR SHE WANTS TO COME TO THIS SCHOOL!
PAPA WAS PANICKING AGAIN.
BUT WHEN MOMO GETS HERE...
...I'LL HAVE GRADUATED ALREADY.

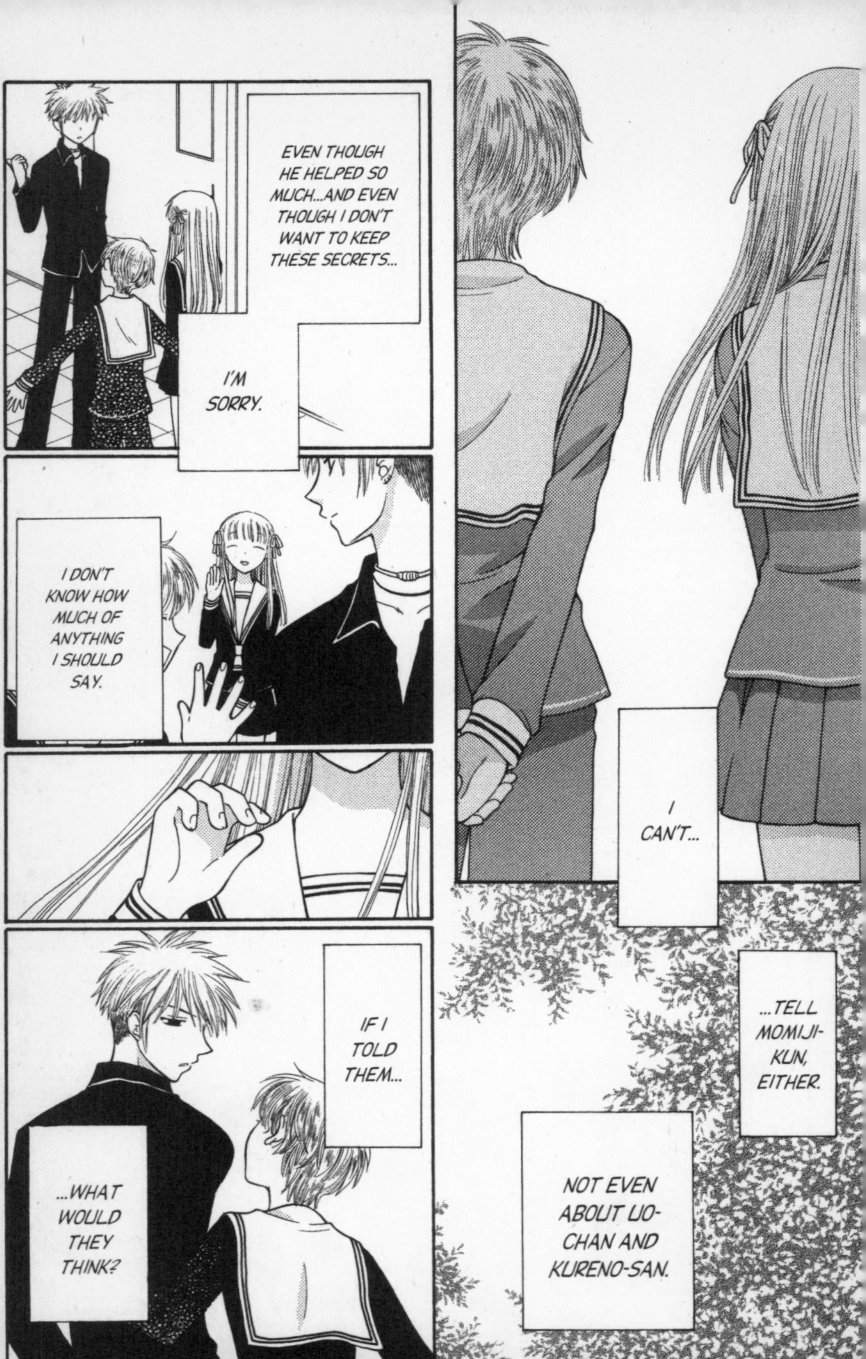
I CAN'T...
...TELL MOMIJI-KUN, EITHER.
NOT EVEN ABOUT UO-CHAN AND KURENO-SAN.
EVEN THOUGH HE HELPED SO MUCH...AND EVEN THOUGH I DON'T WANT TO KEEP THESE SECRETS...
I'M SORRY.
I DON'T KNOW HOW MUCH OF ANYTHING I SHOULD SAY.
IF I TOLD THEM...
...WHAT WOULD THEY THINK?

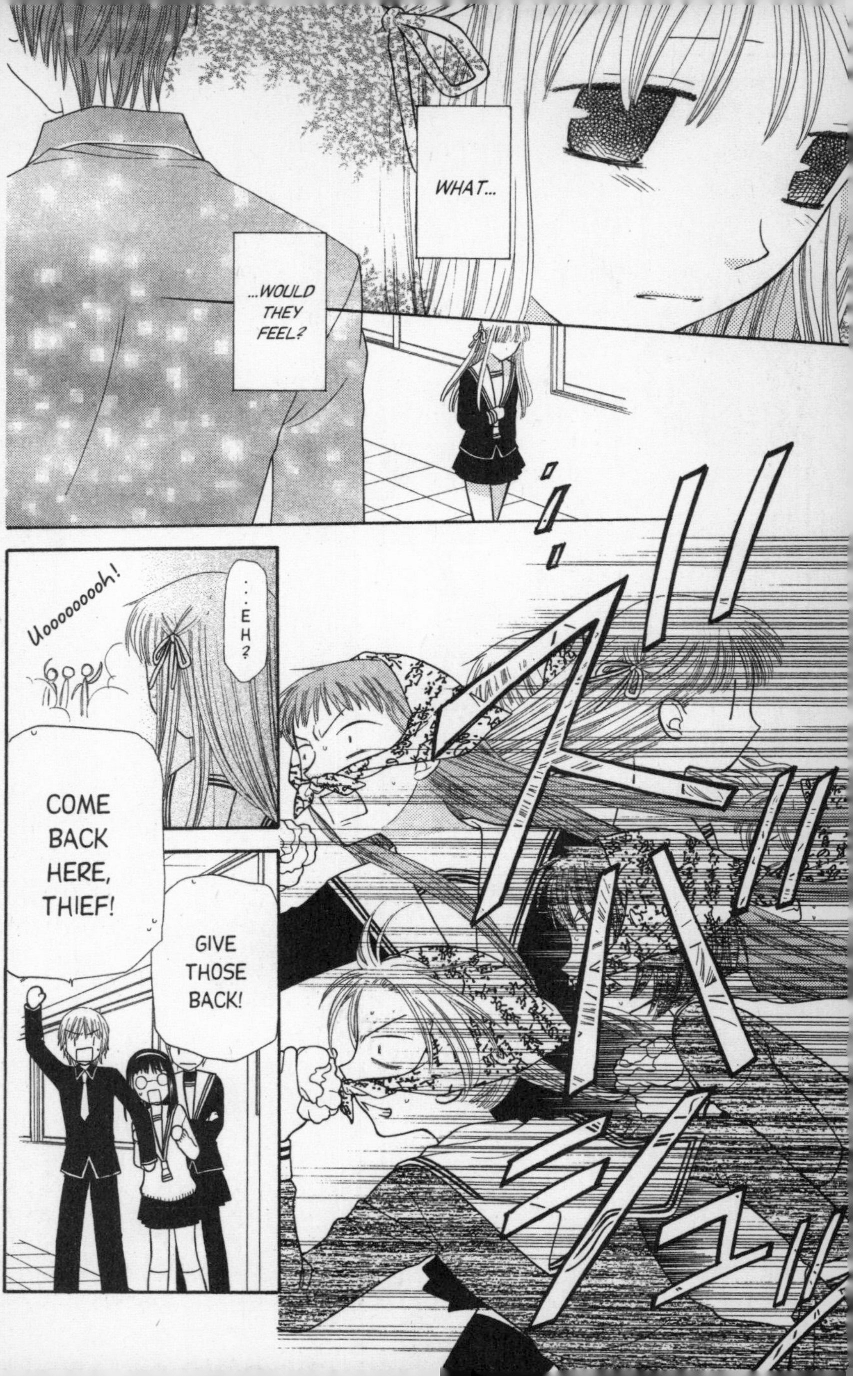
WHAT...
...WOULD THEY FEEL?
...EH?
Uoooooooh!
COME BACK HERE, THIEF!
GIVE THOSE BACK!

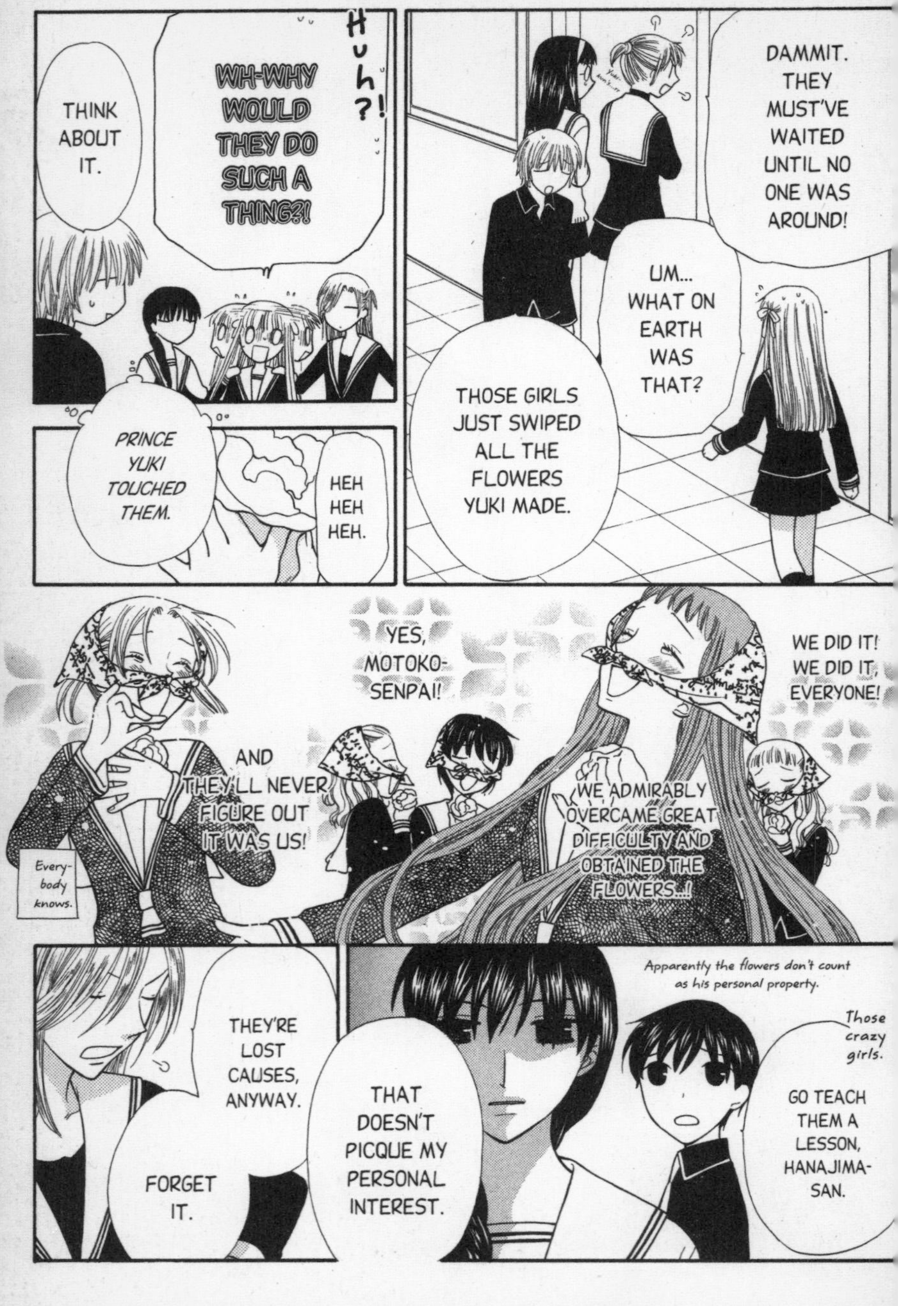

DAMMIT. THEY MUST'VE WAITED UNTIL NO ONE WAS AROUND!
UM... WHAT ON EARTH WAS THAT?
THOSE GIRLS JUST SWIPED ALL THE FLOWERS YUKI MADE.
Huh?!
WH-WHY WOULD THEY DO SUCH A THING?!
THINK ABOUT IT.
HEH HEH HEH.
PRINCE YUKI TOUCHED THEM.
WE DID IT! WE DID IT, EVERYONE!
WE ADMIRABLY OVERCAME GREAT DIFFICULTY AND OBTAINED THE FLOWERS...!
YES, MOTOKO-SENPAI!
AND THEY'LL NEVER FIGURE OUT IT WAS US!
Every-body knows.
Apparently the flowers don't count as his personal property.
Those crazy girls.
GO TEACH THEM A LESSON, HANAJIMA-SAN.
THAT DOESN'T PICQUE MY PERSONAL INTEREST.
THEY'RE LOST CAUSES, ANYWAY.
FORGET IT.

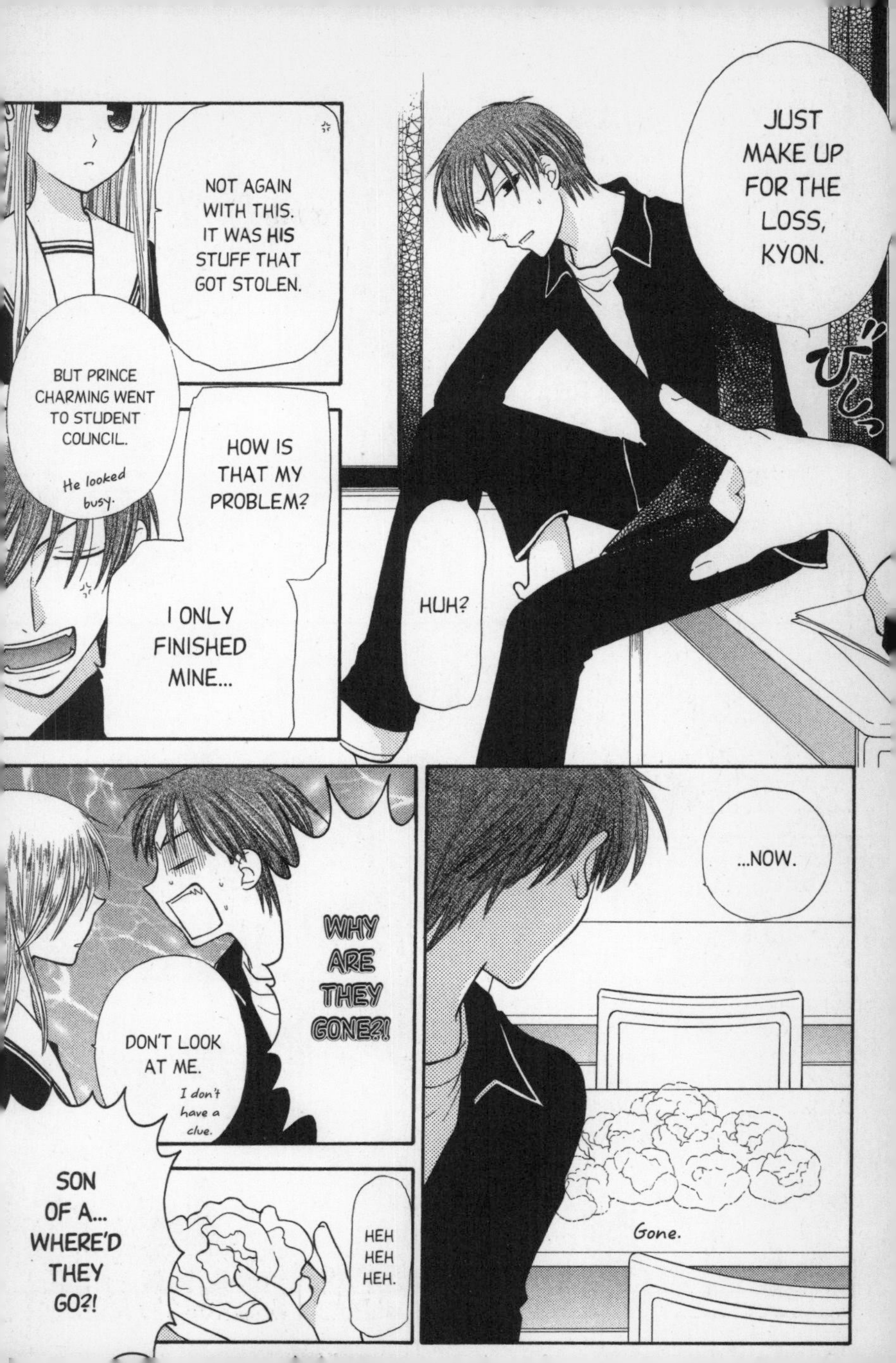
JUST MAKE UP FOR THE LOSS, KYON.
びしっ
HUH?
NOT AGAIN WITH THIS. IT WAS HIS STUFF THAT GOT STOLEN.
BUT PRINCE CHARMING WENT TO STUDENT COUNCIL.
He looked busy.
HOW IS THAT MY PROBLEM?
I ONLY FINISHED MINE...
...NOW.
Gone.
WHY ARE THEY GONE?!
DON'T LOOK AT ME.
I don't have a clue.
HEH HEH HEH.
SON OF A... WHERE'D THEY GO?!

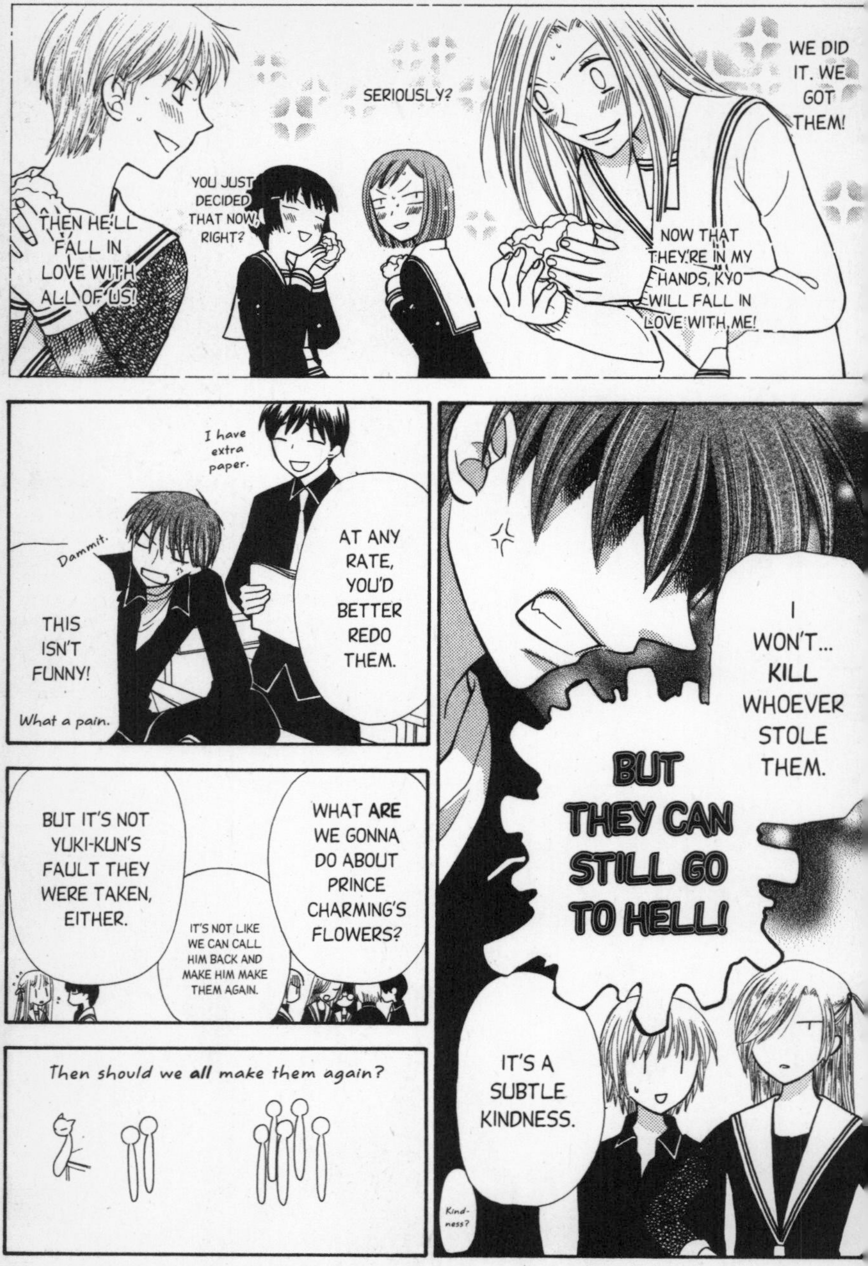
WE DID IT. WE GOT THEM!
NOW THAT THEY'RE IN MY HANDS, KYO WILL FALL IN LOVE WITH ME!
SERIOUSLY?
YOU JUST DECIDED THAT NOW, RIGHT?
THEN HE'LL FALL IN LOVE WITH ALL OF US!
I WON'T... KILL WHOEVER STOLE THEM.
BUT THEY CAN STILL GO TO HELL!
IT'S A SUBTLE KINDNESS.
Kind-ness?
I have extra paper.
AT ANY RATE, YOU'D BETTER REDO THEM.
Dammit.
THIS ISN'T FUNNY!
What a pain.
WHAT ARE WE GONNA DO ABOUT PRINCE CHARMING'S FLOWERS?
BUT IT'S NOT YUKI-KUN'S FAULT THEY WERE TAKEN, EITHER.
IT'S NOT LIKE WE CAN CALL HIM BACK AND MAKE HIM MAKE THEM AGAIN.
Then should we all make them again?

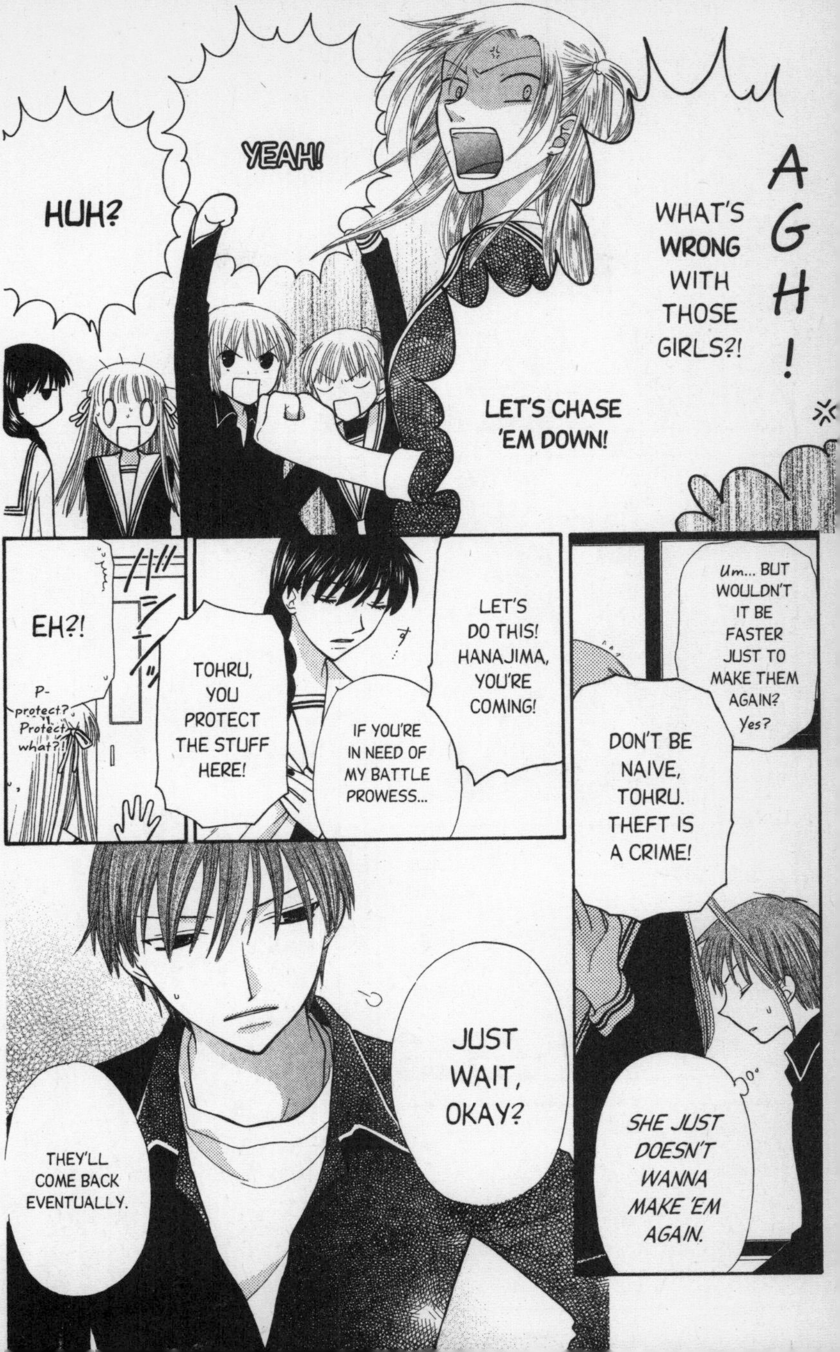
AGH!
WHAT'S WRONG WITH THOSE GIRLS?!
LET'S CHASE 'EM DOWN!
YEAH!
HUH?
Um... BUT WOULDN'T IT BE FASTER JUST TO MAKE THEM AGAIN? Yes?
DON'T BE NAIVE, TOHRU. THEFT IS A CRIME!
SHE JUST DOESN'T WANNA MAKE 'EM AGAIN.
LET'S DO THIS! HANAJIMA, YOU'RE COMING!
IF YOU'RE IN NEED OF MY BATTLE PROWESS...
TOHRU, YOU PROTECT THE STUFF HERE!
EH?!
P-protect? Protect what?!
JUST WAIT, OKAY?
THEY'LL COME BACK EVENTUALLY.

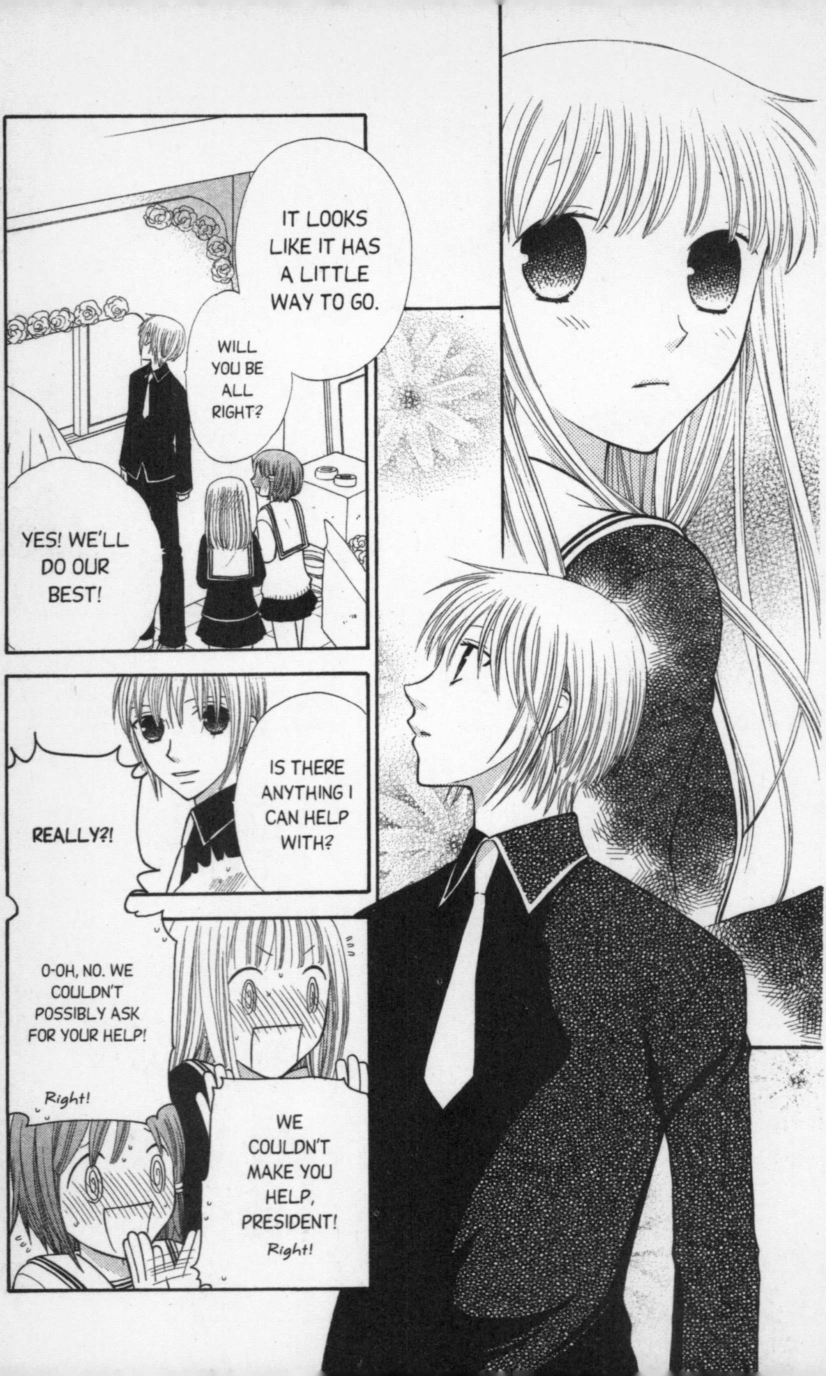
IT LOOKS LIKE IT HAS A LITTLE WAY TO GO.
WILL YOU BE ALL RIGHT?
YES! WE'LL DO OUR BEST!
IS THERE ANYTHING I CAN HELP WITH?
REALLY?!
O-OH, NO. WE COULDN'T POSSIBLY ASK FOR YOUR HELP!
WE COULDN'T MAKE YOU HELP, PRESIDENT!
Right!
Right!

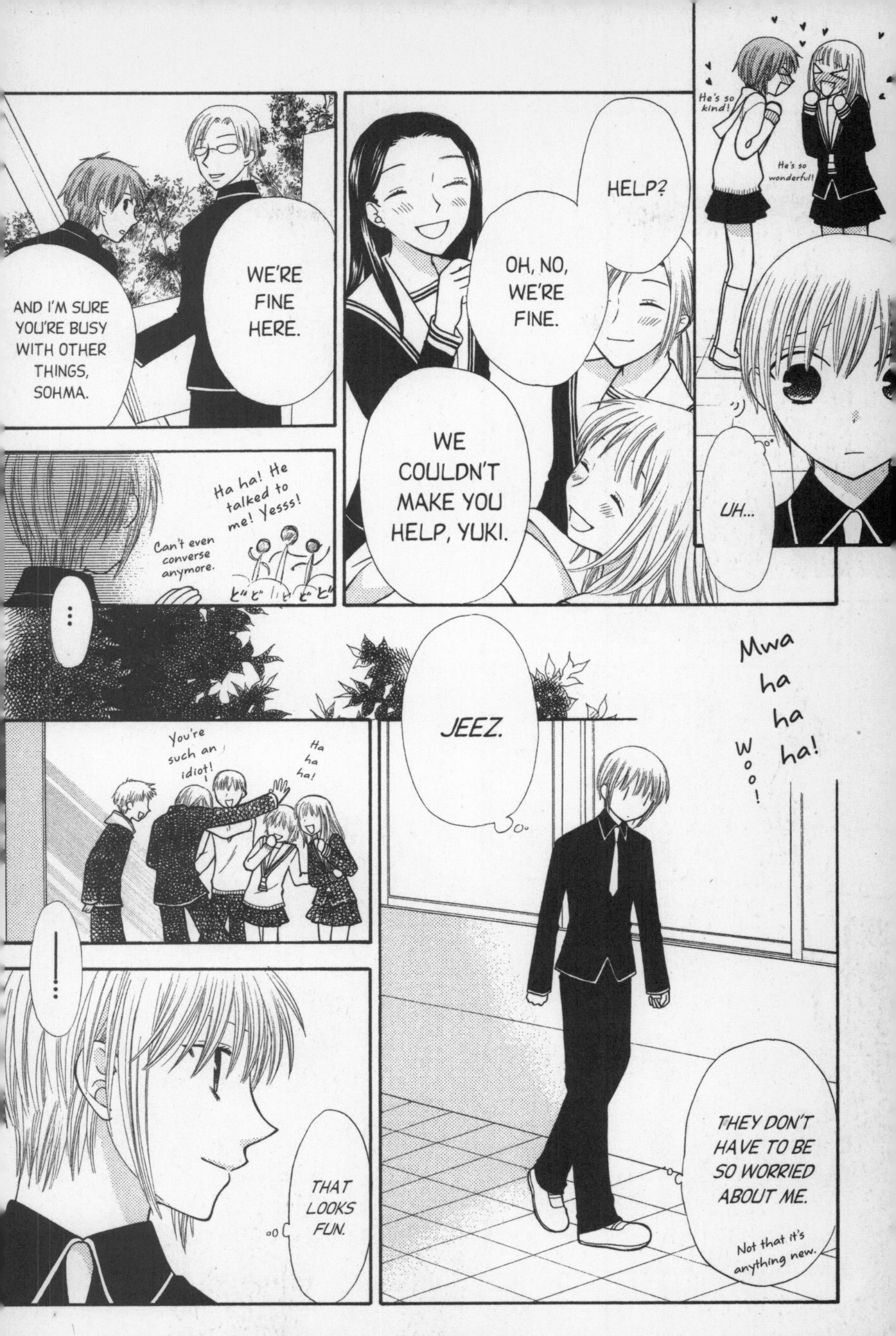
He's so kind!
He's so wonderful!
UH...
HELP?
OH, NO, WE'RE FINE.
WE COULDN'T MAKE YOU HELP, YUKI.
WE'RE FINE HERE.
AND I'M SURE YOU'RE BUSY WITH OTHER THINGS, SOHMA.
Ha ha! He talked to me! Yesss!
Can't even converse anymore.
...
Mwa ha ha ha!
Woo!
JEEZ.
THEY DON'T HAVE TO BE SO WORRIED ABOUT ME.
Not that it's anything new.
You're such an idiot!
Ha ha ha!
...!
THAT LOOKS FUN.

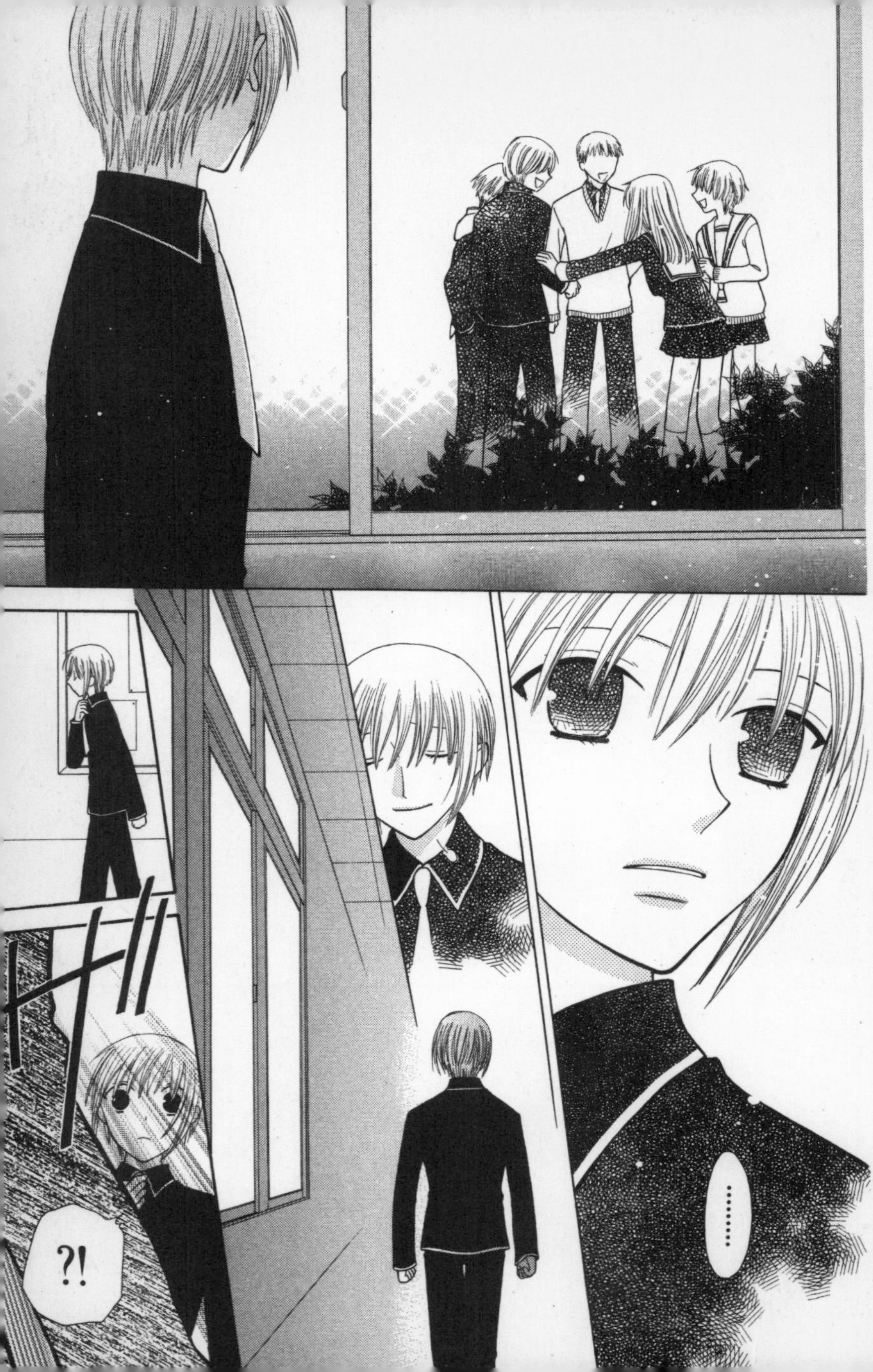

......
?!

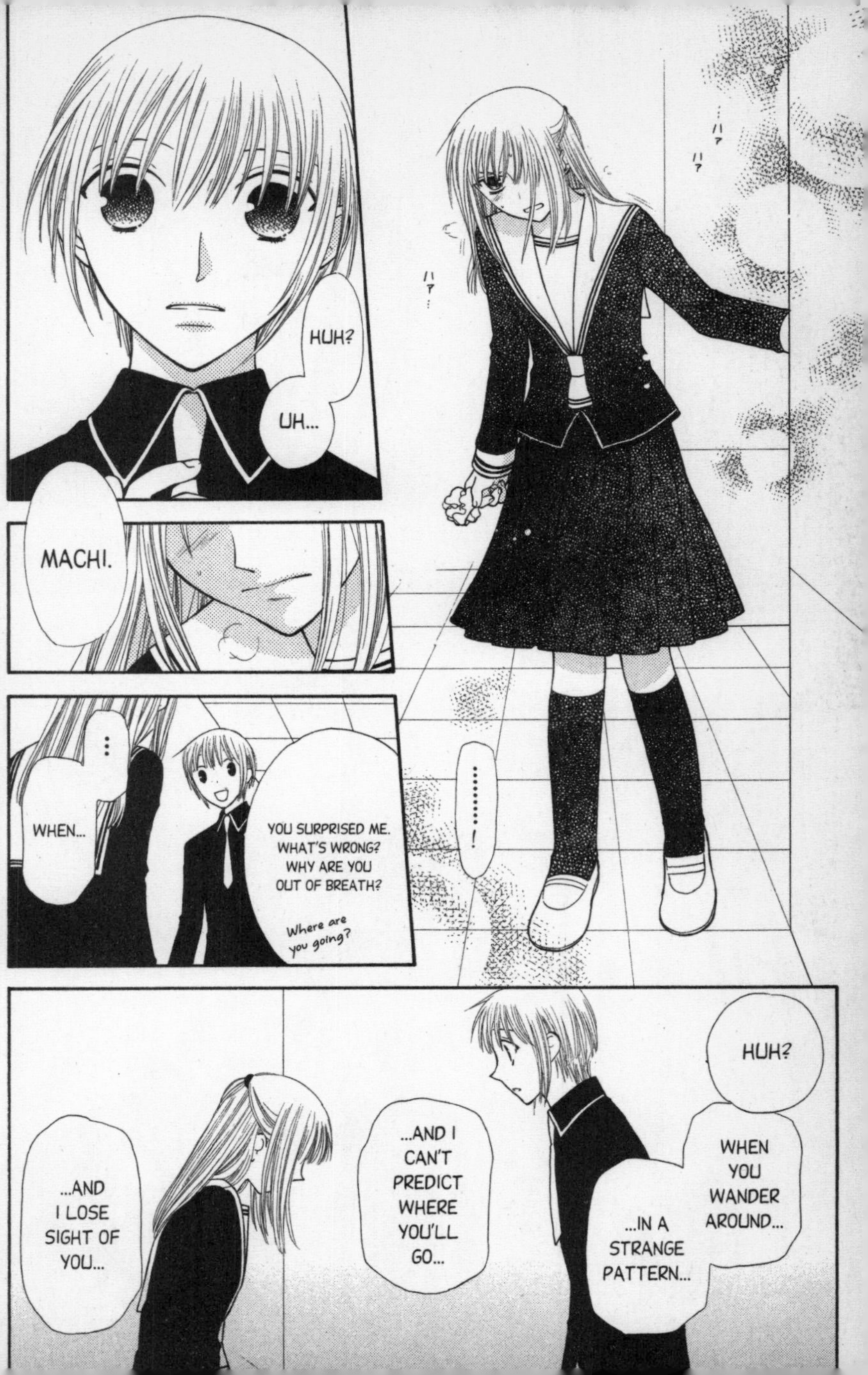

…ハァ
ハァ
ハァ…
........!
HUH?
UH...
MACHI.
YOU SURPRISED ME. WHAT'S WRONG? WHY ARE YOU OUT OF BREATH?
Where are you going?
...
WHEN...
HUH?
WHEN YOU WANDER AROUND...
...IN A STRANGE PATTERN...
...AND I CAN'T PREDICT WHERE YOU'LL GO...
...AND I LOSE SIGHT OF YOU...

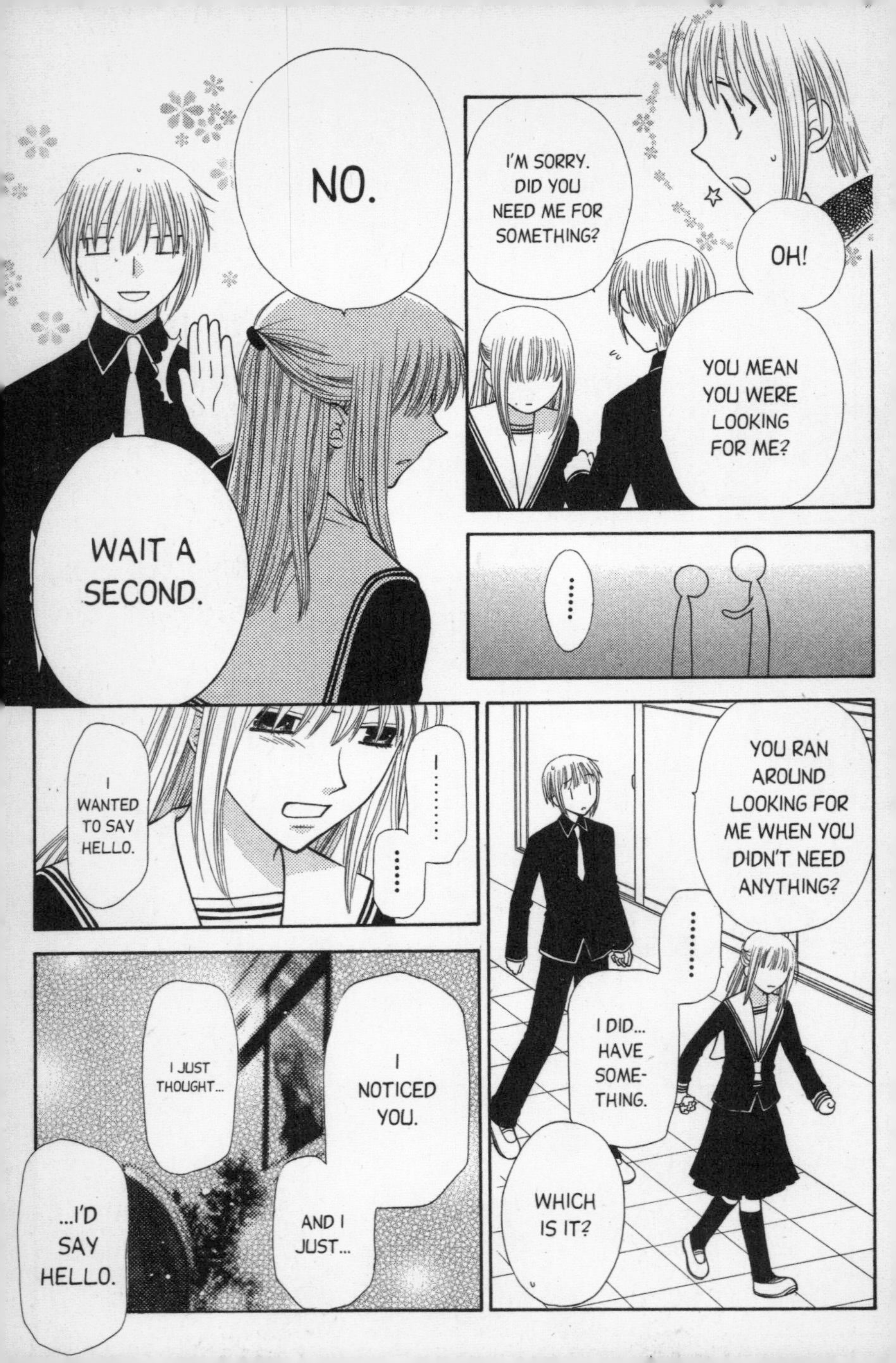
OH!
YOU MEAN YOU WERE LOOKING FOR ME?
I'M SORRY. DID YOU NEED ME FOR SOMETHING?
......
NO.
WAIT A SECOND.
YOU RAN AROUND LOOKING FOR ME WHEN YOU DIDN'T NEED ANYTHING?
......
I DID... HAVE SOME-THING.
WHICH IS IT?
I......
......
I WANTED TO SAY HELLO.
I NOTICED YOU.
AND I JUST...
I JUST THOUGHT...
...I'D SAY HELLO.

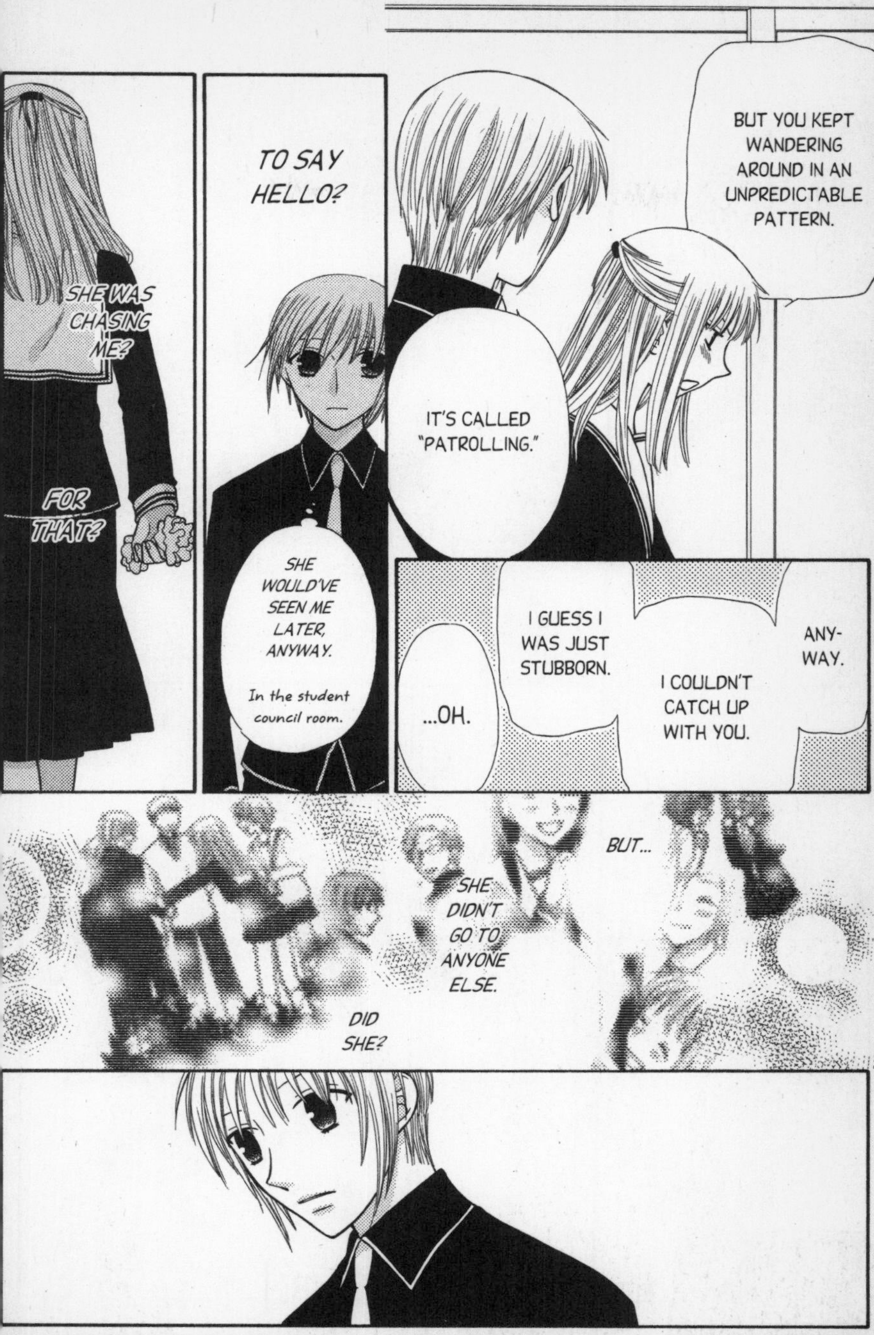

BUT YOU KEPT WANDERING AROUND IN AN UNPREDICTABLE PATTERN.
IT'S CALLED "PATROLLING."
ANY-WAY.
I COULDN'T CATCH UP WITH YOU.
I GUESS I WAS JUST STUBBORN.
...OH.
TO SAY HELLO?
SHE WOULD'VE SEEN ME LATER, ANYWAY.
In the student council room.
SHE WAS CHASING ME?
FOR THAT?
BUT...
SHE DIDN'T GO TO ANYONE ELSE.
DID SHE?

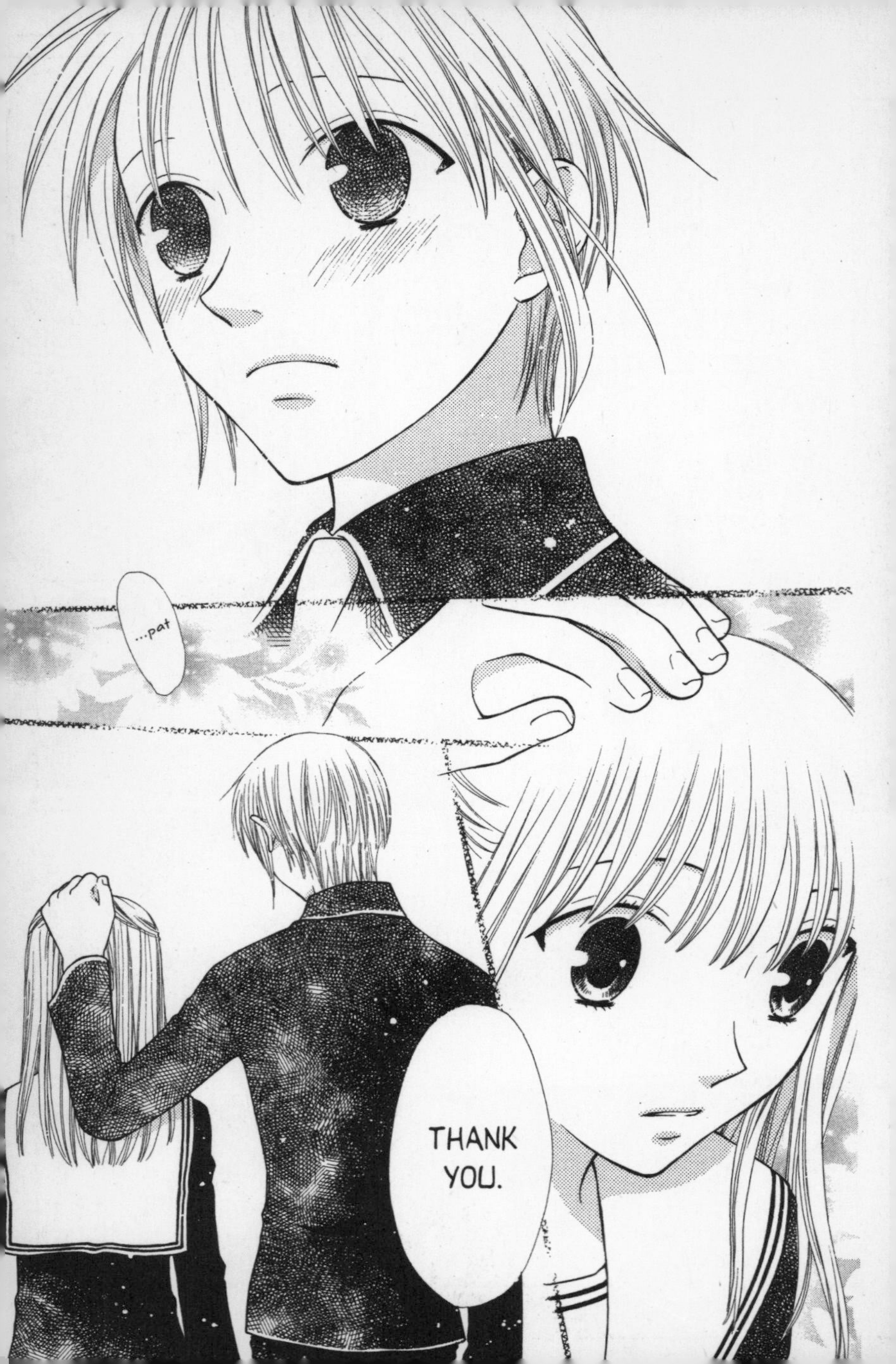
...pat
THANK YOU.

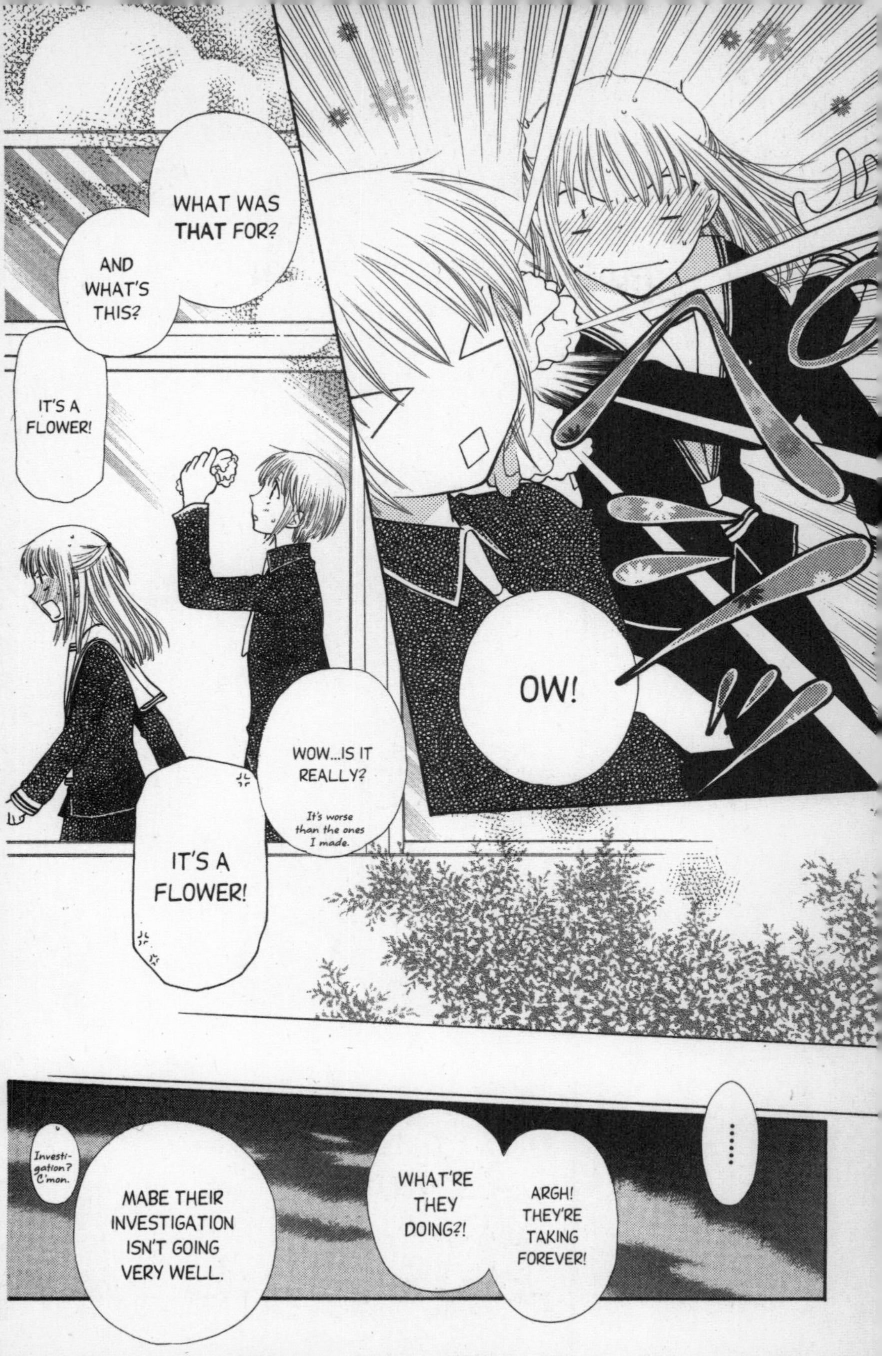
OW!
WHAT WAS THAT FOR?
AND WHAT'S THIS?
IT'S A FLOWER!
WOW...IS IT REALLY?
It's worse than the ones I made.
IT'S A FLOWER!
......
ARGH! THEY'RE TAKING FOREVER!
WHAT'RE THEY DOING?!
MABE THEIR INVESTIGATION ISN'T GOING VERY WELL.
Investigation? C'mon.

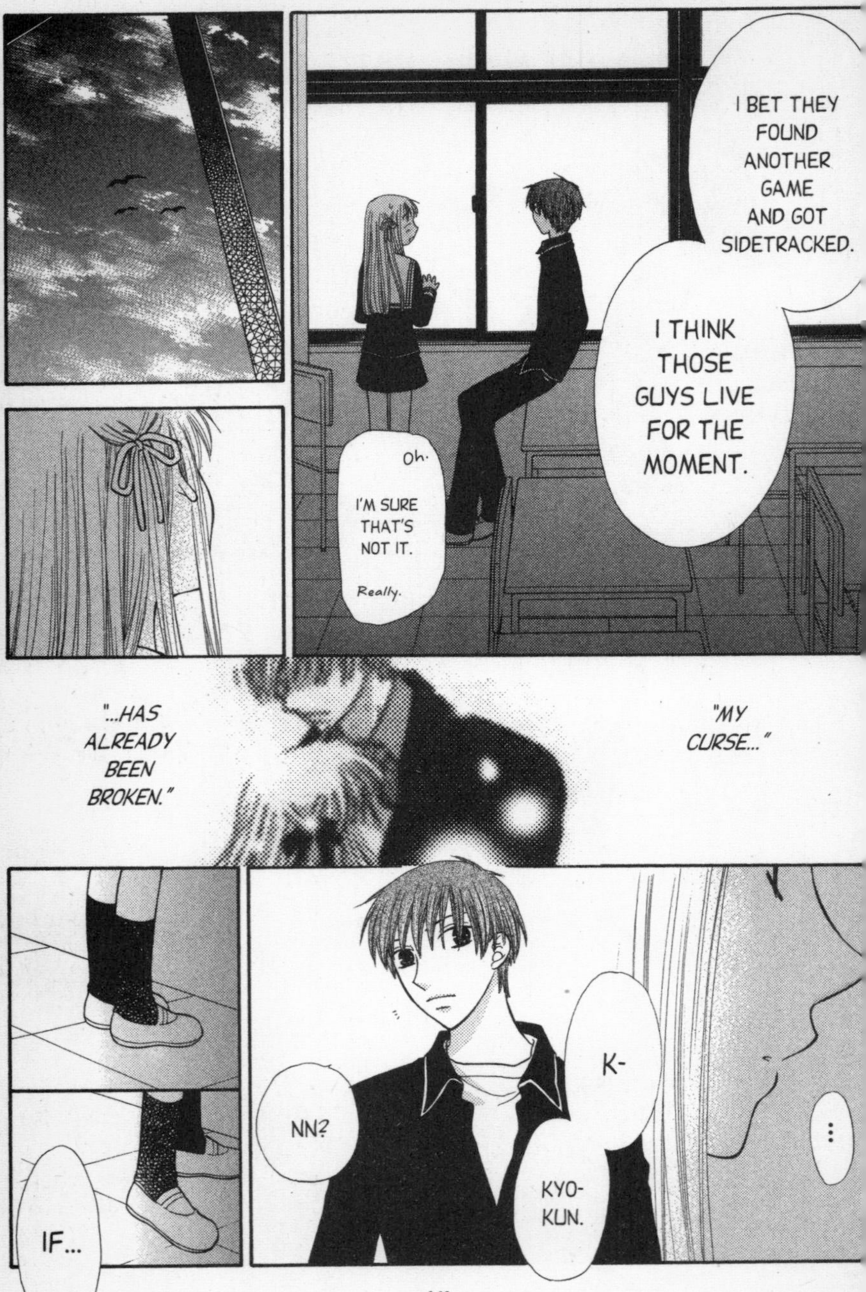
I BET THEY FOUND ANOTHER GAME AND GOT SIDETRACKED.
I THINK THOSE GUYS LIVE FOR THE MOMENT.
Oh.
I'M SURE THAT'S NOT IT.
Really.
"MY CURSE..."
"...HAS ALREADY BEEN BROKEN."
...
K-
KYO-KUN.
NN?
IF...

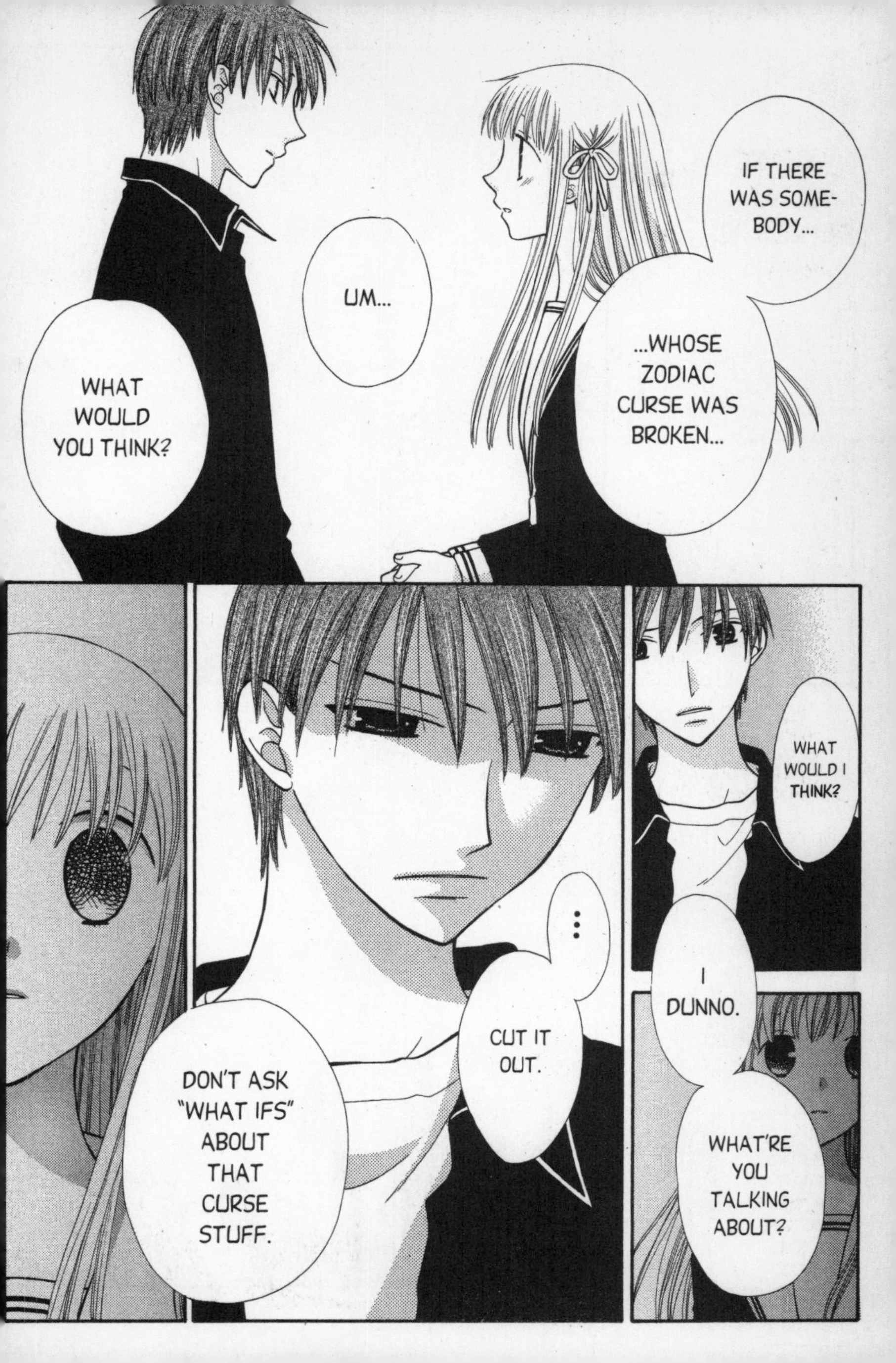
IF THERE WAS SOME-BODY...
...WHOSE ZODIAC CURSE WAS BROKEN...
UM...
WHAT WOULD YOU THINK?
WHAT WOULD I THINK?
I DUNNO.
WHAT'RE YOU TALKING ABOUT?
...
CUT IT OUT.
DON'T ASK "WHAT IFS" ABOUT THAT CURSE STUFF.

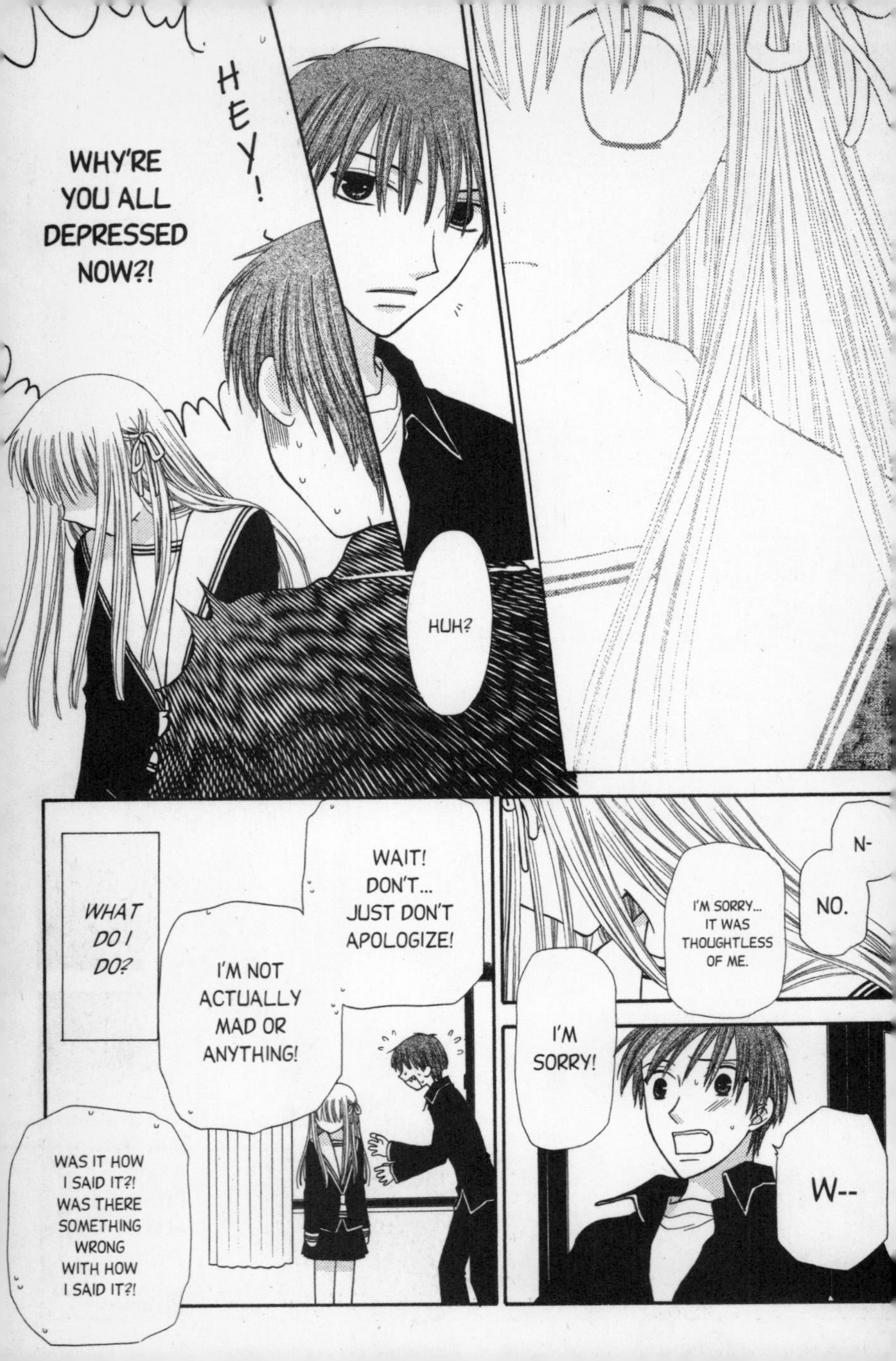
HUH?
HEY!
WHY'RE YOU ALL DEPRESSED NOW?!
N- NO.
I'M SORRY... IT WAS THOUGHTLESS OF ME.
W--
I'M SORRY!
WHAT DO I DO?
WAIT! DON'T... JUST DON'T APOLOGIZE!
I'M NOT ACTUALLY MAD OR ANYTHING!
WAS IT HOW I SAID IT?! WAS THERE SOMETHING WRONG WITH HOW I SAID IT?!

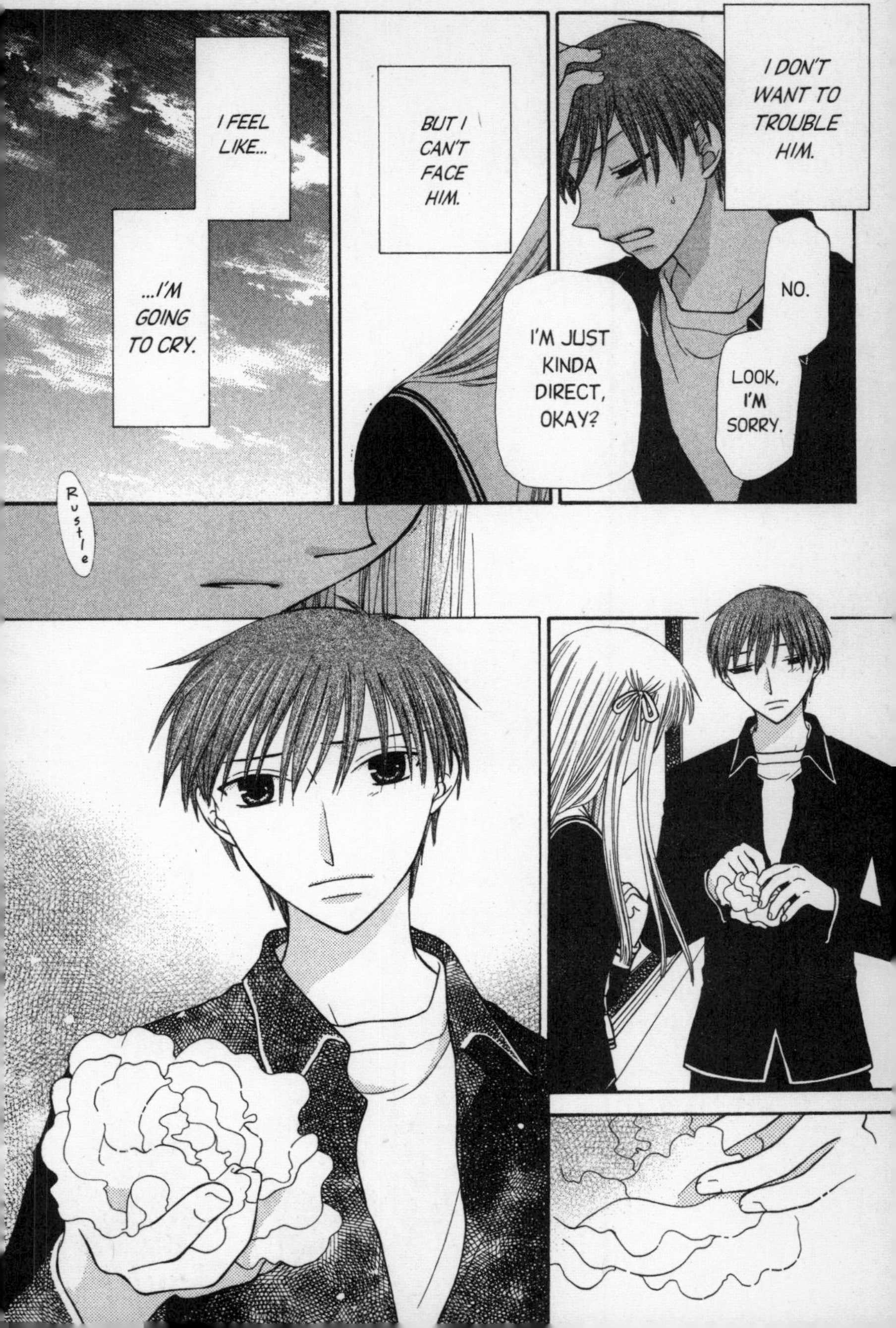
I DON'T WANT TO TROUBLE HIM.
NO.
LOOK, I'M SORRY.
I'M JUST KINDA DIRECT, OKAY?
BUT I CAN'T FACE HIM.
I FEEL LIKE...
...I'M GOING TO CRY.
Rustle

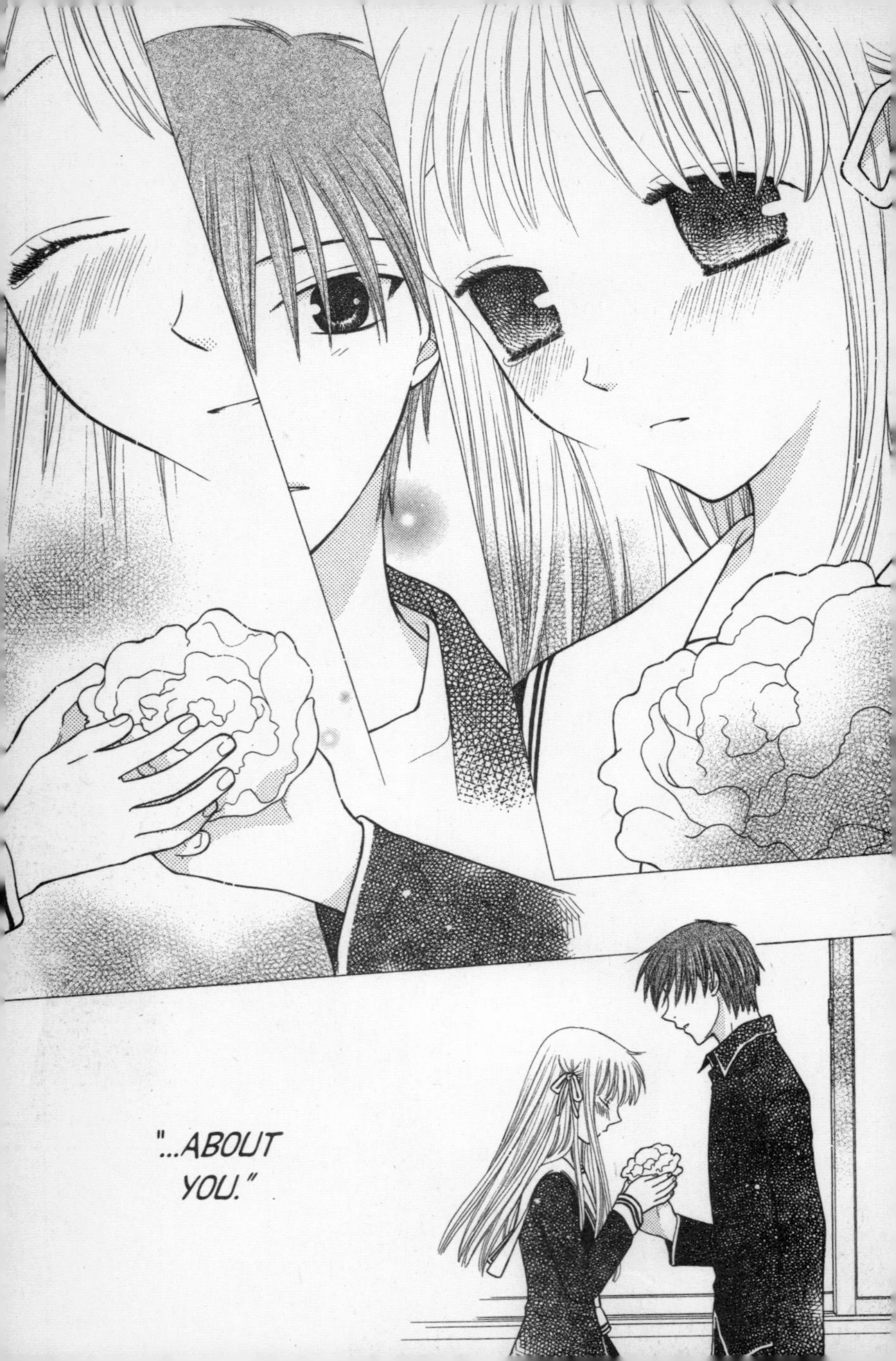
"...ABOUT YOU."

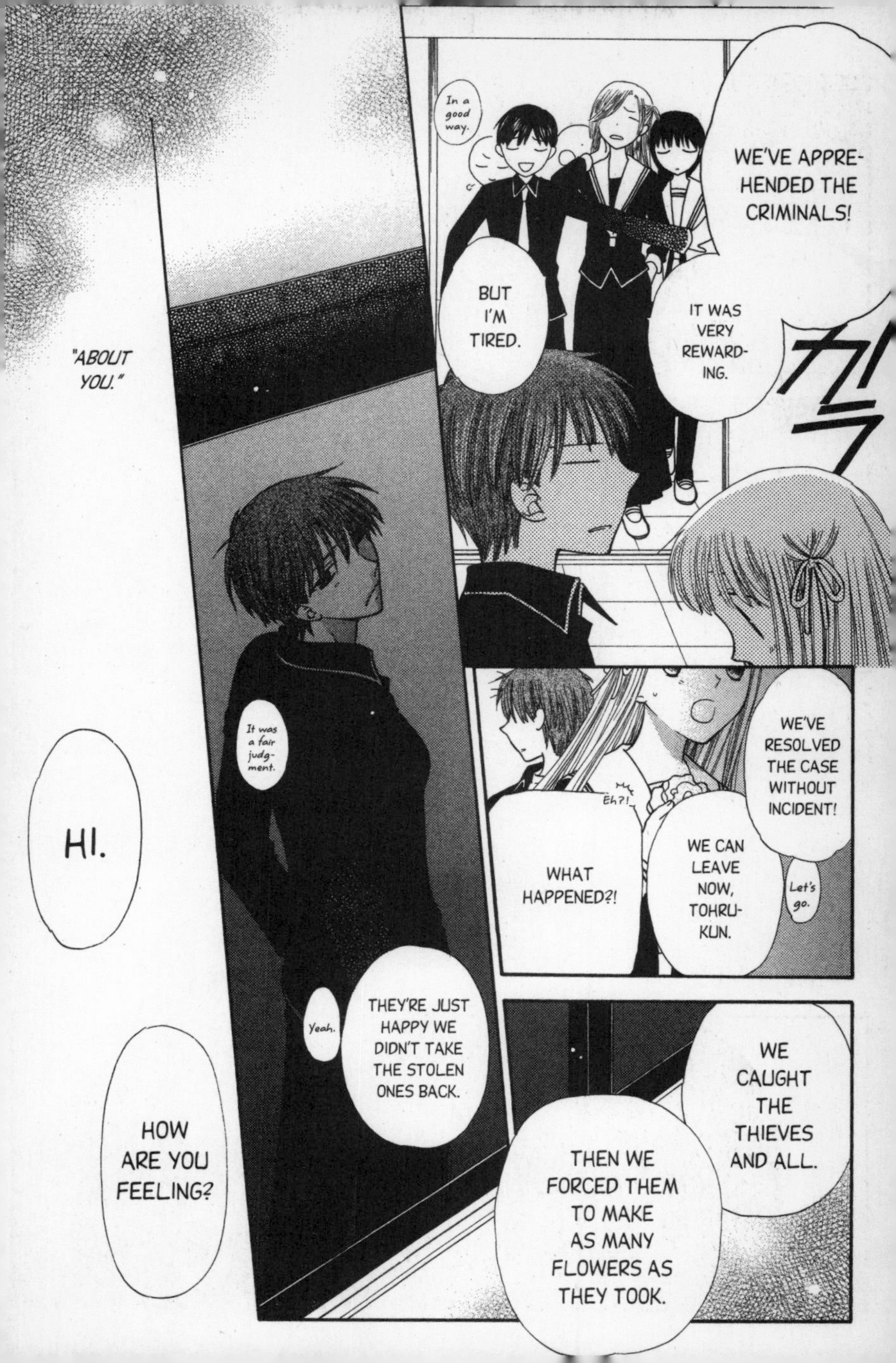

カラ
WE'VE APPREHENDED THE CRIMINALS!
IT WAS VERY REWARDING.
BUT I'M TIRED.
In a good way.
WE'VE RESOLVED THE CASE WITHOUT INCIDENT!
Let's go.
WE CAN LEAVE NOW, TOHRU-KUN.
Eh?!
WHAT HAPPENED?!
WE CAUGHT THE THIEVES AND ALL.
THEN WE FORCED THEM TO MAKE AS MANY FLOWERS AS THEY TOOK.
THEY'RE JUST HAPPY WE DIDN'T TAKE THE STOLEN ONES BACK.
Yeah.
It was a fair judgment.
"ABOUT YOU."
HI.
HOW ARE YOU FEELING?

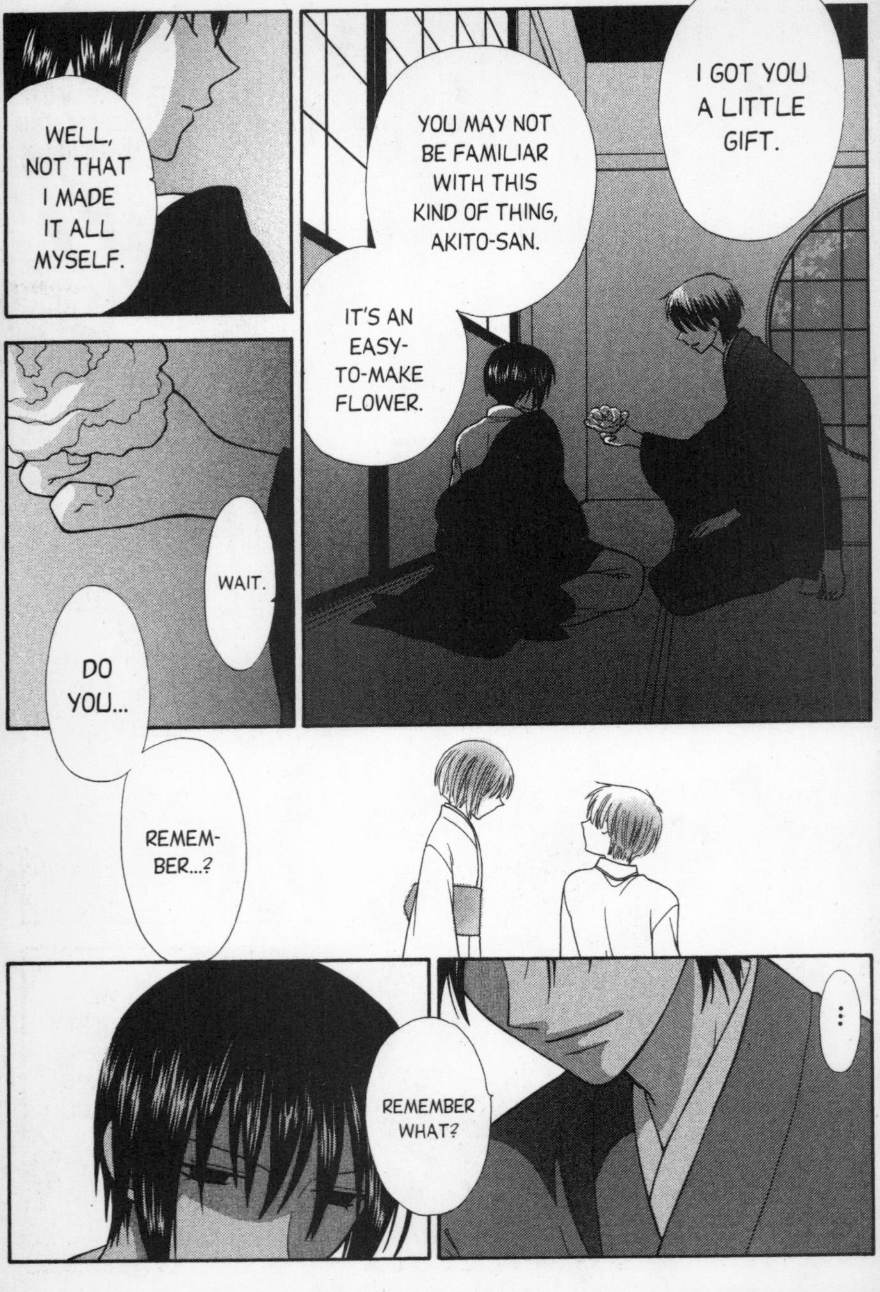
I GOT YOU A LITTLE GIFT.
YOU MAY NOT BE FAMILIAR WITH THIS KIND OF THING, AKITO-SAN.
IT'S AN EASY-TO-MAKE FLOWER.
WELL, NOT THAT I MADE IT ALL MYSELF.
WAIT.
DO YOU...
REMEMBER...?
...
REMEMBER WHAT?

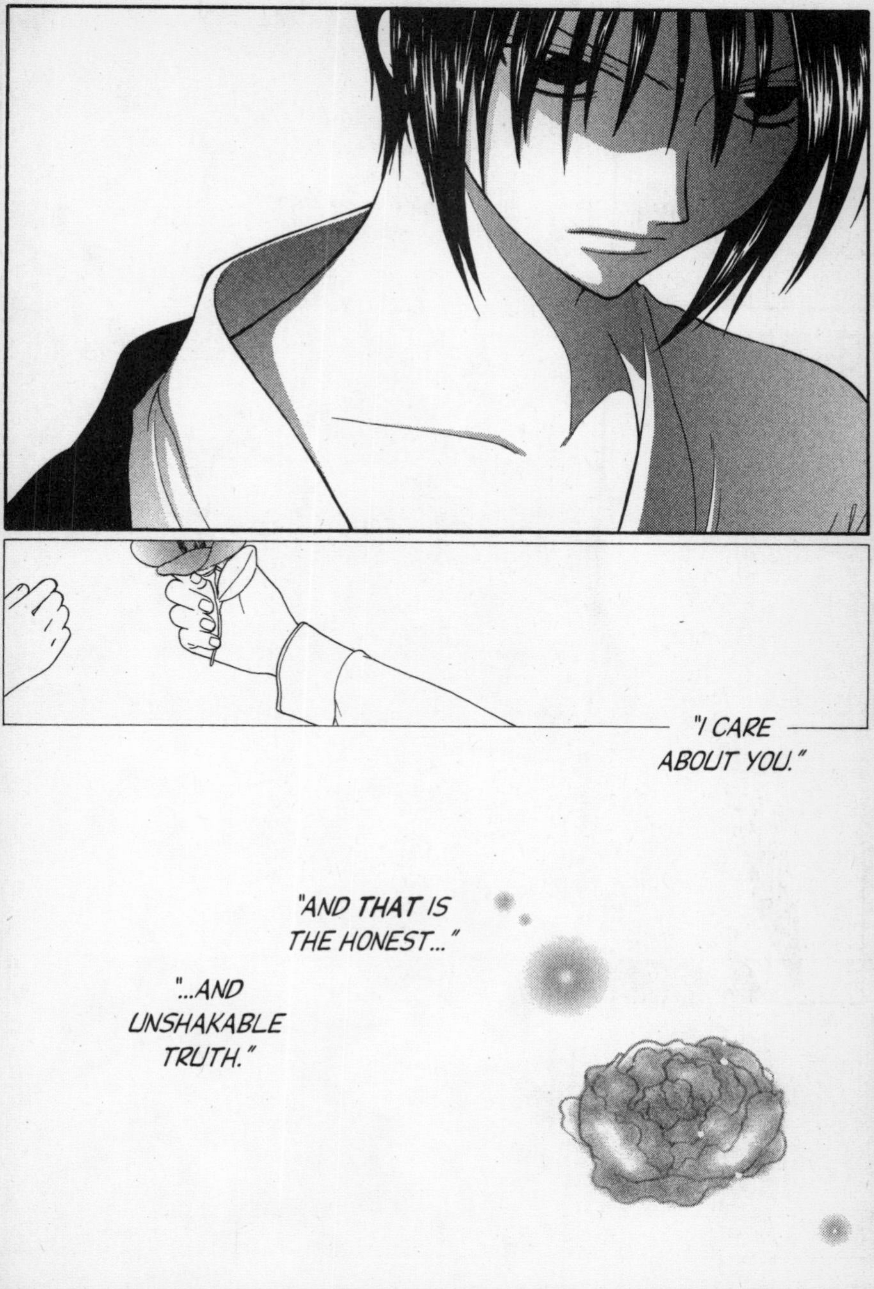
"I CARE ABOUT YOU."
"AND THAT IS THE HONEST..."
"...AND UNSHAKABLE TRUTH."

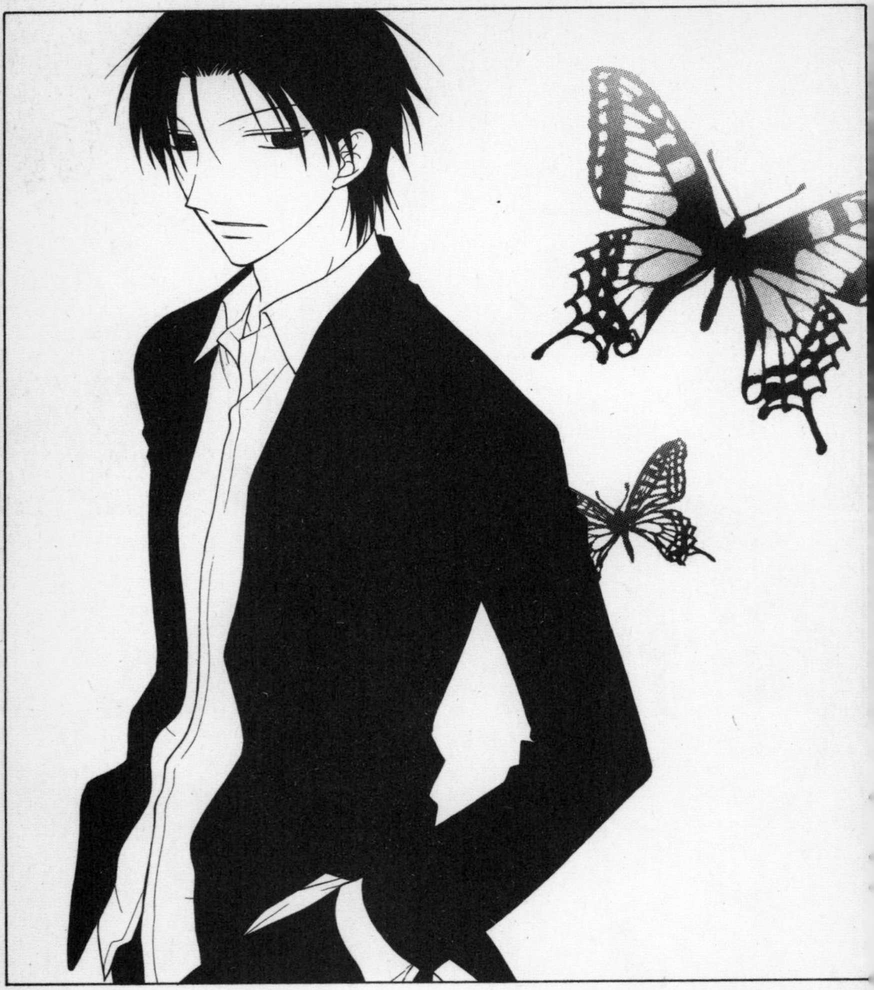

Chapter 101

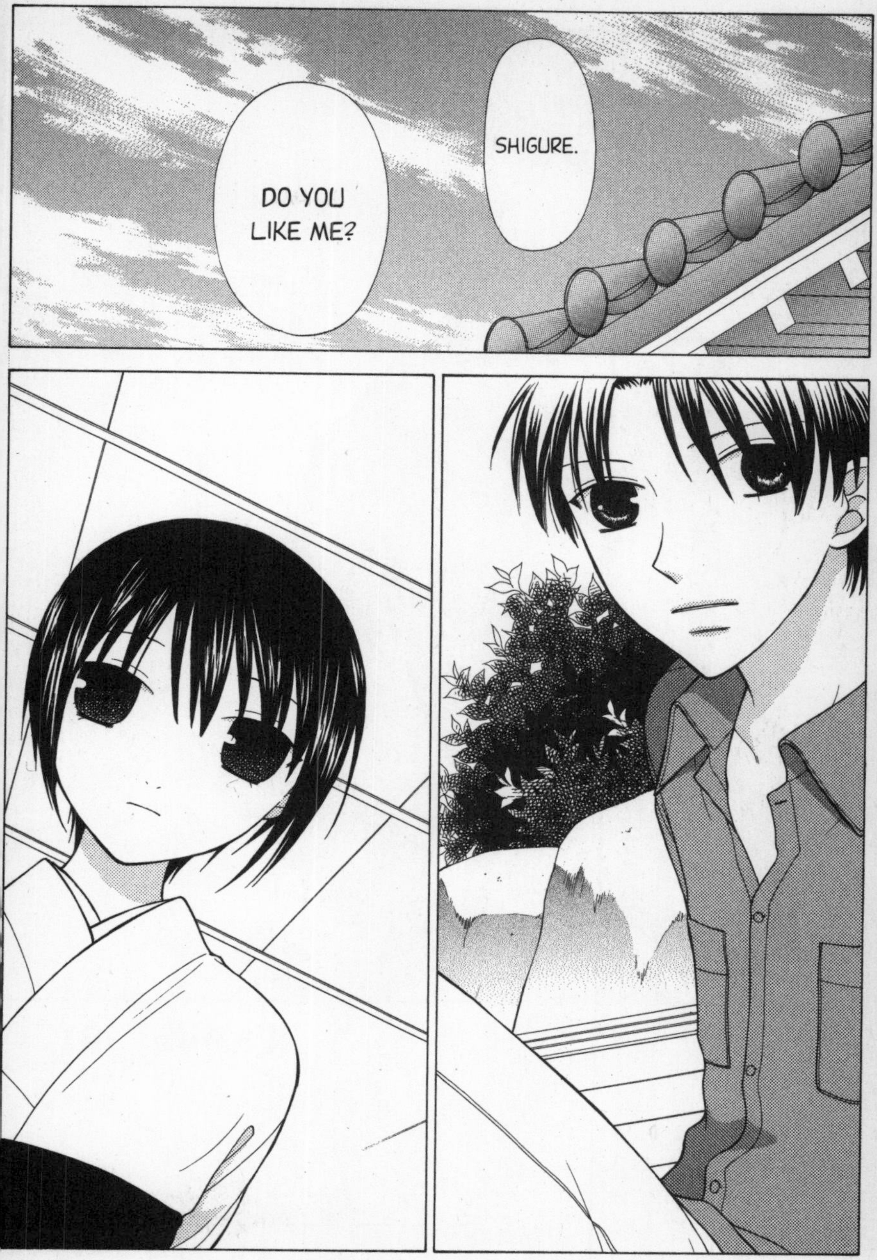
SHIGURE.
DO YOU LIKE ME?

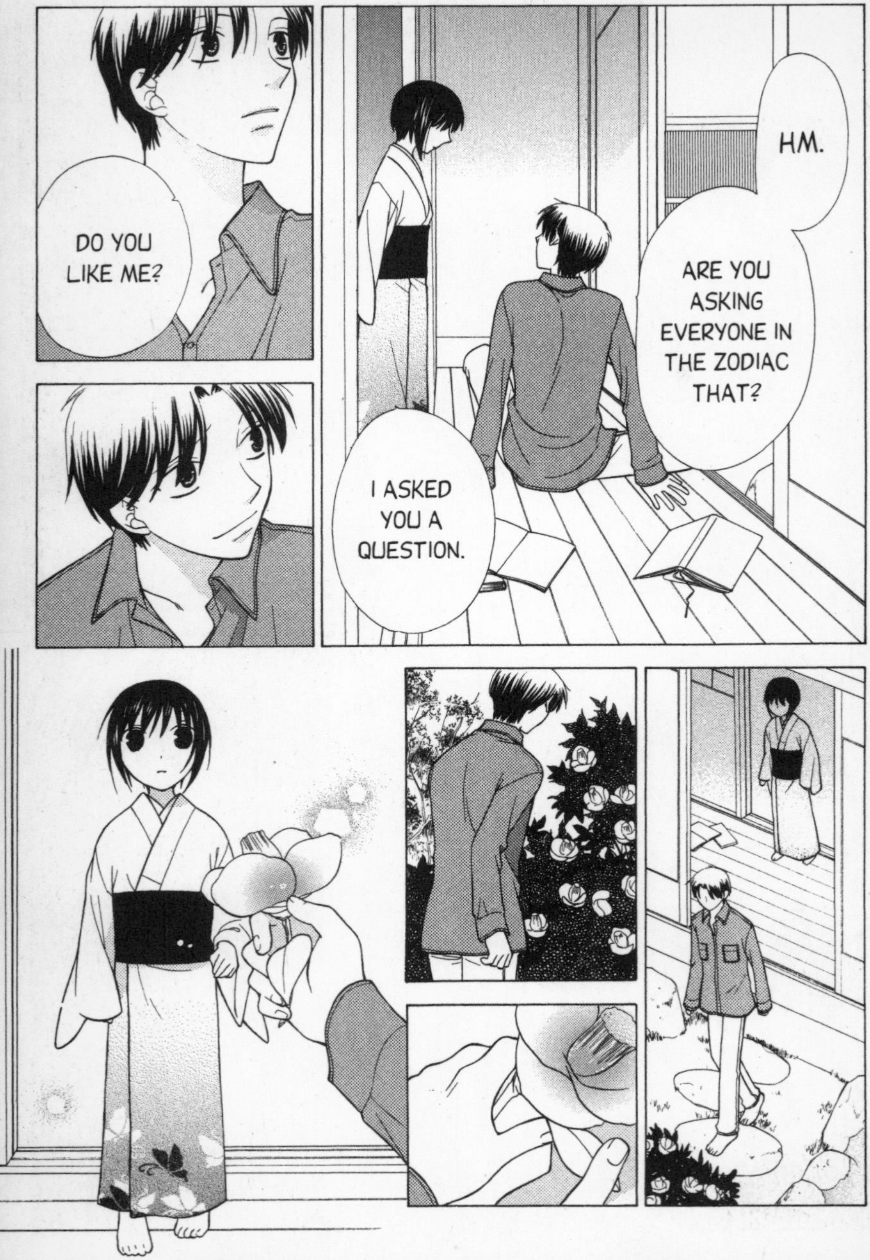
HM.
ARE YOU ASKING EVERYONE IN THE ZODIAC THAT?
I ASKED YOU A QUESTION.
DO YOU LIKE ME?

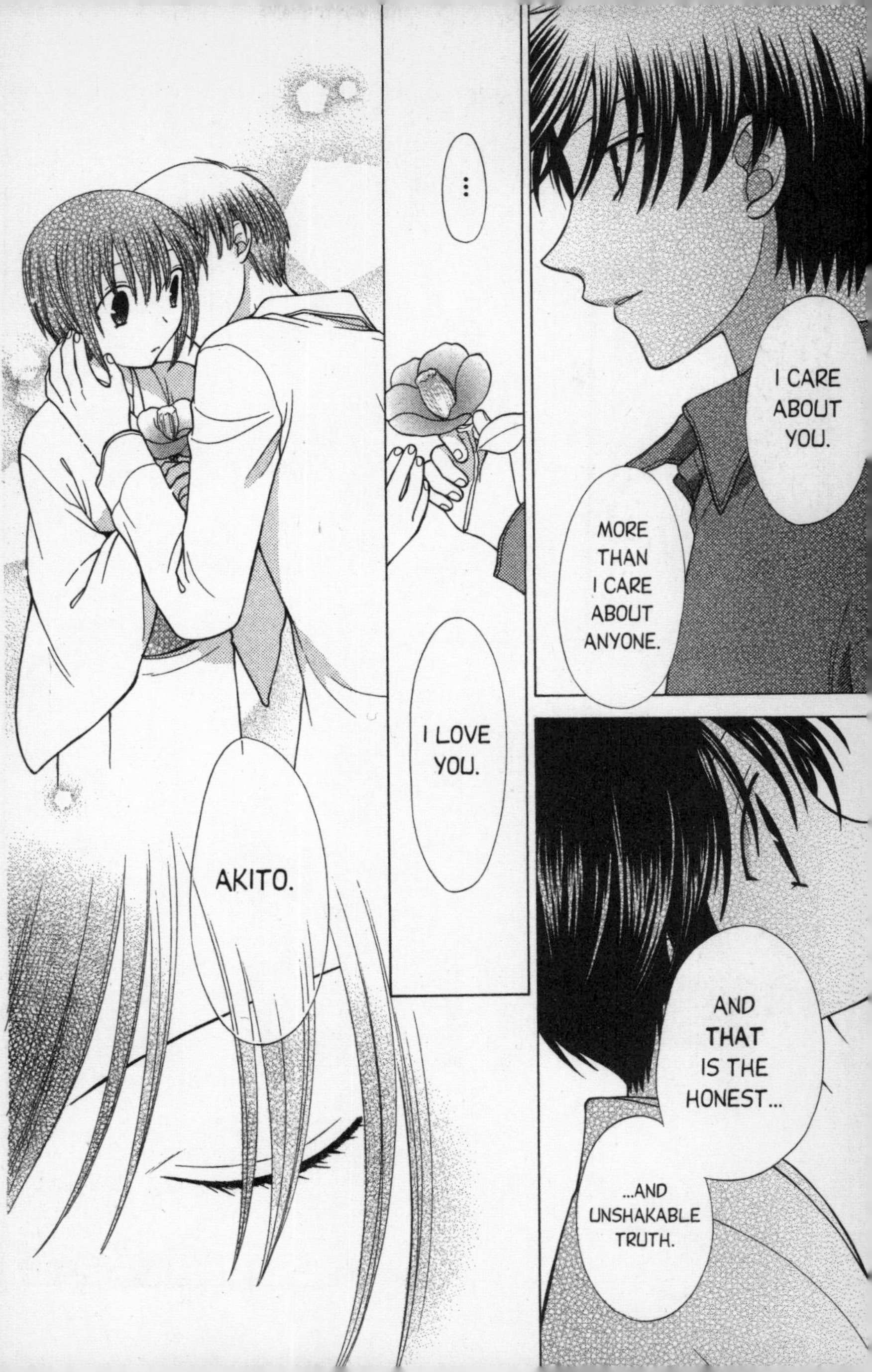
I CARE ABOUT YOU.
MORE THAN I CARE ABOUT ANYONE.
AND THAT IS THE HONEST...
...AND UNSHAKABLE TRUTH.
...
I LOVE YOU.
AKITO.

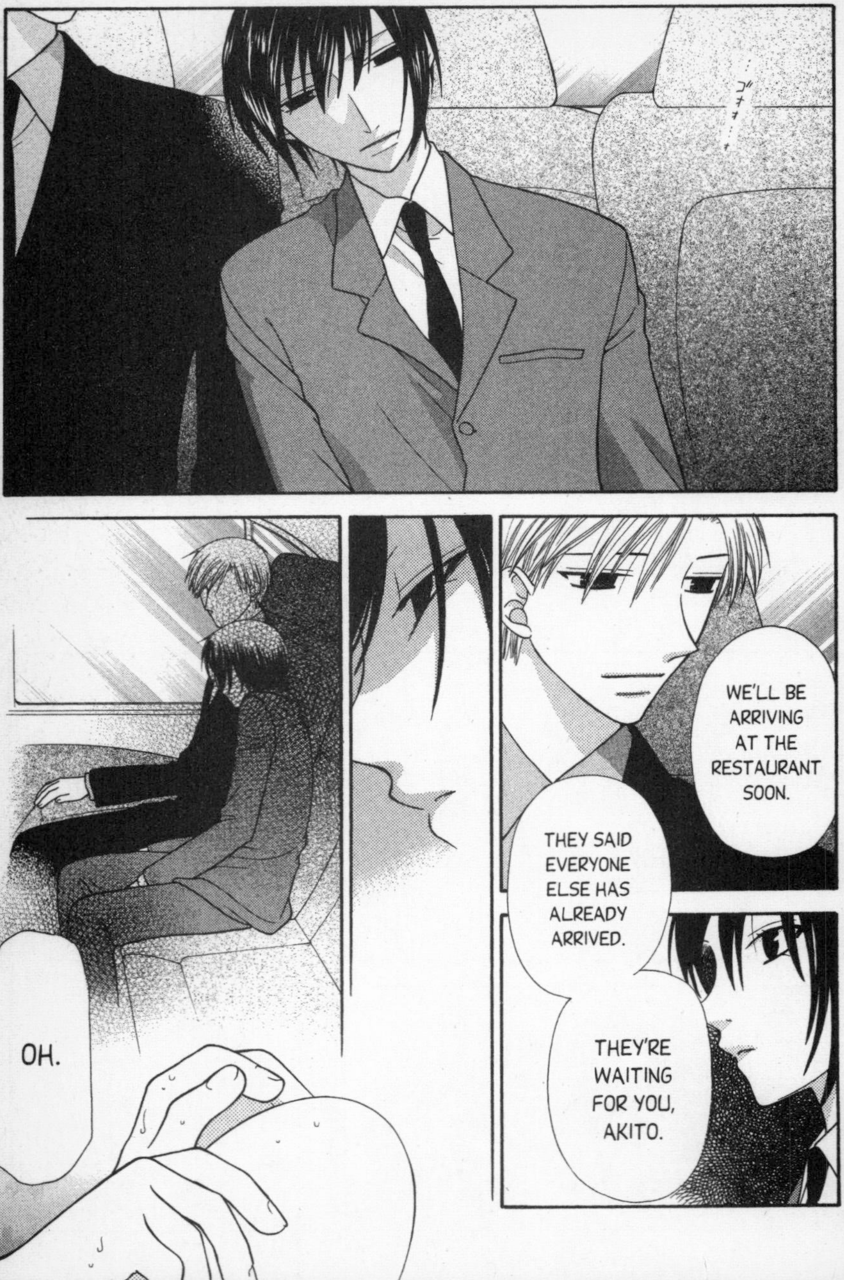
...ゴォォ...ォ
WE'LL BE ARRIVING AT THE RESTAURANT SOON.
THEY SAID EVERYONE ELSE HAS ALREADY ARRIVED.
THEY'RE WAITING FOR YOU, AKITO.
OH.

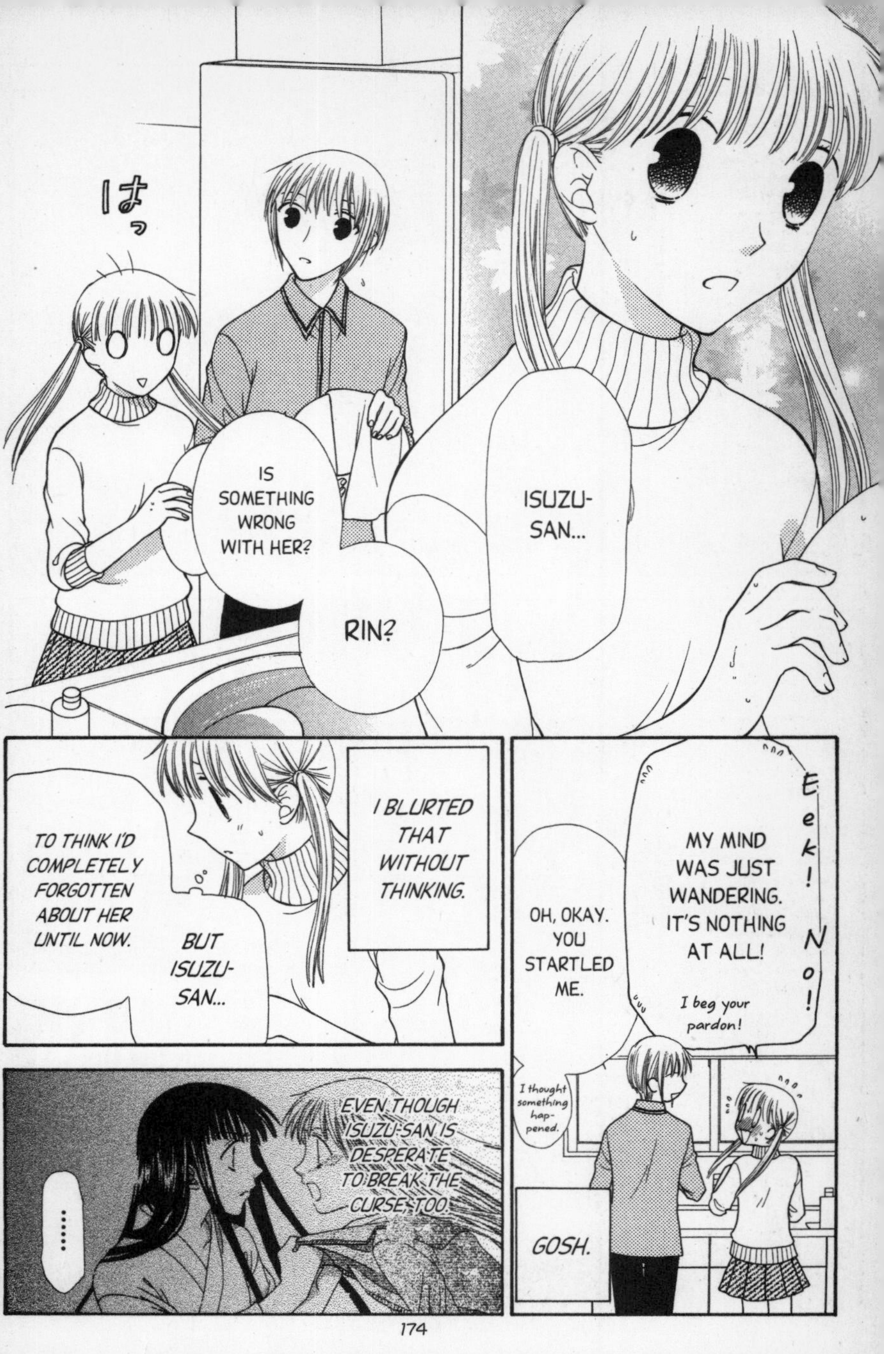
ISUZU-SAN...
RIN?
IS SOMETHING WRONG WITH HER?
はっ
Eek! No!
MY MIND WAS JUST WANDERING. IT'S NOTHING AT ALL!
I beg your pardon!
OH, OKAY. YOU STARTLED ME.
I thought something hap-pened.
GOSH.
I BLURTED THAT WITHOUT THINKING.
BUT ISUZU-SAN...
TO THINK I'D COMPLETELY FORGOTTEN ABOUT HER UNTIL NOW.
EVEN THOUGH ISUZU-SAN IS DESPERATE TO BREAK THE CURSE, TOO.
......

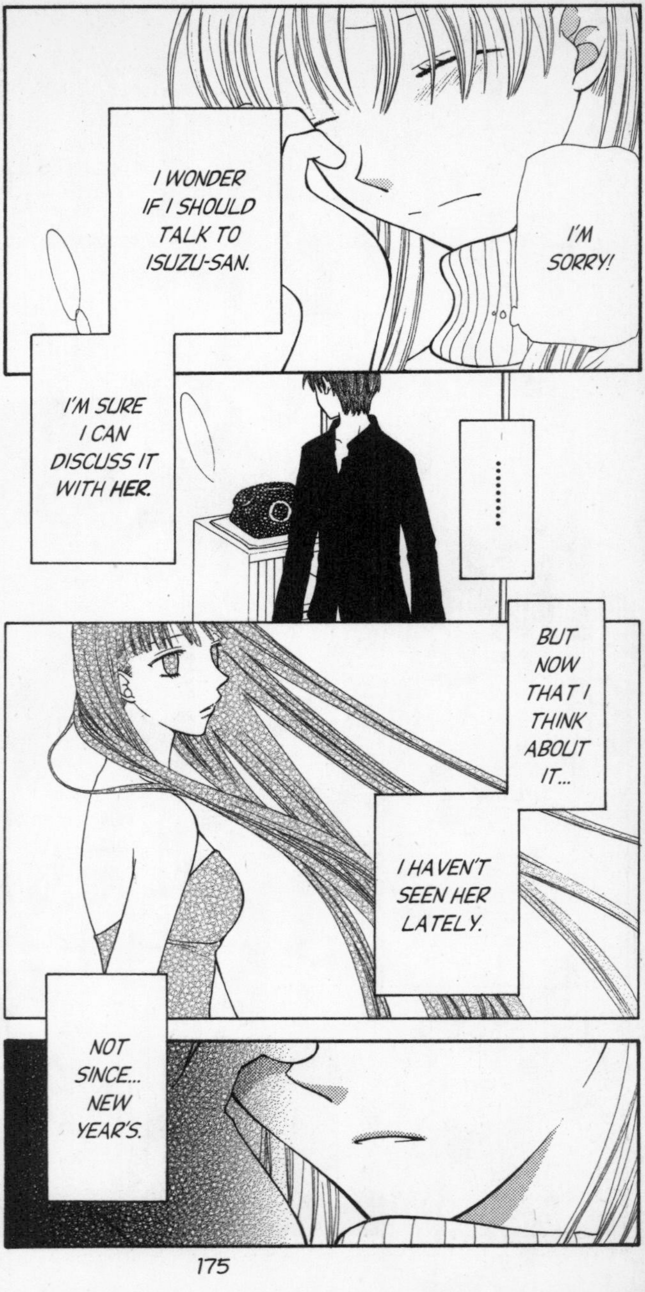
I'M SORRY!
I WONDER IF I SHOULD TALK TO ISUZU-SAN.
....
I'M SURE I CAN DISCUSS IT WITH HER.
BUT NOW THAT I THINK ABOUT IT...
I HAVEN'T SEEN HER LATELY.
NOT SINCE... NEW YEAR'S.

Continued →

- I made Nao-chan a boy who has no relation to the axis of the story as well. That makes me think Nao-chan is uselessly lively, too.
- Women are the majority in his family, and he grew up with his two older sisters taking loving care of him (laugh).
- He's worked like a slave, always being told to go buy this or go get that.
- I think it may be one of Nao-chan's good traits that, even while he's complaining about it, he'll grant their requests.
- But him liking "that person" might actually be because he has a sister complex.
- Kakeru thinks he's taking loving care of him, too, in the way he treats him.
- From the reader's point of view, it might be irritating to have a character whose heart isn't complete yet, but from the writer's perspective, it's pretty fun.

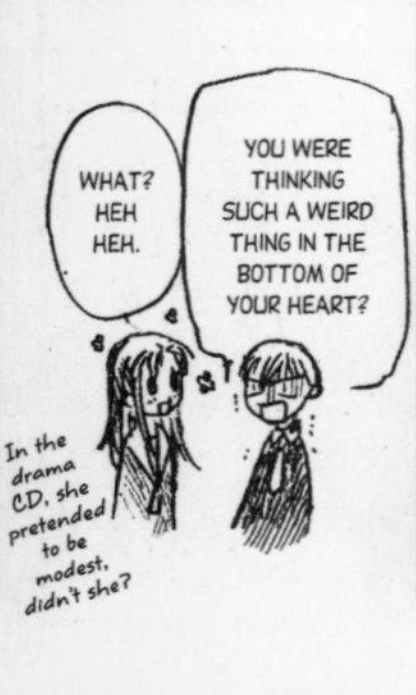
YOU WERE THINKING SUCH A WEIRD THING IN THE BOTTOM OF YOUR HEART?
WHAT? HEH HEH.
In the drama CD, she pretended to be modest, didn't she?

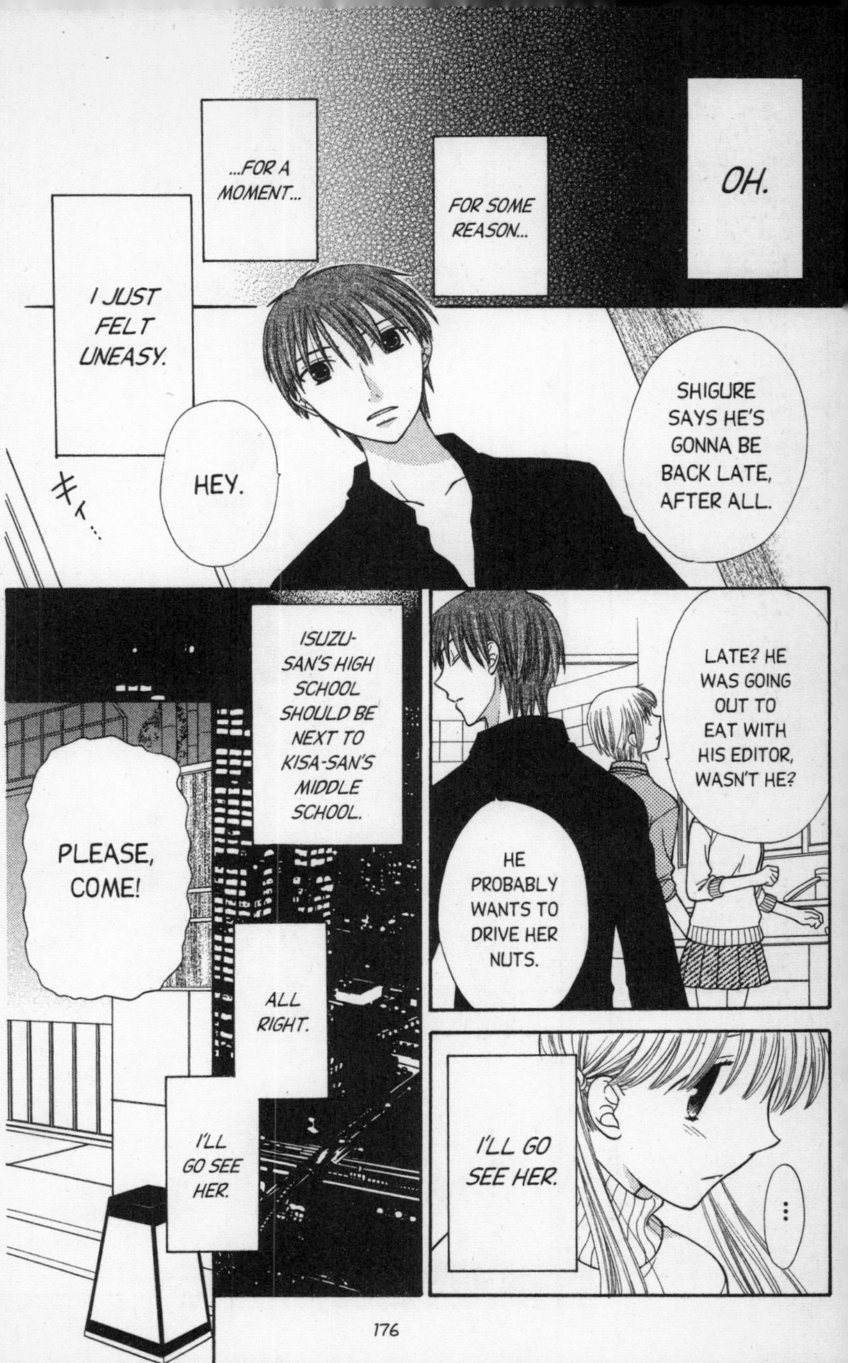
OH.
FOR SOME REASON...
...FOR A MOMENT...
I JUST FELT UNEASY.
SHIGURE SAYS HE'S GONNA BE BACK LATE, AFTER ALL.
HEY.
キィ…
LATE? HE WAS GOING OUT TO EAT WITH HIS EDITOR, WASN'T HE?
HE PROBABLY WANTS TO DRIVE HER NUTS.
I'LL GO SEE HER.
...
ISUZU-SAN'S HIGH SCHOOL SHOULD BE NEXT TO KISA-SAN'S MIDDLE SCHOOL.
PLEASE, COME!
ALL RIGHT.
I'LL GO SEE HER.

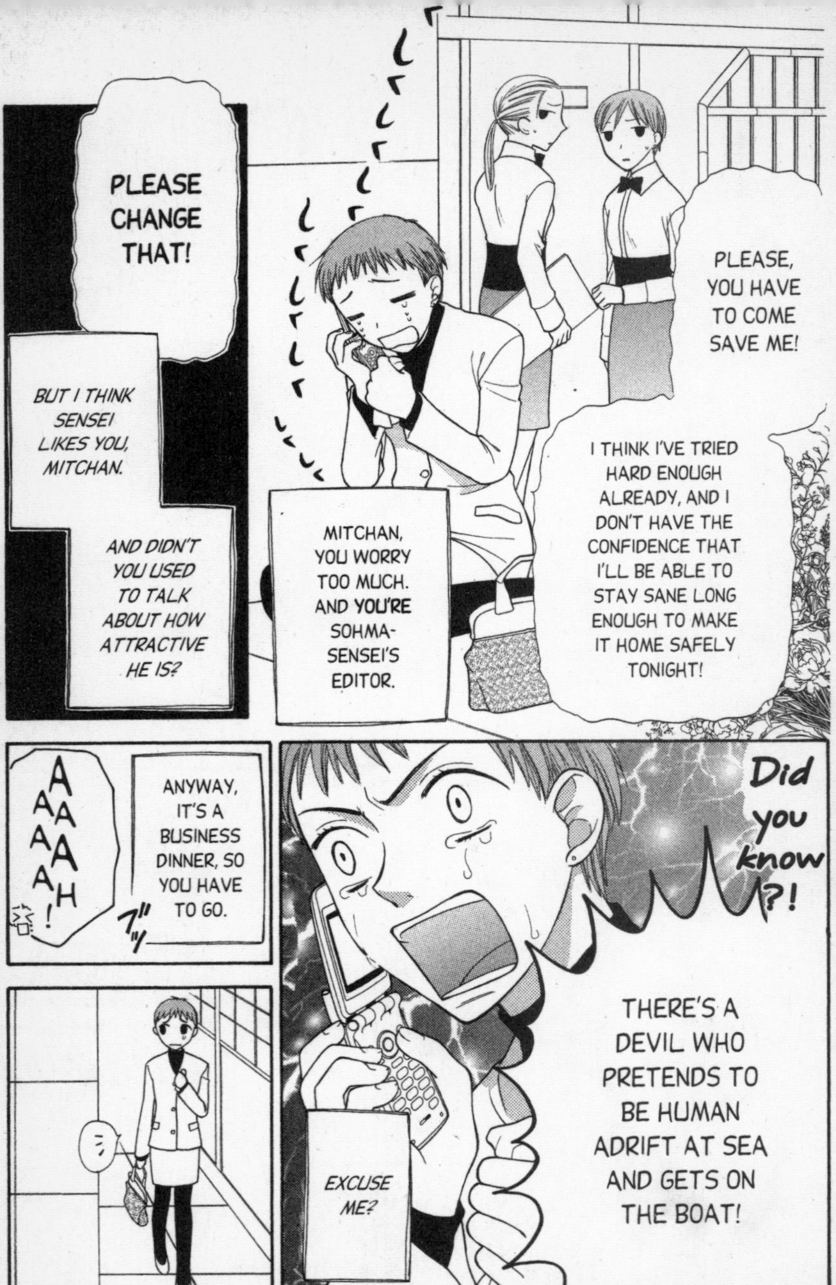
PLEASE, YOU HAVE TO COME SAVE ME!
I THINK I'VE TRIED HARD ENOUGH ALREADY, AND I DON'T HAVE THE CONFIDENCE THAT I'LL BE ABLE TO STAY SANE LONG ENOUGH TO MAKE IT HOME SAFELY TONIGHT!
MITCHAN, YOU WORRY TOO MUCH. AND YOU'RE SOHMA-SENSEI'S EDITOR.
PLEASE CHANGE THAT!
BUT I THINK SENSEI LIKES YOU, MITCHAN.
AND DIDN'T YOU USED TO TALK ABOUT HOW ATTRACTIVE HE IS?
Did you know?!
THERE'S A DEVIL WHO PRETENDS TO BE HUMAN ADRIFT AT SEA AND GETS ON THE BOAT!
EXCUSE ME?
AAAAAAH!
ANYWAY, IT'S A BUSINESS DINNER, SO YOU HAVE TO GO.
ブツ

Talking about a movie.

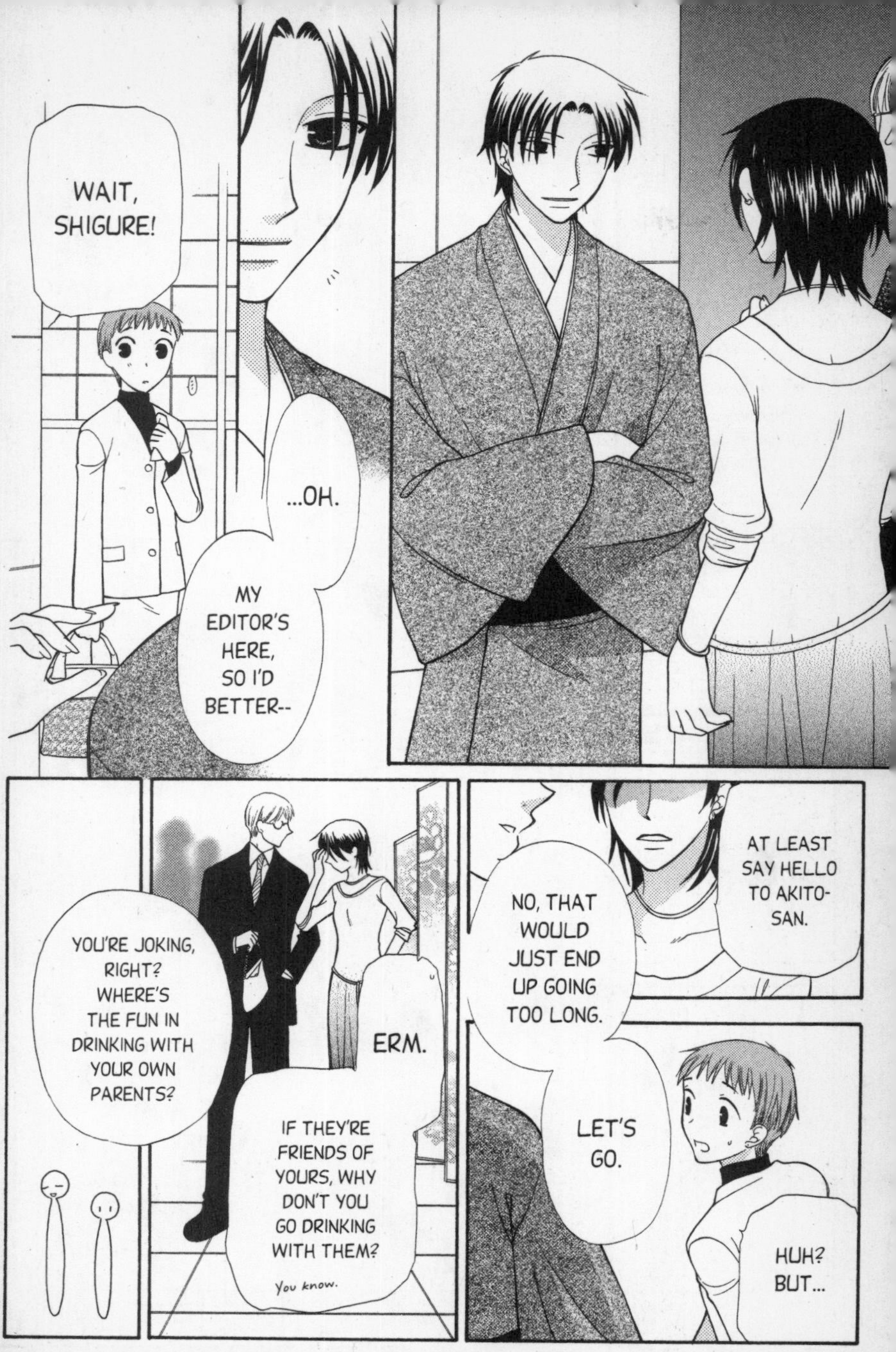
...OH.
MY EDITOR'S HERE, SO I'D BETTER--
WAIT, SHIGURE!
AT LEAST SAY HELLO TO AKITO-SAN.
NO, THAT WOULD JUST END UP GOING TOO LONG.
LET'S GO.
HUH? BUT...
ERM.
IF THEY'RE FRIENDS OF YOURS, WHY DON'T YOU GO DRINKING WITH THEM?
You know.
YOU'RE JOKING, RIGHT? WHERE'S THE FUN IN DRINKING WITH YOUR OWN PARENTS?

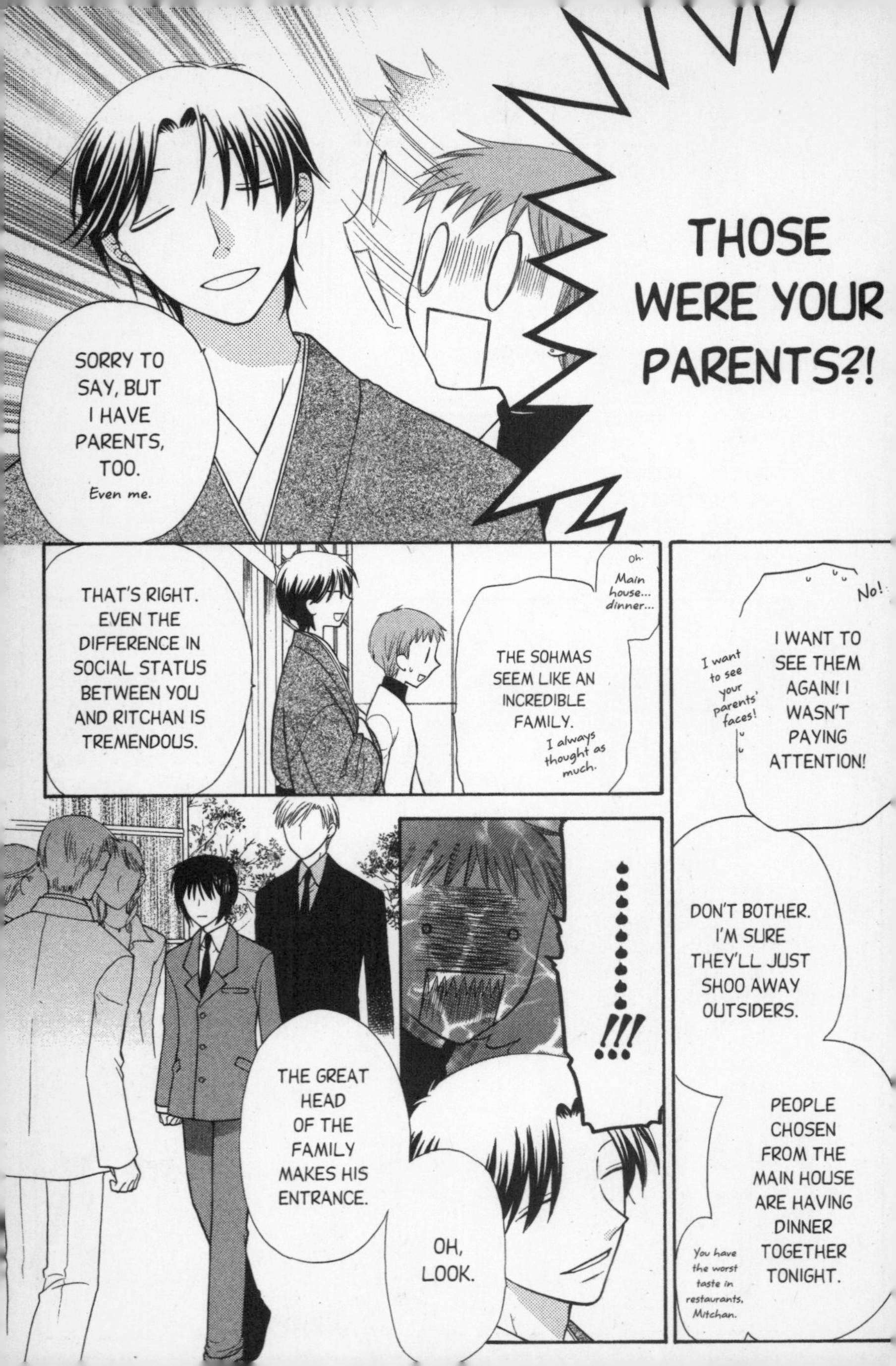
THOSE WERE YOUR PARENTS?!
SORRY TO SAY, BUT I HAVE PARENTS, TOO.
Even me.
No!
I WANT TO SEE THEM AGAIN! I WASN'T PAYING ATTENTION!
I want to see your parents' faces!
Oh. Main house... dinner...
THE SOHMAS SEEM LIKE AN INCREDIBLE FAMILY.
I always thought as much.
THAT'S RIGHT. EVEN THE DIFFERENCE IN SOCIAL STATUS BETWEEN YOU AND RITCHAN IS TREMENDOUS.
DON'T BOTHER. I'M SURE THEY'LL JUST SHOO AWAY OUTSIDERS.
PEOPLE CHOSEN FROM THE MAIN HOUSE ARE HAVING DINNER TOGETHER TONIGHT.
You have the worst taste in restaurants, Mitchan.
......!!!
OH, LOOK.
THE GREAT HEAD OF THE FAMILY MAKES HIS ENTRANCE.

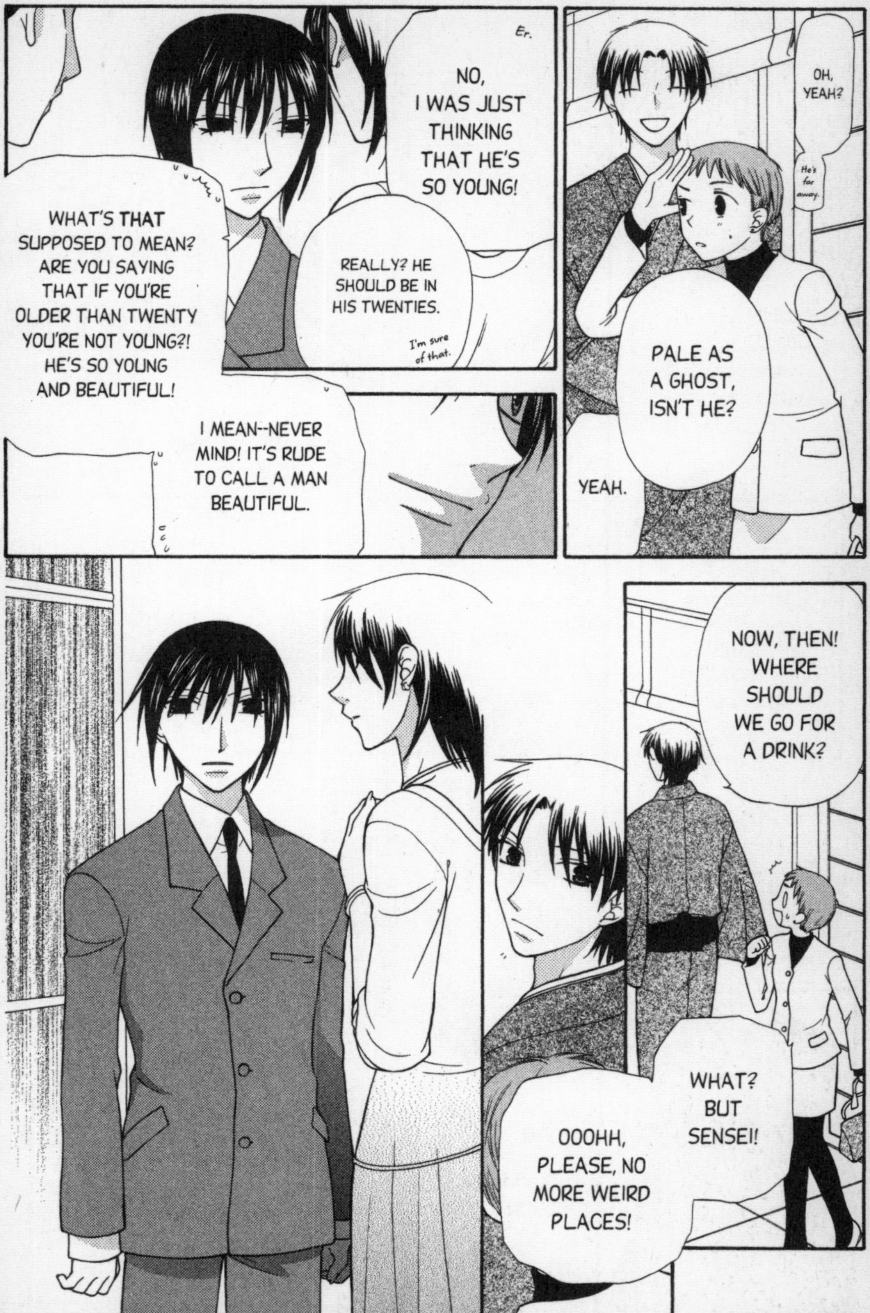
OH, YEAH?
He's far away.
PALE AS A GHOST, ISN'T HE?
YEAH.
Er.
NO, I WAS JUST THINKING THAT HE'S SO YOUNG!
REALLY? HE SHOULD BE IN HIS TWENTIES.
I'm sure of that.
WHAT'S THAT SUPPOSED TO MEAN? ARE YOU SAYING THAT IF YOU'RE OLDER THAN TWENTY YOU'RE NOT YOUNG?! HE'S SO YOUNG AND BEAUTIFUL!
I MEAN--NEVER MIND! IT'S RUDE TO CALL A MAN BEAUTIFUL.
NOW, THEN! WHERE SHOULD WE GO FOR A DRINK?
WHAT? BUT SENSEI!
OOOHH, PLEASE, NO MORE WEIRD PLACES!

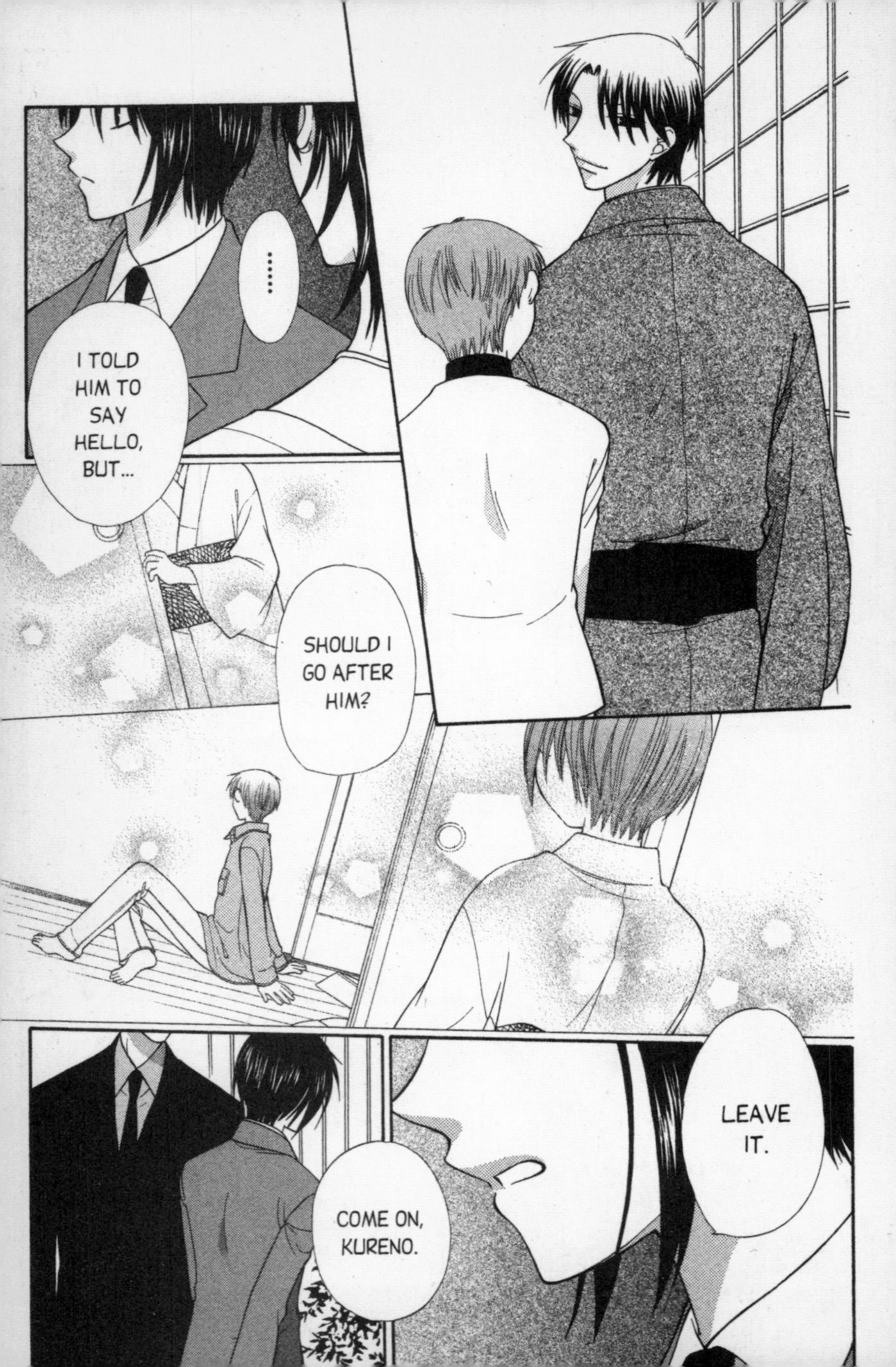
......
I TOLD HIM TO SAY HELLO, BUT...
SHOULD I GO AFTER HIM?
LEAVE IT.
COME ON, KURENO.

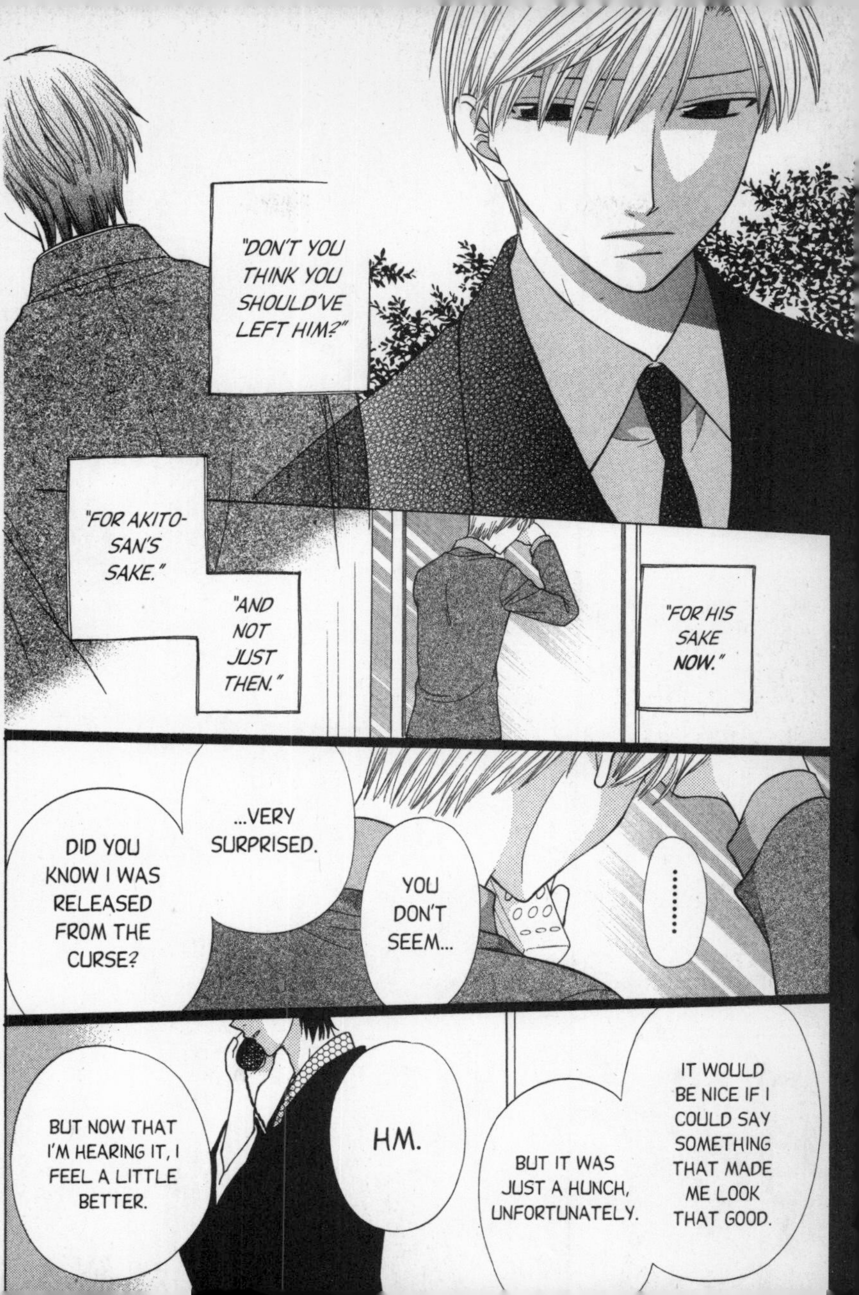
"DON'T YOU THINK YOU SHOULD'VE LEFT HIM?"
"FOR AKITO-SAN'S SAKE."
"AND NOT JUST THEN."
"FOR HIS SAKE NOW."
......
YOU DON'T SEEM...
...VERY SURPRISED.
DID YOU KNOW I WAS RELEASED FROM THE CURSE?
IT WOULD BE NICE IF I COULD SAY SOMETHING THAT MADE ME LOOK THAT GOOD.
BUT IT WAS JUST A HUNCH, UNFORTUNATELY.
HM.
BUT NOW THAT I'M HEARING IT, I FEEL A LITTLE BETTER.

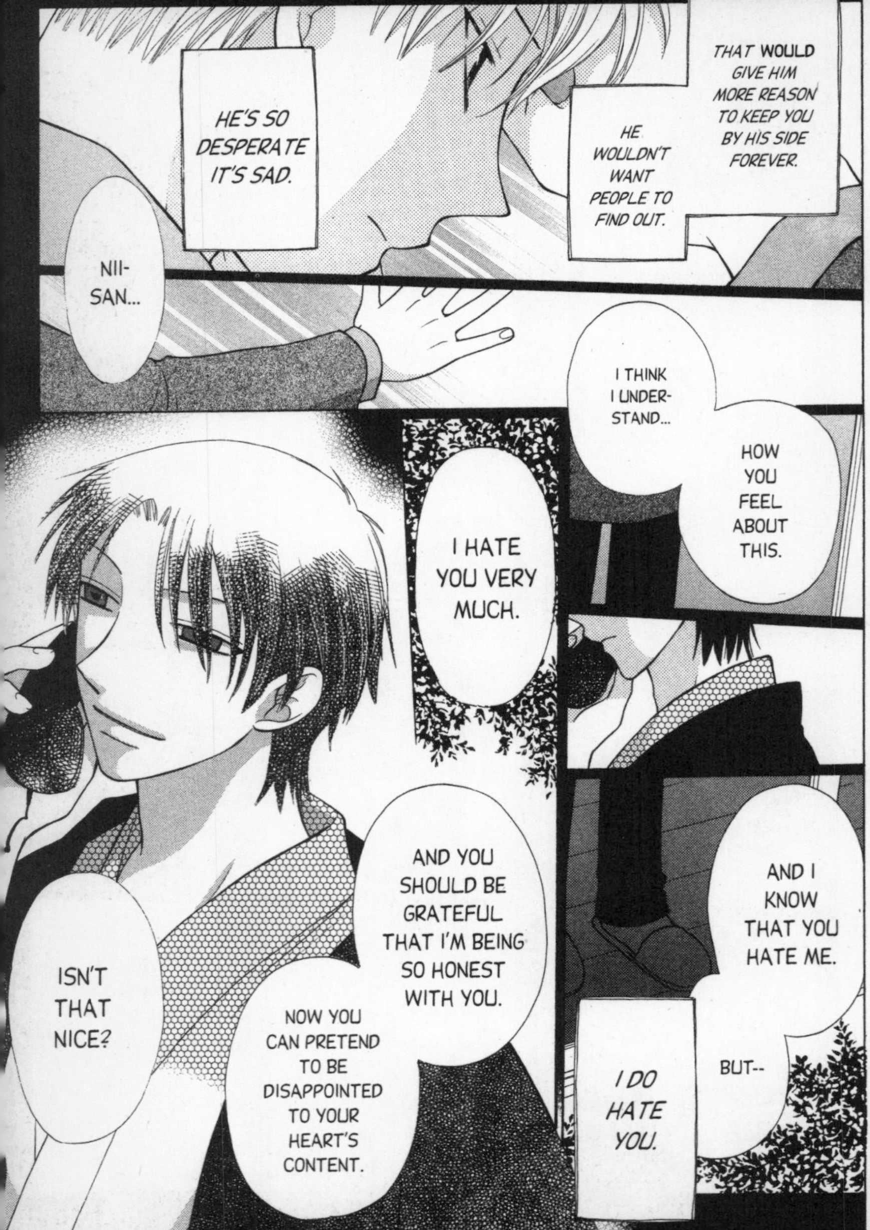
THAT WOULD GIVE HIM MORE REASON TO KEEP YOU BY HIS SIDE FOREVER.
HE WOULDN'T WANT PEOPLE TO FIND OUT.
HE'S SO DESPERATE IT'S SAD.
NII-SAN...
I THINK I UNDER-STAND...
HOW YOU FEEL ABOUT THIS.
AND I KNOW THAT YOU HATE ME.
BUT--
I DO HATE YOU.
I HATE YOU VERY MUCH.
AND YOU SHOULD BE GRATEFUL THAT I'M BEING SO HONEST WITH YOU.
NOW YOU CAN PRETEND TO BE DISAPPOINTED TO YOUR HEART'S CONTENT.
ISN'T THAT NICE?

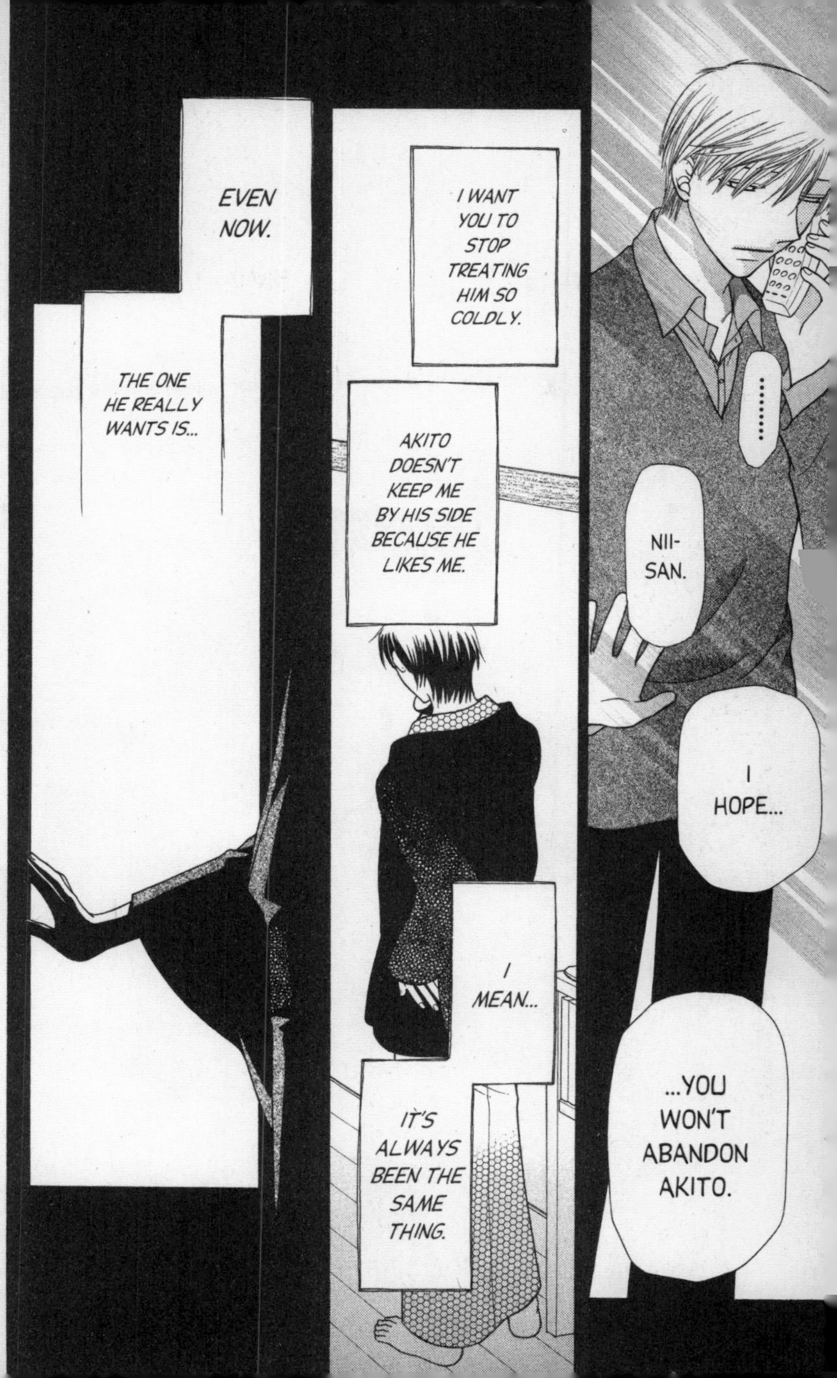
......
NII-SAN.
I HOPE...
...YOU WON'T ABANDON AKITO.
I WANT YOU TO STOP TREATING HIM SO COLDLY.
AKITO DOESN'T KEEP ME BY HIS SIDE BECAUSE HE LIKES ME.
I MEAN...
IT'S ALWAYS BEEN THE SAME THING.
EVEN NOW.
THE ONE HE REALLY WANTS IS...

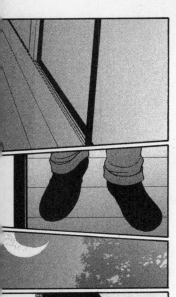

WELCOME HOME.

WELCOME HOME...

AKITO-SAN.

WELCOME BACK.

Sohma

. . . .

HERE IS FINE.

JUST KEEP EVERYONE AWAY.

OF COURSE.

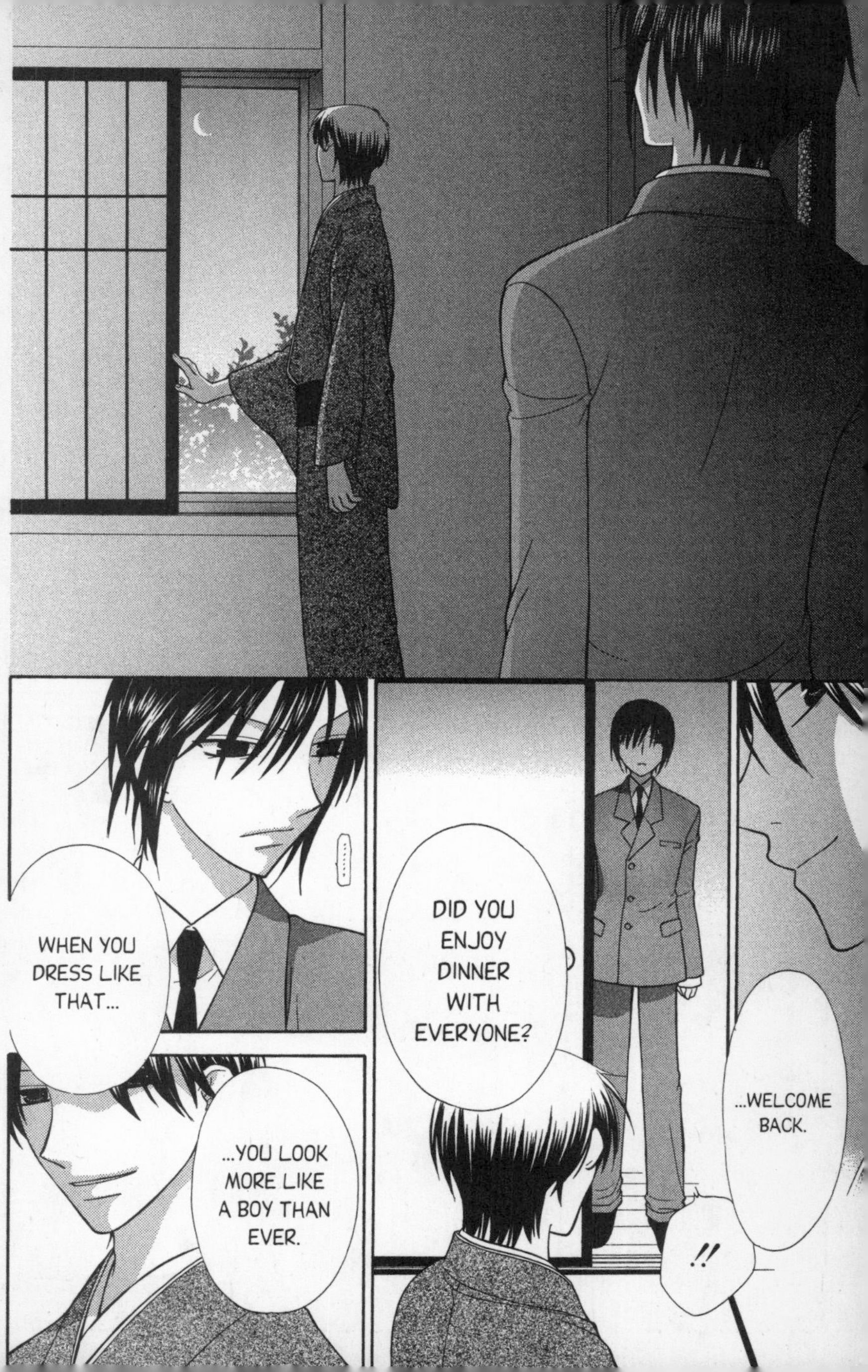
...WELCOME BACK.
!!
DID YOU ENJOY DINNER WITH EVERYONE?
......
WHEN YOU DRESS LIKE THAT...
...YOU LOOK MORE LIKE A BOY THAN EVER.

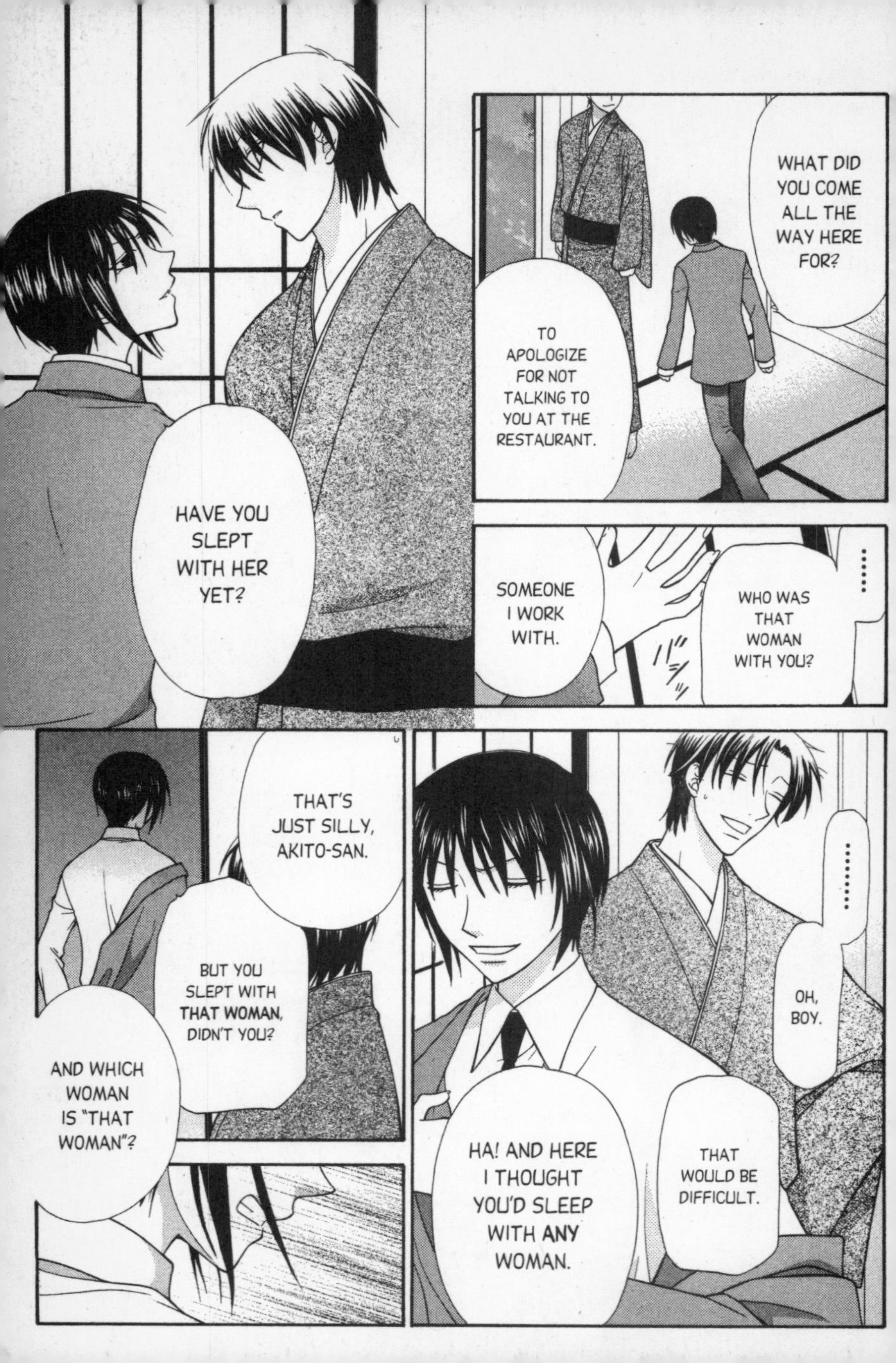
WHAT DID YOU COME ALL THE WAY HERE FOR?
TO APOLOGIZE FOR NOT TALKING TO YOU AT THE RESTAURANT.
......
WHO WAS THAT WOMAN WITH YOU?
バッ
SOMEONE I WORK WITH.
HAVE YOU SLEPT WITH HER YET?
......
OH, BOY.
THAT WOULD BE DIFFICULT.
HA! AND HERE I THOUGHT YOU'D SLEEP WITH **ANY** WOMAN.
THAT'S JUST SILLY, AKITO-SAN.
BUT YOU SLEPT WITH **THAT WOMAN**, DIDN'T YOU?
AND WHICH WOMAN IS "THAT WOMAN"?

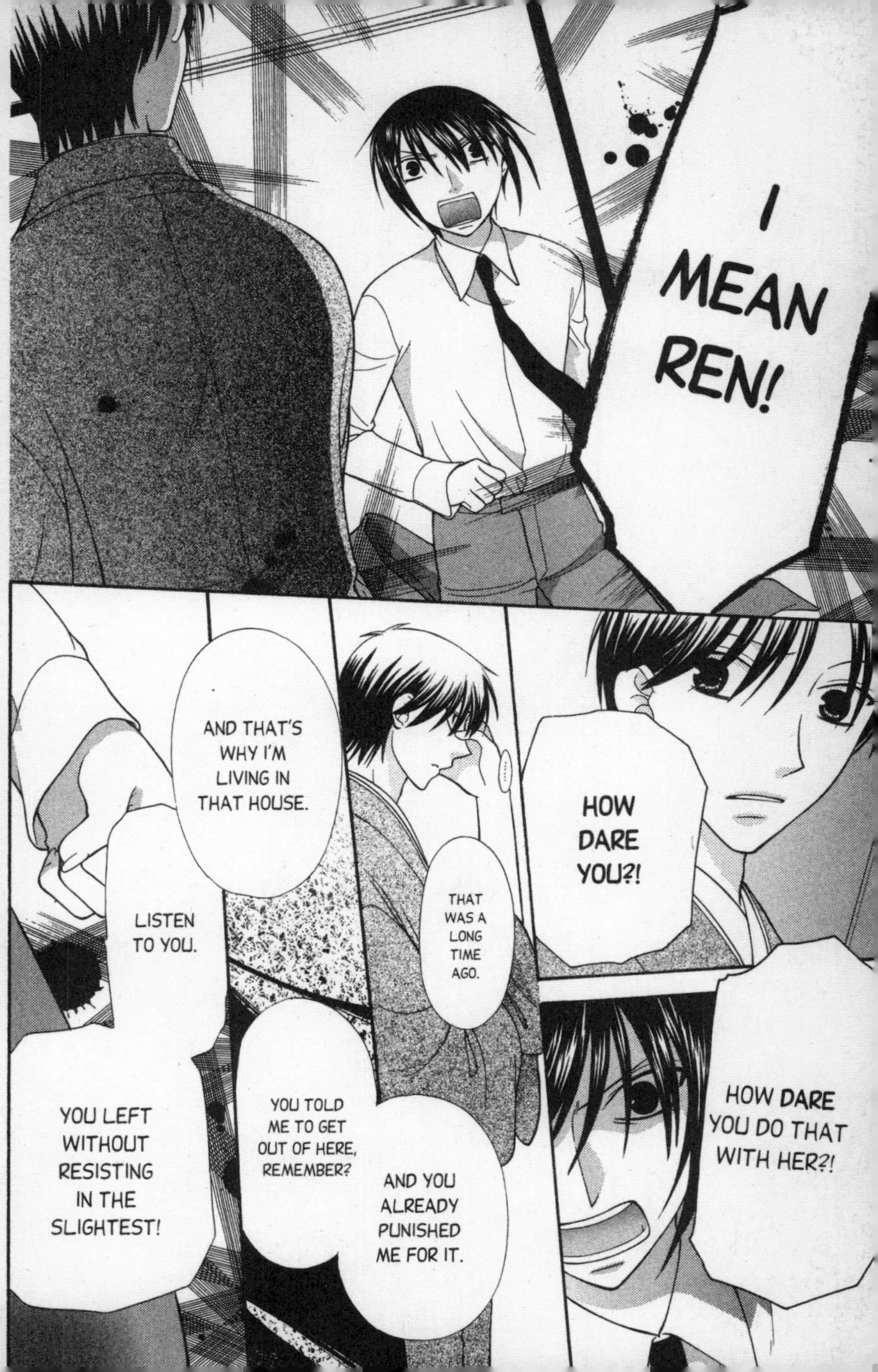
I MEAN REN!
HOW DARE YOU?!
HOW DARE YOU DO THAT WITH HER?!
...
THAT WAS A LONG TIME AGO.
YOU TOLD ME TO GET OUT OF HERE, REMEMBER?
AND YOU ALREADY PUNISHED ME FOR IT.
AND THAT'S WHY I'M LIVING IN THAT HOUSE.
LISTEN TO YOU.
YOU LEFT WITHOUT RESISTING IN THE SLIGHTEST!

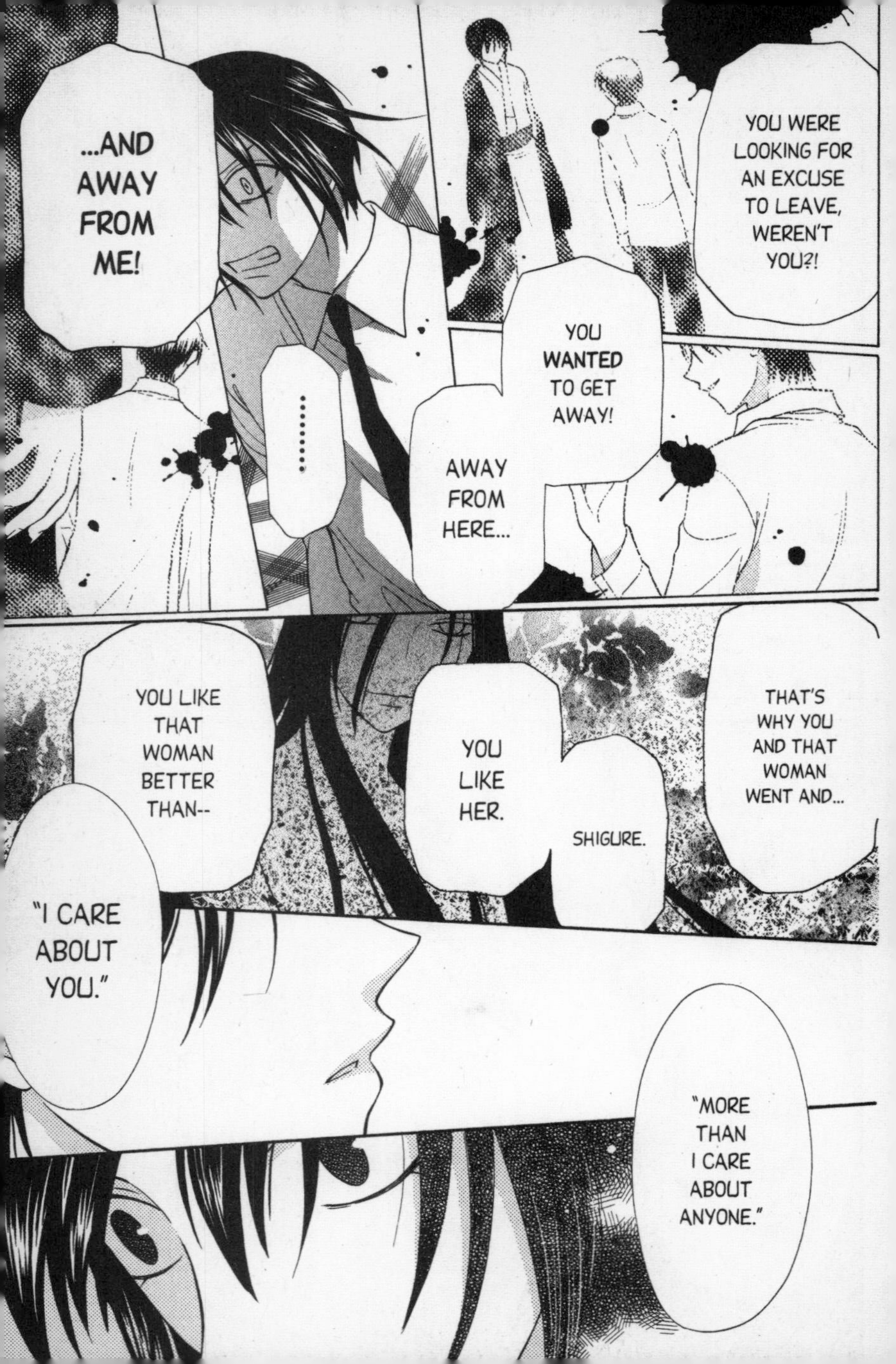
YOU WERE LOOKING FOR AN EXCUSE TO LEAVE, WEREN'T YOU?!
YOU **WANTED** TO GET AWAY!
AWAY FROM HERE...
...AND AWAY FROM ME!
......
THAT'S WHY YOU AND THAT WOMAN WENT AND...
SHIGURE.
YOU LIKE HER.
YOU LIKE THAT WOMAN BETTER THAN--
"I CARE ABOUT YOU."
"MORE THAN I CARE ABOUT ANYONE."

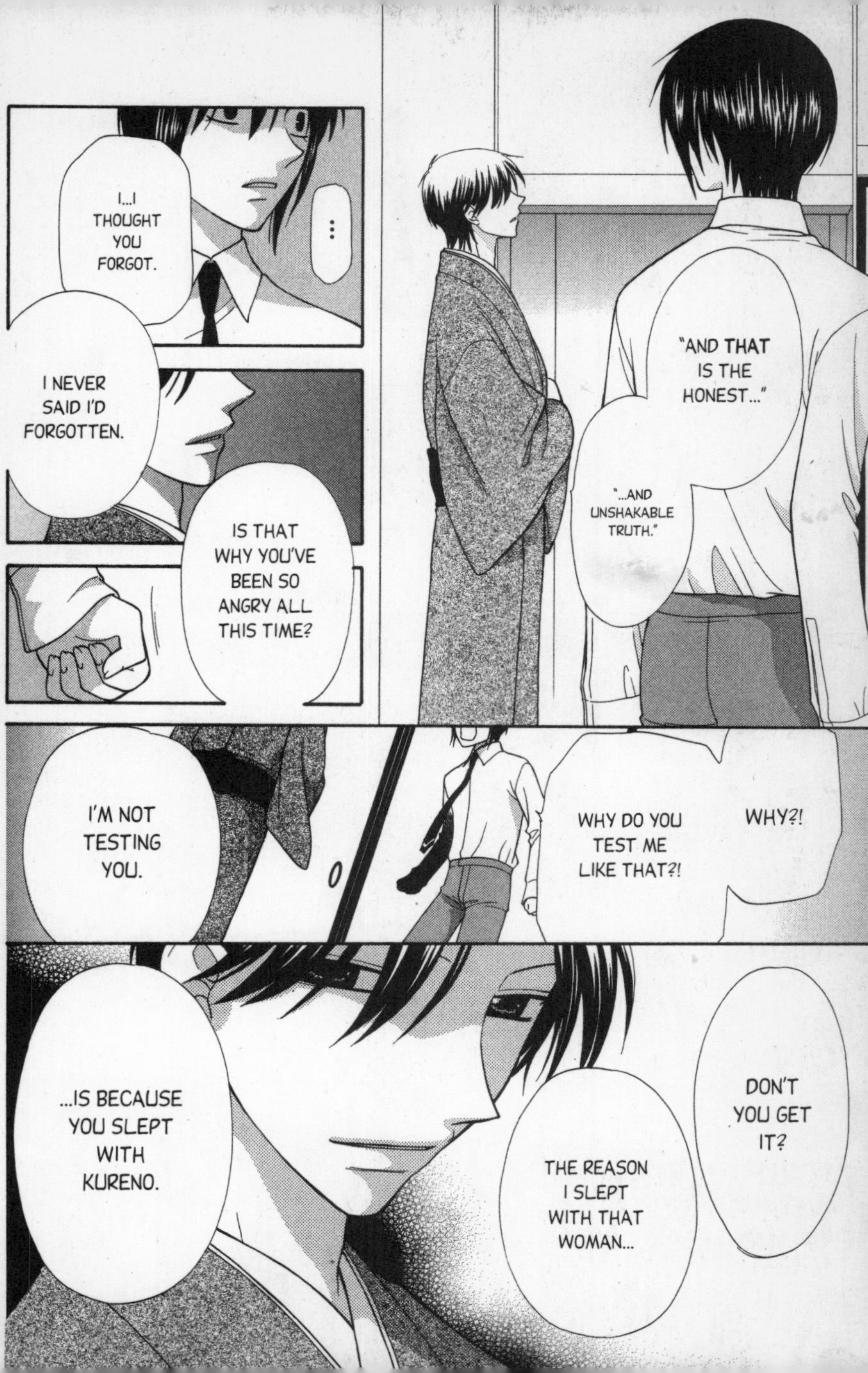
"AND THAT IS THE HONEST..."
"...AND UNSHAKABLE TRUTH."
...
I...I THOUGHT YOU FORGOT.
I NEVER SAID I'D FORGOTTEN.
IS THAT WHY YOU'VE BEEN SO ANGRY ALL THIS TIME?
WHY?!
WHY DO YOU TEST ME LIKE THAT?!
I'M NOT TESTING YOU.
DON'T YOU GET IT?
THE REASON I SLEPT WITH THAT WOMAN...
...IS BECAUSE YOU SLEPT WITH KURENO.

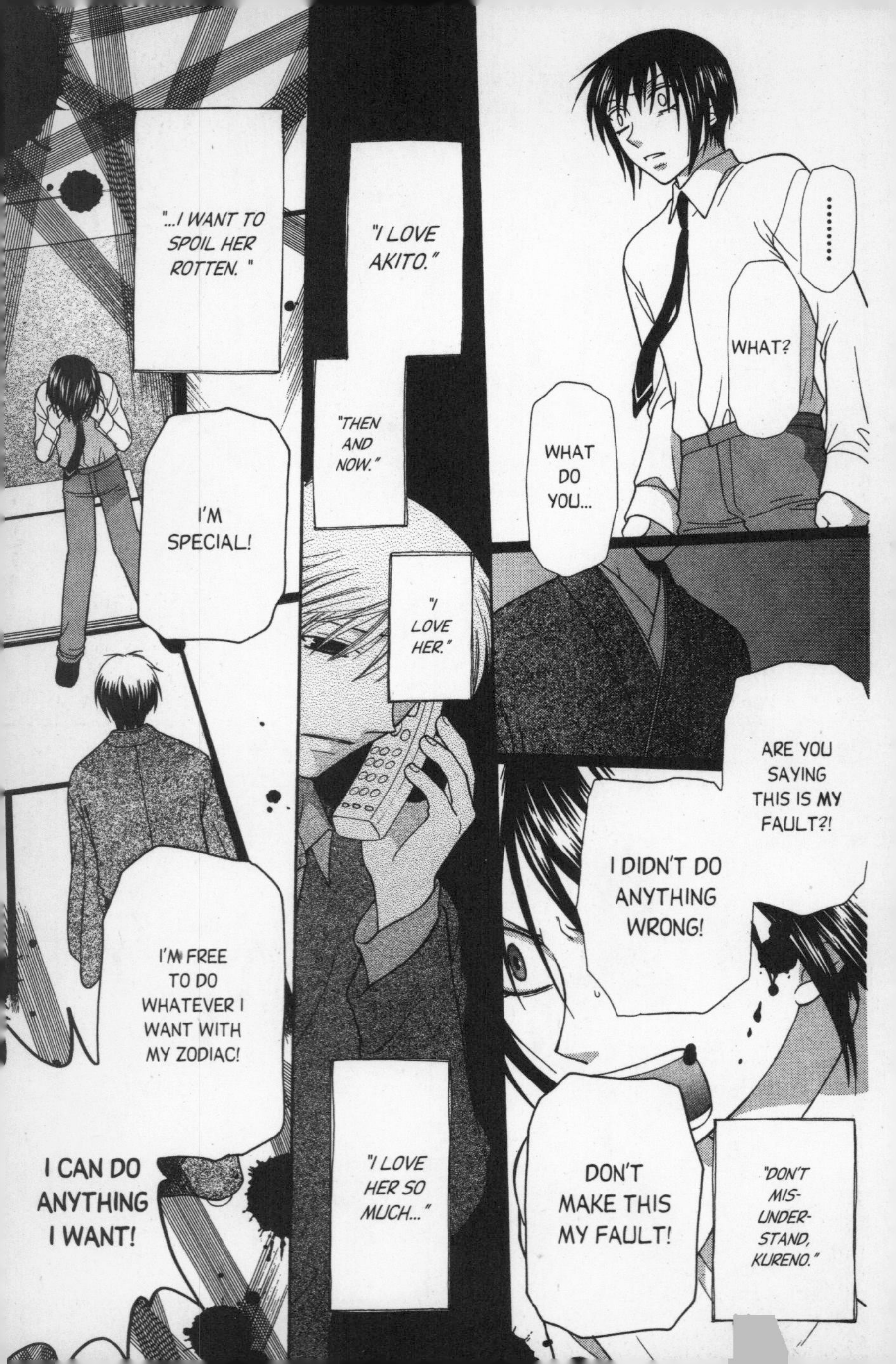

......
WHAT?
WHAT DO YOU...
ARE YOU SAYING THIS IS MY FAULT?!
I DIDN'T DO ANYTHING WRONG!
"DON'T MISUNDERSTAND, KURENO."
DON'T MAKE THIS MY FAULT!
"I LOVE AKITO."
"THEN AND NOW."
"I LOVE HER."
"I LOVE HER SO MUCH..."
"...I WANT TO SPOIL HER ROTTEN."
I'M SPECIAL!
I'M FREE TO DO WHATEVER I WANT WITH MY ZODIAC!
I CAN DO ANYTHING I WANT!

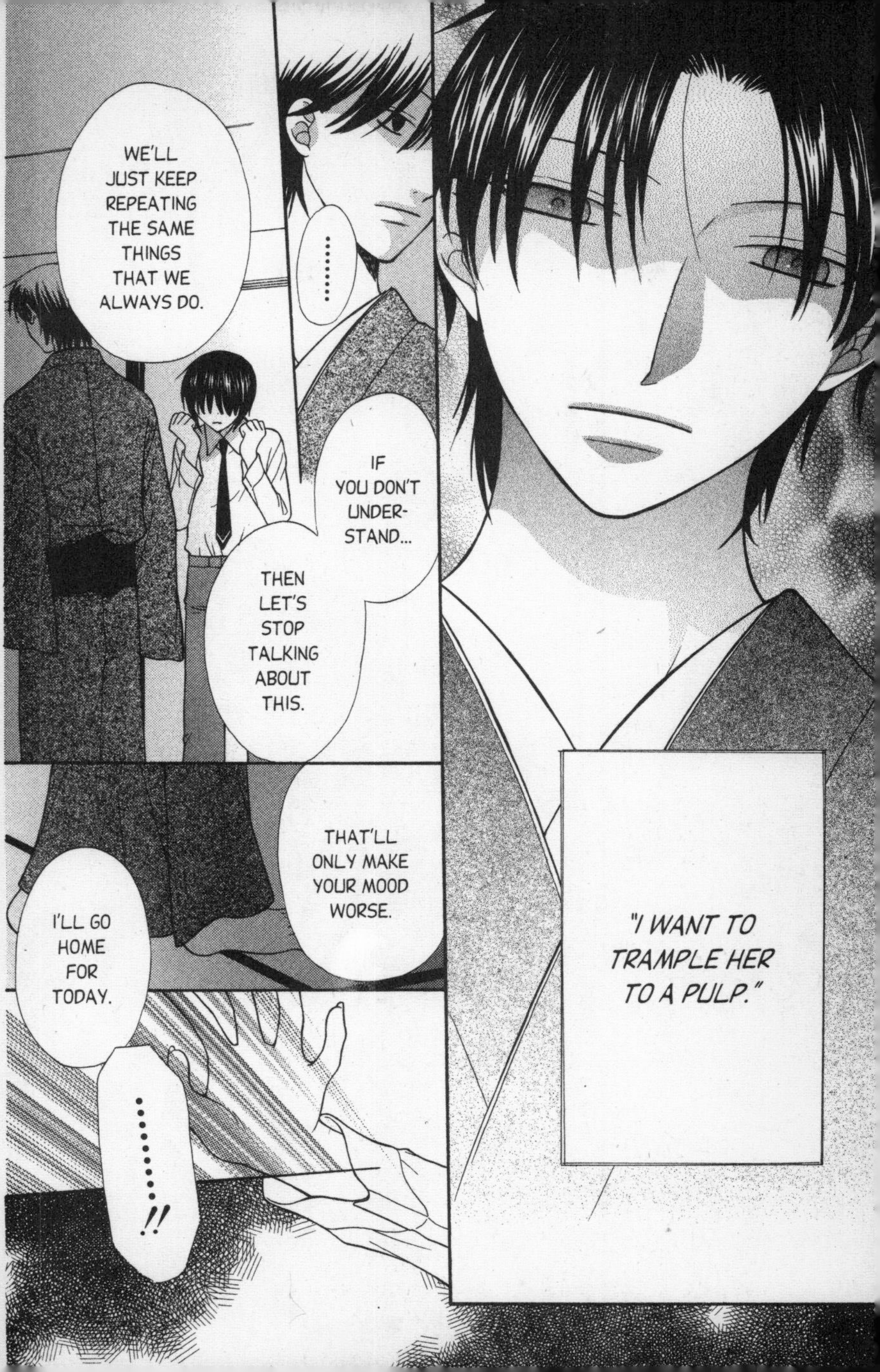
"I WANT TO TRAMPLE HER TO A PULP."
......
IF YOU DON'T UNDER-STAND...
THEN LET'S STOP TALKING ABOUT THIS.
WE'LL JUST KEEP REPEATING THE SAME THINGS THAT WE ALWAYS DO.
THAT'LL ONLY MAKE YOUR MOOD WORSE.
I'LL GO HOME FOR TODAY.
......!!

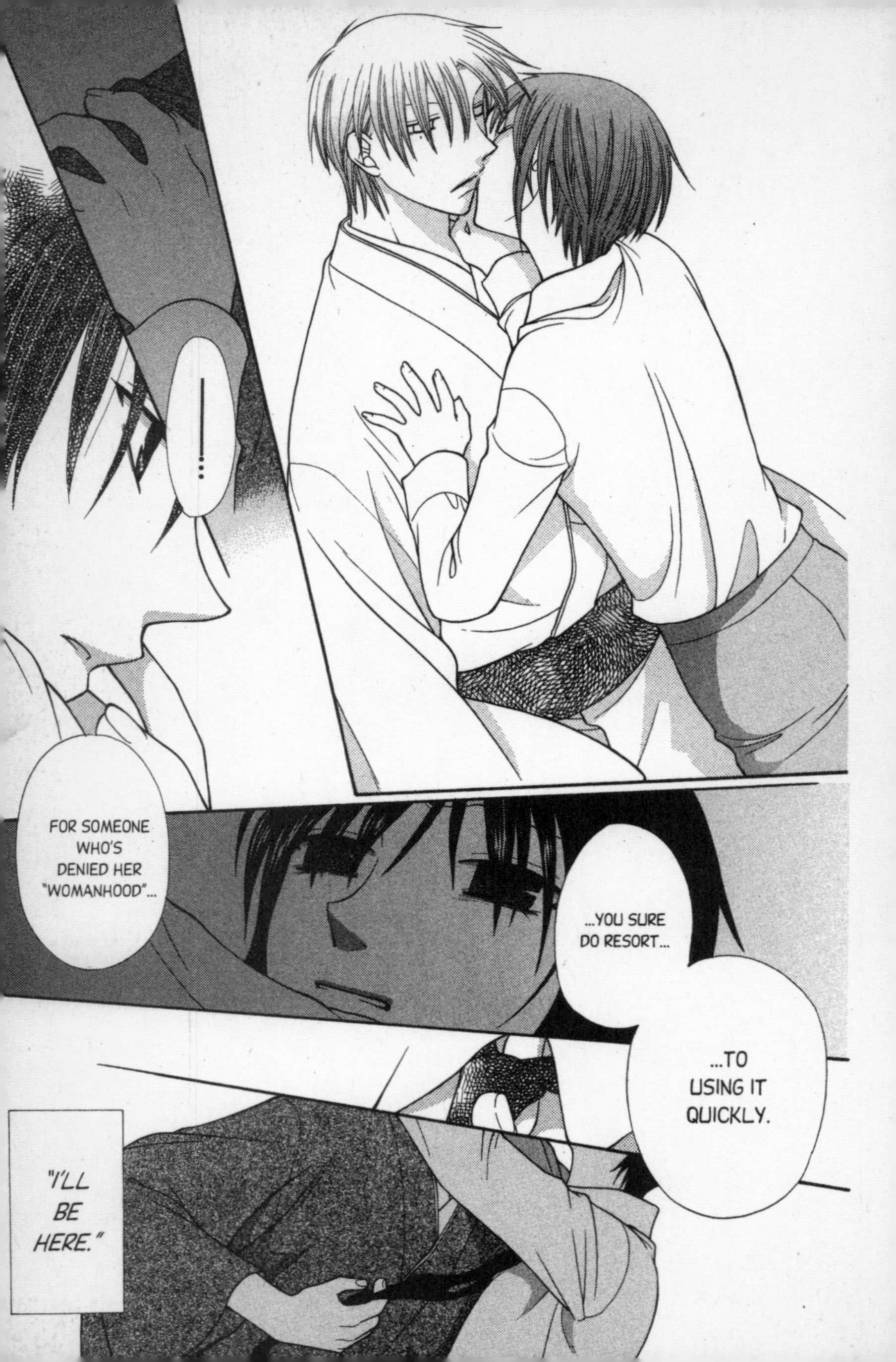
......
FOR SOMEONE WHO'S DENIED HER "WOMANHOOD"...
...YOU SURE DO RESORT...
...TO USING IT QUICKLY.
"I'LL BE HERE."

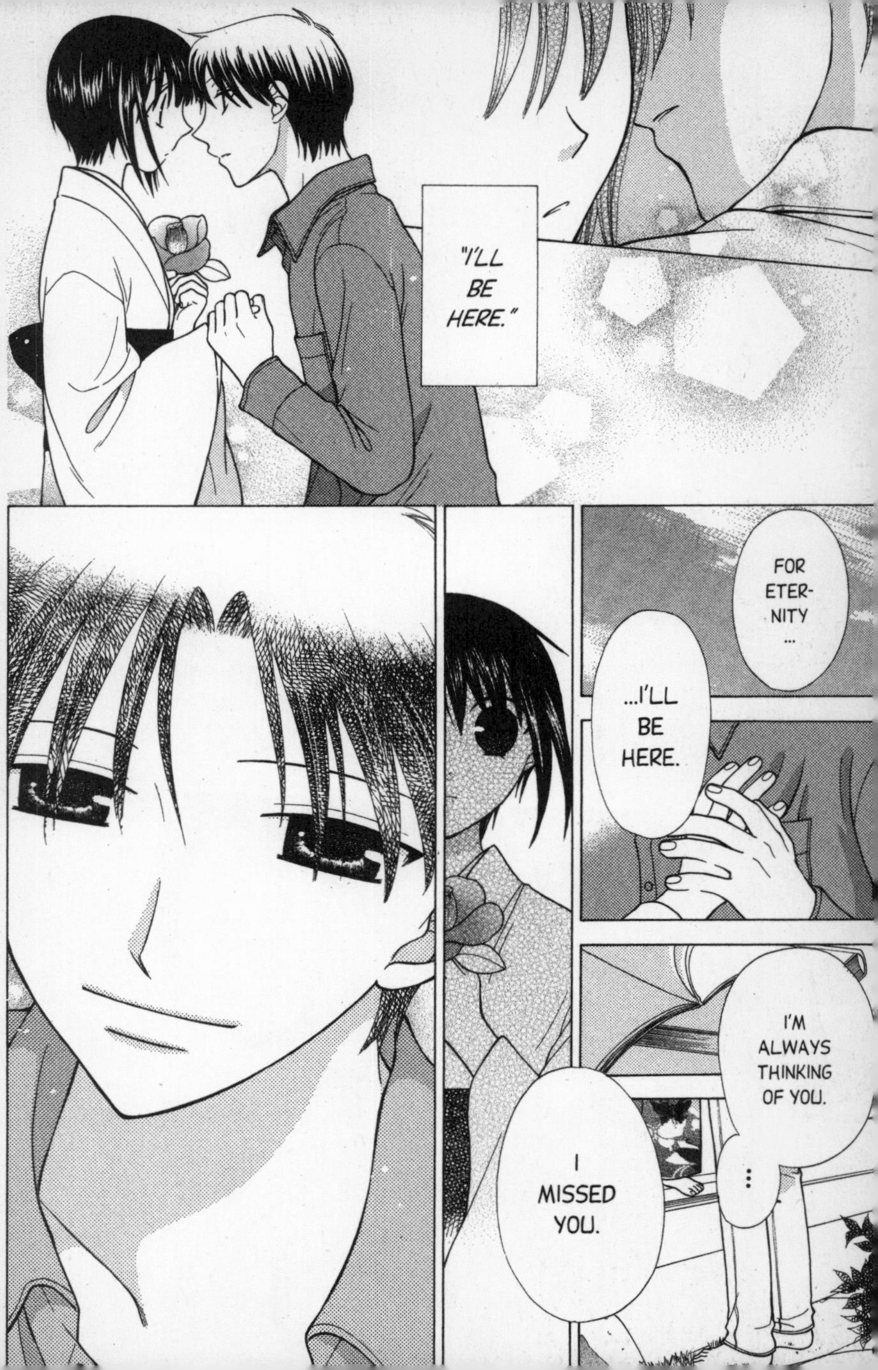
"I'LL BE HERE."
FOR ETERNITY...
...I'LL BE HERE.
I'M ALWAYS THINKING OF YOU.
...
I MISSED YOU.

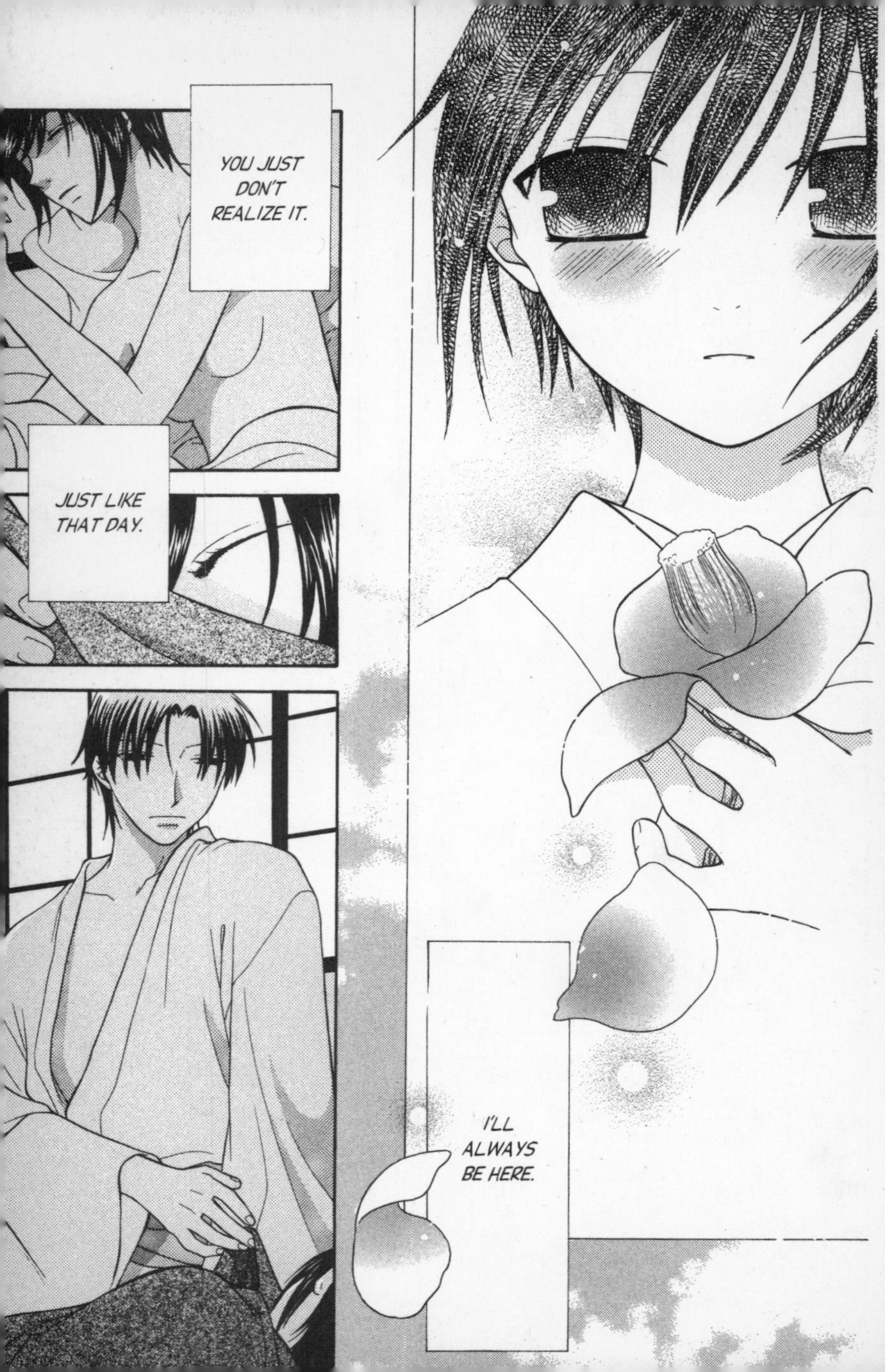
I'LL ALWAYS BE HERE.
YOU JUST DON'T REALIZE IT.
JUST LIKE THAT DAY.

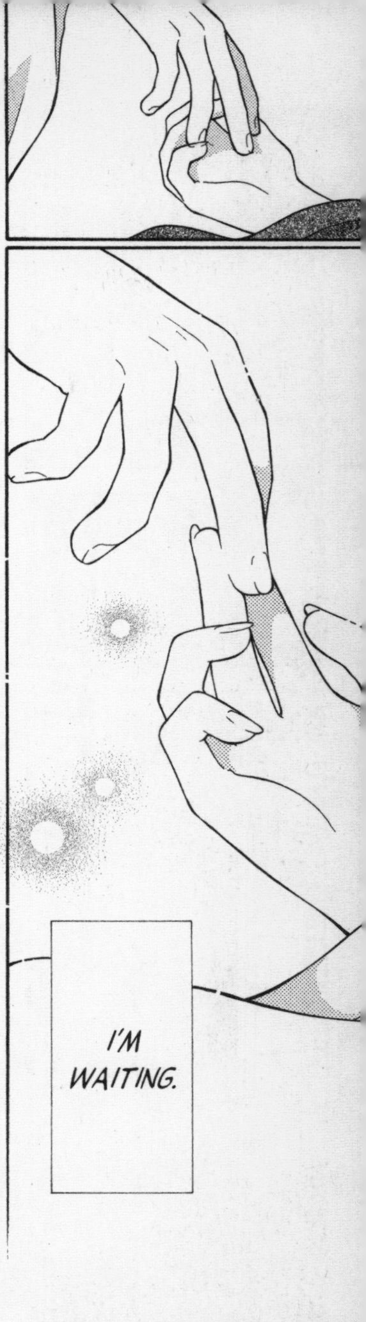
I'M WAITING.
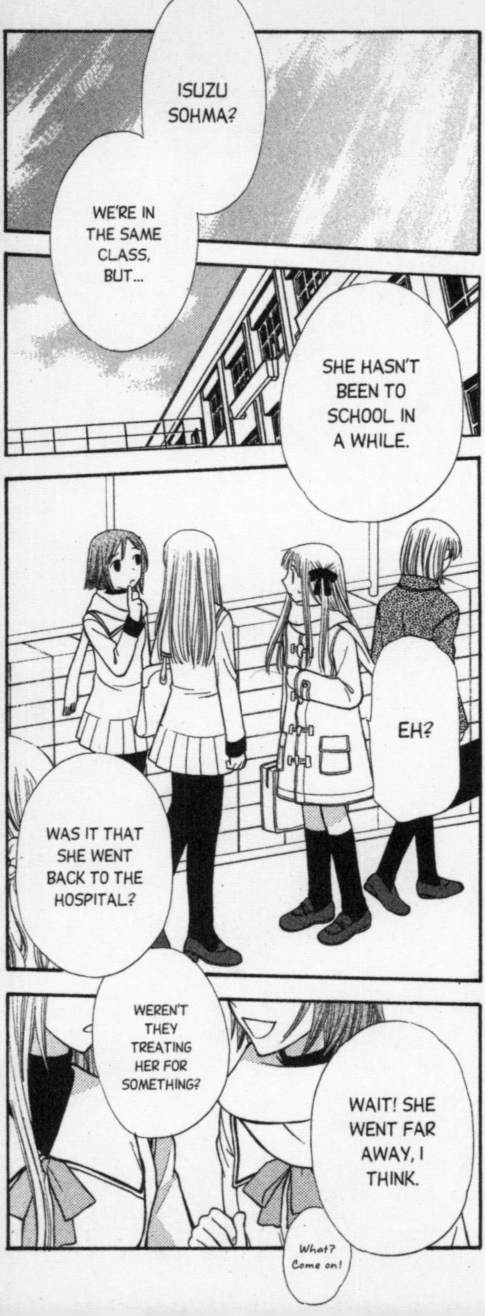
ISUZU SOHMA?
WE'RE IN THE SAME CLASS, BUT...
SHE HASN'T BEEN TO SCHOOL IN A WHILE.
EH?
WAS IT THAT SHE WENT BACK TO THE HOSPITAL?
WEREN'T THEY TREATING HER FOR SOMETHING?
WAIT! SHE WENT FAR AWAY, I THINK.
What? Come on!

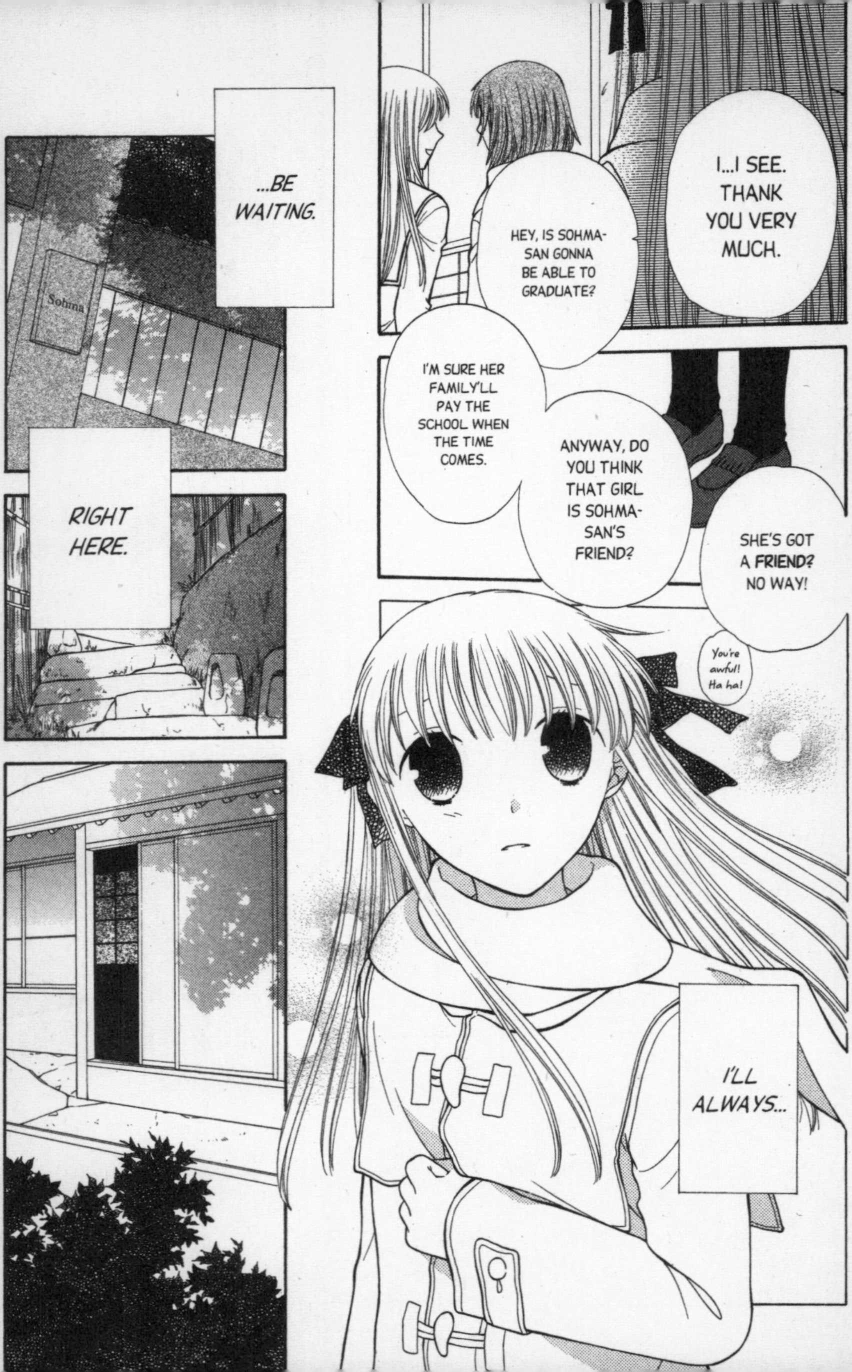
I...I SEE. THANK YOU VERY MUCH.
HEY, IS SOHMA-SAN GONNA BE ABLE TO GRADUATE?
I'M SURE HER FAMILY'LL PAY THE SCHOOL WHEN THE TIME COMES.
ANYWAY, DO YOU THINK THAT GIRL IS SOHMA-SAN'S FRIEND?
SHE'S GOT A **FRIEND?** NO WAY!
You're awful! Ha ha!
I'LL ALWAYS...
...BE WAITING.
Sohma
RIGHT HERE.

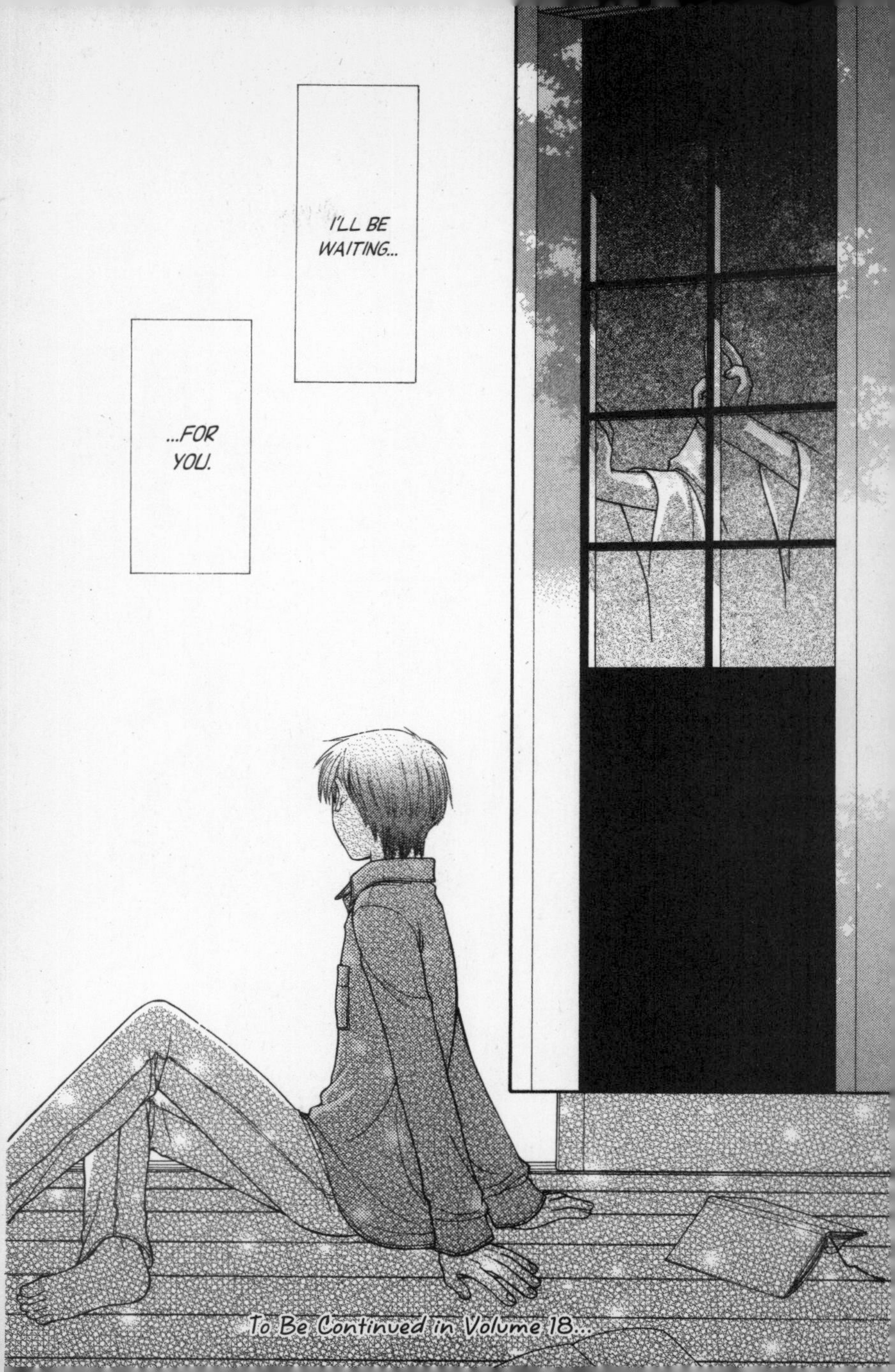
I'LL BE WAITING...
...FOR YOU.
To Be Continued in Volume 18...

I feel so grateful!

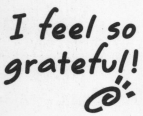

...She says.

Harada-sama, Araki-sama,
Mother-sama, Editor-sama

And everyone who reads and
supports this manga.

Next is the one whom I feel is now
completely recognized as "Kyo's father."

This has been...

高屋 奈月 でじたる
Natsuki Takaya.

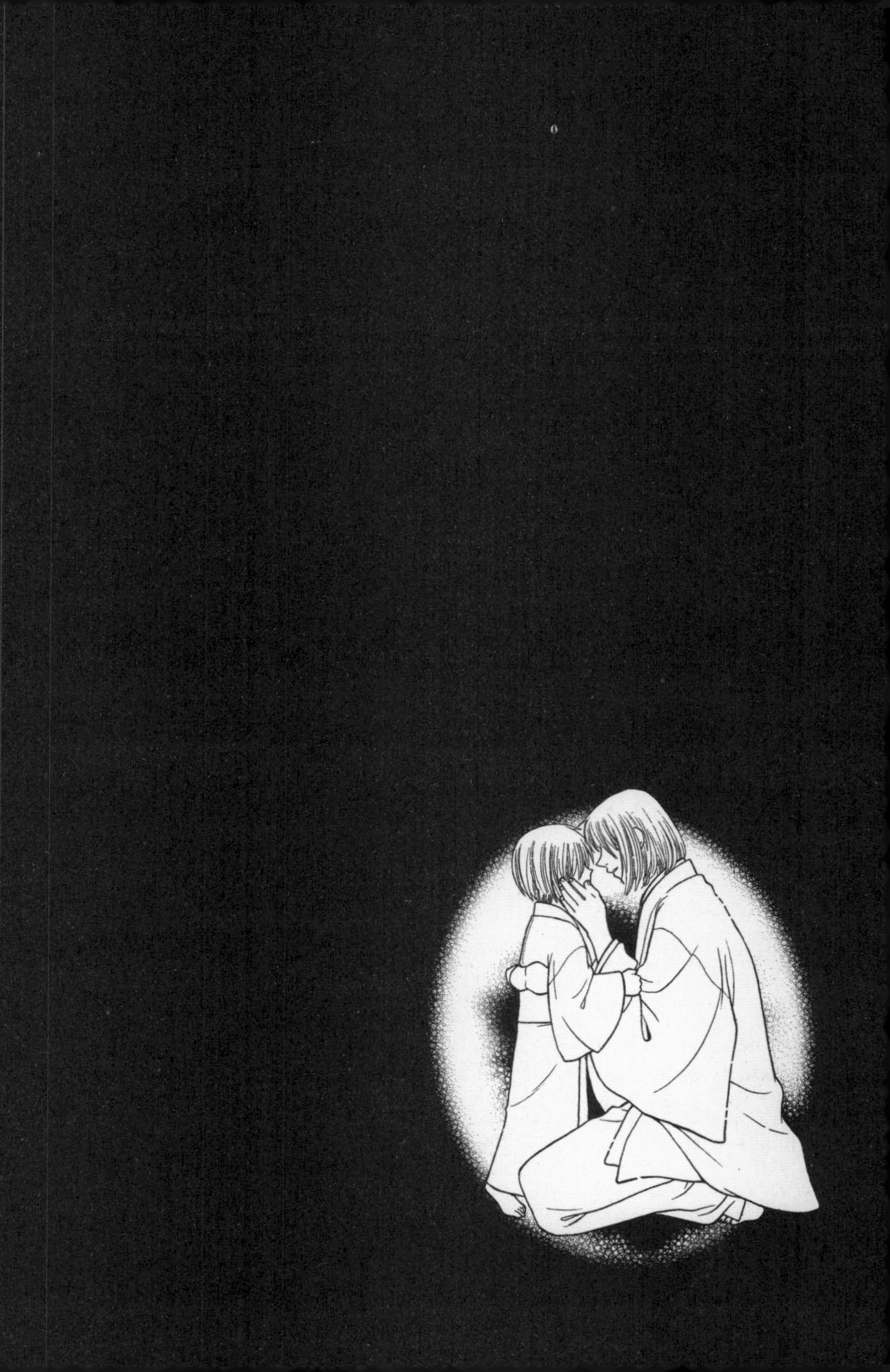

Next time in...

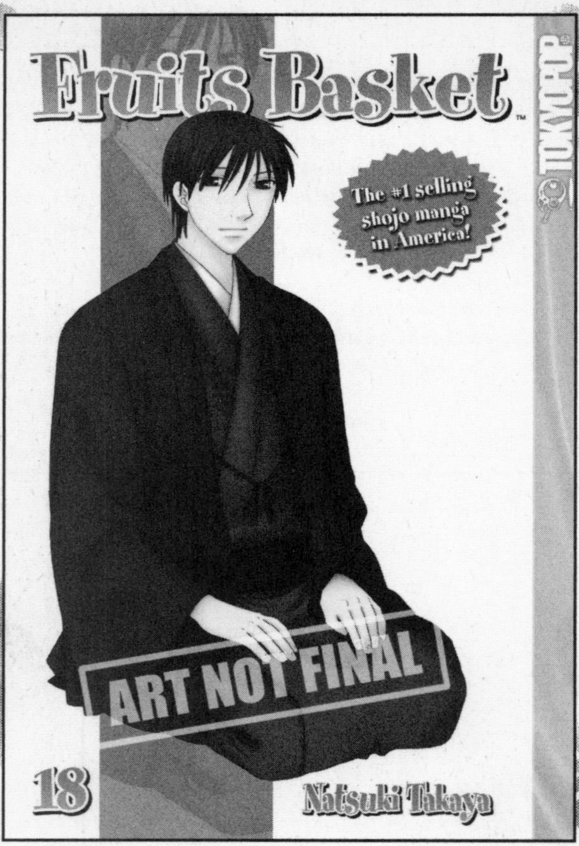

Fruits Basket
TOKYOPOP
The #1 selling shojo manga in America!
ART NOT FINAL
18
Natsuki Takaya

Everyone knows Rin is in the hospital...or is she? While Hatsuharu searches for Isuzu, he discovers that Isuzu had planned to swipe an item from Akito... an item that might just allow her to break the curse! So, what has actually happened to Rin? Read Fruits Basket 18 to find out!

Fruits Basket Volume 18
Available November 2007

Fans Basket

Wow! Volume 17 sure had some shockers, huh? How many of you were suspicious of Akito, I wonder? I'd really like to see some drawings of Akito as a woman, in her true gender! As usual, I have a never-ending mountain of "Fans Basket" mail to dig through... If your art gets picked, it's pretty much just the luck of the draw! But I honestly do read everything you send, and even if it's not ever printed, it probably put a smile on my face. So thanks! Okay, so let's see what's been chosen for this volume!

Oh! And don't stop reading after you've seen all the fan art! Thanks to TOKYOPOP copy editor Stephanie Duchin, we have a Furuba-themed "Cosplay Special" at the end of this volume! Enjoy!

- Paul Morrissey, Editor

Navy H.
Age 16
Calgary, Canada

6/27/06

Take a really close look at Tohru's skirt... What a fun way
to include the other *Fruits Basket* characters in your piece,
Navy! I also really like the badges worn by Yuki and Kyo!

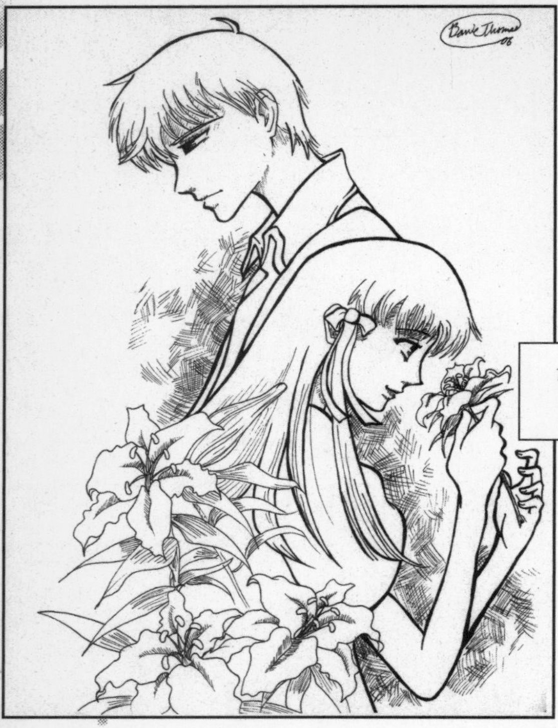

Excellent pen and ink work, Barrie. Your flowers look amazing! Thanks for being such a great fan!

Barrie Thomas
Age 19
Menifee, CA

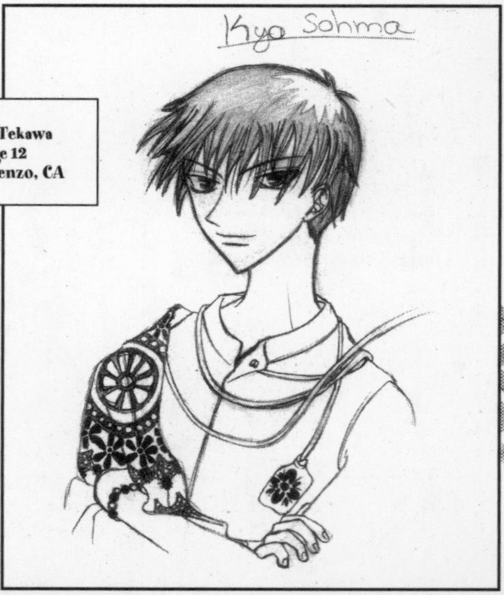
Kyo Sohma

Sarah Tekawa
Age 12
San Lorenzo, CA

Sarah would like everyone to know that she was 11 when she drew this. That's very impressive! I hope you're still drawing, Sarah. You have a lot of talent.

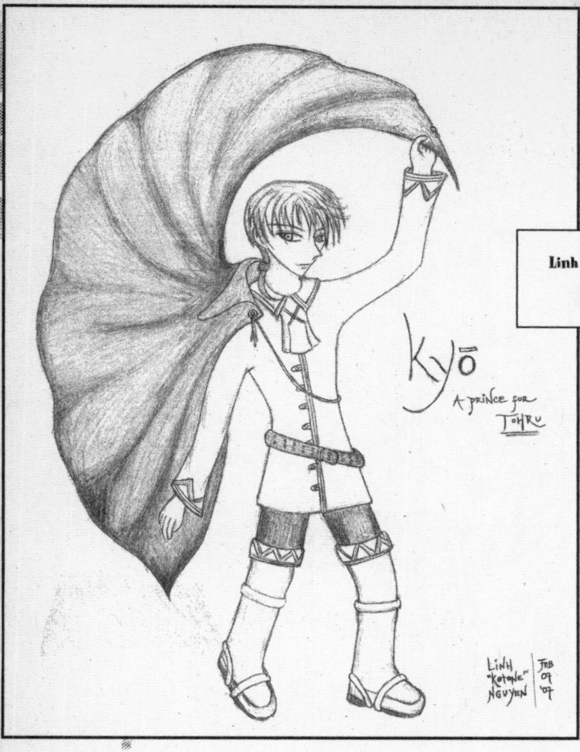
Kyō
A prince for Tohru
Linh "Kotone" Nguyen
Feb 07 '07

Linh "Kotone" Nguyen
Age 21
Corvallis, OR

I love Kyo's princely pose--especially his cape. It seems like you really enjoyed the "Cinderella" play, Linh!

Nikki
Lafayette, IN

I love it when people draw the *Fruits Basket* cast as other manga or anime characters. Here we have a *Tokyo Mew Mew Ala Mode* inspired Tohru! Great idea, Nikki!

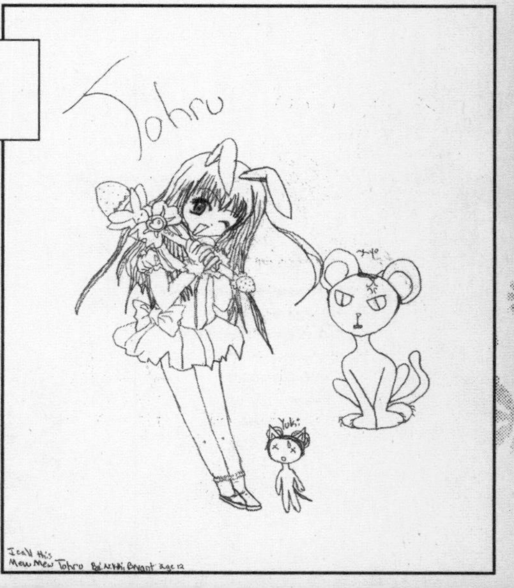
Tohru
Kyo
Yuki
I call this
Mew Mew Tohru By Nikki Bryant age 12

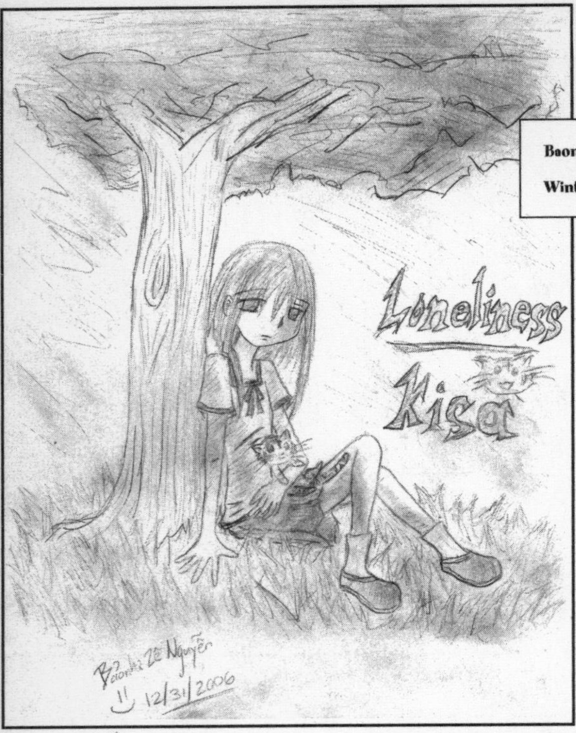
Loneliness
Kisa
Baonhu Le Nguyen
11 12/31/2006

Baonhu Le Nguyen
Age 11
Winter Garden, FL

Awwwwww! Kisa looks so sad here... Great job, Baonhu! It's always great to see awesome work from young artists. Keep it up!

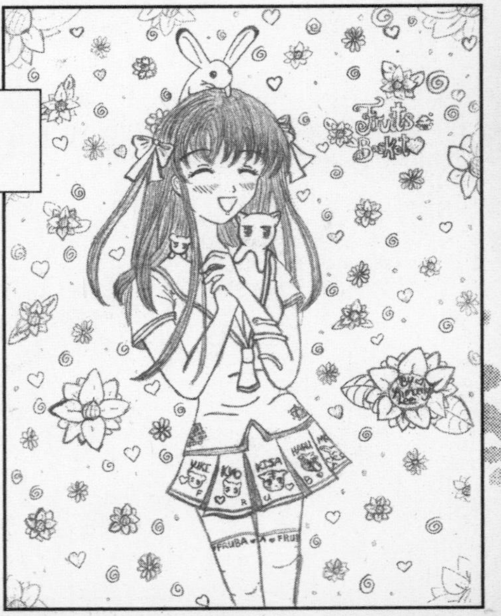
Fruits Basket
YUKI
KYO
KISA
HARU

Kimberly Lee
Age 12
Merced, CA

Here's another picture with Tohru wearing a *Furuba*-themed skirt! I really like your drawing, Kimberly--especially Momiji on top of Tohru's head. Adorable!

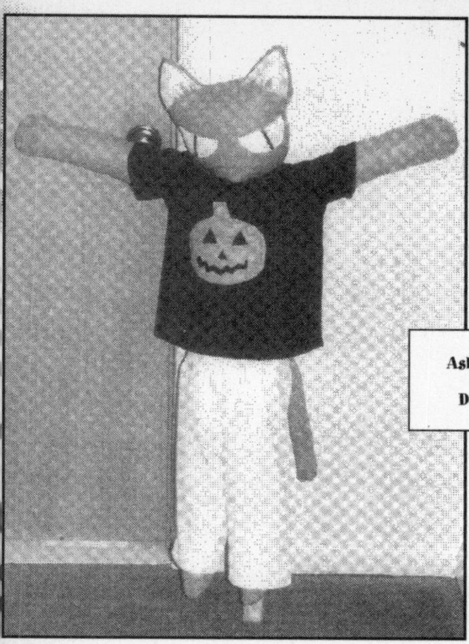

Ashley Randall
Age 17
Dundee, MI

Wow! Ashley made a Kyo scarecrow! How cool is that? According to Ashley, "His glare keeps the birds and rats away!"

Gorgeous art, Eevetta! Kisa has rarely looked as adorable. And her tiger looks soooo cute. Great work!

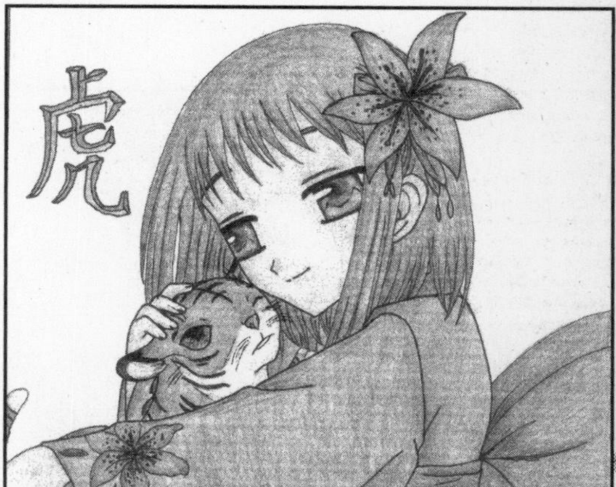
虎
Kisa Sohma

Eevetta
Age 18
Chula Vista, CA

Do you want to share your love for *Fruits Basket* with fans around the world? "Fans Basket" is taking submissions of fan art, poetry, cosplay photos, or any other Furuba fun you'd like to share!

How to submit:

1) Send your work via regular mail (NOT e-mail) to:

"Fans Basket"
c/o TOKYOPOP
5900 Wilshire Blvd.
Suite 2000
Los Angeles, CA 90036

2) All work should be in black-and-white and no larger than 8.5" x 11". (And try not to fold it too many times!)

3) Anything you send will not be returned. If you want to keep your original, it's fine to send us a copy.

4) Please include your full name, age, city and state for us to print with your work. If you'd rather us use a pen name, please include that, too.

5) IMPORTANT: If you're under the age of 18, you must have your parent's permission in order for us to print your work. Any submissions without a signed note of parental consent cannot be used.

6) For full details, please check out our website: http://www.tokyopop.com/aboutus/fanart.php

Disclaimer: Anything you send to us becomes the exclusive property of TOKYOPOP Inc. and, as we said before, will not be returned to you. We will have the right to print, reproduce, distribute, or modify the artwork for use in future volumes of Fruits Basket or on the web royalty-free.

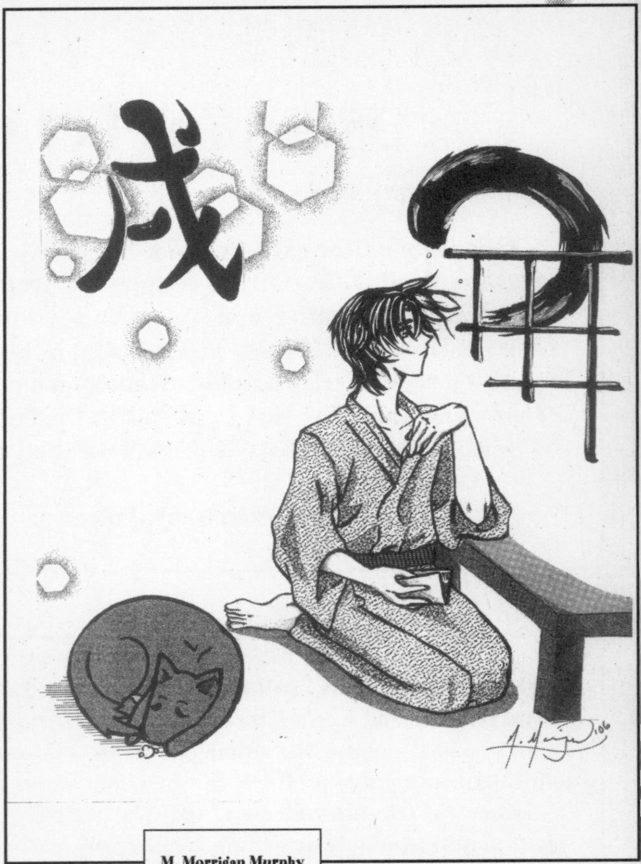
戌

M. Morrigan Murphy
Age 23
Boston, MA

Another really stunning piece of artwork. Your tones and brushwork look fantastic, M. I really like the sleeping dog curled up next to Shigure.

Fruits Basket™

COSPLAY SPECIAL

Our copy editor extraordinare--Stephanie Duchin--
was involved with a Furuba cosplaying group with her
roommate, Zach Shaffer, and we have a section devoted to
their costumes. Wait until you see Kyo in his true form!
Yup, that's right! Zach made the ultimate in a cosplay outfit!
Thanks for insisting that I put this in the book, Steph! I
think the fans will love it! Now, take it away, Zach...

- Paul Morrissey, Editor

I've been a huge fan of Fruits Basket ever since I started reading
it, and after seeing Kyo's true or "monster" form, I was inspired
to make a costume for the anime convention Anime Expo. After
months of thought and effort, the costume began to materialize,
and so did friends who also loved the series! We formed a
group, seventeen of us completed the full zodiac, plus Tohru
and her friends. Once we all got together, we had a wonderful
time, and, worth all of that effort to show our love of the series.
The convention was huge; many other fans came to see what
we'd done and chat about Fruits Basket;
everyone got into it, and could not have been nicer!
(Except maybe our Kagura;
I got squeezed for a good hour...ooph!)

- Zach Shaffer

COSPLAY SPECIAL

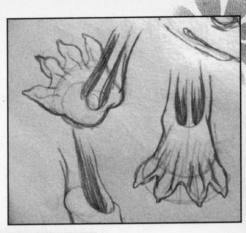

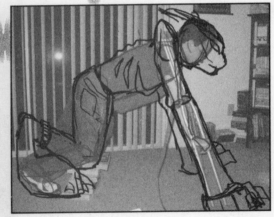

Design sketches were the first step for the costume's creation...to decide how the structure for the legs would be made.

COSPLAY SPECIAL

The skeleton mesh inside the head for
the mask is shown here, with the first
sculpture of the exterior of the head.

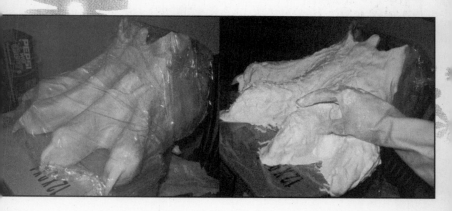

After the clay was sculpted, it was
covered in plaster to create a mold.

COSPLAY SPECIAL

Latex rubber was then applied inside each
mold and allowed to set, in order to form
the sturdy face and feet for the costume.

COSPLAY SPECIAL

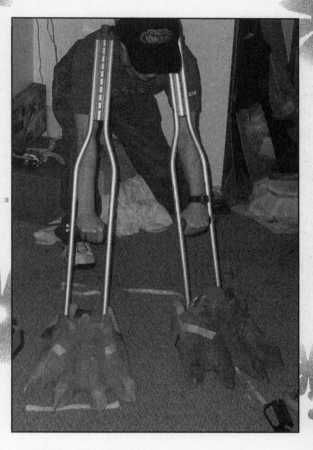

**Supports were needed inside each front leg.
Why not aluminum, lightweight crutches?
The structure proved to be perfect.**

COSPLAY SPECIAL

Each hind leg had a foam section built into the back. This would hide the true location of my legs when worn. The pants followed the false leg sections back, to complete the illusion. My feet are actually just behind the costume feet.

COSPLAY SPECIAL

The members of the Zodiac gathered together (left to right) are: Matt as Haru, Yana as Momiji, Lacie as Rin, Stan as Yuki, Matt as Hatori, Justin as Shigure, Zach as Kyo, Jennifer as Ritsu, Deborah as Kagura, Stephanie as Kisa, and Carolyn as Hiro. *

* This picture was professionally taken by Imagecraft Studios.

COSPLAY SPECIAL

Our full Fruits Basket group, comprised of members of Brilliant Moon
Cosplay and Friends, dressed up for Anime Expo 2006. (All that's
missing is our Akito, who, appropriately, was sick at the time.) Pictured
are: Caroline as Hanajima, Tiffany as Uotani, Angelica as Tohru, Yana as
Momiji, Matt as Hatori, Deborah as Kagura, Tara as Ayame, Zach as
Kyo, Lyn as Kureno, Stan as Yuki, Matt as Haru, Stephanie as Kisa, Lacie
as Rin, Carolyn as Hiro, Jennifer as Ritsu, and Justin as Shigure. *

* This picture was professionally taken by Imagecraft Studios.

COSPLAY SPECIAL

The true--or monster--form of the cat was completed by Zach and worn to Anime Expo 2006.

COSPLAY SPECIAL

Nikki, as Akito, does not care for the
smell of the cat's true form.

COSPLAY SPECIAL

Angelica, as Tohru, pictured with Zach, as Kyo.

COSPLAY SPECIAL

Jennifer, as Kagura, finishes the fun
with her true opinion of Tohru: "Bleeeeeh!!"

Beautiful Color Images from
CLAMP's Most Popular Series!

Chobits Art Book

Your Eyes Only

CLAMP

Luscious, full-color art from the world's most popular
manga studio, CLAMP, fills this stunningly gorgeous book.
This book is a feast for the eyes of any Chobits fan!

STOP!

This is the back of the book.
You wouldn't want to spoil a great ending!

W9-DGE-490

This book is printed "manga-style," in the authentic Japanese right-to-left format. Since none of the artwork has been flipped or altered, readers get to experience the story just as the creator intended. You've been asking for it, so TOKYOPOP® delivered: authentic, hot-off-the-press, and far more fun!

DIRECTIONS

If this is your first time reading manga-style, here's a quick guide to help you understand how it works.

It's easy... just start in the top right panel and follow the numbers. Have fun, and look for more 100% authentic manga from TOKYOPOP®!